Contents

	Acknowledgements	xi
	Abbreviations	xiii
	Illustrations	xv
	Money	xvi
1	'Queen of the Yorkshire Coast': Pre-war Scarborough	1
	The Town	1
	People and work	10
	The Adshead Report	11
2	'Phoney War' Scarborough	15
	War declared	15
	Civil Defence	16
	The 'Phoney War' economy	21
	The 1940 Crisis	26
3	'Pied Piper': Evacuation to Scarborough	33
	Planning	33
	Arrival	34
	Life as an Evacuee	40
	Hotels	43
	The 'Trickle Evacuation'	47
	The Doodlebug Evacuation	48
4	'If the Invader Comes'	56
	The Defence of Britain	56
	Defending Scarborough	57
	'Others'	67

5	'Like A Sea of Khaki': The Army and Home Guard		72
	The Army		72
	Home Guard		79
6	Luftwaffe over Scarborough: 1940		89
	'Tip and Run'		89
	10 October 1940		91
	Air Raid Shelters		96
7	Luftwaffe over Scarborough, 1941-1945		101
	The March Blitz		101
	After the March Blitz		109
8	Through the Tunnel: the mid-war economy		115
	Tourism 1941		115
	Tourism 1942		117
	Tourism 1943		119
	The War Economy		121
9	Scarborough Fishermen at War		126
	Luftwaffe attacks and the threat of mines		126
	Wartime fishing		132
	Fishermen in the Navy		134
10	Wartime politics and personalities		139
	The Constituency		139
	Sir Paul Latham		140
	By-election		144
	Postscript		152
11	The Flyers: the RAF Initial Training Wings		158
	Planning		158
	Life in the ITWs		159
12	Scarborough's Secret War		169
	Background		169
	Wartime Interception		170
	Working at Scarborough		172
	Scarborough's Contribution: A Balance Sheet		176
13	Scarborough Women at War		181
	Women's Work		181

*In memory of my parents,
Anne MacDonald (1920-2010),
who served on the Home Front,
and John Alexander MacDonald (1920-1980),
who served in North Africa and Italy.*

Author biography

Stewart MacDonald taught History at Scarborough Sixth Form College for 30 years, publishing *Charles V: Ruler, Dynast and Defender of the Faith* in 2000. He helps to run the Scarborough Archaeological and Historical Society and the Scarborough Maritime Heritage Centre.

© Stewart MacDonald, 2021

Published by Scarborough Archaeological and Historical Society

All rights reserved. No part of this book may be reproduced, adapted, stored in a retrieval system or transmitted by any means, electronic, mechanical, photocopying, or otherwise without the prior written permission of the author.

The rights of Stewart MacDonald to be identified as the author of this work have been asserted in accordance with the Copyright, Designs and Patents Act 1988.

A CIP catalogue record for this book is available from the British Library.

ISBN 978-0-902416-10-9

Book layout and design by Clare Brayshaw

Prepared and printed by:

York Publishing Services Ltd
64 Hallfield Road
Layerthorpe
York YO31 7ZQ

Tel: 01904 431213

Website: www.yps-publishing.co.uk

Scarborough at War

The Impact of the Second World War on Scarborough, North Yorkshire

STEWART MACDONALD

Scarborough at War

Best wishes,
Stewart MacDonald

	Women's Voluntary Service (WVS)	185
	Women in local politics	189
	Women in the police	190
14	Salvage and Savings	196
	Salvage	196
	National Savings	202
15	Food, fuel and transport	212
	Feeding Scarborough	212
	A 'British Restaurant'?	218
	Fuel and Transport	221
16	'Don't You Know There's a War On?'	228
	Wartime Puritanism	228
	'Good-time girls'?	229
	Youth 'Running Wild'	232
17	End of War Tourism, 1944-1945	239
	Tourism 1944	239
	Tourism 1945	240
18	Peace and Looking Ahead	249
	Peace	250
	General Election	251
	Local Elections	256
19	Post-war Scarborough: housing	262
	The Housing crisis	262
	'Prefabs'	263
	Permanent Housing	265
	Eastfield	268
20	Post-war Scarborough: who governs?	273
	Education	273
	Health	278
	Fire Brigade	279
	Police	281
	Nationalisation	282
	Centralisation	283

21	The post-war economy	288
	Industry	288
	Tourism's post-war prospects	291
	Obstacles to a tourist revival	293
	Post-war tourism	299
	Post-war challenges	301
22	Epilogue	308
	Appendices	316
	Appendix 1	316
	Appendix 2	321
	Sources	322
	Select Bibliography	324
	Index	327

Acknowledgements

Thanks must go to my family in Glasgow for many years of support and encouragement. Special mention must be made also to my cycling companions in Scarborough and elsewhere for helping to keep me sane (or nearly so) during the writing of this book. My gratitude goes to friends who provided feedback on draft chapters: Jo Barron, Richard Cotterill, Amanda Daynes, Tania Exley-Moore, Sue Harris, Jennifer King and Steve Tipple. Patrick Argent has been supportive throughout. On the history of Scarborough fishing, I benefited from the advice of Fred Normandale and Tom Rowley, whilst David Abrutat of GCHQ provided assistance on Scarborough's 'secret' war. I am grateful to Trevor Pearson for volunteering his map-making skills and to Jonathan Eves for helping with photography. I would also like to acknowledge my debt to Richard James Percy, whose unpublished research on Scarborough during the Second World War has, hitherto, been the only work available on this subject. Amongst others who lent their support or expertise along the way are Farrell Burnett, Steve Collins, Kate Evans, Stephen Gandolfi, Chris Hall, Lindy Rowley, Emma Temlett and Marie Woods.

During my research I received help from a number of local and national organisations. Locally, tribute must be paid to Scarborough Library (thanks to Angela Kale and her colleagues), the Scarborough Museums Trust and the Scarborough Maritime Heritage Centre. At the latter, Mark Vesey has been a constant source of practical help, ideas and enthusiasm, whilst Les Shannon helped me to locate photographs and has shared his encyclopaedic knowledge of Scarborough with me. Outside Scarborough, thanks are due to York University Library, the North Yorkshire County Records Office, Historic England, the Second World War Experience Centre, the National Archives and the Imperial War Museum. I am indebted also to the Curtis Brown Group Ltd acting on behalf of the Trustees of the Mass Observation Archive. The editor of the *Scarborough*

News kindly granted permission to use material from the newspaper's archive and the poet Christopher Wiseman likewise gave approval for his work to be quoted. The exemplary Scarborough Archaeological and Historical Society was enthusiastic about publishing the book and has been unwavering in its support. The Society's Treasurer, Martin Bland, has been a great help on financial matters. Keith Johnston has been generous with his time, suggested valuable improvements to the manuscript and has consistently imparted wise advice. As a comparative novice in the local history of Scarborough, I have learned a great deal from Keith and from Jack Binns, another colleague from my teaching days at Scarborough Sixth Form College. The final accolade goes to my son Calum MacDonald, who has acted as an unpaid academic adviser, IT consultant and all-round problem-solver. His help has been inestimable.

Of course, all errors and shortcomings in this book remain the responsibility of the author. Every effort has been made to contact copyright holders for material cited in this volume. The publisher would appreciate being contacted if there are any oversights.

Abbreviations

AFS	Auxiliary Fire Service
AFV	Armoured Fighting Vehicle
ARP	Air Raid Precautions
ATS	Auxiliary Territorial Service (women's branch of the Army)
D/F	Direction Finding, used along with wireless interception
GC&CS	Government Code and Cypher School
HC Debs.	House of Commons Debates (*Hansard*)
HDU	Home Defence Unit or RAF 'watcher' station
HE	High Explosive
HG	Home Guard
IB	Incendiary Bomb
ITW	Initial Training Wing (RAF)
IWM	Imperial War Museum
LDV	Local Defence Volunteers
LEA	Local Education Authority
LNER	London and North Eastern Railway
MO	Mass Observation Archive
NAAFI	Navy, Army and Air Force Institutes, provided canteens, shops etc.
NA	National Archives (Kew, London)
NALGO	National and Local Government Officers' Association
NFS	National Fire Service
POW	Prisoner of War
RNPS	Royal Naval Patrol Service

ROF	Royal Ordnance Factory
SEN	Scarborough Evening News
SHBHA	Scarborough Hotels and Boarding Houses Association
TA	Territorial Army
UXB	Unexploded Bomb
V1	German flying bomb
V2	German rocket bomb
VE Day	Victory in Europe Day
VJ Day	Victory over Japan Day
WAAF	Women's Auxiliary Air Force
WLA	Women's Land Army
WRENS	Women's Royal Naval Service
WVS	Women's Voluntary Service

Illustrations

Thanks to the following for granting permission to use illustrations.

Scarborough Borough Council, North Yorkshire County Council, Scarborough Maritime Heritage Centre, Scarborough Museums Trust, the editor of *Scarborough News*, the Imperial War Museum, GCHQ, Historic England, Les Shannon, Jonathan Eves, Jeannie Swales. It has not been possible to trace the copyright of all photographs. Please contact the publisher if you can help with this.

Money

The sums of money referred to in this book are in the pre-decimal British currency of pounds (£), shillings (s.) and pence (d.). A shilling was 12 pence and a pound was 20 shillings. Translating amounts from the 1940s to present values can be difficult, but a valuable starting point is:

www.measuringworth.com/calculators/ukcompare/

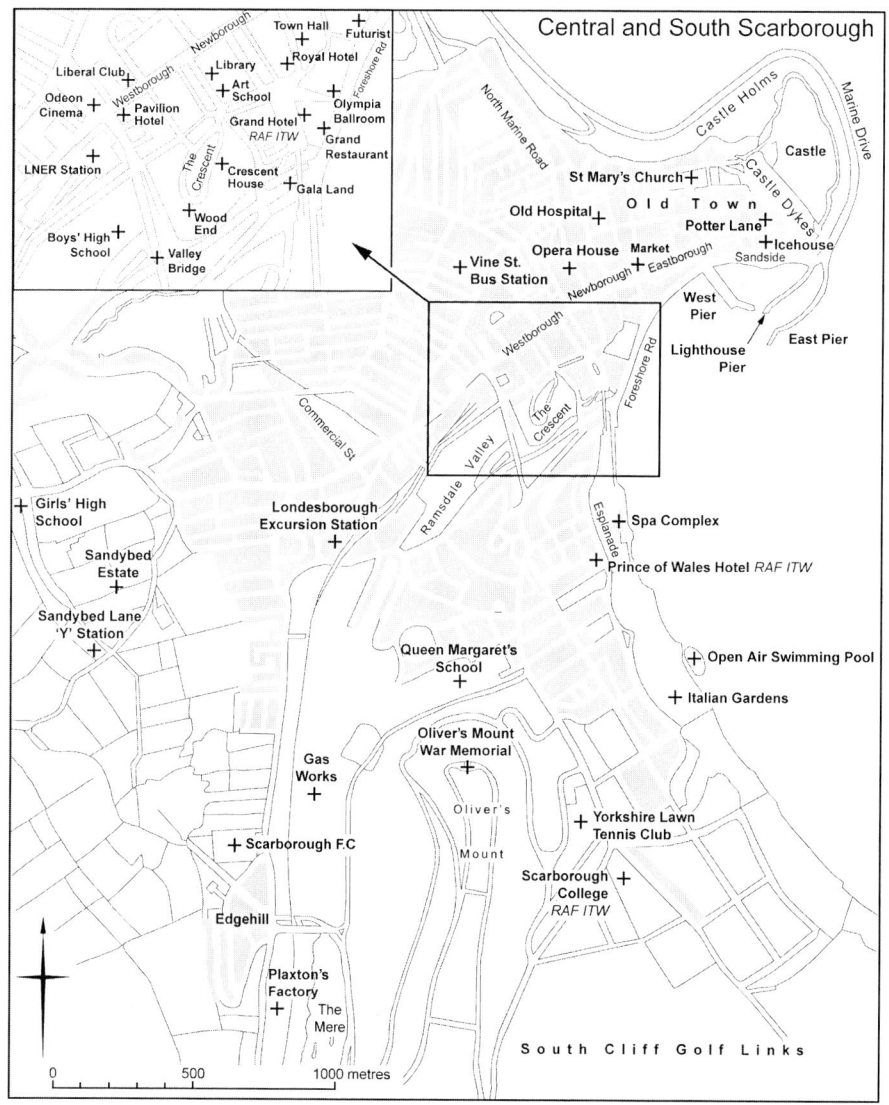

xvii

North Scarborough
Scalby Beck
Scalby Mills
North Cliff Golf Links
Miniature Railway
Northstead Manor Gardens
Corner Cafe
Open Air Theatre
Peasholm Gap
Peasholm Bathing Pool
Floral Hall
Peasholm Park
Queen's Parade
Cricket Ground
Barrowcliff
New Hospital
0
500
1000 metres

Scarborough Area
Whitby
Whitby
Fylingdales Moor
Hayburn Wyke
Cloughton
Burniston
Scalby
North Bay
Scarborough
South Bay
Irton Moor 'Y' Station
Wheatcroft Battery
Cornelian Bay
NALGO Camp
Eastfield Estate
Cayton Bay
Pickering
Wykeham
Seamer
Snainton
Brompton
Filey
Staxton
Ganton
Staxton Brow RAF Radar Station
Butlin's Holiday Camp
Malton and York
Bridlington and Hull
0
5
10 kilometres
Yorkshire Wolds

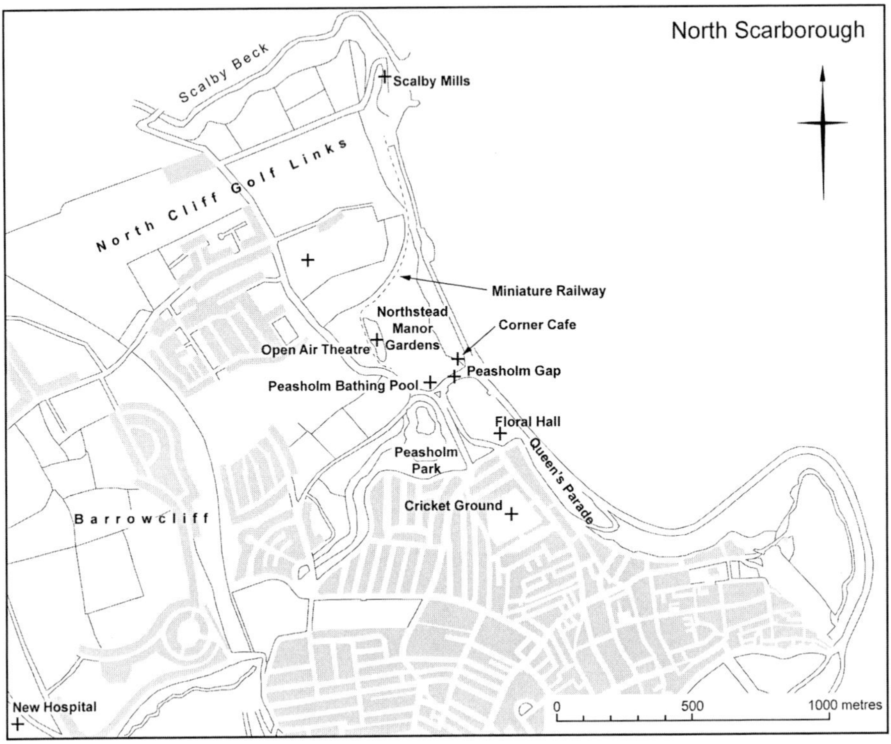

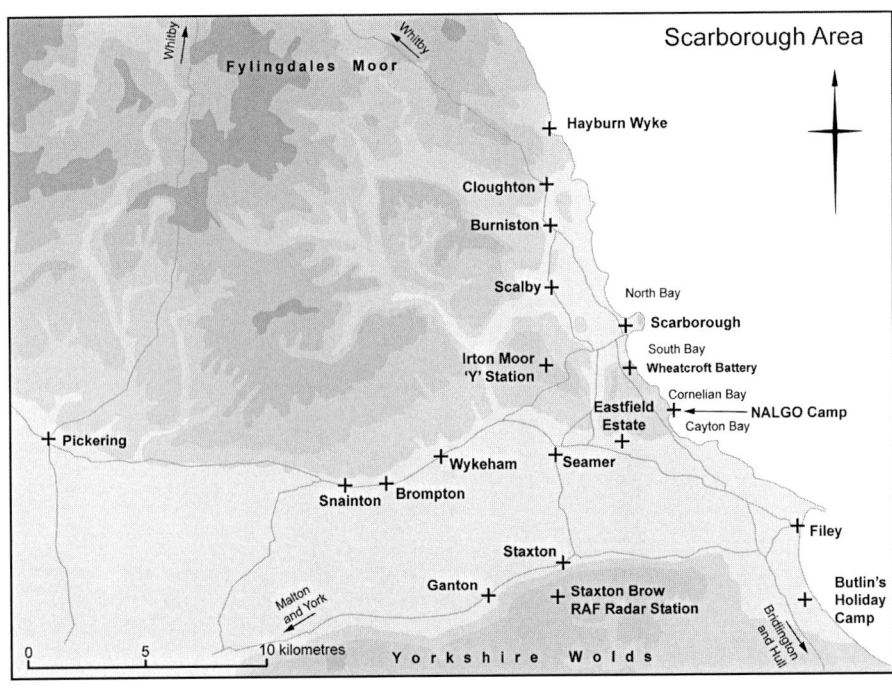

CHAPTER 1

'Queen of the Yorkshire Coast': Pre-War Scarborough

In its [Scarborough's] gradual development through history, and comparing its growth with that of other seaside resorts, it may be claimed that it has led, rather than followed, the panorama of events.[1]

The Town

In the later 1930s, when Scarborough wished to obtain advice on its development as a pleasure resort, it selected a man who was probably the country's pre-eminent authority in such matters. Stanley Adshead had a formidable reputation as an architect and town planner. Born in Manchester, he was appointed the country's first professor of Town Planning at the University of Liverpool in 1909, where he made the university a pioneer in civic design. From 1914 he enjoyed a distinguished career as Professor of Town Planning at the University of London. Retiring in 1935, he took up planning consultancies, advising on the planning of the new capital city of Lusaka in modern-day Zambia.[2] He was invited to Scarborough in early 1937 and, supported by Scarborough's Borough Engineer H.V. Overfield, presented his report to the Council in April 1938.[3] *Scarborough: A Survey of its Existing Conditions and some Proposals for its Future Development* was an ambitious, inventive and ground-breaking document.

What sort of impressions would a visitor to Scarborough like Adshead have had arriving in the later 1930s? Two roads approached the town from the south. Arriving along the Filey Road that followed the coast, the visitor might detect an air of social exclusiveness as they passed the South Cliff Golf

Links and the Yorkshire Lawn Tennis Club. Entering the town, visitors would observe the affluence of the South Cliff area. It was a highly favoured residential neighbourhood for well-off professionals, businessmen and retirees. The prestigious Esplanade, overlooking the South Bay, with its lavish hotels and apartments, was originally developed in a Regency style in the early Victorian period to rival Regency Brighton. Adshead was particularly impressed by the promenade:

> It possesses in its South Esplanade a promenade commanding magnificent views of castle, harbour and sea; a promenade completely cut off from the noise and bustle of the centre of the town, and which for seclusion and the attraction of retirement excels The Leas at Folkstone, or the higher promenade at Bournemouth.[4]

To access the main town from the South Cliff, the visitor would have to cross one of two bridges, one pedestrian, that spanned the steep and landscaped Ramsdale Valley, which ran down to the sea. Sight of 'the Valley' would be an early indication that Scarborough was very much a town of hills and dales and, on the coast, cliffs. Indeed, this was one of its primary charms as a seaside resort. The town's carved up topography, according to the writer V.S. Pritchett, also enabled Scarborough, more than other seaside resorts, to attract working-class visitors to some areas of the town without upsetting more genteel ones elsewhere.[5] A guide to the town could boast that Scarborough welcomed all, 'from the millionaire to the miner, from the society belle to the factory lass'.[6]

Arriving by road from the south, the visitor might also approach Scarborough along Seamer Road. This would provide further clues as to the nature of the town. On the right they would pass the Mere, a historic lake transformed into a picturesque tourist amenity with artificial islands, rowing boats and a lakeside café. Here was evidence of Scarborough Corporation's determination to impress visitors by providing beauty spots and extensive areas of parks, landscaped walks and pleasure grounds. It was common for visitors to commend Scarborough for such facilities, and also to acknowledge the beauty of the surrounding countryside and coastal scenery.[7] Above the Mere rose the steep, 500-foot slope of Oliver's Mount, linked, in legend only, to the presence of Oliver Cromwell in the town during the battles of the Civil War. At the northern end of the flat-topped Mount, an imposing obelisk commemorating the war dead of World War One overlooked the town below.

As the traveller approached the main town along Seamer Road, evidence of the lives of the town's ordinary inhabitants would become more apparent. On the left, they would pass the council housing estate of Edgehill, part of the Corporation's interwar slum clearance programme. Scarborough Football Club was close by. On the right there were factory buildings, notably the large Plaxton's factory built in 1936. Starting as a small joinery business, Plaxton's had diversified into the building industry and metal work. The company now specialised in manufacturing motor coach chassis, spearheading the growth of light and metal industries in a town which many associated only with the business of tourism.

Further travel by road would take the visitor alongside the LNER railway line from York, before arriving in the town centre by skirting around the western end of the Valley. The arrival of the railway in Scarborough in 1845 marked the beginnings of large-scale tourism in the town, starting with an influx of well-to-do middle-class visitors. In the 1930s poorer day or half-day trippers and working-class families heading for a week's holiday poured in on trains in large numbers. The train from York arrived firstly at an Excursion Station, before passing a connecting line to Whitby and finally stopping at the main LNER station in the centre of town, from where there was also a direct line to Hull. The supremacy of the railway, however, was beginning to be challenged in the 1930s by the arrival of private motor vehicles and, for the less well-off, the motor coach or the charabanc.

In the central area of the town the visitor would undoubtedly be struck by the variety of ambitious architecture. At one end of the railway station stood the five-storey, opulently-Victorian Pavilion Hotel. Opposite the station was the art deco Odeon Cinema, reflecting the interwar craze for the 'movies'. It opened in 1936, clad in the chain's trademark cream and black glazed tiling. East of the station could be found the Crescent, an early Victorian, Georgian-style terrace built in emulation of Georgian Bath. Facing the Crescent stood the Corporation's Medical Baths, where residents and visitors could enjoy Turkish and Russian Baths, seaweed solution baths and treatment in the Electro-Medical Department. Nearby was the municipal library, enlarged in 1936.

The Town Hall, once a private home, was another grand Victorian building, though built in a Jacobean style. From here, the non-county borough of Scarborough was governed by a Town Council or, as a legal entity, Corporation.[8] The Council was responsible for a population of some 42,000. Together with the Town Hall staff, the Council managed the borough in a highly interventionist manner, owning and running a large part of the tourist infrastructure of the town, from boating in Peasholm Lake and the Mere to dancing at the Olympia Ballroom and the Corner Café. A good income was derived from cafés, refreshment kiosks, the hire of deckchairs and the manufacture of municipal ice-cream. The Council's Entertainment Department was always keen to promote its healthy outdoor activities. By 1939 it provided visitors with facilities for open-air swimming in the North and South Bays, also hiring out its own unfashionable bathing costumes. In addition to 21 hard tennis courts, the Corporation also offered bowling, putting and 'mini' golf. The Town Hall took direct responsibility for the amenities at Northstead Manor Gardens and Peasholm Park on the North Side of the resort. Some major venues, like the Spa, Floral Hall, Open Air Theatre and Gala Land, were leased out by the Corporation to private companies. Municipal investments in the provision of tourist amenities in Scarborough between the wars was considerable and brought in substantial revenues. In addition, the Corporation's tentacles spread out to control many areas of the everyday life of the community, including public housing, electricity supply, elementary education, police, fire brigade, public health, town planning, weights and measures and veterinary inspection. The reach of the Town Hall was much greater than that of the pared-down local authorities of post-1945 England.

From the railway station a ribbon of adjoining streets (Westborough, Newborough and Eastborough) ran downwards for half a mile to the harbour in the South Bay, passing firstly through the town's business and banking quarter. Shops had by now gravitated from older parts of the town to this main thoroughfare, many expanding upwards to three or four storeys. Adshead commented in his report that the town's shops and stores could compete favourably with any to be found in England's South Coast resorts.[9]

At the top of Westborough, the visitor would encounter the town's Liberal Club, opened in 1895, an imposing building containing a large concert hall. The home of the local Conservative Party, opened in 1888 on Huntriss Row, was nearby, 'A florid mixture of Tudor and Baroque styles.'[10] The town's modern political history had been dominated by the tribal contest between Liberals and Conservatives. Since World War I, and the formation of the Scarborough and Whitby parliamentary seat, the Conservative Party had triumphed over the Liberals, winning the seat in every parliamentary election. In local government too, the Conservatives comfortably outperformed the Liberals, dominating the Town Council before World War II along with Independents.

Looking down Newborough and Eastborough, with the headland and the castle's curtain wall in the background.

As a visitor made his or her way down Westborough and Newborough, they would pass the site of the principal point of entry into the medieval town and further on they would catch their first sight above them of the curtain wall of Scarborough Castle. The Norman castle sat on a prominent, flat-topped headland, 300 feet above sea-level, which separated the North and South Bays. Obscured from view from Eastborough, the ruined castle keep rose up from the headland nearly 100 feet against the sky. Adshead described the castle as 'a striking ruin, possessing much of its ancient grandeur'.[11]

To the north of Eastborough, in the lee of the castle, lay Scarborough's Old Town. 'It nestles in a hollow beneath Castle Hill,' observed Adshead, 'which seems to take it under its wing.'[12] Small cottages clung to the slope, arranged in a rough gridiron of horizontal streets and smaller lanes and stairs running off them. Those that lived here, the 'bottom enders', enjoyed life in a close-knit community in some respects cut off from the rest of the town. There were well-appointed dwellings, but much of the housing was shoddy and overcrowded. Some of the worst slums of the Old Town had been cleared in the 1920s and 30s, replacing inadequate housing, dark alleys and shabby courtyards with new municipal houses and flats. The streets closer to the harbour, above Sandside, constituted Scarborough's historic fishing quarter, where the congested homes of fishermen and their families could often be identified by the nets, lines and baskets attached to the cottages. The tall chimney of the 'Icehouse' rose incongruously above the cottages. Adshead took for granted the inexorable decline of Scarborough's fishing industry, but was optimistic about the potential of the fishing village as a tourist attraction:

> The old fishing village should be regarded not only as a collection of cottages for fishermen, but also as a special feature of interest to Scarborough. As time goes on visitors to our seaside resorts are more and more attracted by the quaintness and beauty of these old relics of the fishing industry.[13]

Near the top of the Castle Hill, looking down over the red-tiled roofs of the Old Town and across to the Castle, sat St Mary's church, which had been the town's parish church for some 800 years. During the Civil War it sustained serious damage when parliamentary forces had used it as an artillery battery against royalist forces in the neighbouring Castle.

Eastborough emerged into the South Bay opposite the town's three piers and inner and outer harbours, the infrastructure of the town's maritime past. The oldest pier, Vincent's Pier, was attached by a bridge to the Lighthouse, the latter illuminated with soft amber lighting in the dark. The lighthouse tower had famously been holed by a naval shell in the German bombardment of Scarborough in December 1914 and had not been rebuilt until 1931. The smells of fish and smoke from steam trawlers would testify to the survival of sea fishing in Scarborough, though business other than fishing was encroaching on the harbours. A strip of the old harbour had been given over to Westall's Amusements: 'The Nicest and Jolliest Amusement Park in the North of England.' Among the vessels in the harbour there were invariably a number of yachts, boats for hire and pleasure boats, whilst the well-appointed *Coronia* and *Royal Lady* were available for tourists who wished to venture out to sea in some comfort. In the 1930s Scarborough had become celebrated for its 'big-game' fishing for 'tunny' (tuna) in August and September, a sport which attracted members of high society from home and abroad. Tourism, then, had long overtaken sea fishing as the town's most important trade. The bigger and more modern boats in the harbour, moreover, were most likely to come from other ports like Hull and Grimsby.

Vincent's and West Piers in the foreground, the Grand Hotel to the right, with the South Cliff Esplanade in the background beneath Oliver's Mount.

Looking southwards from the harbour, in good weather at least, a visitor might notice that the tradition of outdoor bathing in Scarborough, popular since the 18th century, had survived. Bathing took place in the sea itself and in an open-air sea-water bathing pool, opened by the Corporation in 1915 and located to the south of South Bay. It was now 'Renovated – Filtrated, Aerated and Chlorinated'. The pool featured a towering diving platform, beach bungalows and viewing grandstands, where the Corporation organised concerts, beauty contests and diving exhibitions. The South Bay's expansive sands offered space for family play on the beach and for the more recent fashion of sun-bathing. In the 1930s the deckchair became a symbol, according to one writer, of the new enthusiasm for 'the idling away of time in the sunshine'.[14] For Adshead, the main requirements of 'Day Excursionists' and poorer families were the sea and sands, 'and whether they come by train or motor-coach, they make direct for the seashore'.[15]

Close to the open-air swimming pool, Scarborough's Spa complex was a focal point for well-heeled and respectable residents and visitors, attracted to its bands and orchestras, dances, refreshment rooms and shops. The Spa, with its spectacular view across the South Bay, had developed as an undertaking in the

17th century supplying allegedly health-giving waters to visitors. Scarborough, as the self-proclaimed 'Queen of Watering Places', was seeking to rival inland spa towns like Harrogate and Buxton. Now the Spa's leisure and entertainment overshadowed the token provision of medicinal spa waters. The more plebeian visitors, moreover, were often put off by the Spa's high prices, fussy dress code and classical music.

Dominating the South Bay was the up-market Grand Hotel, which was built on a cliff above the South Bay but descended the cliff towards sea level. When the hotel had been completed in 1867, it was the biggest in Europe and took 6½ million bricks to build and required 11 miles of carpeting on its halls and stairs. In front of it stood the Grand Restaurant block and roller-skating rink (unrelated to the hotel).

Respectable visitors who patronised the Grand and the Spa might also venture into the Futurist cinema on the Foreshore for the latest movies or the Olympia Ballroom for its immensely popular evening dances. However, most of the South Bay seafront had been given over to the tastes of the less well-to-do day-trippers and working-class holidaymakers. The sort of diversions available included 'Cheeky Charley' the ventriloquist's dummy, Punch and Judy, donkey-rides, an Indian Village with 'jolly' Indian monkeys and lowbrow seaside shows at the Arcadia Theatre. Multiple sources of cheap and cheerful food and drink were available, with the Grand Restaurant able to provide 2,000 meals at a time. A symbol of the declining social status of the South Bay was Gala Land, originally a three-acre underground aquarium complex located where the Valley meets the Foreshore. It was opened in 1877 as a private enterprise aiming to attract affluent customers who shared the late Victorian interest in aquaria and marine biology. The setting was an extravagant, three-acre environment of tiled Hindu-styled catacombs. Failing to attract sufficient custom, within a few years it became a place of amusement and entertainment. Then it was bought by the Town Hall in 1921, leased to an entertainment company and by the end of the 1930s offered 'Melody, Mirth and Merriment'. Often, it simply offered shelter from the rain. Adshead was not impressed: 'The derelict condition of the Aquarium [Gala Land] is such that Scarborough can no longer afford to have this eyesore in one of the town's most important positions.'[16]

In the 20th century Scarborough began to spread northwards and westwards, as more council and suburban housing was built on the 'North Side'. Smaller hotels appeared, too, supplementing the older and larger ones overlooking the North Bay on Queen's Parade. Holidaymakers had been making their way in greater numbers to the North Bay since the Marine Drive had been forced round the Castle headland by 1908 in a remarkable feat of municipal engineering and roadbuilding.

North Bay, looking south from Peasholm Gap and the Corner Café, with the castle and the headland in the background to the left.

In 1925 the seafront Corner Café was opened at Peasholm Gap, providing facilities for concerts and dancing as well as refreshments. Of a new gas-heated, sea-water bathing-pool nearby, opened in 1938, a journalist commented that it was 'easily the most successful new attraction. It is taxed to the capacity of dressing accommodation and there are queues for as much as an hour morning and afternoon, while midnight bathing carnivals are attracting big crowds each Friday.'[17] Peasholm Park on the North Side, developed before World War I, featured popular open-air concerts and the twice weekly mock naval battles on the lake. The late 1920s witnessed the creation of the 27-acre Northstead Manor Gardens, featuring an artificial boating lake, the hugely popular miniature railway (1931) and the Open Air Theatre (1932), the latter boasting spectacular stage effects. The North Side increasingly attracted visitors who were perhaps not wealthy enough to colonise the South Cliff area, but who felt themselves to be too respectable for the down-market South Bay or who desired a more peaceful or a more family-oriented holiday.

People and work

It is difficult to overstate the importance of tourism in sustaining the interwar Scarborough economy. During the 1930s working-class holidaymaking expanded greatly, culminating in the 1938 Holidays with Pay Act. Middle-class customers, as we have seen, continued to enjoy Scarborough's more refined attractions. Most local people had some sort of investment in the success of tourism. Providing accommodation to visitors in hotels and boarding-houses was at the heart of the tourist economy, whilst other residents made money renting out private apartments, rooms in lodging houses or individual rooms in the family home. Ron Welburn's mother, for example, took summer visitors into her council house in Edgehill in the 1930s: '… these visitors had to cram into one of the front bedrooms and were allowed exclusive use of the sitting room.'[18] Employment and profits were also generated by the catering trades, from selling shellfish on the seafront to serving visitors in fish and chips shops, cafés and restaurants. Local retailing felt the benefit of tourist spending, whether in 'fancy goods' shops and confectioners or in ladies and gents outfitters. Entertainment boosted local revenues, as Scarborough shared in the interwar golden age of movies, dance halls and family shows. Tourism, moreover, generated ancillary economic activities: costumiers serviced entertainments, laundries the hotel sector and market gardeners catering. A buoyant tourist economy brought in handsome returns for the Corporation in local taxes and profits from their own undertakings. The living standards of the town, therefore, depended on incomes directly or indirectly derived from the tourist economy. When tourism boomed, a ripple of prosperity was felt across the borough.

Yet many inhabitants of Scarborough remained economically hard-pressed, and there was a significant number who lived a precarious hand-to-mouth existence. A key reason for this, of course, was the seasonal economic fluctuations of the town as a seaside resort. The average unemployment rate in January in the 1930s, for example, was nearly 9%.[19] Furthermore, wages were poor for many Scarborough workers. A lack of strong trade unionism weakened the bargaining power of labour, whilst the widespread employment of women and juveniles in tourist-related jobs helped to depress wage levels. Some of Scarborough's key areas of employment tended to pay low wages, notably hotels and boarding houses, domestic service, catering, entertainment, shops, fishing and the building industry. Whilst self-employment provided a secure living for many, others remained financially precarious. Such was the fate of the cheaper lodging-house owners and caterers, ice-cream and candyfloss stallholders and hawkers of souvenirs and postcards. It is also difficult to generalise about the situation of the many retirees who settled in the resort. Some enjoyed a comfortable retirement by the sea, whilst others, often widows or 'spinsters', eked out a pinched existence on small independent incomes. Therefore, whilst Scarborough enjoyed considerable prosperity in the 1930s, the town was not without its poorer citizens. In 1936, for example, its Medical Officer of Health found that one in five of the town's children was undernourished.[20] As in the rest of the country, it would be safe to assume that the main causes of poverty were large families, low wages, chronic sickness and old age, aggravated in Scarborough's case by significant levels of underemployment.[21]

The Adshead Report

When the Adshead Report was published in 1938 it displayed a great optimism about Scarborough's future as a seaside resort. This was based on the attractive physical setting of the town, the work already accomplished by the Corporation in attracting holidaymakers and the growing enthusiasm of all social classes in the 1930s for seaside holidays. Knowledgeable about pleasure resorts throughout Britain (and Europe), Adshead asserted: '… as a seaside resort its [Scarborough's] natural features and early development give it advantages possessed by but few seaside resorts in this country.'[22]

Adshead's proposals aimed to capitalise on the current demands of seaside visitors. He indicated that more needed to be done to embrace the age of the motor car and motor coach. New approach roads should be built, he proposed, some urban roads widened and plenty of bus and car parks situated in the town. He also identified the need for enhanced facilities for dancing and swimming in the town. For a modest outlay, Adshead recommended the immediate conversion of the boating pond at Peasholm Gap to an outdoor bathing pool. This had been speedily completed by the time of the publication of the Report. Adshead advocated the demolition of the White House, on the edge of the town centre Crescent, and its replacement by a Sports and Social Centre which would include an indoor swimming pool, along with squash and badminton courts, a sunbathing terrace and a refreshment room. By the time of the Report, detailed plans for this had already been submitted to the Ministry of Health for approval. The Report recommended replacing the 'dilapidated' Gala Land with an underground skating rink, and with gardens and carparking above ground. On St Nicholas Cliff, the Report proposed the construction of a small concert and conference hall with a tea-balcony. This should be built as soon as possible at a low cost. A more ambitious and longer-term proposal involved pulling down the Corporation's Olympia Ballroom on the Foreshore and replacing it with a larger dance hall, which would share the building with a covered swimming pool, shops, a restaurant and a roof-garden.

Other longer-term priorities were suggested for the North Bay. The Corner Café on Peasholm Gap should be razed and replaced by a larger and grander venue for refreshments, concerts and dancing. The most ambitious and expensive scheme (estimated at £150,000) was the Scalby Mills (or Scalby Beck) development. Incorporating the existing and picturesque Scalby Mills Hotel at the north end of North Bay, it was planned as a continental-style illuminated pleasure park, containing an open-air swimming pool, a boating lake and a dance hall, along with a beer-garden, tea-room, sun-bathing terraces and gardens. It was intended that this development would act as a magnet, attracting visitors to the North Side. Adshead also recommended that the Corporation purchase land on the outskirts of the town to enable the development of a Country Club and Sports Centre and proposed an 'aerodrome' in the Irton Moor area.

Adshead's plan for the Scalby Mills area in the Adshead Report (1938).

The Adshead Report, then, was intended to equip Scarborough to take advantage of the striking growth in tourism being witnessed in the 1930s. The Report delivered bold proposals, though Adshead was insistent they were both realistic and 'modest' in comparison with some of the town's great infrastructure projects of the past.[23] The report generated great excitement about the future of the resort. Few appeared to be unduly worried about the dark clouds emerging on the international horizon in the later 1930s.

Notes

1. S.D. Adshead and H.V. Overfield, *Scarborough: A Survey of its Existing Conditions and some Proposals for its Future* (London, 1938), p.13.
2. *Daily Telegraph*, 28 May 1935.
3. *Manchester Guardian*, 13 April 1946, Obituary.
4. Adshead, op. cit., p13.
5. V. S. Pritchett, 'Scarborough' in *Beside the Seaside*, ed. Yvonne Cloud (London, 1934), p.226.
6. Ward, Lock and Co., *A Pictorial and Descriptive Guide to Scarborough and District* (London, prob.1925), p.13.
7. *SEN*, 15 August 1939. For endnote abbreviations, see the 'Sources' section at the end of the book.
8. A non-county borough was subject to the authority of a county council in some matters. The authority in this case was the North Riding County Council in Northallerton, 60 miles distant. Although the Council in Scarborough was responsible for the Borough of Scarborough, it was invariably referred to as the Town Council. Scarborough was bounded in the north by Scalby Urban District and elsewhere by parishes in Scarborough Rural District.
9. Adshead, op. cit., p.17.
10. Raymond Fieldhouse and John Barrett, *The Streets of Scarborough* (Scarborough 1973), p.30. The Liberal Club is now a public house called (appropriately) the *Lord Rosebery*, whilst the home of the Conservative Party was demolished in 2016.
11. Adshead, op. cit., p.13.
12. Ibid., p.28.
13. Ibid., p.29.
14. Fred Gray, '1930's Architecture and the "Cult of the Sun"' in (eds.) Lara Feigel and Alexandra Harris, *Modernism on Sea* (Oxford, 2009), p.161.
15. Adshead, op. cit., p.17.
16. Adshead, op. cit., p.83.
17. *Manchester Guardian*, 23 August 1938.
18. Ron Welburn, *Full Circle: the jottings of a Scarborian* (Scarborough, 1992), p.20.
19. Jack Binns, *The History of Scarborough* (Pickering, 2001), p.342.
20. Ibid., p.338.
21. For the national picture see John Stevenson, *British Society, 1914-45* (London, 1990), pp.134-135.
22. Adshead, op. cit., p.15.
23. Adshead, op. cit., p.12.

CHAPTER 2

'Phoney War' Scarborough

The whole stage was set for an early and intense attack by Germany which would have aroused our stubbornness. The Government had not foreseen a situation in which boredom and bewilderment would be the main elements.[1]

(Harold Nicholson, diplomat and MP)

War declared

Eric Appleby remembered the start of the war in Scarborough: 'When war broke out I was the organist and choirmaster of St Sepulchre Street Methodist Church, which was a building holding 1,200 people ... At 11 am on 3 September 1939 I was playing the organ during the taking of the collection at the morning service. I was actually playing the soft movement of Mendelssohn's first sonata when the door opened and a person came in from one of the houses opposite to tell the minister that he had heard over the radio that war with Germany had been declared.' The minister then informed the congregation. 'After the service, the one topic of conversation was, of course, the news of the beginning of what was to become world war two, but people were too shocked and bewildered to react in any other way but to think what might be the outcome and how it would affect individuals and families.'[2] For the first eight months of the war, the so-called 'Phoney War', Britain was not involved in any large-scale military action, but the strains of war began to have an impact on Scarborough's individuals and families.

Civil Defence

Since the mid-1930s British war planning had identified Nazi Germany as the most likely enemy and had assumed that the Nazis would inflict a mass aerial bombing campaign on Britain, possibly using poison gas. The planners therefore developed a system of Air Raid Precautions (ARP) as a 'Fourth Line' of defence against Germany. This was renamed 'Civil Defence' in 1941.

During the Phoney War Scarborough developed an ARP machinery which was later to prove invaluable. The Town Hall set up an emergency control-room under the north end of Valley Bridge and an ARP Control Centre in the underground Market Vaults. The latter controlled a network of ARP services which helped to prepare the town for the eventuality of air-raids.[3] On the widespread assumption that the enemy would use gas attacks, Gas Decontamination Squads were established. Exercises in decontamination were frequent, though in one simulated gas attack on the Foreshore there was concern that the incident was attended by a large crowd of enthusiastic spectators.[4] First Aid posts, too, were a key part of the ARP infrastructure. Rescue Squads were formed which would search for the survivors of bombings and shore up buildings if required. The Control Centre would also be ready to direct the existing police, fire and ambulance services to the areas of greatest need in the town. At the core of Scarborough's ARP machinery were the salaried full-time and voluntary part-time ARP Wardens (300 at peak strength) stationed at ARP posts throughout the town. The wardens, with their ARP armbands and tin helmets, became a distinctive presence in everyday life. As respected members of the local communities they served, they were, in the words of one historian, 'the eyes and ears of the civil defence machine'.[5] In the Phoney War period they instructed the people of Scarborough on how to fortify their homes against bomb and gas attacks, on the importance of maintaining and carrying gas masks and on the necessity of obeying blackout regulations concerning sources of light in homes, businesses and transport. In the event of an air-raid, Wardens were trained to play a central role in coordinating ARP emergency services, supervising rescue efforts and logging incidents.

Wardens were supported in this work by an array of wartime helpers. Along with the regular police, fire and medical services were auxiliary forces that could be called upon to aid ARP efforts. Scarborough's regular fire brigade was supported by the volunteer firefighters of the Auxiliary Fire Service (AFS). About a hundred part-time and full-time auxiliary firemen were on standby during the Phoney War, supported by three auxiliary fire stations. Similarly, the town's regular police force was backed up by volunteer Special Constables, 302 having been appointed after the Munich Crisis in 1938. There could be rivalries between members of ARP-related services. Unsurprisingly, some resentment existed between paid and unpaid ARP workers, whilst some Special Constables felt hard done by and harboured jealousy towards AFS volunteers, whom they regarded as cosseted. Special Constables, one alleged, were deprived of even a cup of coffee on duty and were obliged to share coats.[6]

ARP and Red Cross vehicles and members on Grange Avenue in Falsgrave, Scarborough. The house on the right is identified as a First Aid Party Depot. The vehicle on the left is a 'First Aid Party Car' and the light lorry on the right is 'ARP Ambulance No.5'. The three private cars in the middle have window stickers identifying them as 'ARP'.

Other volunteers helped too. Women played an important role in air-raid precautions, especially those in the Women's Voluntary Service (WVS), who trained to operate canteens for emergency workers, look after the victims of bombings and provide cars and drivers from their Transport Section (see chapter 12). Local cycling clubs were deployed by the Chief Constable as messengers and lookouts.[7] The Boy Scouts and Girl Guides were trained in first aid, helped to deliver ARP messages and distributed gas masks and sandbags to the public.[8] Groups like the YMCA, the St John's Ambulance Brigade, the Women's Institute and local churches also helped to staff ARP canteens and made ready to provide welfare support to the victims of air-raids.[9]

The implementation of ARP policies in Scarborough generated some tensions and difficulties, triggering something of a turf war between Scarborough and

Scarborough at War

the County Council in Northallerton. ARP in the town was the responsibility of the North Riding County Council in conjunction with the ARP North-East regional headquarters based in Leeds. From the start of ARP preparations in 1938, the Scarborough authorities resented Northallerton's supervision and demanded that they had control over their own ARP arrangements. Scarborough's Chief Constable, Walter Abbott, threatened to resign in protest against the town's impotence.[10] The Town Clerk informed Northallerton that the Town Hall would cooperate with their ARP plans, 'if the scheme is one which will be sufficiently satisfactory reasonably to guarantee the safety of the inhabitants of this town'. 'This is completely non-cooperative,' was the North Riding's blunt response.[11] Scarborough appealed to the Home Office to be allowed to become a separate ARP scheme-making authority. Working with the County Council only generated friction and delays, Scarborough argued. The County Council, moreover, was accustomed to overseeing a largely rural and semi-rural county and lacked an understanding of the ARP needs of a community like Scarborough. 'There is a recurring failure of the County,' claimed Scarborough's Town Clerk, 'to appreciate urban problems and to act upon the suggestions of the Corporation, which are based upon intimate knowledge of urban requirements and local circumstances.'[12] Scarborough, for example, complained in November 1939 that the County's air raid siren system in the town was inaudible to people indoors and practically inaudible outdoors in certain areas of the town. Nothing had been done by the end of March 1940.[13] Scarborough also chaffed at having to obtain Northallerton's permission before it could spend over £2 on ARP or paint white lines on local roads.[14] It was also felt in Scarborough that it was unfair that the town should be subsidising ARP arrangements in the North Riding's rural areas. This was resented especially as inland areas were unlikely to be attacked, whilst the Town Clerk pointed out that '… it is probable that Scarborough will from its geographical position and publicity value, receive very early attention from the enemy'.[15] The Home Office was unsympathetic to Scarborough's objections to County control over ARP and in August 1940, given the country's perilous security situation, Scarborough finally dropped its claim to be exempted from County Council jurisdiction.[16]

In some ways, the greatest challenge to Britain's ARP services in the first eight months of the war was the absence of *Luftwaffe* activity over the country, as public opinion became increasingly complacent about the threat of Nazi bombing. People spoke of the 'Bore War' and became less inclined to carry gas masks. An official war historian detected in the autumn of 1939, 'a chill wind of public criticism which – with what, in retrospect, seems astonishing speed – began to blow on them [ARP workers].[17] As early as 18 September 1939, it was claimed in the local press that civil defence workers had 'nothing to do'.[18] Later, there were grumblings in the press about the 'vast total of hours of boredom' endured by ARP workers, especially volunteers.[19] Similarly, a local unemployed man complained about the injustice of recruiting men for the AFS who already had jobs, and who used their time at AFS posts to catch up on missed sleep.[20] In Scarborough, questions were asked about the scale of ARP arrangements and about their sizeable cost. It was revealed that, by the end of September 1939, the Town Hall had spent some £17,000 on ARP, though it was not always appreciated that much of this was recoverable in the long-run from the County Council and the Home Office. But such costs exasperated the parsimonious Chair of the Council's Finance Committee Alderman Francis Whittaker, who condemned the sums involved as a 'gross extravagance'.[21] Writing in the *Mercury* newspaper as 'Jottings', he reviewed the whole panoply of local ARP services and concluded that the expenditure involved amounted to 'an appalling sum of money'.[22] An awkward debate rumbled on within the Council about the appropriate level of protection for elementary schoolchildren. The left-wing Councillor Sidney Simpson persistently demanded the construction of substantial, purpose-built shelters for the town's school pupils, whilst the Council majority defended the cheaper option of merely sandbagging existing structures.[23]

Criticism of ARP spending had an impact on the ARP authorities and efforts were made to rein in their ARP commitments and expenditure. Towards the end of September 1939, the Council in Scarborough agreed to sizeable cuts to the salaried ARP organisation.[24] At the end of October the Civil Defence Regional Commissioner unveiled a more thorough reorganisation of ARP, involving further cuts to the ARP salary budget.[25] In December Scarborough Council's Emergency Committee took the decision to reduce the number of full-time, paid ARP wardens from 91 to 59 and to reduce the manned stations to 15. The number of auxiliary firemen was also cut.[26] Despite the proximity of *Luftwaffe* attacks on North Sea shipping in the early months of 1940, further cuts to ARP were publicised in April 1940.[27]

There is little doubt that it was the restrictions of the blackout that provoked the greatest public hostility towards ARP activity. A Phoney War slogan criticising the enforcement of the blackout stated, 'Turn on the lights and turn out the ARP workers.'[28] The sense of popular frustration in Scarborough is conveyed in a letter to the local paper whose author failed to see the point of blackening the side windows of his home. This would 'necessitate enemy aircraft being on the ground,' he commented, 'instead of in the air, where they are to be expected'.[29] Regular prosecutions at the Borough Police Court for infringements of the blackout commenced less than a month into the war, with many feeling that the sanctions were unduly draconian. The impact of the blackout could be a serious inconvenience at the least, causing venues offering evening entertainment to lose custom in the darkness, as did fish and chip shops. Early on, there was a serious shortage of blackout material, which inflated its price. Blackout-related accidents were a common occurrence: pedestrians experienced falls (especially at pub closing time), traffic accidents increased and, in early May 1940, the death of an elderly couple in a house-fire was attributed to the blackout.[30] In a later incident, a 67-year-old pedestrian was fatally struck by a bus in what was described as a 'black-out tragedy'.[31] As happened nationally, ARP wardens, supported by Special Constables, were frequently resented as interfering busy-bodies when imposing the letter of the blackout law. Yet Scarborough does seem to have made good progress in relation to the blackout. In mid-December 1939 the Chief Constable paid tribute to his Special Constables, saying, 'You have made this town one of the blackest towns under the sun.'[32] In March 1940 a visiting ARP warden recorded his admiration for the effectiveness of the town's blackout.[33] At the beginning of 1940 the ARP authorities in the borough were able to shift their blackout efforts from homes, businesses and motor vehicles to the lesser priorities of cyclists and torch-wielding pedestrians.[34]

It was inevitable that aspects of ARP would face problems and criticism during the Phoney War, when the threat of air-raids remained theoretical. However, in retrospect the service played an important role in preparing the town for the reality of war. In December 1939, for example, a major dress rehearsal took place at the town's main hospital, involving the simulation of a bombing incident where there were some hundred casualties. Important lessons were learned.[35] In mid-January an ARP 'try-out' tested the arrangements for responding to 23 explosive incidents in the town and a follow-up practice was completed in March 1940.[36] The construction of public air-raid shelters was also commenced (dealt with in chapters 5 and 6). Psychologically, the pervasive presence of ARP was a constant reminder of the perilous state of the country, helping to create a 'civil defence mentality'.[37] And voluntary support for the ARP effort helped to foster a patriotic sense of participation in the defence of the local community.

The Scarborough Auxiliary Fire Service photograph illustrates the civil defence spirit of improvisation. Former United buses have been converted into water tenders.

The 'Phoney War' economy

At about 8.00 a.m. on 16 December 1914 two German battle cruisers, *Derfflinger* and *Von der Tann*, emerged from the early morning mist north of Scarborough. Taking up positions off the South Bay, for half an hour they fired some 700 explosive shells into the town. Eighteen people were killed, 84 injured and there was widespread damage to property.[38]

When the prospect of war loomed in Britain in 1939, the German naval attack on Scarborough in the First World War was still well remembered in the town and the damage inflicted by World War One on its tourist economy had also not been forgotten. There were, therefore, good grounds for pessimism in Scarborough when war was declared on Germany. Bookings for the summer season in 1939 were already well down. The threat of war meant that British families had more to worry about than organising seaside holidays, whilst there was already uncertainty about the availability of transport to holiday destinations. And it was not clear, from the evidence of 1914 at least, that resorts on the east coast would be safe from enemy attack.

The war brought what there was left of the season in September to a premature end. In the words of Alderman Whittaker, 'the season was cut off as by a knife'.[39] This hit the town's hoteliers, boarding house keepers, caterers and traders severely, as many depended upon the summer season to cover their overheads, and the additional September custom to generate an income.[40] The cancellation of the resort's popular cricket festival in September was a further body-blow to the tourist trade. The early months of the war also saw a depletion in the holiday accommodation available in the town, caused, firstly, by the need to billet evacuee children and, secondly, by the Armed Forces' requisitioning of some of the resort's largest hotels. At first it was the Admiralty and the Air Ministry that commandeered substantial hotel properties, to be followed in 1940 by the War Office. Even when accommodation was available, the town had to counter rumours outside the area that it was 'taken over by the military', 'full of evacuees' and 'closed up'.[41] In response to such an unfavourable climate, some hoteliers and traders opted to close their businesses, whilst there was also something of an exodus of well-to-do residents from the town.[42] Many less well-off families, who let out one or two rooms during the holiday season to help make ends meet, had good reason to be anxious about the future.

Other early wartime developments provided challenges to pleasure resorts like Scarborough. Food shortages (and rationing from January 1940) posed difficulties for the town's hotels and catering establishments. The blackout threatened attendance at seasonal evening entertainments. Petrol rationing, introduced at the beginning of the war, and cuts to passenger rail transport made it more difficult to get to the resort in the first place. By April 1940 the Council was having to cut back on tourist publicity and advertising due to paper rationing.[43] Potential visitors were liable to be put off by the security risks of coming to Scarborough, so there was considerable anger in late November 1939 when the BBC broadcast erroneous reports of *Luftwaffe* activity over the North-East Coast.[44]

Despite this backdrop, there were some, like the retiring President of the Scarborough Hotels and Boarding Houses Association (SHBHA), who were confident that the resort would overcome the challenges of war. The town had, after all, enjoyed some good seasons during the later years of World War One. Some leisure activities in the town enjoyed something of a boom in war conditions, notably dancing at the Olympia Ballroom. 'When the horrors of war overtake a nation,' reflected Alderman Whittaker, 'its young people seek relief in such things as the weird noises of jazz.'[45] Others, however, exemplified by the incoming President of the Association, were more pessimistic about the future. The challenge to the town was now greater than it had been in World War I, he pointed out, as it was much more reliant on the hospitality industry. He was not confident that Scarborough would be able to compete with the relatively safer resorts on England's north-west coast. In mid-December the Association formed a War Emergency Committee to provide advice to members who were experiencing economic difficulties arising from the war.[46]

The decline in tourism in the Phoney War period caused extensive difficulties in the town. The Town Hall was dependent on revenues from tourism for financing public services and for helping to lighten its demands on local taxpayers. As we have seen (p.4), the Council profited from running a range of the resort's tourist undertakings and seasonal attractions. From the summer of 1939 profits from such enterprises began to fall. Similarly, privately operated undertakings like the Scarborough Spa saw a rapid drop in profits, necessitating a cut in salaries and the cancellation of dividends in January 1940.[47] Aggravating the situation, many of the town's residents found it increasingly difficult to keep up with the payment of local taxes, or rates. The non-payment of rates proved to be a thorny issue for the Town Hall to deal with. By the end of October 1939 there were much larger sums outstanding than usual. In early December there was criticism of the Council for failing to sympathise with the non-payment of rates caused by the slump in tourism and for issuing summonses to some 800 residents.[48] Some ratepayers, though, were on the side of the Council, feeling that a minority of ratepayers were using the war as an excuse for not paying their due. Similarly, the Council began to experience greater difficulties in collecting council house rents. It again found itself the target of some public criticism when it initiated repossessions from tenants who, it turned out, had family members serving in the army in France. Amidst these difficulties Alderman Whittaker could only appeal to a sense of fair play and 'local patriotism' when it came to the payment of rates and rents.[49]

Whilst the Council's revenues were being eroded, the cost of fulfilling its new wartime responsibilities was increasing. Central government imposed on municipalities a range of additional expenses to deal, for example, with child evacuation, National Registration, food and fuel control and, most onerously, civil defence. Although some of this expense was ultimately defrayed by the county council and central government, there were serious shortfalls in municipal finances. Pressure built up on the Council to make economies. Though staffing was already depleted due to the demands of war work and conscription, the populist Councillor Jackson demanded further reductions in staffing and salaries and the establishment of a Council Economy Committee.[50] Jackson demanded to know why the Council were not making cuts, whilst being quick to issue summonses to 'poor folk' for the non-payment of rates.[51] In the *Mercury* the Council was excoriated for the extravagance of its ARP expenditure. The town's air-raid sirens, for example, were remarkably expensive, each one requiring the support of a whole team of electricians.[52] The majority of councillors did not need to be pushed very hard to adopt a programme of cuts. In November, the Council voted to cut the generous payment it made to Council employees serving in the Armed Forces to compensate them for loss of earnings and in April 1940 the Council withdrew payments to members of the Police Force for doing extra fire duties.[53] Pressure was brought to bear on all Corporation Committees to effect economies.[54]

Against such a backdrop of concern about the resort's economic prospects, there was relief over visitor numbers at Christmas 1939. There were surprisingly few cancellations and the weather was gratifyingly mild. Crucially, train services remained reasonably dependable, with 4,000 visitors arriving by rail for the festivities. Hotels and boarding houses were mostly fully booked, whilst some smaller hotels even put on a festive Christmas effort for the first time. It was largely business as usual, and certainly a vast improvement on the first Christmas of World War One, shortly after the bombardment of the town by the German navy.[55]

There continued to be a reassuring number of winter visitors after Christmas, but attention in the town turned to the economic prospects for the spring season. The people of Scarborough had good reasons for anxiety. Unemployment was rising and by April juvenile unemployment was 31% above the level of the previous year.[56] From mid-January there were regular reports on the BBC and in the local and national press of enemy aircraft attacking fishing vessels off the Yorkshire coast (see pp.126-131), with commentators speaking of the East Coast becoming the country's 'front line' in the war. Rumours circulated about prohibitions on travel to the East Coast, the barricading of the beach in Scarborough and the danger of mines washing up on its shores.[57] The greatest source of pessimism in the town remained concern about the availability of train services. The local authority appealed to the London and North Eastern Railway (LNER) to organise as many trains to Scarborough as possible for the Easter period, within the limits of government restrictions.[58]

There was a determination on the part of the resort's municipal and business leaders to make the most of the opportunities afforded by the Easter holiday season. The Council allocated up to £60,000 in publicity and preparations for Easter and committed itself to maintaining most of the existing municipal entertainments and amusements, apart from the bathing pools. It was hoped that those who had cancelled the previous September would re-book for Easter, but dealing with fears about the safety of the resort was trickier. Local businesses were not keen on the approach of *The Times* newspaper, which speculated that holidaymakers might be attracted to resorts like Scarborough in the hope of enjoying the excitement of an aerial dogfight in the skies above them.[59] Reservations about holidaying in Scarborough are evident in the diary of a Glasgow shipping secretary, who was planning a holiday with her mother. 'I didn't fancy Scarborough again,' she decided in February. 'I should not like the East Coast in the Blitzkrieg.' In April she remained pessimistic:

> Mother wants Scarborough. I feel hesitant for I am not as confident as she that air raids are an impossibility and I also anticipate travelling difficulties and Scarborough is a long way away.[60]

Scarborough's tourist authorities played down the threat of war as much as possible. Instead, they argued that workers deserved a break from the demands of the Home Front, and that they should not allow Hitler to keep them away from a well-earned respite.

When Easter came it was a mixed one for the resort. It started slowly and numbers were down overall for the Easter weekend. Returns for municipal amenities and entertainments dropped from £1,667 in 1939 to £1,054. In 1939 some 21,000 had arrived by train, in 1940 the number fell to about 8,800. It was the shortcomings of rail transport, especially day and half-day excursions, that most concerned the business community. According to *The Mercury* newspaper, the LNER did not 'go all out', and 'must do better next time'.[61]

Yet there was some relief that things were not worse. The weather held up well. Scarborians were reassured to see the sea-front thronged and crowds of holidaymakers taking advantage of the resort's attractions, notably the Olympia Ballroom and the many cinemas. Some hotels had to turn visitors away. A marked increase in motor vehicle transport to the coast helped to compensate for rail shortcomings and suggested that motorists had been conserving petrol for use during the Easter break. The Chairman of the Town Hall's publicity committee was greatly encouraged, having been 'told by no small number of people that no one would come'.[62] An observer was probably correct in describing Easter 1940 as a two-thirds success, with visitor numbers and takings in the region of two-thirds of peace-time figures.[63]

The 1940 Crisis

The Whitsun holiday in May 1940 coincided with the Nazi onslaught on France and the Low Countries and the dramatic replacement of Prime Minister Neville Chamberlain with the more pugnacious Winston Churchill. German military success heightened fears in Britain of aerial bombing and raised the very real possibility of invasion. The existing troubles of the tourist economy in Scarborough were seriously exacerbated as the government cancelled the Whitsun bank holiday and discouraged any unnecessary travel at such a time of national emergency.[64] A flood of telegrams arrived in the town from the West Riding cancelling Whitsun bookings, whilst rumours circulated that the resort was completely closed for business.[65] The National Association of Master Bakers, Confectioners and Caterers cancelled its annual conference in Scarborough and Special Whitsun passenger train services were withdrawn.[66] Whilst some of the larger and more opulent hotels were not so badly hit, with customers arriving by private car, the smaller hotels and boarding houses were dealt a punishing blow. Corporation takings, a good barometer of the health of the tourist economy, were well below one third of the previous year, despite excellent weather.[67] The *Mercury* columnist Jottings, in a series of articles, tended towards the apocalyptic. Whitsun, he felt, had been 'disastrous', parts of the resort's economy would never recover and, indeed, the very future of the town as a pleasure resort had been put in jeopardy.[68]

The forebodings of Jottings were to be partially vindicated during the remaining spring and summer of 1940. At the end of May and beginning of June 1940 the British Expeditionary Force was forced into a hasty retreat from Dunkirk, and France surrendered to Germany on 17 June. In the summer of 1940 Nazi air raids on Britain escalated, including several raids on the Scarborough area. The threat of an enemy invasion loomed increasingly large. Frantic efforts were made to defend the coastline of the east and south-east of the country, and on 19 June the Ministry of Information distributed a pamphlet entitled 'If The Invader Comes'.

The repercussions of this national emergency for holiday resorts on the east coast were drastic. Political leaders exhorted the workforce to maximise war production and forgo recreation and holidays. The money saved by sacrificing holidays could be channelled usefully into National Savings, the government advised. The August Bank Holiday was cancelled, and local 'Wake Weeks' in the North were prohibited to prevent road and rail congestion and disruption to war production.

The culminating body blow for Scarborough came in early July 1940 when the existing east coast Defence Area was extended northwards from the Wash to Berwick, including Scarborough. Citizens were prohibited from travelling to the Defence Areas for the purposes of holidays, pleasure or recreation. The government was keen to protect the already fragile economies of east coast seaside resorts and tried to make exceptions to the ban where tourist numbers were not great and where there were no important military installations.[69] Neither consideration applied to Scarborough. Nonetheless, there was some flexibility in the arrangements. Those entering for reasons other than 'pleasure' could still travel to the coast, for business, visiting relatives or evacuee children and such like, and entry to Defence Areas did not require a permit.[70] Yet rumours that all visitors to the coast were banned only compounded the town's problems.

The impact of the Defence Area regulations, on top of existing difficulties, was calamitous. Throughout the summer of 1940 business in the town was devastated. It was reported that in early July there was 'not more than a handful of visitors' and the August Bank Holiday was described by one resident as looking like 'a wet Wednesday half-term holiday in February'.[71] Major entertainments, like a performance of *Merrie England* at the Open Air Theatre, were cancelled. An impression was being given that the resort was shutting up shop.[72] A report on the town's tourist economy estimated that some £4m of trade was lost over the summer.[73] Jottings warned that if the government failed to provide financial assistance to the town the result might be 'much unrest and even trouble' and looking back at the end of the summer season he concluded that the situation was 'going from bad to worse'.[74]

The disappearance of tourists in the summer was a painful experience for many. Hotels, boarding and lodging houses and the catering trade took the brunt of the collapse of the hospitality trade in the summer of 1940. The Town Clerk judged that the hotel trade had been 'put to an end'.[75] The billeting of evacuees and soldiers, which had previously been perceived as a burden, was increasingly seen as a lifeline, as was having a breadwinner in the family in employment outside the tourism economy.[76] So many hotels, shops and businesses closed down, and so many residents left the town, that the Council was forced to raise the cost of electricity due to a slump in demand of 20-25%.[77] Many of the smaller hotels and boarding houses, often run by elderly retirees to the town, were pushed towards closure and bankruptcy. The *Mercury* embarked on a campaign to champion the victims of the collapse in trade, alerting readers to the fact that many Scarborians were being driven to pauperism and Public Assistance and demanding government assistance and rate relief.[78] The town's shopkeepers also felt the economic downturn keenly. It was indicative of their travails that advertisements began to appear in the local press encouraging shopkeepers to re-locate to other more prosperous areas of the country.[79] What made this situation all the more galling was the feeling that east coast resorts were, through no fault of their own, being asked to pay the price for the nation's predicament in the summer of 1940. Other areas of the country were largely unaffected by the war, or even benefited economically from expanding wartime production. Suspicions were aroused that rival west coast pleasure resorts, notably Blackpool, were taking advantage of the woes of resorts in the east to boost their own tourist business.[80]

The summer of 1940, then, proved to be a very challenging one. The atmosphere in the town remained distinctly pessimistic for the remainder of the year. In November the new mayor, J.C. Ireland, was unambiguous about the cause of the town's crisis, lamenting that, 'hopes for last season were dashed as a result of the Order making Scarborough a Defence Area. But for that Order many people would have welcomed the opportunity of a few days' relaxation at Scarborough.'[81] Later in the month, the retiring President of the SHBHA surveyed the toll taken on his members' livelihoods, bemoaning the collapse in visitor numbers, the struggle to pay the rates, the lack of alternative employment and the insufficient payment for hosting evacuees. One member summed up the mood of frustration, gloom and anger, comparing the town to the impoverished town of Jarrow in the 1930s and lashing out at the Civil Defence Order, which had 'crippled the industry entirely'.[82] Evidence from the SHBHA was reinforced by the local Council of Social Welfare, which reported that its charitable workload had increased markedly in supporting workers in the tourism industry and it also observed that many who were falling into financial troubles were too proud to seek Public Assistance.[83] In December *The Mercury* expanded on the extent of local distress, highlighting the breakdown of the catering trades, concluding that they were 'dead for the duration of the war'.[84]

For the Town Hall, the collapse of the tourist economy during the summer of 1940 created considerable difficulties. Responsibilities for civil defence, and other wartime impositions, continued to expand, necessitating, for example, an increase in staffing and resources for the Borough Engineer's and Treasurer's Departments.[85] Rate arrears continued to rise and municipal revenues from tourism continued to fall. A review of municipal finances in late August 1940 concluded that the designation as a Defence Area had 'completed the destruction of the financial structure' of the Borough.[86] Councillors intensified an economy drive during the autumn of 1940. Most departments were instructed to effect large savings, leading to severe cuts in spending on housing, public health, cleansing, libraries and parks. Funding for the tourism-related departments of Publicity, Entertainment and Cafés was effectively terminated. There were also cuts to the salaries of officials and perks, like the use of official cars, were curtailed. By late September the Council announced that it had saved over £13,000.[87]

Throughout the summer of 1940 there was a chorus of demands from Scarborough and other east coast resorts for aid to alleviate the hardships inflicted by the collapse of tourism.[88] In Scarborough the SHBHA took the lead in appealing for financial help, lobbying MPs and government departments, in conjunction with representatives from other resorts. The most frequent demands were for some form of reduction of the rates (through derating or rate relief) for hotels and boarding houses and for a central government subvention to the local authorities affected. Government responses were not encouraging. The preference of ministers was for local authorities to collect the rates as vigorously as possible, to concentrate on maintaining essential services and to implement robust economies in other areas. They also recommended, where unavoidable, municipal borrowing. Only where it seemed that local authorities were unable to maintain essential services would emergency financial support be considered, and it would come with strings attached.[89] But the determination of the Council in Scarborough not to seek any form of government bailout merely added to the frustration of hard-pressed business people in the town. One wrote to the local press accusing the Chair of the Finance Committee of preferring the prospect of an OBE to protecting local business in the town.[90]

The case for special treatment for east coast towns was weakened in the autumn of 1940 when the *Luftwaffe* launched its *Blitz*, firstly on London, then on other ports and industrial cities. In Scarborough public statements became increasingly coloured by a patriotic spirit of self-sacrifice and national solidarity. In November, for example, the new President of the SHBHA reminded his members that '… things could be worse … A lot of people were suffering a great deal more than they were.'[91] Similarly, when the Scarborough and District Cooperative Society was compelled to reduce its dividend in November 1940, a spokesman observed, 'Whatever we had to face in Scarborough would be accepted with a spirit of fortitude when we consider the tragedy of London, Coventry and other towns.'[92]

Notes

1. Quoted in Brian Bond, 'The calm before the storm: Britain and the "Phoney War" 1939-40', *RUSI (Royal United Services Institute) Journal*, Spring 1990, p.61.
2. SMHC File, *Scarborough Volume 9, Wars and Streets*.
3. *SEN*, 10 October 1939.
4. *SEN*, 4 March 1940.
5. Angus Calder, *The People's War* (London, 1971), p.227.
6. *SEN*, 2 and 5 March 1940.
7. *SEN*, 2 September 1939.
8. *SEN*, 12 February 1940.
9. See, for example, *Mercury* 15 March 1940.
10. Les Shannon, *Conflagrations: Scarborough's Firefighting History* (Scarborough, 2003), p.136.
11. NA HO 207/1035, Clerk of the County Council to Scarborough Town Hall, 10 September 1938.
12. NA HO 207/1035, Scarborough Town Clerk to Home Office, 15 April 1940.
13. NA HO 207/1035, Scarborough Town Hall Memorandum, 29 March 1940.
14. NA HO 207/1035, Scarborough Town Clerk to Home Office, 15 April 1940, SEN 30 April 1940 and SEN 6 May 1940.
15. NA HO 207/1035, Ibid.
16. NA HO 207/1035, Scarborough Town Clerk to Home Office, 8 August 1940.
17. Terence H O'Brien, *Civil Defence* (HMSO London, 1955), p.341.
18. *SEN*, 18 September 1939.
19. *SEN*, 30 January 1940.
20. *SEN*, 6 November 1939.
21. *SEN*, 10 October 1939.
22. *Mercury*, 10 November 1939.
23. See, for example, *SEN*, 2 October 1939 and *Mercury*, 3 November 1939.
24. *Mercury*, 22 September 1939.
25. *SEN*, 28 October 1939.
26. Shannon, op. cit., p.139.
27. *SEN*, 9 April 1939 and O'Brien, op. cit., p.373.
28. O'Brien, op. cit., p.297.
29. *SEN*, 16 October 1939.
30. *SEN*, 6 May 1940.
31. *SEN*, 24 November 1941. Nationally, there was a notable increase in fatal accidents for the young and the elderly in the war years. See R.M. Titmuss, *Problems of Social Policy* (HMSO, 1950), pp.333-335.

32. *SEN*, 16 December 1939.
33. *SEN*, March 26 1939.
34. *SEN*, 10 January 1940.
35. *SEN*, 11 December 1939.
36. *SEN*, 15 January 1940 and 4 March 1940.
37. Richard Overy, *The Bombing War* (London, 2013), p.128.
38. See Jann M. Witt and Robin McDermott, *Scarborough Bombardment* (Berlin, 2016).
39. *SEN*, 1 April 1940.
40. Justice of the Peace and Local Government Review on Scarborough, *SEN* 22 August 1940.
41. The manager of the Grand Hotel, *SEN*, 16 November 1939.
42. *Mercury*, 13 October 1939.
43. *Mercury* 19 April 1940.
44. *SEN*, 3 January 1940.
45. *SEN* 1 April 1940.
46. *SEN*, 29 November 1939 and SEN, 13 December 1939.
47. *SEN*, 20 January 1940.
48. *SEN*, 21 October 1939 and letter in SEN, 2 December 1939.
49. *SEN*, 10 October 1939.
50. *SEN*, 8 December 1939.
51. *SEN*, 27 December 1939.
52. *Mercury*, 8 December 1939.
53. *Mercury*, 12 April 1940.
54. *SEN*, 11 November 1939 and 19 December 1939.
55. *SEN*, 27 December 1939 and *Mercury*, 29 December 1939.
56. *SEN*, 16 February 1940 and 2 April 1940.
57. *Mercury*, 3 February 1940, 14 March 1940 and 19 April 1940.
58. *SEN*, 9 March 1940.
59. *SEN*, 28 March 1940.
60. Simon Garfield, *We Are At War* (London, 2006), pp. 172 and 201.
61. *SEN*, 27 March 1940 and *Mercury*, 29 March 1940.
62. *Mercury*, 12 April 1940.
63. *SEN*, 26 September 1940.
64. *SEN*, 13 May 1940.
65. *SEN*, 14 May 1940.
66. *SEN*, 16 May 1940.

67　*SEN*, 15 May 1940.
68　*Mercury*, 17, 24 and 31 May 1940.
69　NA HO 186/344, T.R. Gardiner to Sir Findlater Stewart, 21 June 1940.
70　NA MEPO 2/3493, Supplementary Police Order 98, 27 August 1940.
71　*Mercury*, 5 July and 9 August 1940.
72　*SEN*, 19 June 1940 and 8 July 1940.
73　*SEN*, 5 July 1940, *Mercury* 9 August 1940 and SEN 22 August 1940.
74　*Mercury*, 9 August 1940 and 13 September 1940.
75　NA HLG 7 /179, Minute, 8 January 1941.
76　*Mercury*, 27 September 1940.
77　*SEN*, 1 October 1940.
78　*Mercury*, 26 July, 9 August and 13 September.
79　For example, *SEN*, 25 July 1940.
80　See, for example, *SEN*, 5 June 1940 and 17 August 1940.
81　*SEN*, 11 November 1940.
82　*Mercury*, 22 November 1940.
83　Ibid.
84　*Mercury*, 6 December 1940.
85　*SEN*, 24 September 1940.
86　*SEN*, 22 August 1940.
87　*SEN*, 10 September 1940 and 24 September 1940.
88　Paul Addison and Jeremy A. Crang (eds.), *Listening to Britain* (London, 2011), p.264.
89　*Mercury*, 6 December 1940 and SEN, 18 December 1940.
90　*SEN*, 13 October 1941.
91　*Mercury*, 22 November 1940.
92　*SEN*, 19 November 1940.

CHAPTER 3

'Pied Piper': Evacuation to Scarborough

The poet Christopher Wiseman remembered the day he was evacuated as a toddler from Hull's railway station to Scarborough:

> …Through barriers to one train,
> ignoring yells, my suddenly bigger mother marched
> the whole length to the engine and asked the driver
> where he was going to. *Scarborough, lady*,
> he said, taken aback. *Just up the coast.*
> Now we have our coffee and walk outside,
> Around the concourse. The journey of my life,
> I think, everything that's happened started here.
> Another train and I'd be someone else.[1]

Planning

The evacuation of British children from potential areas of danger in the event of war with Germany was planned in the later 1930s. The plans arose from a fear that the enemy would launch devastating aerial attacks on the country's ports and cities. In the words of Prime Minister Baldwin, 'the bomber will always get through'.[2] In preparation, Britain was divided into three types of areas: neutral (where there would be no population movement), evacuation (from where children were to be removed) and reception (to where children would be sent). Scarborough was placed in the latter category. It was planned that schoolchildren would be evacuated with their teachers, along with expectant mothers and mothers with pre-school infants. Evacuees were to be hosted as far as possible in private households, where hosts would receive a modest allowance from the state, whilst mothers with infants would pay for their own board. In reception areas volunteers, under the direction of billeting officers, surveyed the housing stock to establish how many evacuees could be accommodated. Generally, the hosting of evacuees was done on a voluntary basis, though the billeting officers did have compulsory powers at their disposal.

In Scarborough, the authorities identified potential accommodation for 25,000 evacuees. In the event, the Ministry of Health, responsible nationally for evacuation, allocated 18,000 evacuees to Scarborough, from Hull, Middlesbrough and West Hartlepool.[3] The Town Hall was highly exercised over the financial implications of the evacuation scheme for its tightly controlled purse strings. A lengthy shopping list was submitted to the Ministry of Health of items it would require financial help with as a reception area, including direction signs, hurricane lamps, tea, milk, biscuits, stationery, mattresses, blankets and the installation of new telephone lines. The Town Hall also wished to ascertain who would meet claims of liability in the event of evacuee accidents. The Ministry was distinctly unsympathetic, declining to take responsibility for most expenses. First Aid equipment, it recommended, could be obtained from hospital stores. The only items it readily accepted financial responsibility for were armlets and badges for evacuees and volunteer workers, 'a not inconsiderable cost' according to the relieved Town Clerk.[4] Next, the Scarborough authorities were concerned that they did not possess sufficient school places for the projected number of evacuee children. '(T)he first consideration must be the safety of the children,' minuted a ministry official, 'education is not of such importance.'[5]

Arrival

By the end of August 1939, it was evident that war with Nazi Germany was imminent. On 31 August the code word 'Pied Piper' was passed to local authorities in reception areas, signalling the commencement of evacuation. On September 1st at 8.13 a.m., two days before Britain's official declaration of war, the first evacuees from Hull began to arrive at Scarborough's Londesborough Road Railway Station. The platform was soon crowded with excited and anxious children, with name labels attached to their coats and gas masks hung around their necks with string. A hyperbolic observer suggested that the arrival 'dwarfs the flight of the Israelites from Egypt'.[6] Over the next week the evacuees continued to arrive from Hull, Middlesbrough and West Hartlepool.

When the evacuees alighted from the trains Town Hall staff provided a welcome. They were supported in checking the health of the evacuees by ambulance workers and voluntary first aiders. ARP workers, Special Constables and members of the Woman's Voluntary Service (WVS) helped to reassure and organise the young arrivals. Staff from local department stores, Woolworth's and W. Rowntree's for example, had prepared emergency rations, including chocolate. A 'plentiful' supply of private cars helped with the distribution of evacuees to temporary accommodation in local schools or to permanent billets.[7]

Evacuee children with mothers and teachers arriving in Scarborough, photographed on Hoxton Rd. Boxes containing gas marks are visible.

There were some inevitable deficiencies in the evacuation process. Some evacuees arrived at hotels, only to find their rooms occupied by paying guests. Temporary accommodation had to be hastily arranged.[8] One evacuee was involved in an awkward situation. Pearl, a 13-year-old, had just arrived in Scarborough and was part of a crocodile of evacuees being dropped off at their allocated billets. One host was assigned a visibly deprived child. Pearl was selected instead, with the comment, 'No, we'll have this one.'[9] However, overall, the Town Hall had organised the reception and distribution of evacuees with considerable efficiency and there was some self-congratulation, as well as relief, at how well the initial process had gone.

One reason for the relatively smooth initial reception of evacuees was that the numbers arriving were well short of what had been expected. Some 9,000 evacuees arrived instead of the planned 18,000, which was broadly typical of the scheme nationally, where about 40% arrived in reception areas.[10] An obvious reason for the sluggish take-up of evacuation was that there was no immediate sign of a German bombing campaign. On a more personal level, it was an emotional wrench for parents to send children off for an indefinite period to live with strangers. Parents were anxious to keep families together, at least until they faced the reality of enemy action. There were, too, obvious disincentives to sending children to Scarborough in wartime. A *Manchester Guardian* correspondent visiting Middlesbrough in October 1939 was reminded of the World War One bombardment: 'What the Germans then did from the sea they are now likely to do from the air'.[11]

The arrival of 9,000 evacuees in a town with a population of some 40,000 inevitably provoked some anxiety and resentment, but is difficult for the historian to measure how widespread such feelings were. Some Scarborians were more directly affected than others, whilst the voices that were most likely to be heard were those that belonged to those that were most inconvenienced. Some felt that the burden of looking after evacuees was not being shared equitably. 'Foster Parent', for example, wrote to the press alleging that some townsfolk were cheating the system by claiming dishonestly that they had relatives occupying spare rooms.[12] Ironically, the fact that less accommodation was required than was planned for could exacerbate irritations by encouraging a feeling of 'Why me?' among those whose hospitality was still required. There were concerns also about the financial burden of evacuation on the town, especially as the war took a toll on the tourist economy in the autumn of 1939. The basic allowance for hosting evacuees, 8s 6d per week, was widely considered to be insufficient.

There were also grievances about the impact of evacuation on education in the town. Local children and evacuees shared many of the town's school premises, one group occupying the school in the morning, one in the afternoon. Parents were unhappy that local children's education was being cut by fifty per cent. A letter to the local paper, signed 'Mother', pointed out that residents still had to pay full fees for a reduced secondary education and that students approaching their leaving exams would be disadvantaged.[13] The Chairman of the Council's Education Committee favoured using spare accommodation in the town for teaching evacuee children, but there was little available and the cost of equipping spare rooms would be formidable.[14]

Questions were also raised about the need for evacuation in the first place, in the absence of any German air raids. The people of Scarborough often shared the concerns of outsiders about the vulnerability of the town to aerial bombing. Hull, moreover, where the majority of the evacuees came from, was alleged to have enviable air raid protection for most of the population.[15] The conclusion arrived at by the more cynically minded Scarborians was that many evacuees were here for the benefit of their household finances. Some evacuees, it was claimed, were returning home for the weekends. The *Mercury* newspaper provided the example of a women and her two children being maintained in Scarborough, whilst her husband, who was earning £7 per week, made no contribution.[16]

Yet what did more than anything to trigger an outcry over evacuation in the town was the abject poverty of many of the evacuees. The people of Scarborough, a relatively well-to-do seaside resort, found it acutely uncomfortable to be confronted with the products of the country's urban slums. Many of the children arrived without a change of clothing, nightwear and winter clothing, prompting the columnist Jottings to insist that the parents of children and their evacuation areas must be responsible for providing clothing for evacuees.[17] Panic about the condition of the evacuees seized parts of the community in the first fortnight of September, reflecting a national 'spasm of horror' in the early days of evacuation over the sorry state of many evacuees.[18] In Scarborough concerns were widely aired in the local press. Evacuee mothers and children were apt to be described as 'wretched', suggesting a degree of squalor that was alien to the people of the town. Jottings was congratulated for taking a stand against 'the evacuation scandal'. This he did in a provocative manner, declaring that the city of Hull had no excuse for sending 'a few demented people, large numbers of mental defectives, children suffering from infectious diseases, and very many women and children in a very filthy bodily condition'.[19] Some residents drew sympathetic conclusions from the revelations of squalor and deprivation, suggesting that more must be done by the country in the future to help those enduring such conditions. Others appreciated the justification for evacuating the vulnerable from wartime target areas, but, given their condition, proposed that they should be housed separately from the rest of the population. Others refused to accept the need for evacuation at all.[20]

Evacuees from deprived urban areas were often deemed to pose a serious health risk to reception areas. The most common evacuee health problems were fleas, head lice, scabies, impetigo and other skin diseases.[21] By the middle of

September 1939 it was reported that Scarborough's Public Health Committee 'is going to have a serious time'.[22] Medical Centres for evacuees were established in local schools and a Cleaning Centre was established to clean and re-clothe evacuees.[23] Before the end of the month the town's Medical Officer of Health was making arrangements for the reopening of the town's old hospital in the Old Town as an Isolation Hospital for evacuees.[24] The *Mercury* was not satisfied by such initiatives. 'Obvious disease carriers could be dealt with,' it pronounced, but 'latent illnesses' would continue to pose a threat to the town and to its tourist industry.[25]

Some Scarborians identified risks not only to the physical well-being of the town, but also to the moral health of the community. The threat, it was proposed, arose from the moral shortcomings of many evacuee parents and children. Some were not willing to attribute the poor physical condition of evacuees to a deprived environment at home. 'No one is compelled to be verminous,' wrote one local.[26] There were, moreover, frequent condemnations of the behaviour of some evacuees. 'Fair Play' wrote to the local paper declaring that the town's hospitality was being repaid with 'foul language, dirty habits, destructiveness and insolence'.[27]

The most vocal charges concerning evacuation were generally not directed against the evacuees themselves, but against the authorities in the city of Hull, from where the most deprived evacuees came. The authorities, it was alleged, had knowingly loaded women and children on to trains in an unfit physical condition, including many with infectious diseases. The Chairman of Scarborough's Public Health Committee stated bluntly that the evacuees from Hull 'should not have been sent in that condition'.[28] A letter in the *Scarborough Evening News* described the state of the arrivals as 'a disgrace'.[29] A councillors' report to the General Committee of the Council was highly critical of the city of Hull, finding that, after despatching the evacuees in such a poor condition, the Hull authorities had been slow to respond to Scarborough's pleas for help. It maintained that the evacuees posed a threat to public health and it stated that Scarborough should be financially compensated for its efforts to look after needy evacuees from Hull.[30] Though sound progress was made in integrating the poorer evacuees from Hull, the initial shock of receiving them bequeathed a legacy of distrust between the people of Scarborough and Hull. At Christmas 1939, a rumour circulated in Scarborough that the Hull authorities had refused to contribute towards festive treats and entertainments for their evacuees. The owner of one hotel alleged that Hull had 'not sent an apple or orange, not a good wish'.[31]

The initial anger about the arrival of evacuees subsided after a number of weeks, assisted by the steady flow of evacuees back to their home towns. By the end of September some 15% had left Scarborough. There was a conspicuous spike in departures in the autumn: 40% by late October, 51% by mid-December. Cynics attributed the rise solely to the government's announcement in October that parents of evacuees would be liable to pay a means-tested contribution towards their upkeep in reception areas.[32] The upward trend of returning evacuees continued in 1940: 57% had returned by late January, over 66% by mid-March and, by mid-April, 72%.[33] Like the proportion of arrivals, the proportion of departures was in line with national trends.[34]

Nationally, mothers with infant children were proportionately most likely to return. In Scarborough it was reported that by early October 1939 adult evacuees were 'fed-up', partly because evacuee mothers with infants commonly found it difficult to share a household with other adults and families.[35] Evacuee mothers from the poorer inner cities found acceptance most difficult. 'So many of these,' a letter writer lamented in the local paper, 'are so definitely of a different social type to the good people who have received them.'[36]

The reasons for the flight of so many child evacuees from Scarborough were innumerable. Many were homesick, departures often following family reunions. Christmas 1939, for example, accelerated the 'homing process' of young evacuees.[37] Observers at the time identified the desire of parents to maintain close contact with their offspring as a problem. '(C)hildren will settle if left alone,' counselled the *Hull Daily Mail*.[38] Parents at home, on the other hand, missed their children and were keen to re-unite their families. In some cases, they found it difficult to endure war conditions without the support of their children. Pearl Harman, for example, a working-class girl from Hull, found herself in a large, well-to-do home in Scarborough. She grew to appreciate the ethos of self-improvement in the household, but after the death of her disabled sister she chose to return to Hull to support her distressed mother. She opted to put aside dreams of a more ambitious future.[39] In a similar case, a young evacuee returned to Hull after entreaties from his mother to the school:

> … I wish him to be at home here with me, now I am at home, because every time he writes he is asking to come home and I am bad with my nerves and he will be able to help me with my little children and be company for me when his Dad is on nights.[40]

Life as an Evacuee

It is impossible to generalise about the experiences of so many young people living with host families in Scarborough, but is probably safe to assume that they ranged widely across a spectrum, from a loving acceptance into a new foster family to various degrees of neglect. However, fraught relations with host families undoubtedly explains some departures. One host, when they were at work all day, gave an evacuee some food and told them to spend the day walking outdoors.[41] Another evacuee came to Scarborough as a nine-year-old with his sister, living in a three-storey house with several other boys and girls, hosted by four women, each referred to as 'aunty'. 'My main recollection was that I was always hungry,' he wrote. His story illustrates some of the tensions and distrust that could exist between evacuees and foster parents, and the unspoken negotiations that helped both to navigate difficult relationships:

> One evening, feeling hungry as usual, I stole downstairs to the kitchen. The aunties were in a seperate [sic] room from the kitchen, and on the table was a cake-stand with four cakes on it, and beside it, a loaf of bread. I grabbed the cakes, and as an afterthought, the bread too. My sister and I ate the cakes and I put the loaf in my chest of drawers for later. Although questioned about the theft of 'aunties [sic] supper' I didn't own up. After all, we never had cakes, ever, for our tea. I don't remember eating the loaf, but I expect when my bed was made, the crumbs were a dead giveaway. Nothing was said however, but we were forbidden to enter the kitchen after that.[42]

In difficult circumstances like these, some children, unsurprisingly, cajoled their parents into taking them home. For homesick children, of course, there was an incentive to exaggerate their unhappiness in Scarborough. For parents who were missing their children, there was an incentive to believe them.

There is little doubt that conditions for evacuees improved over time and that many came to experience evacuation as a largely positive experience. As numbers fell, there was less pressure on the host community and consequently a more sympathetic attitude towards evacuees. Of course, those evacuees that were most unable to adapt to their circumstances in Scarborough were the most likely to leave, especially working-class mothers with infants. Over time, both evacuees and their host community got used to each other, developing a greater degree of mutual understanding and consideration. Jottings, in the

Mercury, identified November 1939 as the time when 'the evacuation problem seems to have settled down'.[43]

The Town Hall played a critical role in alleviating the initial shock waves of evacuation. It endeavoured to meet some of the recreational needs of the newcomers, especially as they only attended school for half days. The Olympia Ballroom was made available in poor weather for PE and games and the Corporation Swimming Baths, normally closed in the winter months, were kept open exclusively for the use of evacuee swimmers.[44] Support was made available for evacuees most in need, and particularly 'difficult' children were transferred from their ordinary billets to a Council hostel in the Old Town.[45] A crèche was founded to support evacuee mothers. And despite some of the early criticism of the authorities in Hull, the city came to provide support for its exiled population in Scarborough. In late October 1939, for example, the Lord Mayor sent a consignment of boots, clothing and blankets to Scarborough.[46]

In Scarborough voluntary organisations complemented the efforts of the local authority in helping evacuees to settle in the town. Prominent among them were the WVS and the Council of Social Welfare, both of which supported needy evacuees and collected donations of clothing, boots, nightwear and prams for them.[47] Trainee teachers from the Leeds Training College, which had been evacuated to Scarborough at the beginning of the war, also played an important role, organising play, games and expeditions for evacuees outside school hours.[48] Sometimes the role of teachers from the evacuation areas, the so-called 'invisible evacuees', is overlooked. As those selected tended to be younger and lacking in parenting experience, accompanying their pupils certainly posed challenges. They often found themselves *in loco parentis* for seven days a week both during and outside school hours.[49] With only half a day of formal schooling, teachers often organised practical lessons outside the classroom. One girl recalled her teachers' efforts to keep their charges busy in their spare time by organising dressing-up and plays.[50] Other evacuees remembered opportunities to participate in dancing, choir, ping pong, board games, quizzes, competitions, playlets and charades.[51] A pupil, hosted at the Astoria Hotel, recalled the disorienting world of evacuation in school groups:

> I used to stand in awe of Miss ____. I certainly never dreamt she would serve my meals, but now it does not seem out of place at all. It is very hard to attend lessons when one has seen the teacher performing queer antics at a concert or toiling to stop a burst pipe, dressed up to the ears in waterproofs, but it does make the mistresses seem more human.[52]

The rapt and gleeful attention of evacuees during entertainment at the Astoria Hotel, with adults looking on. (From John D. Hicks, A Hull School in Wartime).

Evacuees were, of course, keen to take advantage of the diversions provided by a seaside holiday resort and many fondly recall swimming in the sea and playing on the beaches when wartime regulations permitted. As a small town with a rural hinterland, many evacuees took the opportunity of exploring the countryside. Some had their eyes opened to country life for the first time, discovering, for example, that rhubarb did not grow on trees like bananas.[53]

Once evacuees from industrial towns had settled into Scarborough, it was felt locally that they would benefit from the healthy environment of the seaside. When a local journalist accompanied the Director of Education on a visit to evacuee pupils at a local school, he reported on signs of greatly improved health. The children were not only clean and healthy in appearance, but 'pink-cheeked and putting on weight'. A Middlesbrough teacher told the reporter that she hoped that her pupils might catch up with the physical condition of Scarborough children, who she noted were much taller than her own.[54] In late November 1939, the town's hoteliers' association attributed its members' much more positive attitude to evacuees to the fact that the evacuees were now 'physically better than they have ever been in their lives'.[55] The causes of the evacuees' good health in Scarborough were commonly identified as good food, regular hours, early to bed and the town's 'invigorating air'. A boy from Hull identified another privilege of evacuee life: 'What I enjoy most of all, though, is a good bath and a good wash; that's the finest thing of all!'[56]

The arrival of adolescent evacuees seems to have increased the prospects of amorous adventure in the town. Romance developed between an evacuee boy and the daughter of the owners of the Astoria Hotel where he was billeted. They later married, he becoming a distinguished professor of Chemistry.[57] In one school, the local boys, who occupied classrooms in the morning, left letters in the desks for the evacuee girls occupying the school in the afternoon, the letters proposing discreet assignations. When teachers uncovered the plot, the girls were chaperoned safely back to their South Cliff lodgings at the end of each school day.[58]

There were many reasons, then, why young evacuees had much to thank the Scarborough community for. Despite some inevitable problems of adaptation, those evacuees that stayed in the town mostly came to develop a strong sense of gratitude towards their hosts in Scarborough. The Head of English at a Hull school wrote in verse of the overcoming of initial difficulties:

> … But your kind welcome changed distress
> To seven months of happiness.[59]

When a Middlesbrough school departed from Scarborough, the headmaster thanked the people of the town who he judged had 'spared neither time, work nor money to make the boys happy'.[60] Another Middlesbrough head stated, on departure: 'No town in the country could have done more than Scarborough.'[61] The experience of evacuation to Scarborough early in the war was an enormously complex and variegated one, reflecting innumerable individual histories. For many, though, their lives were enriched by the welcome extended by the people of Scarborough at a time of considerable anxiety and economic insecurity.

Hotels

One of the distinctive features of evacuation to seaside resorts like Scarborough was the use of hotels as accommodation for evacuees that could not easily be housed privately. At the planning stage, the local authorities found it difficult to estimate the amount of potential accommodation available in hotels. In season, many rooms would be occupied by paying guests, whilst some of the larger hotels also housed a large number of their own staff. It was, moreover, difficult to know precisely how hoteliers would respond to the evacuation scheme. Some were unwilling to volunteer to take evacuees at the expense of potential paying customers. Others, given that evacuation would be triggered by the outbreak of war, anticipated losing most of their bookings, and gambled that the modest allowance provided for hosting evacuees would be better than nothing. A further complicating factor for billeting officials was that if hotels were not used for evacuees, and had empty rooms during an evacuation, then local householders would be less inclined to volunteer to take in evacuees.

There were 13 schools, eight of which were secondary, billeted in hotels in Scarborough in early 1940.[62] In many ways, hotels could provide suitable and agreeable billets. When a journalist visited the Mount Hotel, where girls from one of Hull's poorer schools had been evacuated, he was greatly impressed by the success of the billet and reported that the girls were having 'a very happy time'.[63] The owner of the Astoria Hotel reported to the Ministry of Health that for the previous six months his hotel had functioned as a school, whilst the resident evacuees had been 'happy, well-fed and free from illness'.[64] For the majority of evacuees, the experience of hotels offered the first taste of the high life. Some of the town's premier hotels were initially occupied by evacuees, including the Prince of Wales, the Crown and the Royal. One evacuee felt that staying at the Prince of Wales was 'something new and worth writing home about', whilst another, in the same hotel, recalled an occasion when he left his shoes outside his room, finding them cleaned the next morning.[65] Dennis Spurgeon found it hard to believe that he was staying in a hotel billet 'where, in summer, people would pay much money to stay'.[66] The fact that such billets were situated in a famous holiday resort, usually near the sea-front, was a bonus. Evacuation could seem more like a school trip or a holiday than a flight from the terrors of aerial bombing. When evacuees learned that their destination was Scarborough, the news conjured up images, in the words of one, of a 'never-ending seaside holiday in the months to come'.[67] Moving into an hotel overlooking the Italian Gardens and the South Bay, another recalled, 'I thought it was a great joke.'[68]

But there were challenges and difficulties for many of the evacuees who were billeted in hotels. Life in out-of-season hotels did not always live up to expectations, especially during the exceptionally cold winter of 1939-40. An evacuee poetaster expressed the feelings of some in a school magazine:

It's cold – it's freezing hard – it blows:
The pipes won't run – it's dark – it snows;

> We'll all be here to crack of doom,
> For generations – till our tomb.
> …For Scarborough is a bitter pill;
> We want to grumble – and we will.[69]

Overcrowding in hotels was a problem, particularly during the earlier days of evacuation. Rooms could be occupied by six children, sometimes as many as ten.[70] Children of a young age had to learn quickly how to look after themselves and to contribute to the running of the hotel: cleaning, helping with the laundry, lighting fires, preparing and serving food and washing up. 'A culture shock for those of us used to being looked after by our mothers!' recalled one evacuee.[71]

For Scarborough's hoteliers, in the lean times of the Phoney War, receiving evacuees was seen as a means of bringing in some regular revenues from the government's billeting allowance, as well as making a contribution to the war effort. However, hoteliers commonly found that the allowances hardly covered their overheads, a difficulty exacerbated by rising food prices. The arrival of significantly fewer evacuees than had been expected, and the subsequent return of many more, left hoteliers with more empty rooms than they had budgeted for. Proprietors were also unsure how long evacuees would be staying for, making it difficult to plan ahead and make decisions about advertising their hotels for forthcoming holiday seasons.[72]

As complaints from Scarborough hoteliers increased, Ministry of Health officials were not sympathetic. They did not approve of the Town Hall's 'indiscriminate' use of hotels for evacuation purposes and felt that costs would be easier to control in household billets. Nor were they much moved by the protests of hoteliers, convinced that a room of evacuees was better for them than an empty room. The Ministry's attitude is reflected in a departmental minute (in relation to the Adelphi and Astoria Hotels):

> It may be that the proprietors would have made more money if they had kept open for normal visitors, and it may be that they are unable to recover the whole of their overhead costs from the billeting money, but in offering the premises for evacuees they presumably took the risk as a war hedge.[73]

The Ministry was determined not to change official regulations, nor to establish precedents, by making concessions to Scarborough hoteliers. Nor was it interested in requisitioning hotels for evacuees. No increase in the billeting allowance was countenanced, but it was hoped that some hoteliers could be bought off by reasonable compensation for damages and by the payment of rent for the use of extra hotel rooms for educational purposes. The Ministry's preferred solution was to move evacuees out of hotels and into household billets, wherever possible. As evacuee numbers fell, this became more practical. And if hoteliers remained dissatisfied with the arrangements, they could apply, like anyone else, to a local evacuation tribunal to have the evacuees removed.[74]

Two Scarborough hotels posed particular difficulties for those responsible for evacuation policy in Whitehall. The Fairview Hotel was an up-market hotel on the town's South Cliff, whose owners agreed to take pupils from a Hull residential special school for the physically and mentally disabled and from a day school for deaf children in the city. Thirty-four pupils arrived from the special school and ten from the deaf school, which was significantly less than had been promised, the hotel possessing accommodation for 230 evacuee children. Whilst the evacuees were there, it was not considered feasible for the hotel to host any paying guests. The hotel was already in a parlous financial situation before the arrival of the evacuees. The Wessex Hotel, another 'high-class' hotel on the South Cliff, faced similar challenges, receiving a nursery school of 2 to 6-year-olds from Hull, precluding the accommodation of paying guests. Of the 130 children promised to the owner, only 52 arrived. Both hotels made it clear to Ministry of Health officials that the billeting allowance was inadequate for meeting the needs of such evacuees. Unfortunately, neither hotel had concluded negotiations with the authorities about the amount of money required when the evacuees arrived. Both hotels then complained bitterly that the normal billeting allowance was wholly unsatisfactory. The Ministry accepted that the billeting circumstances were in both cases 'exceptional', but remained opposed to establishing the precedent of compensating owners for the loss of customers:

> ... the Government would be adamant in refusing to acknowledge any liability in respect of a hypothetical loss of profit due to the outbreak of war. It was common knowledge that there was a great exodus from the holiday resorts in the period immediately preceding and following the outbreak of war and it could not be assumed that guests would have remained or that bookings would not have been cancelled.[75]

The Ministry was prepared, however, to make some concessions and agreed to provide financial help for staffing, heating and the hire of 'chattels' (furnishings, crockery etc.). The Wessex reluctantly accepted the settlement, whilst the Fairview continued to insist it needed greater financial support. In the summer of 1940 the Ministry got its way when the evacuees from the two hotels were distributed to other billets in Scarborough and elsewhere.[76]

The 'Trickle Evacuation'

Scarborough experienced two further and smaller waves of evacuation during the war. The difficulties of the 1939 evacuation were to cast a shadow over them. The first was the so-called 'Trickle Evacuation', which arose from the Blitz on London and other cities and took place from September 1940 till late 1941. Like its predecessor, the scheme was voluntary for evacuees. By mid-December 1940 there were 350 refugees from the Blitz in Scarborough, 254 from the London area and 96 from other bombed cities. By late April 1941 there was a total of 549 and by July 1941, 764.[77] Evacuees on this occasion were a mixed group, mostly parents with young children, but also expectant mothers, the elderly, disabled and those made homeless by bombing. Some were described as being in a 'deplorable' condition, having abandoned their bombed-out homes with nothing, whilst a few seem to have been in a precarious mental state after their experiences.[78] One Old Age Pensioner from London fell out with her host family and was brought before the local magistrates for 'one of the worst cases of drunkenness we have come across for years'. Tragically, an adult male Londoner hanged himself from his bedpost in March 1941.[79]

The writer Bob Holman has observed: 'Much was learned from the first evacuation and the result was a virtually complete reversal of policy.'[80] Evacuees were free to make their own way to reception areas, the government providing free travel vouchers. They could choose from a number of different types of accommodation: host families, 'digs' or hostels. The government also made financial assistance available if evacuees wished to arrange their own accommodation under the 'assisted private evacuation scheme'.[81] This phase of evacuation ran more smoothly than the original one, more alive as it was to the needs of the evacuees and the reception areas.[82] The numbers were, of course, much smaller and arrivals were spread over a longer period. When the Ministry of Health had appealed in March 1940 for volunteers to host refugees from anticipated air raids, there was some reluctance in Scarborough, as elsewhere, to repeat the unhappy experience of September 1939.[83] When the Blitz commenced in earnest in the autumn, however, there was a greater sympathy for the suffering of the victims of the German bombing campaign.

In an effort to persuade evacuees to remain in reception areas, the government also relaxed the restrictions on local authorities' expenditure on welfare measures for evacuees. Scarborough was able to develop a specialist team of social workers and 'psycho-therapists' to help support child evacuees.[84]

The Doodlebug Evacuation

The summer of 1944 witnessed a new stimulus to civilian evacuation: '... on the night of June 12/13th, an unusual spluttering noise was heard over south-eastern England. Astonishingly powerful explosions took place in several parts of London and the home counties.'[85] The new threats from Nazi-occupied Europe were firstly the V1 pilotless planes, or 'Doodlebugs', followed in September by the deadlier V2 rocket bombs. Some 9,000 civilians died as a result of this new wartime terror.[86] Most of the weapons landed on the London area. The Ministry of Health reactivated its assisted evacuation scheme and asked local authorities again to provide accommodation for an official evacuation from vulnerable areas. Scarborough was told to expect over 1,000 arrivals. It is difficult to be precise as to how many arrived, as some arrived independently and others arrived under official arrangements. But the bulk of evacuees arrived on two dates. Firstly, 763 arrived on 27 July 1944: 71 mothers with 180 children, 481 unaccompanied children and 31 aged and infirm. A further 676 arrived on 20 August: 203 mothers, 176 children under age 5, 194 children over age 5 and 103 unaccompanied children.[87]

A great deal of effort was made to provide a hospitable welcome for this new wave of evacuees. The WVS went to considerable lengths, providing welcoming meals, a mobile canteen for tea and biscuits and running Rest Centres as temporary accommodation for new arrivals. The evacuees were assessed at the Medical Centre, which found that children from the London area in 1944 were generally in a much better physical condition than those of the mass evacuation of 1939, a testament, perhaps, to the welfare state that had developed alongside the warfare state.[88] Some of the children, it was said, appeared indistinguishable from typical young pre-war tourists.[89] As ever, however, the mental strain of fleeing a war-torn city and arriving in an alien place registered with some of the youngsters, one journalist recording that 'not all could maintain a brave show of cheerfulness'.[90]

Like the 'trickle evacuation', a range of different types of accommodation was made available. Many evacuees, especially mothers with young children, remained in Rest Centres for a week or so until permanent shelter could be found.[91] The local authority scrambled to find hosts for unaccompanied children. Most of the aged and infirm were accommodated in a local War Refugee Hostel.[92] For the majority of adult evacuees, with or without children, the Town Hall's preference was to find them empty accommodation where they could look after themselves, and some such properties were duly commandeered. For the mayor, this sort of arrangement was 'the best for all concerned'.[93] It was deemed to be particularly appropriate for mothers with children, who had proved to be the most difficult to integrate in the 1939 evacuation. This solution, however, was dependent on receiving sufficient donations of household goods and furniture from the public, hence exhortations were made to local people, churches and businesses to contribute essential goods. The appeal was reinforced by the message, or threat, that, where shortages persisted, evacuees would have to be compulsorily hosted in private households.[94]

The Council, however, remained in need of private households in which to place unaccompanied children and those evacuees who could not be found empty properties and essential equipment. The public response to appeals from the billeting authorities for volunteer households was described as 'fairly good'.[95] But it was not so good as to enable the authorities to avoid the problems of compulsory billeting. There was a sense of injustice among those selected as suitable hosts for evacuees, as there was a suspicion that other householders were dishonestly denying that they had any spare rooms.[96] After the August arrivals there were 56 written appeals to the billeting authorities and a 'score' of townsfolk made appeals before a billeting tribunal.[97] It was also found necessary to deploy the local police to assist with the placing of some evacuees in private households.[98]

There were obviously divided opinions in the town about the arrival of evacuees from the London area in 1944. Unlike the 'Trickle Evacuation', the arrivals were quite sudden and unexpected. Those who were knowledgeable about the devastation being wrought in the south-east by V bombs were more likely to be sympathetic, but others felt that Scarborough had already suffered enough disruption in wartime. Given also that the numbers were relatively small, those selected for compulsory hosting often felt unfairly or arbitrarily targeted. As usual, there was evidence nationally of 'class-engendered hostility' in 1944.[99] A culture clash is evident in the memoirs of one Scarborian:

> It would probably have been around 1943 [presumably 1944] when we were allocated, and forced to take, two evacuees from the east end of

London. They were two brothers, much older than us – they would be around 9 and 10 – and much rougher and tougher. Mother must have been pulling her hair out as they were reported to her by neighbours for defecating in an air raid shelter not far from the house. In the house they swung on curtains, had very poor cleanliness habits and tried to encourage Phoebe [his sister] and me to follow their bad examples. Eventually Mother persuaded the authorities that they must be found other accommodation. They were. But we were then allocated a woman with a parrot![100]

A London bus driver felt so aggrieved at the uncaring attitude of some Scarborians towards London refugees that he proposed that they be sent to London to experience for themselves the terror of the latest Nazi attacks.[101] Alderman Wilkinson apologised for the insensitivity of some members of the community who felt that evacuees should be sent back to London. It was, he insisted, 'one of the joys and privileges of Scarborough to entertain these people'. As in September 1939, the *Mercury* columnist Jottings appointed himself as a spokesman for the town's wronged and put-upon, alleging that London's working class were lacking in the respectability that ordinary folk in Scarborough possessed. He revived the old complaint about the inadequacy of government allowances for hosting evacuees and highlighted the importance of spare rooms as a means of generating extra income in the holiday season. Jottings, therefore, opposed any form of compulsory billeting and advised that no evacuees should be sent to Scarborough unless they had already arranged their own accommodation, or it had been allocated by the local authority.[102] Other types of accommodation were available, Jottings argued. There were, he noted, plenty of empty properties that could be taken over, including those taken over by the military and now lying empty, whilst there were also unused military camps in the area. When the national *Daily Mirror* picked up on the sentiments being expressed by Jottings about evacuees, it was incensed: '… if the paper [The *Mercury*] represents Scarborough, then Scarborough stinks,' was its riposte.[103] Some locals were scandalised too, one writing to the *Mirror*: 'I wish to apologise on behalf of all decent Scarborough people.'[104] As in 1939, evacuation remained a divisive issue in the Scarborough community, as it did in most reception areas.

Some historians take an 'optimistic' view of Britain's experience of evacuation, emphasising the patriotic and unifying spirit of the experience and its positive legacy of welfare reforms which aimed to tackle some of the social problems exposed by evacuation. Writers of a more 'pessimistic' point of view more readily acknowledge the disruptive and polarising effects of evacuation. Angus Calder, for example, identified a negative legacy:

> Without denying that evacuation stimulated the social conscience of many 'worthy' middle-class people, and gave credibility and urgency to projects for social reform, it seems fair to enquire whether it did not also have a bearing on the strong class prejudices so marked in post-war Britain.[105]

The experience of Scarborough would seem to bear out Calder's concerns. The evacuation of citizens from poorer urban areas of the country to the town triggered a good deal of anxiety and not inconsiderable anger. This was lent some legitimacy by the hostile sentiments expressed in the *Mercury* newspaper. The story of Scarborough highlights, however, the extent to which tensions over evacuation fed off existing wartime difficulties and stresses, especially the economic damage inflicted on the hospitality industry in Scarborough's case. The pessimistic view also tends to underestimate the progress, albeit incomplete, that was made during the war in helping to bring evacuees and the host community together, a process aided considerably by Town Hall interventions, the voluntary efforts of local organisations and the patriotic instincts of people of goodwill in the town.

Notes

1. Christopher Wiseman, *36 Cornelian Avenue* (Montreal, 2008), p.72-73.
2. *Hansard, House of Commons,* 10 November 1932.
3. NA HLG 7/179, Scarborough, Summary of Accommodation, 27 February 1939 and Ministry of Health to Town Clerk, 28 March, 1939.
4. NA HLG 7/179, Ministry of Health to Evacuation Officer, Education Office, 12 May 1939 and Borough of Scarborough, Education Office, Evacuation Officer to Town Clerk, 2 June, 1939.
5. NA HLG 7/179 Town Clerk to Ministry of Health, 20 April 1939 and departmental minute, 28th April, 1939.
6. *Mercury,* 1 September 1939
7. Ibid.
8. Ibid.
9. IWM, Pearl Harman, Catalogue Number 13662.
10. See *SEN*, 13 December 1939, which gives the total number of evacuees as 8,811. Nationally, see Daniel Todman, *Britain's War: Into Battle, 1937-1941* (London, 2016), p.248.
11. *Manchester Guardian*, 12 October 1939.
12. *SEN,* 5 October 1939.
13. *SEN,* 4 October 1939.
14. *SEN,* 10 October 1939.
15. *Mercury*, 15 September and 10 October 1939.
16. *Mercury*, 22 September 1939.
17. *Mercury*, 24 November 1939.
18. H.C. Dent's phrase, quoted by Geoffrey G. Field in *Blood, Sweat and Toil* (Oxford, 2013), p.14.
19. *Mercury*, 8 September 1939.
20. See *Mercury, 15 September 1939* for debate about what to do with evacuees.
21. Bob Holman, *The Evacuation: A Very British Revolution* (Oxford, 1995), pp.76-77.
22. *Mercury* 15 September 1939.
23. Ibid.
24. *SEN,* 3 October 1939.
25. *Mercury* 22 September 1939.
26. Ibid.
27. *Mercury* 8 September *1939.*
28. *Mercury,* 15 September 1939.
29. *SEN,* 11 September 1939.

30 *SEN,* 19 September 1939.
31 *SEN,* 20 and 27 December 1939.
32 Juliet Gardiner, *Wartime* (London, 2004), pp.36-37.
33 For the statistics, see SEN, 3 and 25 October, 13 December 1939 and 23 January, 13 March, 30 April 1940.
34 Gardiner, op. cit., p.44.
35 *Mercury,* 6 October 1939.
36 *Mercury* 15 September 1939.
37 *SEN,* 4 January 1940.
38 *Hull Daily Mail,* quoted in John D. Hicks, *A Hull School in Wartime: Kingston High School's Evacuation to Scarborough* (Beverley, 1990), p.27.
39 IWM, Pearl Harman, Catalogue Number 13662.
40 Hicks, op. cit., pp.27 and 29.
41 *SEN* 9 November 1939.
42 IWM, R.A. Child, Catalogue Number 5504.
43 *Mercury,* 17 November 1939.
44 For Council initiatives, see *SEN,* 4 and 27 November and *Mercury,* 8 December 1939.
45 *SEN,* 24 October 1939.
46 Ibid.
47 *SEN,* 23 November 1939.
48 *SEN,* 18 November 1939.
49 See *SEN,* 4 November 1939.
50 IWM, Pearl Harman, Catalogue Number 13662.
51 Hicks, op. cit., p31.
52 Hicks, op. cit., p.12. Surname omitted in original.
53 *SEN,* 5 December 1939.
54 *SEN,* 4 November 1939.
55 *SEN,* 28 November 1939.
56 Hicks, op. cit., p.12.
57 Ibid., p.31.
58 Ibid., p.13.
59 Ibid., p.13.
60 *SEN,* 7 March 1940.
61 *SEN,* 20 March 1940.
62 NA HLG 7/179, Ministry of Health to Board of Education, 22 February 1940.
63 *Mercury,* 8 September 1939.

64   NA HLG 7/179 Owner of Astoria Hotel to Senior Regional Officer, Newcastle, 16 March 1940.
65   Hicks, op. cit., p.9 and Len Markham, *Homefront Yorkshire*, 1939-1945 (Barnsley, 2007), p.99
66   Hicks, op. cit., p.9.
67   Hicks, Ibid., p.8.
68   IWM, Lilias Walker, Catalogue Number 13578.
69   Hicks, op. cit., p.23.
70   Hicks, op. cit., p.9 and www.keepmilitarymuseum.org, Source H.
71   BBC, WW2 People's War, Fred Stearman, A6711095, (accessed 11 June 2018).
72   NA HLG 7/179 Ministry of Health files contain numerous complaints from Scarborough hoteliers.
73   NA HLG 7/179 Senior Regional Officer, Ministry of Health, 29 July 1940.
74   NA HLG 7/179, Ministry of Health files contain a great deal of discussion about what should be done concerning Scarborough hotels.
75   NA HLG 7/179, minute, Finance Officer, Northern Region, Ministry of Health, 11 October 1940.
76   NA HLG 7/179, minute, Finance Officer, Northern Region, Ministry of Health, 11 October 1940 and 8 January 1941.
77   *SEN*, 14 December 1940, 22 April and 1 July 1941.
78   *SEN*, 22 April 1941.
79   *SEN*, 3 March 1941.
80   Bob Holman, *The Evacuation: A Very British Revolution* (Oxford, 1995), p.48.
81   B.S. Johnson (ed.), *The Evacuees* (London, 1968), p.15.
82   Richard M. Titmuss, *Problems of Social Policy* (HMSO, 1950), p.257.
83   *Mercury*, 15 March 1940 and SEN 20 March 1940.
84   Report on School Medical Service, *Mercury*, 13 July 1945.
85   Angus Calder, *The People's War* (London, 1971), p.645.
86   Gardiner, op. cit., p.560.
87   *SEN*, 25 July and 20 August 1944.
88   *SEN*, 25 July 1944.
89   *SEN*, 21 August 1944.
90   *SEN*, 25 July 1944.
91   *SEN*, 24 August 1944.
92   *Mercury*, 14 July 1944.
93   *SEN*, 10 August 1944.
94   Ibid.
95   *SEN*, 25 July 1944.

96 *SEN,* 22 August 1944.
97 *SEN,* 22 and 23 August 1944.
98 *SEN,* 22 August 1944.
99 Travis L. Crosby, *The Impact of Civilian Evacuation in the Second World War* (Beckenham, 1986), p.57.
100 David Fowler, *I've started so I'll finish…A Memoir* (Scarborough, 2017), p.49.
101 SEN, 23 August 1944.
102 *Mercury,* 21 and 28 July, 11 and 25 August and 8 September 1944.
103 *Daily Mirror,* 16 September 1944.
104 *Daily Mirror,* 22 September 1944.
105 Angus Calder, *The Myth of the Blitz* (London, 1995), p.59. The classic 'optimistic' view can be found in R. M. Titmuss, *Problems of Social Policy* (HMSO London, 1950).

CHAPTER 4

'If the Invader Comes'[1]

The Army's Northern Command, responsible for the defence of Scarborough, distributed a transcript of a Commander's talk to civilian representatives on Invasion Committees:

> ... For the period of fighting there will be, there must be, no respite, no quarter. Only one thought and purpose lies before us, and that is to fight and destroy, no anxiety for the care of the wounded, no fears about food or water supply, no thought for the immediate safety of our homes, families, factories, must deflect us even for one moment from destroying the invader. There will be no quarter – you will live or he will live but not both. It must be you.[2]

The Defence of Britain

Once Germany had overrun Norway, Denmark, the Low Countries and France in the spring and summer of 1940, Hitler hoped that the British would accept some form of face-saving capitulation. As this became increasingly unlikely under Winston Churchill's leadership, Germany began to prepare for the invasion of Britain. Hitler issued a directive in July 1940 ordering his commanders to assemble invasion troops and equipment, with air and naval support.[3]

British military planners were aware of enemy preparations, yet could only guess at possible landing sites. They were confident that the main danger was in the south and south-east of the country, but there were concerns also about the east coast. At a meeting of the Home Defence Executive on 25 May it was agreed that Britain was vulnerable to attack 'from the Shetlands to Swanage'.[4]

Later, Churchill identified the coastline from the Cromarty Firth to the Wash as the sector second in importance after the south-east.[5] The Chiefs of Staff remained concerned about diversionary attacks on the North-East of England in 1941 and 1942.[6]

The British policy in response to such an unpredictable threat operated at several levels. In combatting a German invasion, a major role was accorded to the Royal Navy and RAF, aided by the extensive mining of the North Sea. The primary objective was to stall a German invasion force before it reached Britain's coastline. If the enemy broke through, the Commander-in-Chief of Home Forces, General Walter Kirke, had not been optimistic about coastal defences preventing an invasion force from establishing a bridgehead. His overriding priority was, therefore, to enlarge, equip and train a home army capable of counterattacking.

On 27 May 1940 a new man, the charismatic William 'Tiny' Ironside, was put in charge of Home Forces. He, with Churchill's backing, was committed to heavily fortifying Britain's eastern coastline in a so-called defensive 'crust', where fixed coastal defences would be used to harry and delay invading forces. The intention was, according to Ironside, 'to inflict all the losses we can'.[7] Further inland there would be a second line of defence, in the shape of 'stop-lines' and well-fortified 'nodal points'. Finally, Ironside continued to build up mobile reserves capable of hastening to confront enemy incursions.[8] On the east coast Ironside was responsible for initiating the construction of a line of substantial defensive works in one of the greatest building programmes in British history. This transformed the landscape for the remainder of the war, Britain's defiance symbolised by barbed wire and the ubiquitous concrete pillbox. Ironside was replaced by General Sir Alan Brooke on 19 July 1940. As more home troops became available, Brooke was to put greater emphasis on mobile defensive tactics, withdrawing some field artillery and anti-tank guns from coastal fortifications.[9] Nevertheless, the consolidation of coastal defences continued.

Defending Scarborough

Those military commanders responsible for the defence of Scarborough were made aware in June 1940 that an invasion of Britain was highly likely. They were also informed that 'it is known from a most reliable source that the German Air Force is studying the coast of Yorkshire'.[10] Such a fear was shared by Ironside himself in a diary entry on 4 July 1940, where he identified the

Yorkshire coast as a possible target.[11] Two key reasons were suggested for a potential German attack on the Scarborough area: to draw British forces away from the main invasion area in the south-east and to establish a bridgehead that would allow for a breakout towards the ports of Hull or Middlesbrough or towards Yorkshire's industrial centres. It was also noted that such an attack on a popular holiday resort would be likely to damage British morale.[12]

For those responsible for defending the Yorkshire coast, there was some comfort in the fact that much of it was rocky with steep cliffs. There were, however, considerable anxieties about the North and South Bays of Scarborough, and about the neighbouring bays to the south. Some of them matched the military definition of 'Dangerous Beach Areas':

> ... defined as essentially those upon which tracked and wheeled vehicles may be landed and from which there are exits inland. The danger is accentuated when a sheltered sea anchorage abuts on to them.[13]

The cliffs of Cayton Bay to the immediate south of Scarborough provided an obstacle to the exit of Armoured Fighting Vehicles (AFVs) from the beach, but the extensive sands offered a welcoming landing area for the enemy. The fields above Cayton Bay were considered suitable for the landing of enemy troops and supplies by air, whilst the coast just north of Cayton Bay was thought to be passable by tanks. Scarborough's South Bay gave rise to two sources of concern. Firstly, its firm and lengthy sandy beach provided an attractive landing site for enemy troops and equipment. Secondly, for much of the beach the sea wall was so low that it provided little obstacle to hostile AFVs crossing from the beach to the tarmacked foreshore and then to routes into the town. The harbour itself was mainly used by fishing vessels, and at high water was unsuitable for boats over 1,000 tons.[14] However, it could still prove to be useful to the enemy for the offloading of troops, equipment and supplies. Around the Castle headland, North Bay provided military planners with only slightly less serious concerns. The coastline was rockier in places and substantial cliffs dominated most of the bay, whilst the sea wall was also much higher than it was in South Bay. However, there were numerous slipways from the beach to the promenade and the coastal road was close to sea level in places.[15]

Military forces in Scarborough expected that an attack would arrive with little or no warning, most likely at dawn or dusk. There were concerns that the enemy would deploy poison gas and smokescreens to cover their landings.[16] A

Cayton Bay to the south of Scarborough. Scarborough is located on the most distant headland (photograph by Jonathan Eves).

combined assault involving air, sea and land forces was anticipated. Infantry would land on Scarborough's or nearby beaches, along with armoured vehicles and light tanks, supported by an aerial bombardment of the town's defences. The assumption was that enemy forces would attack the town from the flanks and the rear as well as from the beaches. To this end, German parachutists and airborne troops were expected to descend inland, the Vale of Pickering, to the west, providing numerous potential landing places for troop-carrying aircraft. Anti-invasion exercises also had airborne enemy landings on Oliver's Mount and the old Racecourse, both flanking the town itself.[17] There were few natural barriers to the south and west of the town, and the main routes into the town, except from the north, were difficult to defend. News from continental Europe encouraged the military planners to fear the employment of secret agents and saboteurs by the Nazis, with the aim of spreading as much disruption and panic as possible. Again, British exercises shed light on military fears. In one scenario, a fifth columnist member of the Auxiliary Territorial Service (the female branch of the army) sabotaged local military communications by destroying the telephone switchboard of 37 Signal Training Regiment, which was engaged in the defence of the town.[18] There were suspicions, too, that some enemy troops could land wearing British military uniforms.[19]

What, then, was the impact of coastal defence preparations on the Scarborough area? One of the most substantial components of the town's defences was the Wheatcroft Battery.[20] On 11 June 1940, two 6-inch naval guns of World War One vintage, affectionately known to the garrison as Gert and Daisy, were installed on a cliff edge overlooking the South Bay from the south.[21] The guns were intended to target enemy ships and amphibious craft up to four miles out to sea. Later, the gun houses were banked up and turfed, to provide for camouflage and greater protection. A decoy battery was also added on the end of White Nab to the south, comprising telegraph poles and camouflage netting. Deception, concealment and camouflage played a vital part in coastal defence, so the military authorities instructed local troops to make visible tracks leading to dummy positions like the decoy battery to deceive enemy air reconnaissance.[22] The range and direction of the battery was controlled from a Battery Observation Post in a building disguised as a bungalow, whilst two searchlight emplacements on the undercliff supported the battery. The guns required a complex of outbuildings and underground magazines, along with a mess and billets for servicemen. The battery was manned by naval personnel until the army took over, when thirty odd regular troops manned the fortified area, supplemented by a similar number of Home Guard. At one stage the number of men stationed at the battery exceeded 160.

The battery would have been a key target in the event of a German invasion. Frequent inspections, firing practice and 'dummy' attacks were intended to ensure a state of constant readiness. One training exercise did not go well. The measured official account hides, it can be assumed, a developing state of panic:

> At 00.54 hrs the 'enemy' laid smoke screens and threw thunder-flashes etc., our patrols opened up with 'blank ammunition'. At 00.55 hrs the gorse on left flank of Battery North of Main Magazine was observed to be on fire. Fire gongs were sounded. There was a high wind at the time, and with the recent fine/dry weather the gorse and small bushes were soon going well and the fire burnt and spread rapidly. All Fire Fighting equipment was brought into effect, and later on the Local Fire Brigade was called for owing to the rapid progress and serious danger involved with the vicinity of the Magazine. All ammunition was removed to a 'presumed' place of safety. The fire was eventually under control and extinguished by 01.45 hrs. A patrol was detailed in the event of the fire breaking out again. The Umpires for the exercise held a discussion privately and it was decided to call the exercise off.[23]

The defence of Scarborough's beaches, and of the neighbouring beaches at Cayton and Cornelian Bays, remained a key part of anti-invasion planning.

Lancashire Fusiliers and Royal Artillery units were among those who took up positions on the beaches.[24] In May 1940 troops defending Scarborough's beaches were instructed that they must engage any invaders 'energetically and ruthlessly' and that 'there will be no case of withdrawal'.[25] The first priority was to resist and slow down the enemy on the beaches, where their difficulties were considered to be greatest.[26]

At first, beach defences were hastily improvised, employing heavy boulders, earthworks, sandbags and barbed wire to block exits from the beaches. Northern Command admitted its earlier defence works were far from perfect and were a product of 'a race against time'.[27] In Scarborough troops were advised to use empty caravans and beach huts for cover. Throughout June more substantial defences were built. Soldiers working on beach defences were reported to be very content with their initial accommodation in bathing huts and chalets, but were said to have felt 'demoralised' at having to mix on the beach with 'visitors and bathing belles' before Scarborough's designation as a Defence Area at the beginning of July 1940.[28] Thereafter, civilians were banned from Scarborough's beaches until the summer of 1941, when limited access was granted to parts of the beach for small periods of the day. Northern Command advised that it would not be politic for soldiers to enjoy any recreation on the beaches whilst the public was prohibited.[29]

Throughout the summer of 1940 more permanent defences continued to be constructed, the authorities aiming to economise on scarce military manpower and to concentrate on physical barriers to enemy advances. A chain of concrete pillboxes and support structures was constructed on Cayton, Cornelian and Scarborough North and South Bays. The purpose of the pillbox was to create a killing ground on the beach by firing machine guns obliquely across the beach as the enemy came ashore. In Scarborough's South Bay, for example, one was built immediately to the south of the West Pier, in North Bay 200 yards from Monkey Island (at Scalby Mills). High building standards were vital, as pillboxes risked damage from flooding, high tides or subsidence. They were largely constructed by troops garrisoned in the town, with help from the Scarborough Labour Exchange and private builders. The practice of outsourcing work to private contractors was not always a happy one. It was concluded that the work of a Hull contractor 'would scarcely bear close inspection in civil life' and the contract was transferred to the Scarborough builder Plaxton's.[30] Once completed, pillboxes were camouflaged with paintwork and shrubbery. One corporal stationed locally demonstrated such skill in the art of concealment that he was farmed out by his unit for others to employ.[31] When the camouflage of Scarborough's pillboxes was checked from the sea, it was found that they were very difficult to detect, 'even from fairly close to the shore'.[32] Not everyone was convinced by Britain's unrestrained building of pillboxes in 1940, General Majendie of 55 Division feeling, for example, that the Army had succumbed to 'the lure of concrete' and was going 'pill-box mad'.[33]

The lanky figure of the Foreign Secretary Lord Halifax inspecting Scarborough's beach defences in 1940, while a soldier poses conscientiously for the camera. The pillbox has been disguised with woodwork. Metal uprights have been planted to hold barbed wire.

The pillboxes were backed up by an assortment of anti-invasion obstacles. To slow down enemy advances, rolls of barbed concertina wire were laid across the beaches, along with upright wire fences. All British gun emplacements were defended with wire, at a sufficient distance to prevent enemy hand grenade assaults. The barbed wire defences were prone to shifting and being flattened during high tides and stormy weather, especially on the exposed North Bay. The beaches were also equipped with electric Mazda lighting to illuminate them in the event of a night-time attack, a measure considered of the highest importance by army commanders.[34] The pillboxes and the beaches were covered by an assortment of fortified gun positions, employing machine-guns, anti-tank rifles, mortars and artillery. Machine gun emplacements could be found in the South Bay at the open-air Bathing Pool, the Grand Hotel and the outer harbour wall. By August 1940 North Bay had an 18-pounder and a 6-pounder artillery piece.

The enemy had to be prevented at all costs from gaining control of Scarborough's piers. Anti-tank concrete cubes and barbed wire were installed on them and a pillbox was built on West Pier, whilst a small minefield was laid on the Lighthouse Pier.[35] Arrangements for the immobilisation of pier equipment and cranes were rehearsed, and plans were drawn up for the sinking of trawlers to obstruct approaches to the piers.[36] The piers were prepared with demolition charges and were to be blown up in the event of an enemy landing, the plunger to detonate the charges being manned by soldiers in a pillbox disguised as an ice-cream kiosk. Northern Command pronounced that the mantra in 1940 was 'If in doubt, blow'. As invasion became less likely, it changed to 'for goodness sake, do NOT blow prematurely'. In 1943 the charges were removed when the invasion threat had receded.[37]

Should the enemy land, it was the military's top priority to prevent a breakout from the beaches, especially if it involved tanks, armoured vehicles and wheeled transport. Throughout June 1940 substantial barriers to exiting the beach were constructed. Scarborough's Marine Drive, linking North and South Bays, was blocked with anti-tank concrete cubes and the slipways from the beaches in North and South Bays were similarly obstructed. It was not felt feasible to entirely impede access from the beach to the Foreshore in South Bay. Here the main priority here was to prevent access to the town itself, at the entrances to the Valley and to Eastborough.[38] Anti-tank cubes were also sited at Peasholm Gap in North Bay, barricading another route into the town.[39] All such obstructions were accompanied by barbed wire and sometimes by minefields. They were covered by defended trenches and static gun positions, from where defending troops would fiercely resist any attempts to remove anti-invasion obstacles.

The laying of minefields played an important part in anti-invasion defences. The castle undercliffs were extensively mined. The danger of landmines was demonstrated in June 1941 when three local brothers crawled under barbed wire onto the Castle Holms minefield. Nine-year-old Percy Elven was killed instantly when he stepped on a mine.[40] In another incident in April 1943 many windows were smashed on Queen's Parade, overlooking North Bay, when, it was assumed, a dog had detonated a mine on the cliff below.[41] To illustrate the size and extent of the minefields in Scarborough, in North Bay there were nine minefields. To take four examples, 24 mines were laid at the Castle Holms, 42 on Royal Albert Drive, 9 at the bathing huts and 9 at Monkey Island. South of Scarborough, mines were sown behind Osgodby Point, Cornelian Bay and Cayton Bay. Minefields were protected by barbed wire and red flags signalled danger to civilians.[42]

Troops stationed on Scarborough's beaches were an everyday sight for most of the war. One incident in September 1940 illustrates the dangers of life in a fortified town. Mary Wardell, a 25-year-old who had been living in Scarborough for ten years, met up with her sister and two soldier acquaintances. Just after midnight they went down to a prohibited area of the beach. Mary was singing, and the sound of the wind and the sea prevented her from hearing the two challenges issued by a jumpy sentry. Unable to discern who was approaching, the private issued a warning shot. Mary was struck in the head and died.[43]

There were also some risks for the soldiers involved in defending the beaches, even when the most serious threat of invasion had abated. April 1941 saw a series of tragic incidents when military personnel dealt with sea mines washing up on the shores. On 5 April a sea mine exploded in Burniston Bay. Two soldiers of the Loyal Regiment (North Lancashire) 7th Battalion were killed. The following day a mine exploded near the South Bay Bathing Pool, killing a further two soldiers, on this occasion of the 9th Battalion, Loyal Regiment. On 12 April another sea mine exploded when it was brought ashore. A member of a Bomb Disposal Company was killed, and another lost a leg.[44]

It is tempting to picture the threat of invasion in the summer of 1940 in terms of British soldiers anxiously scanning the horizon at sea for the approach of German ships or landing craft. As we have seen, however, the military authorities were greatly concerned about airborne landings inland from the coast. Early warning of an airborne attack was vital. Anti-aircraft Searchlight Units were stationed near to the coast, one in the village of Scalby, adjacent to Scarborough.[45] Also part of the early warning system for the Yorkshire coast was an RAF Radar Station at Staxton Brow, some six miles to the south of Scarborough. It was completed in April 1939 and during the war was defended by troops against sabotage or ground attack.[46]

A series of defended localities, fortified road blocks and pill-boxes was set up around Scarborough in preparation for potential attacks from the rear and flanks.[47] They would also serve to delay any potential enemy breakout after a coastal landing and to control any mass movement of the local population trying to escape in the event of an invasion.[48] One military exercise betrayed a fear that police and civil defence personnel might lose control of the civilian population if the *Luftwaffe* chose to machine-gun civilians fleeing from Scarborough to maximise panic.[49] Another exercise had the enemy landing on the inhospitable shoreline north of Scarborough, at Cloughton and Hayburn Wyke, and advancing on Scarborough behind a shield of captured civilians.[50] As there were particular concerns about the establishment of enemy bridgeheads on the beaches to the south of Scarborough, a number of fortified localities between Cayton Bay and Scarborough were developed, with the aim of checking any enemy advance on Scarborough.[51]

By the end of August 1940, the military were concentrating more on improving the defences of the town's perimeter than on those of the coastal 'crust'. Some of Northern Command's military planners were sceptical about the siting of roadblocks on the perimeter of towns. 'Too often,' one reported in August 1941, 'the arrangements are such that they merely delay well-disposed persons, and are quite unprepared to deal with hostile ones.'[52] A similar argument was made that regular and Home Guard troops would be of greater use against the enemy within a town than spread thinly on a wide perimeter.[53]

Demolition charges were attached to bridges in a wide area around Scarborough. 242 Field Company, Royal Engineers, for example, prepared for the demolition of bridges at Flixton, Staxton, Willerby, Brompton and Ganton, amongst others.[54] To prevent the enemy using the railway line in Scarborough, two 20-ton wagons, loaded with concrete and old rails, were to be run onto a bridge and their wheels blown off.[55] Cliff paths to the north and south of the town were obstructed with barbed wire, and in some cases the cliff itself was cut away. The cliffs were regularly patrolled by the military.[56] Extra precautions were taken to protect so-called 'vulnerable points', like the secret naval wireless station on the edge of the town.

Throughout the country a secret guerrilla force of Home Guard 'auxiliary units' was set up to harass German forces once they had landed. Initially, the military authorities were not confident that these auxiliaries would survive more than a few days in the event of an invasion, but by September 1940 it was hoped that they could 'remain in security behind the enemy lines for a considerable period'.[57] Two substantial underground bunkers were constructed for local Scarborough auxiliaries in higher ground at Middle Deepdale Farm, one with a sweeping view of the coastline.[58]

For the event of an invasion, a secret 'H' (Home) Transmitter was erected in 1940, manned by a small BBC engineering staff, along with the Publicity

Manager of Scarborough Corporation and the secretary of the Scarborough and Whitby Conservative Association. It would be their task to communicate government instructions to the townspeople if the Germans captured the area.[59]

Scarborough's dominant coastal feature is its extensive headland, separating the two bays and providing a vantage point looking out over the North Sea. In the summer of 1941, 'as a matter of urgency', a top-secret RAF station was built in the castle grounds, comprising two small wooden huts and an eight-foot-high protective wall.[60] The station, referred to as a Home Defence Unit (HDU), was controlled by RAF Kingsdown in Kent, which was responsible for a network of small RAF 'watcher' stations along the British south and east coasts. Their main responsibility was to conduct jamming and other electronic countermeasures against the *Luftwaffe*'s radio navigation system. This was part of the so-called 'Battle of the Beams', in which the RAF tried to send enemy bombers off their pre-set courses. Oral testimony also indicates that German-speaking WAAFs (Women's Auxiliary Air Force) were employed on the Scarborough headland in radio interception work, listening in to *Luftwaffe* pilots and their ground controllers. Patient Lambert, a German-speaking WAAF, recalls being stationed here and monitoring German night-fighters and airfields in the Netherlands.[61] Information from Scarborough would be passed on to local fighter command and to HQ Fighter Command at Stanmore. In 1944 the headland was further utilised, when a Civil Defence brick-built Observation Post was erected on an ancient gun emplacement on the Castle's south wall.[62] It has not been possible to ascertain the purpose of this post from the historical record.

The military was keen to take advantage of the ample spare land available on Castle Hill and its undercliffs. During the Phoney War the army built a rifle range on the Holms, at the foot of the north face of the headland.[63] The RAF was given operational control over the headland itself, where it established a clay pigeon shoot for the use of the local Initial Training Wings. RAF personnel at the nearby 'watcher' station were not impressed by the impact of such shooting on their equipment. Peter Giles remembers: 'We lost a lot of (ceramic) insulators to shot-gun pellets!'[64] As Crown property and a scheduled ancient monument, the Ministry of Works retained overall jurisdiction over the historic castle grounds. When the RAF proposed extending its clay pigeon shooting to the inner bailey of the castle, the Ministry of Works rejected this, conscious of its role as a guardian of the headland's historical legacy. An official commented: 'I fail to see what is wrong with the present clay pigeon shoot, which is on the Castle Hill where there is plenty of space.'[65] Similarly in 1943, when the RAF suggested building an assault course involving the digging of trenches and the erection of wooden obstacles on the headland to the east of the castle, the Ministry of Works again refused, an official minuting that 'the site is, in fact, regarded by archaeologists as of exceptional importance'.[66] Unsurprisingly, when the Ministry of Agriculture proposed that the headland be ploughed out for arable crop production in 1942, it too received short shrift from the Ministry of Works.[67]

'Others'

The invasion scare of 1940 heightened suspicions of potentially disloyal residents living amongst the country's otherwise patriotic population. One tiny minority in the country that faced public distrust was that categorised as 'enemy aliens': German, Austrian and, from June 1940, Italian residents in Britain. The military and security authorities were worried by the role played by pro-Nazi 'fifth-columnists' in the German conquests on the Continent, whilst some right-wing newspapers in Britain whipped up a campaign of popular antagonism towards foreigners from enemy countries. A *Daily Mail* headline, for example, demanded 'INTERN THE LOT!'.[68] Two 'enemy alien' residents were removed from Scarborough in May 1940, whilst another 27 were registered as lesser threats.[69] In June the windows of an Italian ice-cream shop were smashed the day after Italy declared war on Britain, whilst two Italian residents in the town were detained by the authorities and interned.[70] When a ship, the *Arandora Star*, was torpedoed in the Atlantic on 2 July 1940, carrying allegedly dangerous enemy aliens to Canada, the long-standing Italian head waiter of the Crown Hotel in Scarborough was reported missing.[71] Most of those who died in the sinking, it became apparent, were above suspicion.[72]

Others who failed to support the war effort fully in 1940 were also deemed to be letting the community down. The small number of Scarborough pacifists, who mostly had roots in the town's nonconformist religious heritage, faced accusations that they were shirking their responsibilities. In October 1940 the pacifist newspaper *Peace News* was withdrawn from the public library.[73] Similarly, the Communist Party newspaper, the *Daily Worker*, was withdrawn from the library and replaced by the *Financial Times*. The small number of local Communists did not support Britain's war effort until Soviet Russia joined the Allies in June 1941.[74]

In 1940 Scarborough was rapidly transformed from a scenic pleasure resort into a heavily fortified garrison. The local beaches, which had formerly welcomed children, bathers and sun-worshippers, became a potential stage for a fight to the death against the enemy. Entry to and exit from the town was controlled by military roadblocks and checkpoints. It would be difficult for civilians to suppress a sense of foreboding in such an environment. Fortunately, the defences were never put to the test.

Notes

1. Ministry of Information pamphlet, June 1940.
2. NA WO 199/1417, Invasion Committees.
3. H.R. Trevor-Roper, *Hitler's War Directives, 1939-1945* (London, 1964), pp.76-79.
4. Leo McKinstry *Operation Sealion* (London, 2014), p.54.
5. Quoted in Joe Foster, *Guns of the North-East* (Barnsley, 2004), p.37.
6. Captain G.C. Wynne, *Stopping Hitler* (Barnsley, 2007), Appendices 21 and 22.
7. Foster, op. cit., p.374.
8. Bernard Lowry, *British Home Defences* (Oxford, 2004), p.11.
9. Daniel Todman, *Britain's War: Into Battle, 1937-1941* (London, 2016), p.405.
10. NA WO 166/1050, 197th Infantry Brigade HQ.
11. (eds.), R. Macleod and D. Kelly, *Ironside Diaries* (London, 1962), p.380.
12. NA WO 166/1050, 197th Infantry Brigade HQ and WO 166/1086, 215th Infantry Brigade.
13. NA WO 166/1086 215th Infantry Brigade, North Riding Home Defence Scheme, August 1941.
14. NA WO 166/1086, 215th Infantry Brigade.
15. Ibid., and NA WO 166/1050 197th Infantry Brigade.
16. NA WO 166/6770 North Riding Sub-Area HQ.
17. Ibid., Exercise 'Simon'.
18. Ibid.
19. NA WO 166/1050 197th Infantry Brigade.
20. See Christopher Hall, 'The Wheatcroft Battery', *Transactions of the Scarborough Archaeological and Historical Society*, No.32, 1996 and Joe Foster, *The Guns of the North-East* (Pen and Sword, 2004), pp.38-39 and 157.
21. At the seaward end of Wheatcroft Ave. *SEN*, 12 July 2005. Gert and Daisy were a comedy double-act of the time.
22. NA WO 199/1411 Minutes of Army Commanders' Conference, 19 August 1941.
23. NA WO 192/92, History of the Fort, April 1942.
24. See, for example, NA WO 166/4408 2/5 Lancashire Fusiliers.
25. NA WO 166/1050, 197th Infantry Brigade HQ.
26. NA WO 199/1423, Northern Command, Beach Defences.
27. NA WO 199/1429, Northern Command, Beach Defences: Long Term Policy, n.d.
28. William Foot, *Beaches, Fields, Streets, and Hills* (CBA Research Reports, 2006), pp.183-189.
29. NA WO 199/1423, Northern Command, Access to Beaches 26 August 1941.
30. NA WO 166/3726 257th Field Co. RE.
31. Ibid.

32. Ibid.
33. Quoted in Robert Liddiard and David Sims, 'A Piece of Coastal Crust: The Origins of a Second World War Defence Landscape at Walberswick, Suffolk', *History*, Vol. 97, No. 3, (July 2012), p.426.
34. NA WO 199/1411 Notes on Army Commanders Conference, Northern Command, 28 April 1941.
35. NA WO 166/1086, 215th Infantry Brigade.
36. NA WO 166/6770, 257th Field Co. RE.
37. SEN 11 October 1945.
38. NA WO 166/3726 257 Field Co. RE.
39. SEN 5 February 1946.
40. Police Report, 29 June 1941 in James Richard Percy, *Scarborough's War Years*, p.154.
41. Police Report, 10 April 1943 in James Richard Percy, *Scarborough's War Years*, p.234.
42. NA WO 166/6770, HQ North Riding Sub-Area, Appendix D.
43. See *SEN* 16 and 24 September 1940 and *Mercury* 20 and 27 September 1940.
44. ARP and Police Reports, 5, 6 and 12 April 1941, in Richard James Percy, *Scarborough's War Years*.
45. NA WO 166/1050, 179th Infantry Brigade and WO 166/3726 257th Field Co. RE.
46. *SEN* 15 August 1945.
47. At, for example, Scalby Beck, Falsgrave, Knox Hill and Cayton Bay.
48. NA WO 166/1050 179th Infantry Brigade.
49. NA WO 166/6770, Home Forces: North Riding Sub-Area HQ, Exercise "Scott".
50. Ibid., Exercise "Simon".
51. Cliff House, for example, was fortified.
52. NA WO 199/1411, Minutes of Army Commanders Conference, 19 August 1941.
53. NA WO 199/1482, Home Guard – Formation and Reorganisation of Battalions, Memo by G.I. (H.G.), n.d.
54. NA WO 166/3711, 242 Field Co. RE.
55. Michael Williams, *Steaming to Victory: How Britain's Railways Won the War* (London, 2014), p.56.
56. NA WO 166/4408, 2/5 Lancashire Fusiliers.
57. Peter Fleming, *Invasion 1940* (London, 1957), pp.270-71 and NA CAB 120/241.
58. I am indebted to Martin Simpson, a local farmer, for this information.
59. *SEN* 7 July 1945.
60. NA WORK 14/1824, Scarborough Castle, Yorks: Use by the Air Ministry during the War.
61. IWM, Patience Lambert, Catalogue Number, 11879.

62 NA WORK 14/1824 Northern Region Civil Defence Regional Officer to Ministry of Works, 4 April 1944.
63 NA WORK 14/1137, Scarborough Castle 1919-1940.
64 Laurie Brettingham, *Royal Air Force Beam Benders: No.80 (Signals) Wing 1940-1945* (Leicester, 1997), p.144.
65 NA WORK 14/1824 Scarborough Castle, Yorks: Use by Air Ministry during war, 1941-1965.
66 Ibid.
67 NA WORK 14/1824, Exchange of letters between Agricultural Executive Committee, North Riding and Ministry of Works, December 1941.
68 Robert MacKay, *Half the Battle: Civilian Morale in Britain during the Second World War* (Manchester, 2002), p.64.
69 *SEN*, 13 May 1940.
70 *SEN*, 12 June 1940 and IWM, William Blewitt, Catalogue Number 28896.
71 *SEN*, 10 July 1940.
72 Neil Stammers, *Civil Liberties in Britain During the Second World War* (London, 1983), p.46.
73 *SEN* 8 October 1940.
74 *SEN* 30 May 1940.

CHAPTER 5

'Like A Sea of Khaki': The Army and Home Guard[1]

Who do you think you are kidding Mr Hitler,

If you think we're on the run...?[2]

The Army

The arrival of a considerable number of troops in Scarborough had a significant impact on everyday life in the town. The army numbers soared in the fraught years of 1940 and 1941, when most were involved in defending the town against invasion (see chapter 4). Falling off in the mid-war years, the numbers climbed again as part of the nationwide preparations for D-Day. Armoured and infantry battalions involved in D-Day exercises on the Yorkshire Wolds were billeted in Scarborough, whilst exercises also took place in the Scarborough area.[3] Margaret Grafton (nee Bird) lived with her parents at High Deepdale Farm on Oliver's Mount. The army, having commandeered some of the farm, brought hundreds of soldiers up to the Mount every day where they trained in tank assault tactics and where her mother ran a NAAFI for them from the dairy window. The atmosphere was frenetic until they abruptly removed all their equipment and disappeared in the run up to D-Day.[4] In the town the hotels were full of troops and military vehicles clogged the South Bay, as D-Day landing craft practised landing on the beach. Sometimes vehicles got trapped in the sea and had to be rescued before they were submerged. When pupils at the nearby Friarage School had to rush home during an air-raid alert, some would fail to reappear in class afterwards, drawn irresistibly to the drama taking place on the beach.[5]

Soldiers of the Green Howards at Peasholm Gap.

What sort of relationship, then, did the locals have with the military during the war? The army was not always successful in restraining the energies and behaviour of its young men in uniform. Now and again soldiers upset residents with episodes of drunkenness or petty theft. One serviceman insisted that he could not recall stealing handbags from a dance hall due to intoxication.[6] It was not uncommon for many young conscripts to become, in the parlance of the time, 'browned off' by the routines and privations of military life, especially in the earlier years of the war.[7] One soldier, for example, was stationed in Scarborough as a signalman. Writing to his sister in February 1941, he complained of the boredom, the petty discipline, the cold and discomfort of army life. 'I have found that if you obey orders to the full in the army, you would forever lasting be buggering about.' He felt that his billet at the Hotel St Malo would have been better named 'St Maggots'.[8] Young men, removed from their home environment and facing the reality of war, could lose their ethical bearings and self-restraint. One young soldier conducted an affair with a local married woman, then deserted the army and fled the town, stealing the identity of the woman's husband as well as his clothes. During the war a number of visiting soldiers were exposed as bigamists after marrying local girls.[9]

One of the most common sources of complaint in Scarborough was the driving habits of servicemen in military vehicles. Soldiers were prone to speeding and ignoring traffic lights, and there was also some frustration at the reluctance of the police to intervene in the case of military driving offences. In September 1941 one army driver drew unwelcome attention to the issue when he knocked down Councillor Catchpole, who sustained serious injuries.[10] The military authorities tried to impose greater discipline on military drivers. Soldiers of the 5th Battalion of the East Lancashire Regiment were told by their commanding officer in Scarborough that they must only ignore traffic lights in cases of 'urgent operational necessity, such as troops moving to take up positions in battle'.[11] But poor driving was often a matter of deficient training. One signaller with the Royal Artillery in Scarborough recalled being appointed as a driving instructor on the grounds that he was one of a few who had passed a driving test:

> The method was to start at the beginning of a straight part of the promenade culminating near the swimming pool adjacent to Peasholm Park. The non-drivers were collected there and allocated to individual instructors. We were allocated more by management than luck a typical Yorkshire mill type, good of nature but lacking a little in the appreciation of mechanical vehicles. We gradually coaxed him into second gear but by that time the runway was becoming shorter and desperate measures were required. To the command of Stop! Stop! Brakes On! came a quick stab at the pedal BUT unfortunately his foot attacked the accelerator. The thoughtfulness of the Royal Engineers now became apparent because they had placed concrete tank barriers at the end of the promenade and we hit this with a resounding crash.[12]

The buildup to the D-Day landings in 1944 saw an influx of more soldiers and military vehicles. The heavy use of military vehicles and some poor driving seems to have pushed up the number of road accidents. Tragically, young children were sometimes the victims. A four-year-old died when she ran out in front of an army truck in May 1944. In June a seven-year-old was fatally struck by a military vehicle as she alighted from a bus.[13] The often-gruelling routines of military life were, moreover, not always conducive to road safety. In March 1944 an army lorry travelling in a convoy crashed into a civilian car. As the driver had only had eight hours sleep out of the previous 54, the case against him was dismissed in court. The magistrate accepted the defence that circumstances were beyond the control of the driver.[14] As the Normandy landings approached, a range of nationalities, American, Canadian, French and

Polish, also took to the local roads. This, too, could end in tragedy. In June 1944, for example, a member of the Polish forces died in a collision between two military vehicles at Ganton, near Scarborough.[15]

In an unfortunate incident in 1941 involving not road transport but an RAF aircraft, a Westland Lysander struck the chimney of a house on the north-side of the town and crashed into nearby allotments. The two airmen were killed. An RAF accident investigation concluded:

> As the accident took place in the very near vicinity to the home of P/O [Pilot Officer] Mould's mother, it may be assumed this officer lost control of the aircraft whilst circling the house.[16]

A young girl who was playing with friends on the Peasholm Lake island witnessed the incident. She recorded in her diary: 'It was very sad. I felt sorry for the boys and prayed for them.'[17]

The record of the British Army on the Home Front, nevertheless, was a good one, as one historian has concluded:

> … for the most part, British servicemen in World War II were extremely law-abiding. Violent crimes were rare, theft and men going absent without leave (AWOL) were the largest category of offenses, and the number of courts-marshal remained low.[18]

Examples of bad behaviour and tragic accidents attracted attention and publicity in Scarborough but were not necessarily typical of the military presence. The military authorities were sensitive to the impact of the army on the local population and encouraged servicemen to behave sensibly and to set an example to the civilian population. In October 1940 the following was decreed in relation to the blackout by the 5th Battalion East Lancashire Regiment: 'The military are expected to set a perfect example in this respect. All blackouts will be adjusted at least half an hour before the published blackout times.'[19] When the regiment found that frequent reports were being received from civilians that officers and other ranks were engaging in 'careless talk' in the town, the message to their men was unambiguous: 'KEEP YOUR MOUTHS SHUT'.[20] The army were keen to stamp out a number of habits that inconvenienced or antagonised locals. Servicemen were instructed to try harder in avoiding the digging up of underground cables and pipelines when constructing defences.[21] Roadblocks could be a source of irritation to the civilian population. In an unhappy case, a civilian died in an ambulance as it was held up at a roadblock 'for an unnecessarily long time'.[22] Orders went out that such delays must be kept to an absolute minimum. Army commanders also banned the soliciting of lifts from private motor cars by soldiers, by either standing on the road or by using a police halt gesture.[23] The irresponsible discharge of weapons was especially reprimanded after a soldier fired at a light in the town during an air-raid.[24] The 183 Special Tunnelling Company was anxious to maintain good relations with the civilian population:

> Avoidable damage done to requisitioned buildings and billets through wantonness and negligence on the part of individuals and units, not only wastes valuable material but causes considerable irritation to owners.

The considerable irritation of many owners when properties were derequisitioned suggests that this was more honoured in the breach than in the observance (see p.241). The military authorities showed some appreciation of the strains that the war was imposing on civilians and, for example, tried to contain the level of noise coming from army billets before 'lights-out':

> Consideration <u>must</u> be shown to civilians living in the close proximity. Some of these civilians are working very long hours in their war effort and they require the maximum amount of sleep, and all ranks must realise that any interference to their efforts is detrimental to the common cause.[25]

Making an effort was invariably worthwhile. An officer in the Green Howards, for example, remembered arriving in Scarborough and finding that the local townspeople were somewhat unfriendly and 'always more ready to serve RAF lads rather than soldiers'. This disappointed him, as Scarborough had historic links to the Green Howards. However, when his Armoured Division organised a 'tattoo' to raise money for Green Howard POWs, including some from Scarborough, relations improved considerably.[26] Such efforts on the part of the army helped to build trust between the military and the civilian population.

There was, moreover, widespread civilian admiration for those who were prepared to make the ultimate sacrifice for their country. The least they deserved, it was widely felt, was a warm hospitality. During War Savings campaigns (see chapter 14) the town celebrated the efforts of the Armed Services in patriotic community activities. Canteens and recreational facilities were made available to servicemen at Westborough Methodist Church and at the old hospital, whilst the Liberal Club offered honorary membership and hospitality to all HM Forces.[27] The Odeon Cinema organised a scheme where local families 'adopted' a young soldier. Elsie MacKenzie remembers one such visitor 'who soon became part of our large family'. He kept in touch when he was posted overseas and later invited her mother to his wedding.[28] Most visiting soldiers, therefore, appreciated their stay in Scarborough and enjoyed harmonious relations with the local population. G. Griffiths (of the Green Howards), for instance, remembered the experience fondly:

> For me Scarborough was a happy time – friendly people, football on the sands, dancing at the Royal Hotel, and an occasional invitation to tea at the now demolished Pavilion Hotel.[29]

Friendships were forged between townspeople and visiting forces, and, inevitably, romantic liaisons developed. One story must serve to illustrate the capacity of the war to transform the lives of local people and visiting servicemen alike. Paddy Fox found himself stationed near Helmsley in North Yorkshire in 1943, serving in the 15th/19th The King's Royal Hussars. He had been born and raised as a Protestant in Southern Ireland, the eldest of a family of 12. Visiting Scarborough on a 48-hour pass, he chose to attend a film at the Futurist Theatre on the Foreshore while his fellow Hussars went off drinking. At the cinema he got chatting to a local girl, Kathleen Barker, like him in her mid-20s. When he asked if he could walk her home, she hesitated, explaining that she was six months pregnant and unmarried. Indifferent to the widespread social stigma attaching to such a situation at the time, Paddy walked her home, and saw her again the next day. They married in January 1944, Paddy a few months later adopting the boy Kathleen had been carrying when they first met. They went on to enjoy a long marriage and a further six children.[30]

The presence of soldiers like Paddy Fox from outside Yorkshire, and, indeed, from many far-flung parts of the globe, helped to generate a sense of excited curiosity about the new visitors. Pat Fleming remembers:

> There was an awful lot going on in Scarborough because it was a garrison town. We were absolutely packed out with service people from all over the world and as a child I can remember they all had flashes on their shoulders … and I liked to read them. There was New Zealand, Australia, Canada, Rhodesia, South Africa, Czekoslovakia [sic], Poland, from everywhere they were coming into the country.[31]

As is well known, well-paid and self-assured American GIs made a big impression on the British people. Pat Fleming added:

> And Dad was always bringing soldiers home and some Americans came once and you met all sorts of interesting people you wouldn't otherwise have seen. And the Americans gave me a pile of comics – now that was something![32]

One 14-year-old Scarborough boy idolised the Americans so much that he followed them around the town, and joined them illegally in pubs. In the Children's Court he announced that American soldiers were better than British ones, whilst he had to be told not to speak with an American accent.[33]

Locals, of course, benefited economically from the presence of the military (see p.121). Personnel billeted in the town paid for their accommodation. Property owners benefited financially from requisitioned properties. There were, indeed, complaints that too few soldiers were being stationed in the town to compensate for the loss of tourists. The spending of visiting servicemen in the town provided a fillip to hard-pressed local businesses, local dance halls

Scarborough had close historic ties to the Green Howards Regiment (formerly known as the Yorkshire Regiment), which had barracks in the town. In September 1945 the Battalion was granted the Freedom of the Borough of Scarborough, the first time the honour had been conferred on an organisation.

proving to be especially popular, along with public houses, cafés and cinemas. The Opera House stayed open throughout the war, staging shows for the troops.

The British Army in Scarborough, therefore, tried to avoid appearing as an army of occupation. There were frustrations on both sides, but a joint commitment to the war effort, and a mutual interest in cooperation, usually allowed difficulties to be overcome.

Home Guard

Few developments in 1940 have generated so much popular interest as the formation and activities of the Home Guard. Such a citizens' defence force had not been planned for. However, in May 1940 British public opinion became highly exercised by the ease with which the Nazis were overrunning the Low Countries and France. There was some panic about the prospects of an invasion of Britain and about the potential menace of enemy parachutists. When demands arose for popular participation in the defence of the country, the authorities decided to canalise such sentiments into a citizens' army under official control.[34] On 13 May 1940 Anthony Eden, Secretary of State for War, broadcast to the nation, appealing for volunteers to join the Local Defence Volunteers (LDV). He highlighted the parachutist threat and, among other things, the urgency of mobilising volunteers in the countryside and in small towns.[35] From the beginning, the government saw the benefits of the initiative in boosting the morale of the public.

Nationally, the LVD recruited a remarkable half a million volunteers in the first 24 hours after Eden's appeal, an historian comparing this to the rush to the colours at the beginning of World War One.[36] Churchill advised that the name be changed to the Home Guard in late July 1940, necessitating a change of official armbands. He felt that the potential association of the LDV with local government would fail to inspire recruits. In Scarborough 50 men had volunteered at the police station by 10.00 a.m. of the first morning of recruitment. Two days later there were over 700. They included a 76-year-old, an example of the widespread laxity over age limits.[37] In June and July the number of volunteers stabilised around 800, a large proportion of whom had served in World War One.[38] The local authorities initially found it difficult to recruit beyond this figure. The Emergency Committee of the town council and the mayor made appeals for more volunteers and late in June an LDV parade was organised in the town centre to encourage interest. Progress was made but it proved difficult to find enough men who would commit to night duties.[39] It also remained difficult to recruit local farmers, whose proficiency with firearms was prized.[40] Within a year, however, it was felt that the Home Guard locally was 'up to strength'.[41]

Scarborough volunteers for the LDV (later Home Guard) in May 1940.

In its earlier days the LDV was chronically short of equipment and resources. The Scarborough battalion was given a temporary office in the old hospital at the beginning of June, and at the same time an appeal was made for the donation of rifles and shotguns.[42] In the meantime, volunteers in Scarborough were taught to make their own weapons by lashing carving knives to broom handles.[43] Subsequent weapons training seems to have reflected the ill-equipped and inexperienced nature of the early local Home Guard. One training exercise on the Racecourse was remembered as involving the use of a German Luger pistol, and a colonel who accidentally dropped his live grenade in his own men's trench instead of throwing it.[44] Mobility was vital for such an anti-invasion force, but in late June an appeal had to be made for locals to make private cars available to the LDV. In July the mayor launched a fund (target

£400) for the purchase of bedding, furniture and 'gumboots' for the force.[45] In early August the guardsmen were still without uniforms.[46] A striking feature of the Home Guard was that they were not initially subject to military discipline, and therefore felt free to express their grumbles and dissatisfactions publicly. One volunteer wrote peevishly to the press 'that what was needed was not regimental badges, but proper uniforms'.[47] Another wrote that it was 'depressing' to find such slow progress being made in arming the Home Guard. 'Let us learn to shoot,' he stated, 'and be responsible for our own rifles.'[48] There was also some disappointment about the initial deployment of the Home Guard. The *Mercury* newspaper complained at the use of the Home Guard on a range of mundane tasks when they should have been actively on the look-out for parachutists.[49] A volunteer, frustrated by the lack of equipment and his insignificant role, was equally gung-ho: 'I joined to defend this town and my home,' he wrote.[50] When uniforms did arrive later in 1940, they were often ill-fitting. Eric Mason recalled getting his uniform altered to fit him. But Scarborough folk could be hard to please and this only elicited the response, 'who the hell does he think he is?'[51]

The early volunteers had signed up for very perilous work, as the threat of invasion seemed a very real one. One local volunteer who joined the Post Office company of the Home Guard in Scarborough recalled thinking that it was 'obvious' that the Nazis would invade the area from Norway. The advice given to him on resisting the enemy did not inspire confidence. Several stratagems were suggested for his defence of the telephone exchange. Firstly, he could hang a clothesline across the approach road, on the supposition that an enemy tank, uncertain of what lay ahead, would be forced to stop. Its commander would make an appearance, exposing himself to attack. Hessian screens were indeed widely used in coastal defence to conceal roadblocks and anti-tank obstacles. Secondly, he could use a length of railway line to jam the caterpillar tracks of an approaching German tank. If an enemy soldier got as far as the exchange, he was advised to use a large pepper canister and a heavy spanner as defensive weapons. Later he was given what he described as a 'cowboy revolver' with six rounds of ammunition, and finally a Thompson sub-machine gun with 30 rounds.[52] If the Nazis had landed, the Home Guard would have been shown little mercy, as it likely that German commanders would have regarded the volunteer force as partisans and not as legitimate combatants.[53]

During the tense summer crisis of 1940, the Home Guard gradually expanded its military responsibilities. Volunteers kept watch for enemy parachutists, often patrolling the Scarborough area by bicycle. They held positions on the cliff tops and defended routes in and out of the town. Their roadblocks were backed up by riflemen and 'Molotov bombers' in nearby houses and gardens. Instructions from the army authorities were upbeat:

> They will conceal themselves in houses and gardens and pick off the enemy troops as they appear. When necessary, they will improvise road blocks with cars or furniture, making sure that the cars are not usable.[54]

Volunteers also provided a mobile reserve, with its own transport, ready to reinforce areas under attack.[55]

In late 1940 and 1941 a major effort was made nationally to provide volunteers with firearms and to establish the Home Guard on a firmer military footing. By November 1940 two-thirds of volunteers nationally had their own weapons.[56] As the Scarborough Battalion acquired more weaponry and training, it was able to develop its capacity to resist invading troops. Training was provided at the Racecourse, Scalby Mills and Oliver's Mount in weapons proficiency and anti-tank warfare. Ken England remembers training in the use of rifles, machine-guns, mortars and Mills bombs.[57] Volunteers learned some of the techniques of guerrilla warfare, for example field craft, concealment and unarmed combat. As the battalion developed it became better able to fulfil the important role of relieving regular troops of their more routine duties. At first it manned vital local installations like the railway bridges, waterworks and Falsgrave reservoir. In time it was entrusted with supplementing Army personnel in defending key strategic points like the harbour, the Foreshore and Oliver's Mount. A member of the Wheatcroft Battery recalled joint training with the Home Guard at night and on Sunday mornings. 'They did a great job and were willing …', he remembered.[58] Volunteers continued to perform gruelling night watches and patrols in the town and surrounding countryside. These could betray the inexperience of the local volunteers, whose look-out duties could prompt false alarms. Eric Mason, for example, recalled witnessing shadows and hearing strange noises on night duty, and receiving public ridicule for raising the alarm unnecessarily.[59]

There has been some debate amongst historians about the effectiveness of the Home Guard in the defence of Britain.[60] In propaganda terms, by mid-1941 the force offered some reassurance to the British public at a time of considerable strain. In military terms, it fulfilled the role which it was set up to perform, providing essential patrols and lookouts and relieving the army of some of its more routine military duties. In the case of an invasion, the volunteers in Scarborough, as elsewhere, may have provided a minor obstacle to an invading army, but probably not much more.

After the Nazi invasion of Soviet Russia in June 1941 the prospect of an invasion of Britain receded. However, the Home Guard continued to expand its military roles and capacities. Nationally, the organisation became more disciplined and developed closer links with the army. In December 1941 the organisation lost its voluntary status and membership became compulsory for men not otherwise engaged in war work. Northern Command prioritised training exercises, often coordinated with the Army, over routine drill. As the Scarborough Battalion acquired greater military proficiency it was used in mock attacks to test the defences of nearby coastal communities such as Filey and Robin Hood's Bay. Army commanders were keen to test the Home Guard's own defensive capabilities by subjecting them to simulated assaults by the army:

> In framing these exercises as many Home Guard units and sub-units as possible were to be attacked even if from the point of view of the attacking Bn [battalion] the exercise might be unreal.[61]

A Home Guard exercise in North Bay. Guardsmen in German uniforms are rounded up whilst spectators watch from Queen's Parade above.

Such training experiences often highlighted the importance of the skill of improvisation in battle. In one exercise in July 1941 Scarborough was subjected to a simulated attack by an enemy force and the Home Guard were instructed to act on the assumption that their lines of communication had broken down. It rose to the challenge by utilising carrier pigeons from the Home Guard pigeon loft at their St John's Road HQ.[62] The value of some of these exercises came at some inconvenience to the town. In August 1941 the town was subjected to another dummy assault, this time by alleged special forces who carried loaded weapons and inflicted considerable damage to gardens and fences as they infiltrated the town.[63]

Military exercises involving the Scarborough Home Guard provide some insight into the role the force would have played in the event of an invasion or of enemy commando or sabotage raids. At the first sign of an attack the Home Guard was given the responsibility of immobilising some of the town's important facilities, such as civilian petrol pumps, to ensure that they did not fall into enemy hands.[64] Manning roadblocks and other strategic locations remained an essential Home Guard duty. In the event of enemy landings, the importance of Home Guard patrolling and intelligence gathering was stressed: 'The value of patrolling with the consequent collection of information both positive and negative cannot be over emphasised,' declared Home Forces Command in the North Riding.[65] If enemy troops were identified, patrols were advised to keep them under observation from a distance and report their movements to HQ, unless they were small enough to engage with.[66] Patrols needed also to be alert to the threat of spies and fifth columnists.[67] Some Home Guardsmen were to be transferred to regular army units if the enemy invaded, to take advantage of what one commander referred to as 'their intimate knowledge of their respective localities'.[68] That the 10 North Riding Home Guard was considered to be a valuable military asset is evident in battle planning conducted by North Riding Home Force commanders. The Scarborough Battalion was amongst those deemed to be 'numerous enough to enable a proportion of them to occupy definite positions either alone or in conjunction with Field Force Troops'.[69] John L. Burt remembers a Home Guard exercise where, acting alone, Scarborough guardsmen aimed to retake the Butlin's Filey Holiday Camp from the enemy, in reality the resident RAF. Deploying a smokescreen, the guardsmen were awarded victory in the battle, and were congratulated by their colonel who told them they 'hadn't done too badly'. They were, in fact, so successful that the RAF refused to allow them to use their bar after the exercise. The men had to return to their own barracks before they could enjoy a celebratory drink.[70] In another anti-invasion exercise the battalion operated on the front line of the defence of the town, occupying positions at the South Bay Bathing Pool, the

Grand Hotel and the West Pier. Their anti-tank Blacker Bombards (mortars) were considered to be an invaluable weapon against enemy beach landings.[71] Even when the prospect of Nazi incursions had become highly unlikely by the spring of 1944, the Battalion participated in a major North Riding exercise which assumed that the Germans had responded to the opening of the Allied Second Front in Europe by launching suicide parachute raids against the North Riding.[72]

A spontaneous product of the 1940 national emergency, the Home Guard came to occupy a significant place on the Home Front and in the national mythology of the war. As a demonstration of a sense of local patriotism, the volunteers helped to boost morale. The Scarborough Battalion, as did others, gathered strength over time and in military exercises later in the war proved itself to be a serious military force. In taking over many of the duties of regular troops in the North Riding, the Home Guard perhaps made its most important contribution to the war effort, allowing the Army to concentrate on preparing for overseas operations and, ultimately, for D-Day.[73] The Home Guard was stood down nationally in December 1944. Ironically, it had by this time developed into a force capable of causing serious problems for an invading army, but only after such an eventuality had become highly unlikely.

Notes

1. Margaret Scott's description of the main street in wartime Scarborough, *SEN*, 12 September 2009.
2. Signature tune of *Dad's Army*, BBC TV comedy series, composed by Jimmy Perry and Derek Taverner.
3. *SEN*, 4 December 1944.
4. BBC, WW2 People's War, Margaret Grafton, A3666855 (accessed 18 June 2018).
5. Reminiscences of Kenneth Rollinson, available at: http://smhc.hqtdevelopment.co.uk/article.php?article=676 (accessed 3 March 2019).
6. *SEN*, 27 September 1940.
7. See, for example, J.A. Crang, 'The British Soldier on the Home Front: Army Morale Reports, 1940-45', in Paul Addison and Angus Calder (eds.), *Time to Kill: The Soldier's Experience of War in the West, 1939-1945* (London, 1997).
8. IWM Private Papers, Catalogue Number 25879. Sadly, he was killed in action in North Africa in June 1942.
9. See, for example, *SEN*, 24 April 1944.
10. *SEN*, 4 June 1941.
11. NA WO 166/4252, 17th September 1940.
12. IWM, Cyril Medley, Catalogue Number 12337.
13. *SEN*, 25 May and 6 June 1944.
14. *SEN*, 23 March 1944.
15. *SEN*, 27 June 1944.
16. NA AIR 81/6746, Report on Accident, n.d.
17. BBC, WW2 People's War, Pat Fleming, A8968431 (accessed 19 June 2018).
18. Geoffrey Field, 'Civilians in Uniform: Class and Politics in the British Armed Forces, 1939-1945', *International Labour and Working-Class History*, No.80, Fall 2011, p.129.
19. NA WO 166/6770, 5th Battalion East Lancashire Regiment, Battalion Orders 23 October 1940.
20. Ibid., 14 September 1940.
21. Ibid., 28 Sept 1940.
22. Ibid., 31 August 1940.
23. Ibid., 23 October 1940.
24. Ibid., 18 Sept 1940.
25. NA WO 166/3656, 183 Special Tunnelling Company R.E. War Diary 1941.
26. BBC WW2 Peoples War, David Rogers, A3830104 (accessed 10 June 2018).
27. NA WO/4252 5th Battalion East Lancashire Regiment, War Diary 1940.
28. WW2 People's War, Elsie MacKenzie, A4971954 (accessed 12 June 2018).

29   Richard James Percy, *Anecdotes of Scarborough* (unpublished MS, 2006), p.23, SMHC.
30   Thank you to Lindy Rowley for sharing her family history with me.
31   WW2 People's War, Pat Fleming, A8968341(accessed 12 June 2018).
32   Ibid.
33   *SEN*, 13 June 1944.
34   S.P. MacKenzie, *The Home Guard: A Military and Political History* (Oxford, 1995), pp. 20-30.
35   Juliet Gardiner, *Britain 1939-1945* (London, 2004), p.193.
36   Daniel Todman, *Britain's War: Into Battle, 1937-1941* (London, 2016), p.375.
37   *SEN*, 15 and 20 May 1940.
38   *SEN*, 5 and 12 June 1940.
39   *SEN*, 15 June 1940.
40   *SEN*, 4,12, and 20 June and *Mercury* 7 June 1940.
41   *SEN*, 10 September 1941.
42   *SEN*, 5 June 1940.
43   *SEN*, 28 February 1997.
44   Frank and Joan Shaw, *We Remember the Home Guard* (Edbury Press, 2012), pp.214-16.
45   *SEN*, 5, 12, 15 June, *Mercury,* 12 July and *SEN*, 5 August 1940.
46   *SEN*, 5 August 1940.
47   *SEN*, 5 August 1940.
48   *SEN*, 22 July 1940.
49   *Mercury*, 7 June 1940.
50   *SEN*, 5 June 1940.
51   Frank and Joan Shaw, op. cit., pp.304-05.
52   Memoir of D. Goy – LEEWW.2000.698, *The Second World War Experience Centre*.
53   S.P. MacKenzie, 'The Real Dad's Army: the British Home Guard, 1940-44', in (eds.), Paul Addison and Angus Calder, *Time to Kill: The Soldier's Experience of War in the West, 1939-1945* (London, 1997), p.58.
54   NA WO 166/4408, Notes on the LDV – Duties, In Connection with the Defence of Scarborough (n.d.).
55   Ibid.
56   David K. Yelton, "British Public Opinion, the Home Guard, and the Defense of Great Britain, 1940-44", *The Journal of Military History* 58 (1994), p.471.
57   David Fowler, *God Bless the Prince of Wales* (Scarborough, 2009), p.223.
58   *SEN*, 12 July 2005.

59 Ibid. pp.198-200.
60 See Yelton, op. cit., pp.461-62 and Craig Armstrong, 'Tyneside's Home Guard Units: An Able Body of Men?', *Contemporary British History*, 22:2 (2008), p.257-58.
61 NA WO 199/1411, Notes on Army Commanders Conference, 28 April 1941.
62 *SEN,* 28 July 1941.
63 *SEN,* 27 August 1941.
64 NA WO 166/6770, Home Forces, North Riding Sub-Area, Scarborough Immobilisation Scheme, August 1942.
65 Ibid., Defence Policy, Section 7, the Home Guard, n.d.
66 Ibid., Defence Policy, Section 3, General, n.d.
67 Ibid., Exercise "Tumble", Narrative n.d.
68 Ibid., Defence Policy, Section 7, the Home Guard, n.d.
69 Ibid.
70 Shaw, op. cit., p.283.
71 NA WO 166/6770, Home Forces, North Riding Sub-Area, Exercise "Scott", Appendix B.
72 *SEN,* 4 and 8 May 1944.
73 NA HO/2951, History of Northern Region, No 1 (Northern), Civil Defence.

CHAPTER 6

Luftwaffe over Scarborough: 1940

A Falsgrave (Scarborough) clergyman visited an elderly member of his flock on a particularly dangerous night. 'How do you manage during these terrible raids?' he asked. 'Well, you see, sir,' she replied, 'I reads a chapter out of the Bible, I says a little prayer, I snuggles down under the bedclothes, and then I says, b………'em and goes off to sleep.'[1]

'Tip and Run'

In the summer of 1940 there were widespread light air-raids across Britain, involving single aircraft or small formations. From 18 June raids began to take place across the country every night, and from 10 July there was a new phase of daylight attacks. The entire east and south coasts, from the Tyne to the Bristol Channel, were subject to raids, as was South Wales. However, the North-East was particularly affected in this first phase of *Luftwaffe* attacks, 'enemy activity in the North-east' becoming a staple of the BBC's 8 o'clock morning news.[2] Scarborough and its surrounding area were hit numerous times. These light 'tip and run' raids persisted in the autumn of 1940 and into 1941, though they were overshadowed by the large-scale German bombing campaign of the 'Blitz' on British ports and cities.

It is difficult to generalise about the motivations behind these *Störangriffe*, or 'nuisance raids'. Sometimes they were part of a reconnaissance operation, especially of ports, airfields and coastal defences, which could involve testing Britain's ground-air defences or luring the RAF into battle. Sorties, in addition, offered the *Luftwaffe* excellent training opportunities and were used to familiarise crews with locating targets and deploying munitions.[3] It was also hoped that these repeated air-raids and the triggering of air-raid alerts would fuel fatigue and despondency in the British people. Many of the raids can be seen, too, as a continuation of the economic warfare that had earlier played out in the North Sea. Thus ports, large and small, were a favoured target, with the aim of dislocating the importation of food and raw materials into Britain.[4] Scarborough harbour seems to have been a target of some *Luftwaffe* attacks, evidenced in some of the Nazis' own communiques. After a raid on Scarborough on 15 August 1940, for example, when some minor damage was done on the outskirts of the town, the Nazis boasted that 'serious damage' had been inflicted on the town's harbour installations.[5] However, identifying the intention behind particular raids is further complicated as, in some cases, pilots were merely acting opportunistically. In the course of pursuing another mission, they took the chance to bomb or machine-gun random targets on the ground or to off-load unused ordnance. In retrospect, the *Luftwaffe* has been criticised by some military historians for dissipating its efforts in pursuing such erratic 'tip and run' raids.[6]

The first attack on the Scarborough area took place on 26 June 1940, when the nearby village of Burniston was hit in a night-time raid. Five cottages were badly damaged, though only one person received serious injuries. Remarkably, eight occupants of one house (including three evacuee children) escaped unscathed when the building collapsed around them. The town's first daytime raid took place on 15 August, a Junkers bomber strafing and bombing the gas works in the Seamer Road area on the western outskirts of the town. Six workers were machine-gunned, four of them required hospitalisation. An eight-year-old boy, Ernest Gates, became Scarborough's first air-raid fatality of the war. He had been playing in woods nearby and, hearing the enemy guns overhead, he ran for home and was struck by flying debris from the blast of a bomb. On the night of 19/20 August the *Luftwaffe* hit the village of Scalby, adjacent to the north of the town. The end wall of Scalby Lodge suffered a direct hit, but only one person was treated for slight injuries.[7] During these summer 'tip and run' raids a number of bombs landed relatively harmlessly in gardens, fields and the sea, providing evidence of the *Luftwaffe's* difficulties in hitting a relatively small target like Scarborough.

The press and local discussion of the raids emphasised the bravery of those on the receiving end and the good fortune bestowed upon local people. This was especially true of the Burniston attack, where the survival of the family of eight was certainly a lucky deliverance. The victims benefited from the

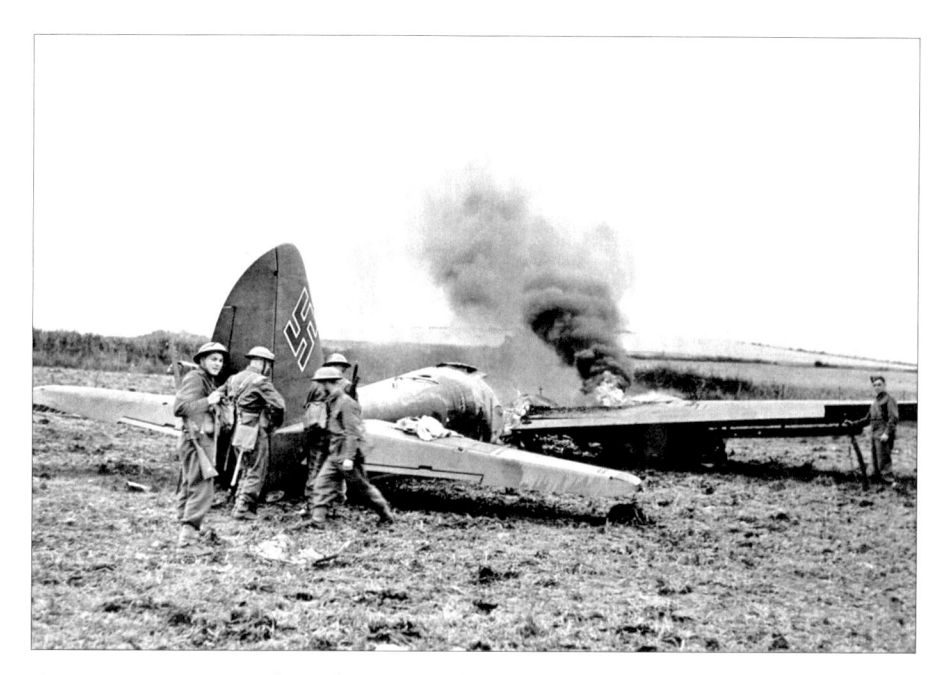

On 15 August 1940 a large formation of Junker 88 German bombers penetrated the Yorkshire coast in daytime. One bombed and strafed the Seamer Rd area of Scarborough, killing 8-year-old Ernest Gates. The radar station at Staxton Wold alerted RAF Spitfires and Hurricanes, which shot down seven of the bombers. The photograph shows one that crashed near Scarborough. (© Imperial War Museum).

efforts of a Special Constable and a local volunteer who rushed to their rescue whilst bombs continued to fall. In the same raid a bomb exploded in a garden, showering a mother and her baby in a bedroom with glass, but injuring neither. Another resident went to adjust his blackout blinds during this raid, whilst an incendiary bomb landed on the bed on which he had just been lying. In a nearby cottage, it was claimed, the occupants had been saved by a family bible on the sideboard, which had helped to stop the fall of a heavy beam after the collapse of the roof. In the case of the Seamer Road attack, rescue came from the RAF, when a Spitfire chased the enemy aircraft out to sea where it was downed. There was some satisfaction that Scarborough was playing a part in the RAF's well-publicised successes against the *Luftwaffe* in the summer of 1940.

10 October 1940

From September to November 1940 London bore the brunt of Nazi aerial bombing. However, despite the *Luftwaffe's* concentration on the Battle of London,

German raids on other ports and industrial centres in Britain continued.[8] Calamity struck Scarborough on 10 October. On a clear night with light rain, shortly before 9.00 p.m., a single enemy aircraft flew over the South Bay at about 1,500 feet, before returning towards the harbour, its engines screaming as it descended. It released a parachute mine which landed on Potter Lane in the Old Town of congested housing above the harbour area. A further one or two parachute mines landed in the sea, 100 yards from Castle Hill.[9] The explosive device was most likely a naval '*Luftmine*', which were widely used against London. Once the parachute opened, it would descend at some 40 m.p.h. and was detonated by a clockwork mechanism shortly after landing. Such mines had a far greater explosive power than anything else deployed by aircraft at this time.

The record of a Spitfire Fund whist drive on the Foreshore on the evening of 10 October 1940. The 20th deal was interrupted by the explosion of the German landmine in Potter Lane, when card players rushed outside to find out what had happened.[10]

Although small-scale in comparison with many cities bombed in the Blitz of 1940, the impact of the bomb on a small area of dense housing was dramatic and shocking. Alice Hick, who lived on Castlegate, adjoining Potter Lane, remembered the moment of the explosion:

It [the mine] hit Castle Gardens [a post-war renaming of Potter Lane] the force of the hit blew out all the windows and doors of our house.

Castle Gardens went down like a pack of cards. We just got through the door when there was a bang, the house seemed to lift and drop down again. The shutters, doors, roof and all the glass from the windows were gone.[11]

Another occupant of a Castlegate property was Winifred Cappleman. She had brought her three boys to Scarborough to escape the horrors of the London Blitz, along with Louis, a Belgian refugee who had been billeted with her in London. Moving in with Scarborough relatives, she was writing a letter to her husband serving in the army to say that the family had arrived safely in Scarborough when she heard the landmine whistling landwards, a sound that was familiar to her from the bombing of London. Next came 'a terrible explosion'. All the lights went out and the house came crashing down, leaving her choking and covered in soot and plaster. Louis was bleeding heavily from glass wounds to the face. She struggled upstairs to the children's bedroom, where she found two of the children trapped under the bedroom door, which had been blown off its hinges. Her third son was still in bed in the far corner of the room: '… the roof and all the walls were missing, the bed just resting on the corner of the floorboards and a sheer drop all around him.' The children were unscathed, though terrified.[12]

Damage to Castlegate in the Old Town after 10 October 1940 bombing.

Scarborough at War

The mine completely destroyed eleven houses and damaged some 500 more, many seriously. In the aftermath 71 had to be demolished, whilst seventy-odd non-residential buildings were also found to be seriously damaged. The explosion left a crater some 60 feet across by 30 feet deep and the immensity of the blast caused damage across 24 streets.[13] A 12½ pound stone crashed through the roof of the nearby Market Hall and St Mary's parish church sustained damage and broken windows.

Remarkably, there were only four fatalities, plus 31 seriously wounded. Two of the dead were an elderly grandmother and her grandchild. The grandmother was babysitting for the parents, who had taken the opportunity to go to the cinema. The other deaths were of a 45-year-old widow and a child of two. That the casualty figures were not much higher was due to a Spitfire Fund dance that was taking place at the Olympia Ballroom, attracting many 'bottom enders' from the Old Town to the safety, on the night, of the Foreshore. Others were attending a Spitfire Fund whist drive. There were many stories of lucky escapes. An elderly couple also went to the cinema, only after the wife had 'natted' (nagged) her husband to go. They returned to find their home destroyed. Among those made homeless were seven-year-old twins who had been evacuated from the London Blitz.

Damage to the Old Town following 10 October 1940 bombing. The outline of the Grand Hotel is visible towards the top right.

In the immediate aftermath of the bombing the 'Phoney War' ARP preparations were put to good use. Rescue squads with hand lamps rushed to the scene to locate the wounded and those trapped in the rubble, taking the wounded to St Mary's Hospital and the Sea Bathing Infirmary on the Foreshore. The rescuers were supported by a community effort, with the Police, Fire and ARP personnel joining in, as did volunteers from the Home Guard. Members of the Women's Voluntary Service (WVS) manned Rest Centres at the Jubilee Chapel and the Bar Church. Corporation workers and members of the public also threw themselves into rescue efforts. However, not everything went completely to plan in the town's first experience of serious bombing, and some criticisms were made of the efficiency of the Rest Centres on the night. It was their responsibility to look after the immediate needs of those who had been made homeless.[14]

After the attack, the priority was to provide shelter for the homeless. 462 families were found temporary billets, the Council's Billeting Officer trying, where possible, to find accommodation with family or friends (who were eligible to receive a small government allowance). The Council reserved the power to requisition properties for the homeless.[15] Winifred Cappleman, referred to above, was initially accommodated with friends who owned a boarding house on North Marine Road. Later, the Council provided her, fatefully, with an empty house on Queen's Terrace on the north side.

Clearance efforts came next. Nearly 300 men, including soldiers billeted locally, were put to work. The initial aim was to effect 'First Aid' repairs on damaged homes by making them reasonably waterproof. The target was 266 properties in the first week, involving the Council employing the services of 22 local firms of builders and plumbers, who provided some 180 tradesmen. An employee of the local Gas Company recalled one aspect of the recovery effort: 'All the staff at the Gas Company able to cope with gas leaks and gas mains were employed in the area for weeks.'[16]

The area affected was one of the more deprived areas of the town. With a poor housing stock, the Borough Engineer advised the mayor that many of the older damaged properties were hardly worth repairing permanently.[17] The people who were most affected by the bombing were often those least able to cope with the consequences of the destruction. The local Labour movement was concerned about the longer-term hardships of such victims. The Trades Council, representing local trades unions, condemned the low payments for injuries to civilians and the niggardly pensions for disablement or loss of life.[18]

The area was also home to the town's fishing community, who relied upon easy access to the harbour from their homes, so those who were moved to billets further afield suffered serious inconvenience. The disruptive impact of the October 1940 attack was, therefore, an additional burden on an already beleaguered fishing community. Although the Old Town of 'bottom enders' often appeared to have a separate existence from the rest of Scarborough, the extensive damage to this part of the town exposed the vulnerability of the rest of the town to Nazi bombing, and raised a question mark over the viability of the tourist industry in wartime.[19]

The scale of the damage inflicted in October 1940 induced a degree of shock in the town, but also a determination to face up to the likelihood of further attacks and a quiet satisfaction that the community had coped with the emergency. The outgoing mayor of Scarborough saluted the 'fortitude and courage' of the victims of the October raid.[20]

Early in 1941 initiatives were taken to enhance the town's ability to cope with the *Luftwaffe* menace. Supplies of sand, along with large water receptacles, were distributed more widely throughout the town to help counter incendiary bombs. Every household was asked to place one bucket of sand and one bucket of water outside their homes. The policing of the blackout was intensified, targeting early morning as well as night-time infractions. Two new emergency communal feeding centres were established at local schools. The Council printed 10,000 circulars for households, providing further information on what to do in the event of an air raid. In the first week of February 1941 a Civil Defence Film Week was organised to disseminate the latest advice on ARP and to stimulate further recruitment to the voluntary emergency services.[21] Despite official efforts at reassurance, it is likely that the town remained very much on edge after 10 October. Towards the end of the year air raid alerts became almost a daily and nightly experience, one day in December 1940 having six warnings within 24 hours.[22]

Air Raid Shelters

A national policy on air raid shelters had developed during the 'Phoney War'.[23] In responding to the threat of air raids, it was felt that the optimal policy was one of 'dispersal', scattering the population around a town or city instead of concentrating people in large public shelters vulnerable to a direct hit. This approach was reinforced by fears about the health risks and threat to public order associated with large public shelters.[24] The best means of achieving a dispersal was to encourage civilians to shelter in their own homes; in cellars, under the stairs or in family shelters dug in the garden. Scarborough took its cue from national policy. The Scarborough writer David Fowler remembers his father's efforts to protect his family:

> It was decided that this cupboard [under the stairs] would be the family's refuge in case of attack, so he decided to reinforce the hall ceiling and one Saturday around March 1940 a lorry arrived bearing planks of wood and sacks of sand. Supply had been easy as Uncle Bill – dad's brother – worked in the office of Sinclair's, a large local firm of joiners and builders. A framework of wood was built across the hall to give additional support to the ceiling, then, sacks of sand were placed on top of this and to the sides, to absorb any blast.

During later alerts, he records:

> … [the family] were usually joined by spinster Miss Weathers who lived on her own next door. Gas and electric were all turned off and we took flasks of tea and Camp coffee (which was the only coffee available unless you had black market contacts!) to the 'shelter'. We even took the galvanised dustbin lid! Phoebe [his younger sister] reminded me that this was included to protect her – then still a baby – from falling masonry should the house be hit.[25]

From October 1939 government-produced corrugated steel Anderson Shelters became available in Scarborough to reinforce the protection provided by outdoor domestic shelters.[26] The aim of shelter policy was, therefore, to encourage civilians to shelter at home and to help them secure what was termed 'moderate' protection against bomb blast and splinters.[27] More than this was considered to be impracticable and too burdensome on financial and material resources. Guided by the North Riding County Council, the Council in Scarborough, therefore, saw as its first responsibility the protection of adults unable to get home after an alert, embarking upon a programme of public shelter building in the autumn of 1939. It was estimated that shelters would need to cope with some 10% of the town's adults. These shelters were built in public gardens, car parks, buildings deemed to be particularly robustly constructed and in sites like subways, underpasses and below bridges.[28] Usually rows of park benches provided seating. Some twenty public shelters were completed during the Phoney War period, at the cost of £11,765.[29] The Council's responsibility was, secondly, to protect schoolchildren during the school day. For children, reinforced and covered trenches were constructed at local schools, intended only to provide for those children who would be unable to get home quickly or to shelter in other homes nearby in the event of a raid. As Mary Bird remembered, the dispersal of schoolchildren was encouraged:

> If the siren sounded at school, you were supposed to go to a billet at other people's houses, to protect at least some family members if there was a direct bomb hit. But living so close to school [Gladstone Road], me and my brothers and sisters ran home to mum, because we felt safer there ...[30]

The October 1940 raid had the effect of concentrating minds on the protection of the civilian population of the town. A Labour Councillor, Sidney Simpson, persevered with a campaign for substantial shelters for all schoolchildren.[31] He was unable to change the general policy of the Council, but the Education Committee did approve the erection of two additional shelters for infant schools, which could also be used by the public outside school hours.[32] In late 1940 the Council embarked on the building of 124 'communal' shelters: brick and concrete surface structures built in residential areas for groups of local householders.[33] These had been recommended by the government when steel shortages prevented the further production of Anderson Shelters. Elsie MacKenzie remembers that no seating was provided in them and that 'These shelters were not at all popular and very seldom used.'[34] Prior to the March 1941 'Blitz', then, most of the population were content to look after themselves in their own homes during air raids. Terry Baker, a Scarborough 'bottom ender' recalls: 'There was a shelter down the street but it was dark, damp and smelly so we usually got under the stairs or the table. I don't remember feeling frightened. It was just normal life for me.'[35] Another 'bottom ender' remembers sheltering in the underground Market Vaults at night. The cold in the winter was made worse by the storage of frozen meat for the market above.[36]

By the end of 1940, therefore, Scarborough had witnessed some serious physical destruction, five air raid fatalities and a wearying cycle of 'nuisance raids' and false alarms. However, the impact of the *Luftwaffe* was minor in comparison with that on cities and ports 'blitzed' in the autumn of 1940. The town had been fortunate. There was worse to come.

Notes

1. *SEN,* 15 May 1946.
2. NA HO 186/2951, History of Northern Command, No. 1 (Northern) Civil Defence: Air Raids.
3. Richard Overy, *The Bombing War: Europe 1939-1945* (London, 2013), pp.71 and 80.
4. Terence H. O'Brien, *Civil Defence* (HMSO, 1955), pp. 358 and 382.
5. *Mercury* 16 August 1940.
6. Daniel Todman, *Britain's War: Into Battle, 1937-1941* (London, 2016), p.442.
7. For the raids, see Richard James Percy, *Scarborough's War Years 1939-45*, pp.21-22, *SEN,* 27 June 1940, *Mercury,* 28 June 1940, *SEN,* 15 August 1940, *Mercury,* 16 August 1940, *SEN,* 20 August 1940. The town is not mentioned by name in the press. See also NA WO 166/4408, 2/5 Lancashire Fusiliers War Diary, August 1940.
8. O'Brien, op cit., pp.403-404.
9. SEN, 10 and 12 October 1940.
10. From unpublished diary of George W. Birley, n.d.
11. SMHC, File WW2, *Scarborough Today,* n.d.
12. Richard James Percy, *Anecdotes of Scarborough* (unpublished MS, 2006), p.10, SMHC.
13. NA WO 166/4252, 5th Bn. E. Lan. R., War Diary, 10th August. The four streets most affected were Potter Lane, Anderson Terrace, Short's Gardens and Castlegate.
14. *Mercury*, 17 January 1941.
15. *Mercury,* 18 October 1940.
16. David Fowler, *God Bless the Prince of Wales* (Scarborough, 2009), p.224.
17. *The Citizen,* 8 November 1990.
18. *SEN,* 19 November 1940.
19. Press reports on German raids did not identify precise targets, but it can be assumed that word spread quickly well beyond the target area.
20. *SEN,* 9 November 1940.
21. See *SEN*, 7 January 1941, *Mercury,* 17 January 1941, *SEN,* 3 February 1941, *Mercury*, 7 February 1941 and *SEN,* 25 February 1941.
22. *Mercury,* 27 October 1944.
23. O'Brien, op. cit., pp.285-289.
24. Richard Overy, *The Bombing War, Europe 1939-1945* (London, 2013), p.137.
25. David Fowler, *I've started so I'll finish…A Memoir* (Scarborough, 2017), pp.37-39.
26. Percy, op. cit., p.17.

27 O'Brien, op. cit., p.285.
28 Examples include Alma Square and St. Nicholas Cliff gardens, car parks at Northway and Victoria Road, in the Market Hall and a number of churches, under Valley Bridge and in the miniature railway tunnel, which was adapted to accommodate 115 persons. See *SEN*, 11 November 1939.
29 *SEN*, 11 November 1939.
30 *SEN*, 3 September 2009.
31 *SEN*, 29 October 1940 and *SEN*, 12 March 1941.
32 *Mercury*, 7 February 1941.
33 *SEN*, 24 December 1940.
34 BBC, WW2 People's War, Elsie MacKenzie, A4919420 (accessed 12 June 2018).
35 Terry Baker, *A Merry Dance: Tales of a Scarborough Lad from the 'Bottom End' of Town* (Richmond, 2010), p.7.
36 http://smhc.hqtdevelopment.co.uk/article.php?article=676 (accessed 19 September 2019).

CHAPTER 7

Luftwaffe over Scarborough, 1941-1945

On the night of 18th March, 'Jerry' decided to offer Scarborough a chance of 'redevelopment'. It was to be a very sustained bombing raid.[1]

The March Blitz

In the first quarter of 1941 the *Luftwaffe* shifted some of its efforts from the 'Battle of London' to other parts of Britain. In a directive of 6 February Hitler emphasised the crucial importance of the economic blockade of Britain, and the need for concerted attacks on ports and shipping.[2] From February to May some 80% of all raids were directed against the country's ports, in March the enemy striking at London, Southampton, Plymouth, Bristol, Merseyside, Clydeside and Hull. The last, less than 50 miles south of Scarborough, saw major raids on the nights of 13/14 and 18/19 March. The attack on 18/19 was the most serious on Hull since the start of the war, lasting six hours and resulting in nearly 200 deaths. It was on the same night that Scarborough faced its most extensive and deadly raid of the war. It is possible that this raid was part of the *Luftwaffe* campaign against ports and shipping, but it is more likely that the *Luftwaffe* bombers struck Scarborough in error. This view was stated officially in late 1944 when the Northern Regional Commissioner for Civil Defence visited the town and pronounced that, 'You, I know, got a few bombs intended for Hull …'[3] Supporting this, other commentators have noted that after two hours of the raid some of the enemy planes appeared to head off in the direction of Hull. It has also been pointed out that Scarborough was on the receiving end of an 'astronomical' number of incendiary bombs, whilst the more important target of Hull got very few.[4] Another motivation considered during the war was that the raid on Scarborough aimed to lure the RAF away from the defence of Hull.[5] By the end of the war, it was reported in the local press that the attack was 'obviously intended for Hull'.[6] Another view that emerged after the war was that some *Luftwaffe* aircraft missed their target of Hull because of RAF electronic counter-measures, which distorted the German air force's pathfinding 'beam' system (*Knickebeim*).[7] Until the German archives are inspected, it will not be possible to pin down authoritatively the reason, or reasons, for the notorious 'Scarborough Blitz' of 18 March 1941.

Around 8.00 p.m. on 18 March 1941, German bombers appeared over Scarborough, though sirens were not sounded till an hour later.[8] After the war this was described as 'one of those infuriating delays which have never been satisfactorily explained'.[9] Intensive bombing continued until about 10.30 p.m., with enemy pilots taking their time over the selection of targets followed, in the words of a local journalist after the war, by 'the desultory dropping of incendiaries and occasional HE (high explosive) bombs for some hours'.[10] Bombs were also dropped around the Filey, Flixton and Seamer areas to the south of Scarborough.[11] There is no record of any RAF intervention, explicable, presumably, by the intensity of the enemy activity over other parts of the north-east coast. The all-clear was not sounded until 4.30 a.m. It is estimated that nearly one hundred planes were involved, dropping some 55 HE bombs, several parachute mines and thousands of incendiaries. Many fires illuminated the sky in red and orange, whilst ARP and firefighting teams from the town and surrounding districts tackled the fires and searched the debris of bombed-out buildings for survivors.

As with many air raids, there were conflicting assessments of the number of fatalities, but this author's calculation of all fatalities arising from the March 'Blitz' is 29. This includes the deaths of a Canadian Squadron Leader and his wife who died soon after the raid as a result of a gas leak caused by bomb damage. It includes, too, Henry Crawford, a local fisherman who had been bombed out of Castlegate in the Old Town on 10 October 1940. He was relocated to New Queen Street, where he was injured in the March Blitz and died as a result of this on 26 April 1941. Another victim was Kate King, who was injured on 18 March whilst visiting her parents on New Queen Street. She died of her injuries on 5 October 1941. Hundreds more Scarborough residents were injured, many seriously. Two incidents were particularly tragic. A direct hit on a house on North Marine Road (number 120) killed a family of six and a maid.[12] The family, including two daughters and two sons, had moved to Scarborough as evacuees. On Commercial Street seven houses were demolished, resulting in the deaths of four women and three children.

Few parts of the town escaped damage to property and throughout windows were blown out by blast. Over 1,300 buildings were damaged or destroyed, many burnt out by incendiaries. A number of hotels and boarding-houses suffered, whilst tourist amenities were hit too. The Opera House and the Olympia dance hall sustained damage, a café adjoining the Floral Hall was destroyed by fire and the Corner Café, on the North Side, was struck. Overall, though, the tourist infrastructure of the town was not affected as greatly as one might have expected. An 'urban myth' emerged that Hitler had instructed the *Luftwaffe* to save the monumental Grand Hotel that dominated the South Bay, as he wished to use it as his Chancellery in a conquered England. In fact, incendiary bombs crashed through the roof of the Grand Hotel, setting fire to the ballroom, whereupon the fires were promptly extinguished by RAF fire parties belonging to the resident 10 Initial Training Wing.[13] The harbour was hit, but minimal damage was done, whilst the Castle Hill overlooking the harbour was showered with incendiary bombs, which bounced down 'like a cascade of fire'.[14] A parachute mine exploded 100 yards from the Corporation's Springhill Reservoir, cracking 45 of its supporting columns. The new hospital, schools and churches sustained damage.[15] A local landmark was seriously damaged when a parachute mine landed on the hall of Queen Margaret's School. The pupils had been evacuated to Castle Howard, but a young evacuee, who happened to be passing at the time, was killed in the blast. Though an expensive new block had been built in 1932, the school was demolished after the war. Some major business premises were damaged or destroyed. Tonks' warehouse (the former Waddington's piano factory), close to the Mere, was destroyed, along with its entire contents of furniture – much of it belonging to residents who had abandoned their homes or businesses in wartime. Perhaps the most spectacular incident was the destruction of E.T.W. Dennis and Sons print works in Melrose Street, shortly after the end of the last shift. It was hit early on by incendiaries and gutted in the ensuing inferno. The metal type was said to have melted on to the floor in the searing heat. A witness the following morning was met with, 'the smell of burning charred paper … and burnt picture postcards blowing around'.[16] An AFS fireman fell from a wall and broke both legs.[17] For months after the raid, unexploded bombs were to be discovered in the town. The reservoir was checked in April 1942 and was found to be leaking 19,000 gallons per day.[18] The

'Blitz' of March 1941 undoubtedly sent psychological shockwaves through the community, greater in magnitude than those produced by the more localised incident in October 1940 in the Old Town. When the Vicar of Scarborough somewhat imprudently suggested a month after the 'Blitz' that the town had 'commiserated with itself too much', given the suffering in other parts of the country, it was pointed out that the town had suffered disproportionately in relation to the country as a whole.[19]

The blaze at E.T.W. Dennis, an image comparable with the Blitz photography of the country's major cities and ports.

E. T. W. DENNIS AND SONS LTD. ARE VERY GRATEFUL FOR MANY KIND MESSAGES AND OFFERS OF HELP RECEIVED.

THEY HAVE OPENED A TEMPORARY OFFICE AT 10 YORK PLACE, AND ARE STILL CARRYING ON.

The Scarborough 'Blitz' was not reported in the press due to censorship, which explains this laconic announcement in the local paper after the inferno at Dennis's. The reference to 'carrying on' suggests Ministry of Information propaganda was being effective.

To appreciate the horror of the March 'Blitz' it is illuminating to explore some of the individual stories of those who lived through it. Pat Fleming was a schoolgirl in Scarborough at the time, living in a tall Victorian house with a cellar that was used as an air raid shelter.[20] The cellar had been decorated in a homely manner by her father to provide some reassurance for the family. Her memory of the bombs falling was of a great 'THUD' and a 'THUMP' and of the tremors of the explosions rising up from her feet. As the bombs drew closer, her father threw himself over her in the cellar. She also recalled the sound of the siren, which, she said, 'gives you a horrible feeling at the bottom of your tummy'. When she ventured out, assuming that all was clear, she saw a German aircraft. 'It was very, very low,' she remembered, and she could see its *Luftwaffe* insignia on the fuselage. She then witnessed the plane machine-gunning and killing a passing postman. Pat felt lucky to have survived, as a number of nearby houses were hit and some of the occupants killed.

William Sanderson was 17 at the time of the 'Blitz'.[21] Being too young for the Navy, he served as a volunteer messenger in the AFS. The attack took place during one of his shifts at the old tram shed off Scalby Road. As the raid intensified, a 'very flustered' firewatcher arrived at the tram shed and informed William that his home street (Commercial Street) had been badly hit.[22] William immediately sped home on his bike, 'with my heart in my mouth,' he remembered. To his relief, at home he found the two frightened faces of his brother and his grandmother peering out from under the stairs. However, nearby houses had been bombed out and rescue parties were attempting to locate victims buried in the rubble. 'That was the first time I realised,' he reflected, 'the war wasn't just a skylark or a bit of excitement.'

One of the houses sustaining a direct hit on Commercial Street belonged to Margaret Willis and her family. Her two-year-old sister Sylvia was killed, while it took nine hours to dig the eleven-year-old Margaret, her parents and her aunt out of the collapsed building. She recalled that it was the first time she had heard bad language, as her rescuers were receiving electric shocks from live wiring. Progress was also slowed when they had to put out their Davy Lamps whenever an aircraft flew overhead. Margaret later received a Girl Guides Gilt Cross for the bravery she displayed awaiting rescue and was commended for adhering to the Guides' law to 'smile and sing' in the face of adversity. Her aunt and mother required leg amputations, and her father received serious leg burns, from which he never fully recovered. As a result of ill-health, he lost his job as a baker, where he had worked for over 30 years. The family's wartime misfortune then propelled them into long-term financial hardship.[23]

A twelve-year-old Roy Hall had moved out of the family home on Commercial Street to keep his grandmother company down the road. On the night of 18 March he was suddenly disturbed by 'a huge rumbling'. Next, his severely injured father appeared at the door. Roy, finding his family home reduced to rubble, helped rescuers to dig his four-year-old brother Norman out and comforted his mother, who was also buried in debris. As a result of the incident, his father James and brother Norman survived with serious injuries. He lost his mother Lavinia, a ten-year-old sister Sheila and a two-year-old brother Alan.[24]

Some of the devastation on Commercial St after the March 1941 'Blitz'. On the left, local children are inspecting the damage.

Elsie MacKenzie, a young women engaged in war work and voluntary fire-watching duties, spent the night of the Scarborough blitz under the stairs at her sister's house, with her sister and her two children.[25] Taking a break from the cramped conditions, the two sisters sat on the stairs. 'Suddenly,' she relates, 'we heard the loud whistle of a bomb and we were sure that this was our lot: without a word we just hugged each other, bent our heads down and waited and waited.' Nothing happened. A delayed action bomb had fallen 100 metres from the house and was later safely defused. Elsie lost three of her friends on the night. Her brother was on leave from the Navy at the time, and, though he had taken part in the Battle of the River Plate, informed his sister that he would rather endure a naval bombardment than the likes of the Scarborough 'Blitz'.

The testimony of Michael Nellis, another survivor, vividly describes the horror of the night. He was a young boy who lived in a flat with his mother on the outskirts of Scarborough.[26] Recollecting the evening of the 'Blitz', he also vividly recalled the sounds of the night; the wail of the siren, the 'steady crump' of the bombs as they drew closer, the 'VROOM' as they fell nearby, the whistle of the ARP warden and the 'CRUMP! – CRUMP! -- CRUMP!' as the bombs fell near his home. Finally, there was a 'tremendous whoosh' when the blast struck, which, he said, 'I will remember till the day I die.' The blast 'seemed to take the last vestige of air from our lungs, yet lifted us and propelled us backwards down the steps, over the wooden gate, across the road to deposit us in a heap outside the front door of the house opposite!' Coming round, he marvelled at an ARP worker: 'No longer neat and tidy, his coat billowing around him, filthy black and blood stained, with his helmet looking as if it was trying to strangle him.' Yet what struck him most forcibly was the total silence of the aftermath. He had been deafened by the blast and had blood running from his ears and nose. He was to be troubled by hearing problems for years to come. Michael, along with another boy, was helped to another house. When his hearing returned he was puzzled to hear another unexpected sound: 'the swishing sound the sea makes when it runs back over loose gravel on the beach.' The house was on fire. He was helped away from this latest danger and led towards the nearest public air raid shelter. When Michael's mother returned to her flat in the morning she found that the chimney stack had collapsed and landed on Michael's bed. If he had gone to bed at his usual time it is unlikely that he would have survived.

As a final testament to the grisliness of war, Winifred Cappleman, whom we met when she was bombed in October 1940, recalled the events at York House on Queen's Terrance on the night of the 'Blitz'.[27] Her brother-in-law Arthur (a nineteen-year-old) and father-in-law were killed in a direct hit. Also killed were a soldier and his wife and baby girl. Body parts had to be put in sacks for burial. Arthur had been sitting at the opposite side of the room from the others, hence his body parts were more recognisable:

> Dad [Winifred's husband and Arthur's brother] had to go to the mortuary to identify Arthur as far as possible, as they had made a ball of rags and fitted pieces of his face and head around it – it must have been a terrible experience for Dad.[28]

There was considerable relief in the town that the emergency services had responded effectively to the March 1941 incident. Genuine gratitude was felt towards the ARP workers, fire-fighters and rescue squads who had risked their lives throughout the attack, and afterwards in dealing with unexploded bombs. The regular firemen and AFS volunteers were praised for tackling widely scattered incendiary bombs and dangerous conflagrations.[29] Resident troops also pitched in. One, a Captain Miller of the Royal Army Medical Corps, received a George Medal for rescue work during the raid, working in close proximity to a delayed action shell.[30] This was the first *Luftwaffe* attack that had tested the town's civil defence for a substantial period of time and across most quarters of the town. There appears to have been some gripes about aspects of the emergency responses, though it remained muted in the patriotic spirit of the time. Jottings in the *Mercury* dismissed negative comment as 'ignorant criticism' and emphasised the opportunity to learn from the experience.[31] Similarly, a correspondent in the local press defended the AFS against criticism from 'those who refuse to do their bit'.[32] After the raid there was some beefing up of the fire services. More paid auxiliary firemen were recruited and the distribution of stirrup pumps throughout the town was extended.[33] A new Youth Service, modelled on examples elsewhere in the country, was initiated at the beginning of April, incorporating 14 to 18-year-old boys and girls into the civil defence apparatus. By later May there were over 500 volunteers. Boys trained as messengers for the ARP, AFS and first aid parties. The girls were put to first aid training and supporting the WVS.[34]

The March 'Blitz' also triggered some changes in public attitudes to air raid shelters and in official thinking. It became more common for townspeople to seek refuge in public shelters at the first sign of an alert and to remain there for the duration of any threat. Overcrowding and insanitary conditions became more common.[35] The Council committed itself to an expanded provision of public shelters, embarking on six new ones in the month following the Blitz. By the end of August 1941, the town had over 30 substantial public shelters distributed throughout the town, each allocated a voluntary shelter warden.[36] The Council also made impressive progress in the provision of communal shelters. By the end of May, 500 communal shelters were available to local communities, with a capacity for 11,000 people.[37] By late September the Council had built nearly 800 such shelters. In a satisfying vindication of the dogged campaign of Councillor Simpson, in late May the Regional Commissioner for Home Security instructed the Council to provide shelters for all schoolchildren. 'It would be better,' noted

Simpson, 'if the Council had a mind of its own and acted upon it.' Tenders were put out for a further 22 shelters for schoolchildren.[38]

After the March Blitz

After the destructive impact of the Potter Lane and March 'Blitz' air-raids, the *Luftwaffe* returned to a pattern of lighter, intermittent raids for the rest of 1941 and 1942. There was a lucky escape towards the end of March 1941 when a parachute mine exploded harmlessly at Cromer Point, about a mile north of Scarborough. On 4 May 1941 bombs fell on Scarborough's rural hinterland, around the villages of Burniston, Cloughton, Staintondale and Harwood Dale. Tragically, a stray bomb also landed on the more distant village of Brompton-by-Sawdon, killing a local man, Captain Yorke, and destroying his house. His wife survived with minor injuries.[39]

There were two further incidents in 1941 that merit some attention. Firstly, on 10 May 1941 a lone raider dropped a considerable number of bombs on South Cliff and the centre of town. Scarborough's Art School, on the corner of Vernon Road and Falconer's Road, was damaged beyond repair. Hundreds of hotels, boarding houses, businesses and private houses were damaged, and windows were blown out over a wide area. A large number of public buildings in the heart of the town were damaged: the Post Office, Public Library, Labour Exchange, omnibus depot and Corporation Medical Baths.[40] Two hotels occupied by RAF 11 Initial Training Wing (the Weston and Waldorf) were hit and a trainee airman at the Weston died of his injuries.[41] Surprisingly few local people were injured. Fourteen months after the incident, on 14 July 1942, the Albert Hall, a disused billiard hall in the town centre, partially collapsed. The owner, a local builder, appealed to the War Damages Commission for compensation. His justification for the claim was that the structure of the building had been fatally weakened by the German bombing of 10 May.[42] However, the authorities were not convinced, as no other properties had been affected in the area of the Albert Hall.[43] The clinching evidence came from a Building Inspector who concluded that the building had been in 'a very bad state of repair': a leaking gutter had caused roof timbers to rot, eventually producing a 'spreading' of the structure and precipitating the partial collapse. The case for war damages was not, then, well-founded.[44] Yet the extent of the bureaucratic paperchase which surrounded the investigation is a testimony to the careful attention to detail of the country's wartime bureaucracy.

Scarborough at War

On 14 September 1941, an early evening air-raid provided further evidence of the random and arbitrary nature of the violence unleashed by the *Luftwaffe* over Scarborough.[45] Two bombs were dropped by a single plane on the Woodland Ravine area of the town. One landed on Prospect Mount Road, severely damaging four houses and bursting a gas main, and the other landed by the railway line to Whitby, damaging the track.[46] There were some typical tales of good fortune. One householder had left his home shortly before an explosion threw a large boulder onto his bed and a kerbstone into his bath. A woman who was washing her hair was blown out of her window and landed on her lawn, surviving unhurt. At another address, an elderly couple were dug out from the debris of their home suffering only light injuries. Not all were so fortunate. A nine-year-old was pushing her pram in the vicinity, accompanied by her family. She remembered 'a terrible bang and a vivid blue flash, then all went black'. Her pram ended up suspended from telephone lines and she came to at the bottom of a large crater, having sustained serious injuries to her back and legs. Meanwhile, a 31-year-old cyclist, Nellie Thornton, who was returning to feed her child after visiting a relative in hospital, was decapitated by flying debris. She had found herself in the wrong place at the wrong time. Mercifully, there were to be no more air-raid fatalities in the town.

Locals viewing repairs to the Whitby railway line at Woodland Ravine after the 14 September 1941 raid.

Later in 1941, the *Luftwaffe* started targeting trains on the railways, presumably in the hope of hitting troop movements or disrupting the movement of supplies. On 10 November, a train between Scarborough and Bridlington enjoyed a lucky escape when a bomb passed between the engine tender and a guard van, exploding after the train had passed over it.[47] Such tactics were repeated in 1942. On 27 March a passenger train was bombed alongside the Mere on the outskirts of the town. Carriages were damaged, as were nearby houses and Plaxton's factory, where war production was interrupted. Twenty-seven passengers required medical treatment, mostly for broken glass injuries.[48]

In late 1941 there were a number of ineffectual 'tip and run' raids, with bombs landing on farmland, open ground, allotments and the sea.[49] Nevertheless, 1941 was a year of prolonged psychological strain in Scarborough. From early spring there were frequent night alerts of several hours' duration, and in the later spring and summer warnings often lasted for the whole night. There were 153 alerts over the whole year, or some 260 hours.[50]

The *Luftwaffe* threat diminished markedly after 1941. There were 62 alerts in 1942.[51] Actual attacks on Scarborough were infrequent and relatively inconsequential. There was some light raiding in early September 1942, hitting barley and turnip fields near Seamer. Later in the month another single raider machine-gunned the southern outskirts of the town. A resident of Cornelian Drive reported that this plane had passed so low that she could smell the plane's exhaust down her chimney. Houses and shops were strafed with cannon fire, but the only injury was to a woman in bed who was cut by flying glass.[52] 1942 marked the end of recurrent *Luftwaffe* raids on Scarborough. The number of alerts fell to 29 in 1943 and continued to fall for the remainder of the war. There were some minor 'tip and run' raids in the North Riding and Scarborough but there were few serious attacks from 1943 onwards.[53]

The final raid of the war in Scarborough took place on 5 March 1945. Bungalows at the NALGO camp and 36 houses off Filey Road were damaged when an aircraft cannon-shelled the area. The poet Christopher Wiseman remembered the incident and the accompanying 'noise like world's end'.[54] A schoolmaster at the Boys' High School was seriously injured in the shoulder and in the black humour of the time, he was said, after receiving a plaster cast at the hospital, to have had his arm stuck forward, 'in a perfect Nazi salute'.[55]

During the years 1940-1942, therefore, Scarborough was frequently under attack by the *Luftwaffe*, suffering two particularly severe raids in October 1940 and in March 1941. The unnerving cycle of scanning the horizon for dangers, seeking safety during air-raid alerts and experiencing the sight and sound of enemy aircraft overhead no doubt generated considerable fatigue, anxiety and fear. There were over 20 raids in the war years. Given the extent of *Luftwaffe* activity over the district, it is surprising that the number of fatal casualties was as low as 37.[56] Many more were seriously injured.[57] The most visible sign of the raids was, of course, the bombed-out and burned-out buildings that pockmarked the town, over 3,000 buildings damaged or destroyed. However, the destruction was light in comparison with many other areas of the country. In 1944, Jottings reflected the town's sense of relief that the cost of the war had been relatively small, writing that 'there was much to be thankful for as a town'.[58]

It is impossible to measure the effects of the air raids on the people of Scarborough. They would have coped with the experience and psychological legacy of air-raids in their own individual ways. That the strain should not be underestimated, however, is evidenced in a poem by Christopher Wiseman, looking back from a vantage point in the 1970s on his experiences as a young evacuee facing air-raids:

To A German Pilot (extract)

I know I shouldn't care any more
The way I did then, crouching under
The steel dining room table with my mother
And baby brother, blankets over our heads,
Hearing the sky exploding over the house.
My hate went up like tracers at you then.

…

You hit no military target that night
But your mission accomplished something
If only that a hundred people would never be
The same. I still dream of you and your black plane.
I dream of the world ending in noise and flame.[59]

Notes

1. BBC, WW2 People's War, Michael E Nellis, A1975304 (accessed 20 June 2018).
2. Richard Overy, *The Bombing War: Europe 1939-1945* (London, 2013), p.109.
3. *SEN*, 8 November 1944.
4. *SEN*, 11 November 1944.
5. Ibid.
6. *Mercury*, 11 May 1945.
7. See p.66 on Scarborough's role in this.
8. For accounts of the raid, see Percy, op. cit., *Mercury*, 21 March, 1941. For wartime summaries of air raids, 1941-45, see *SEN*, 27 October 1944 and 29 October 1954.
9. *SEN*, 18 March 1947.
10. *SEN*, 29 October 1954.
11. *SEN*, 18 March 1947.
12. The Siddle family of 120 North Marine Rd.
13. NA AIR 29/634, RAF 10 ITW, Operations Record Book 19.3.41 and IWM, Flight Lieutenant G.S. Irving, Catalogue Number 2100.
14. *SEN*, 29 October 1954.
15. Churches damaged included St. Peter's, St. Columba's and the Queen St. Methodist Central Hall.
16. BBC WW2 People's War, Pat Fleming, A8968341 (accessed 12 June 2018).
17. Les Shannon, *Conflagration: Scarborough's Firefighting History* (Scarborough, 2003), p.147.
18. NA, HO192/125 Air Raid Damage, Region No.1, Northern. Newcastle. Scarborough.
19. *Mercury,* 25 April, 1941.
20. BBC WW2 People's War, Pat Fleming, A8968341 (accessed 12 June 2018).
21. BBC, WW2 People's War, William Herbert Sanderson, A3855684 (accessed 10 June 2018).
22. 7 were killed and 6 injured on Commercial St.
23. *Mercury*, 22 May 1942 and see also *Scarborough Comet*, 2 June 2015.
24. *SEN*, 18 March 1991.
25. BBC, WW2 People's War, Elsie MacKenzie, A4971954 (accessed 12 June 2018).
26. BBC, WW2 People's History, Michael E Nellis, A1975304 (accessed 20 June 2018).
27. See p.93 on her experience in the October 1940 air raid.
28. Richard James Percy, *Anecdotes of Scarborough* (unpublished MS, 2006), p.10, SMHC.

29 *SEN*, 25 March 1941.
30 *SEN*, 18 June 1941.
31 *Mercury*, 28 March 1941.
32 *SEN*, 15 May 1941.
33 *SEN*, 27 May 1941.
34 *SEN*, 24 May 1941.
35 *Mercury*, 25 April 1941 and *SEN*, 4 June 1941.
36 *SEN*, 23 August 1941.
37 *SEN*, 2 and 22 April 1941 and 27 May 1941.
38 *SEN*, 5 June 1941.
39 Percy, op. cit., p.27.
40 *SEN*, 10 May and *Mercury*, 30 May 1941.
41 NA AIR 29/634, 11 I.T.W. Operations Record Book, 10 May 1942.
42 He also suggested that the building could also have collapsed due to the detonation of an unexploded bomb from the May 10th raid or that such a detonation could have fractured the gas main and triggered an explosion which knocked down part of the building.
43 It landed on Vernon Rd.
44 NA HO 192/127, Albert Hall, Aberdeen Walk, Scarborough, 13-7-42, signed W.I. Williamson, 1 March 1944.
45 *SEN*, 15 September 1941.
46 The houses destroyed were on Prospect Mount Rd.
47 *Mercury*, 27 October 1944 and *SEN*, 29 October 1954.
48 *SEN*, 29 October 1954.
49 *Mercury*, 27 October 1944.
50 Ibid.
51 Ibid.
52 *Mercury*, 25 September 1942 and *SEN*, 26 September 1942.
53 *Mercury*, 27 October 1944.
54 Police Report 5 March 1945 in Richard James Percy, *Scarborough's War Years*, p.247 and Christopher Wiseman, *36 Cornelian Avenue* (Montreal, 2008), p.13.
55 Christopher Wiseman, *36 Cornelian Avenue* (Montreal, 2008), p.24.
56 See Appendix 1 on War-related Deaths.
57 For the wartime statistics, see *SEN*, 29 October 1954.
58 *Mercury*, 27 October 1944.
59 Wiseman, op. cit., p.25.

CHAPTER 8

Through the Tunnel: the mid-war economy

Sea-side resorts on the East Coast are among the most strangely changed places one can visit in the third year of the war. Most of us have a mental picture of deserted esplanades, barbed-wire entanglements, and impoverished boarding-house keepers.

(*Observer*, 31 May 1942)

Tourism 1941

Many of the troubles of Scarborough's economy in 1939 and 1940 (see pp.21-29) carried over into 1941. As news of the March 1941 'Blitz' spread, questions continued to be raised about the safety of the resort for holidaymakers. Although the ban on all recreational travel, introduced at the height of the invasion scare in 1940, was not renewed, the government continued to discourage trips to seaside resorts and other unnecessary travel. It was reluctant to make extra food supplies available for visitors to Scarborough and no extra trains were put on for the town's seasonal periods.[1] There was also a resigned feeling that, as the war progressed, the town was increasingly unable to offer visitors what they desired. The Corporation had cut back on municipal facilities for holidaymakers, like municipal cafés and the Open Air Theatre, and the Spa and the Floral Hall had been requisitioned. Access to most of the beaches was prohibited, whilst the South Bay had become particularly bereft of attractions for the visitor. To compete with the neighbouring resort of Filey, some limited early morning and evening swimming was permitted in July 1941, but this was felt to be inadequate.[2]

Many feared that the physical fabric of the resort was deteriorating to such an extent that the town's appeal to holidaymakers was being jeopardised. In addition to the ugly security features of concrete barriers and barbed wire, which often served as rubbish traps, the precariousness of the Council's financial position meant that it was unable to maintain the physical environment of the town at previous standards. Gardens, roads, road verges and footpaths were left in a poor condition. Private as well as municipal buildings were prone to poor maintenance, vandalism and peeling paintwork, whilst the remnants of innumerable official wartime notices and posters disfigured many walls. Buildings that had been requisitioned were especially liable to mistreatment and periods of abandonment.[3]

Despite difficult circumstances and gloomy prognoses, the summer of 1941 was not as bad as had been feared. From July onwards the number of visitors picked up and there was talk of 'a season of sorts'.[4] Takings by municipal enterprises rose. The Corporation's Café's Department generated some good returns (though it was now also providing for local schools and service personnel). The Olympia Ballroom remained very popular with visitors, whilst municipal facilities on the North Side, notably Northstead Manor Gardens and Peasholm Park, witnessed increased visitor numbers.[5] The North Bay Bathing Pool benefited from restrictions on sea-bathing and attracted twice the previous year's number of visitors.[6] Profits from municipal entertainments were up by £2,490 at the close of the season.[7] By the end of October the Council surprised many by declaring that it was in credit by £20,000.[8] Reflecting on the year as a whole, Jottings in the *Mercury* felt that the town's worst fears had not been realised and that the business of tourism had done 'reasonably well' in the circumstances.[9]

However, there was a worrying omen in the summer. In July 1941 the Ministry of War Transport asked the Ministry of Information to conduct a propaganda campaign to encourage people to take 'Holidays at Home'. Local authorities and voluntary bodies were exhorted to provide local amenities and amusements and to persuade people to enjoy a holiday in their home town.[10] The campaign came too late to make a major impact on the summer of 1941, but anger was provoked in Scarborough at the muddle and inconsistency of government policy. Whilst some northern towns were congratulated for offering recreational activities for local workers as a deterrent to holiday travel, it seemed that extra trains were still being provided to carry passengers to Blackpool and other resorts on the West Coast.[11]

Tourism 1942

Undeterred by the failings of the 1941 campaign, the government decided to reinvigorate the 'Holidays at Home' policy in 1942. The Ministry of Information launched its second campaign prior to Easter, urging citizens to do their patriotic duty and forgo the attractions of seaside resorts.[12] The Ministry of War Transport called upon the holidaymaker to plan the Easter holidays 'according to the country's need and not according to his [sic] own wishes'.[13] There would, moreover, be no extra trains or buses over the Easter period. According to a national newspaper, 'restrictions and prohibitions made travel to the seaside less inviting than ever.'[14] Such an approach by government severely exacerbated the existing problems of the tourist economy in Scarborough. Easter was a great disappointment, being quieter than the two previous wartime Easter weekends. Arrivals by bus were little different from those of an ordinary Sunday, whilst most of the alighting train passengers were, it was suspected, locals who were working away from home.[15] There was real concern that the idea of 'holidays at home' was catching on.[16] Though Scarborough had become somewhat inured to a sluggish wartime tourist trade, it was feared that holidays at home might retain some popularity post-war, if the 'home' offer was made sufficiently attractive.

Looking ahead to Whitsun and summer, there was little optimism in Scarborough. A further tightening of travel restrictions was anticipated, and northern towns and cities were planning to expand 'Holidays at Home' opportunities. Huddersfield in the West Riding had acquired a reputation as a pioneering champion of 'Holidays at Home' amenities. The mayor, indeed, was distinctly apologetic about stealing custom from Scarborough, and tried to reassure the resort that only a minority of his townspeople had ever enjoyed holidays away from home before the war.[17] In addition to the 'Holidays at Home' campaign, other challenges were developing in Scarborough. As military requisitioning of properties advanced, there was a growing shortage of tourist accommodation, only two of the five largest hotels remaining unrequisitioned. The demands of conscription and the war economy, moreover, were creating labour shortages in tourism and catering. Young women, for example, were having to leave the town to take up work in war industries.[18]

Nationally, the 'Holidays at Home' Whitsun campaign was more effective than it had been the previous summer. Throughout the country many workers enjoyed time off work at home, in the surrounding countryside or at organised local amusements. Even Blackpool was quieter at Whitsun than it had been for years. In Scarborough the 'Holidays at Home' movement had a keen effect on visitor numbers during the Whit holiday. Most travellers arriving at the station over Whit came with little luggage and were reckoned to be, as at Easter, locals coming home. Taking advantage of the quiet roads, many cyclists arrived in the resort, including a party of 200 from Leeds.[19]

At Whitsun Scarborough attracted the attention of the *Observer* newspaper, which sent a reporter to the town to investigate the plight of seaside resorts in wartime. The copy was not very flattering, noting the bleak environment of sandbags, barbed wire and concrete blocks. It continued: 'The front was completely deserted with a few soldiers and airmen wandering about and the shops nearly all boarded up.' Furthermore, 'An ice-cream shop with a high reputation for its products was open but empty. "Might be the middle of winter," the girl serving said.' The Corporation's programme of entertainments was described as 'a shadow of the peace-time programme'.[20] Such a portrayal of the town in the national press at Whit exasperated locals. 'It will not result in a single person being attracted here,' was a typical response.[21]

In the summer, the 'Holidays at Home' movement tried to bring more of the appeal of the seaside to the inland town or city. York, for example, borrowed donkeys from Bridlington, whilst Leeds sold 'rock' and other seaside souvenirs.[22] However, it proved to be difficult to deflect people from their desire for a traditional summer break. Throughout July substantial numbers from Lancashire and Yorkshire towns headed for resorts like Blackpool, Morecambe, Weston-Super-Mare and those in North Wales. The initial response in Scarborough was to denounce the railway companies for organising extra train services to the west coast and to question how Blackpool managed to feed such large numbers of holidaymakers.[23] However, by the August Bank Holiday Scarborough, too, began to benefit from a breakdown of the 'Holidays at Home' policy and from the provision of some extra seasonal trains to the coast. What had gone wrong with government policy? Conflicting signals emanated from government departments. Whilst the Ministry of Information was conducting its 'Holidays at Home' campaign, other ministries (notably the Ministry of Labour) believed that providing workers with a traditional holiday break in wartime was good for morale and productivity. For the British people, government policy appeared as 'a typical example of Government muddle'.[24] This only made them more inclined to make up their own minds, which inevitably favoured the opportunity of a holiday away from home. According to the National Council of Social Service, people enjoyed 'Holidays at Home' entertainments in their own towns and cities, but 'everyone who could do so has had a proper holiday as well'.[25]

During the August Bank Holiday weekend in Scarborough there was an unexpected influx of visitors. Though well below peacetime numbers, the weekend was much more successful than Whit and the previous year's Bank Holiday. The takings at municipal ventures were reassuring. The North Bay Pool and concerts at Peasholm Park were heavily patronised, whilst a sound Bank Holiday and summer season enabled the Council to increase its receipts from entertainments by 35% compared with 1941.[26]

Council finances benefited from the boost to the tourist economy in the second half of 1942. The level of rate arrears fell and the Council remained in credit.[27] Overall, the town had weathered another wartime year. 'Compared to 1940,' concluded Jottings, 'and to a lesser extent 1941, many more thousands of pounds were taken'.[28] Such progress helped to shore up the living standards of the town. A decrease in the number of pupils eligible for free school meals testified to a falling level of poverty.[29]

Tourism 1943

Spring 1943 witnessed further economic progress in Scarborough. A revival of the conference trade in the town took place, with visits from the National Federation of Retail Newsagents and the Clerical and Administrative Workers Union, though there were considerable challenges in accommodating the 200 delegates of the latter organisation.[30] In welcoming them, the mayor apologised for the accommodation difficulties and for the fact that the town was 'not arrayed in all her glory at present'.[31] Despite poor weather, Scarborough enjoyed a strong Easter season.[32] Traffic for the whole of the week was 'comparatively heavy' and one day exceeded some peacetime arrivals. There was a record Easter Sunday attendance of paying customers at a Peasholm Park concert (4,170) and a three-hour queue for boat-hire. Takings in municipal amenities were over two times those of the previous Easter. There was relief that people, despite the patriotic invocation of 'Holidays at Home', were determined to have a seaside holiday, even if they had to 'put up with a lot'.[33]

The Whitsun and summer seasons in 1943 witnessed a significant turning-point in the wartime economic fortunes of Scarborough as a seaside resort. There were early signs of optimism when the number of applications for alcohol licenses for new catering establishments rose in May.[34] Efforts were made to provide a wider range of traditional seaside amenities. Commenting on the re-opening of the Marine Drive for pedestrians, now toll free, Councillor Catchpole observed archly that 'people who come to the seaside wanted to see the sea'.[35] Over the Whitsun weekend rail arrivals were more than double those of the previous year and the Town Hall saw an increase in receipts from £687 to £1,171. Attendances at Peasholm Park concerts and boating, at the North Bay Bathing Pool and the Olympia Ballroom compared well with peacetime. Substantial queues were in evidence at shops, cafés and restaurants.[36]

The summer months saw a break with the economic doldrums of the early war years. In July, the Open Air Theatre re-opened with a Scarborough Amateur Operatic Society production of *The Pied Piper*. No artificial lighting was permitted because of Defence Regulations and a shortage of male actors influenced the choice of show and provided opportunities for local children.[37] In mid-July a Peasholm Park concert was attended by an audience of 5,000, a record for peacetime as well as wartime.[38] The August Bank Holiday surpassed all wartime visitor numbers hitherto, the railway stationmaster estimating a 100% increase on the previous Bank Holiday's numbers. A correspondent from *The Times* newspaper was intrigued by the arrival of so-called 'ghost trains', packed trains that did not seem to appear on any timetables or official announcements.[39] In the town the North Bay Pool attracted over 5,000 visitors on the Bank Holiday Sunday, whilst receipts for the Olympia Ballroom and Peasholm Park were each up by over £1,000. Throughout the town there were queues for food and refreshments and public houses operated restricted opening hours or ran dry. Intense pressure was put on accommodation and some new arrivals spent their first nights in the inhospitable environment of an air raid shelter.[40] There was widespread relief that the resort had recaptured some of the energy and bustle of its former peacetime self during the Bank Holiday. The *Times* journalist noted the further opening up of the beaches:

> Gaps in the defensive barbed wire let excited children, with veteran spades and pails, and their elders pass through to the golden sands and the sea. And he would be a hard man who, even amid the demands of total war, could deny the young ones the happiness they so obviously find on this long denied visit to the seaside.[41]

The fact that there was so little for families to spend their incomes and savings on at home was a bonus, one commentator advising the town to embrace the 'squandermania' of the visitors.[42] The success of the Bank Holiday persisted for the remainder of the summer. Receipts from municipal cafés and entertainments remained high. Council proceeds from the North Bay Bathing Pool, for example, exceeded all previous records.[43] Council rate arrears continued to fall, the sign of a slowly rising tide of economic security. The worst of the war, it appeared, was over. The year ahead was viewed with some confidence.

The War Economy

There were additional developments that helped cushion the town from the economic damage of the war. The requisitioning of properties by the Armed Services brought in regular, if not over-generous, payments to owners, as did the billeting of servicemen and evacuees in local properties. Local workers also enjoyed employment in war industries away from the town, notably in the West Riding. Some of their earnings found their way back home. Local labour was required for substantial programmes of military construction in the area.[44] Scarborough builders had helped in the erection of large-scale anti-invasion defences in 1940, whilst special trains ferried workers from the town to work on nearby aerodromes in the Helmsley and Bridlington districts. Local workers played a part in the construction of an artillery range at Fylingdales, including a three-mile-long concrete road across the moors. In 1942 and '43 contracts for the building of the top-secret naval listening station outside the town mostly went to local firms.[45]

Servicing the military stationed in the area, up to 30,000 of them, and the various civil defence organisations, was profitable for some Scarborough firms. Local bakers supplied up to 100,000 loaves of bread a week and vegetable suppliers enjoyed profitable contracts with the military. A single butcher supplied thousands of pies and buns to the town's NAAFIs weekly.[46] Scarborough printers were kept busy satisfying the military's voracious appetite for paperwork and there was also a considerable military demand for local laundry facilities. The military purchase of camouflage netting helped to sustain jobs in W. Rowntree and Sons and John J. Fell and Son.[47] Sandbags were produced *en masse* by P. Glaves and Son in nearby East Ayton. A good example of a Scarborough business that capitalised successfully on wartime opportunities was the Trinity Chair Works, which supplied bunkbeds, tables and chairs, rifle stocks and field telegraph poles to the military. Local timber was used, sawing and seasoning taking place at the Scalby Road Sawmills.[48] Similarly, extensive work on RAF requisitioned properties helped launch Dale Electric into a very successful post-war career.[49]

If the town had a specialism in war production, it was in the manufacture of customised crates and containers for the military. The concentration of such contracts in Scarborough allowed for collaboration and sub-contracting between local firms. Although packing cases may not appear to be a very glamorous part of war production, Britain's war effort was dependent on the safe movement of essential supplies and munitions to many theatres of war around the world. H. Pickup Ltd won contracts to manufacture specialised packing cases for the RAF. Swift and Sons produced specialised metal containers for civil defence and the military, including 650,000 metal drums for gas, oil and paint. Swift's also boasted the manufacture of enough army hut stovepipes to encircle the world. The leader of the pack was F.W. Plaxton and Son, whose coachbuilding was brought to an end by the war. Under the control of the Ministry of Aircraft Production, it specialised in the production of ammunition boxes and engine casings. It manufactured a quarter of a million tin-lined flare boxes and 400,000 tin-lined incendiary bomb boxes during the war. Engine casings for Rolls Royce and Bristol aero engines benefited from the company's pre-war coachbuilding expertise.[50]

Scarborough enjoyed an expansion of other war-related jobs in metalwork and light-engineering. Spavin Ltd, a machine tools company, produced nearly two million machined parts for the Admiralty, the Ministry of Aircraft Production and the Ministry of Supply. H. Pickup Ltd, in addition to producing a wide range of metal components, won the contract to manufacture the steel gun emplacements for the 6-inch naval guns at Filey, Scarborough, Whitby and the Tees. At Killerby Garage, near Scarborough, over 1.25 million machined and partly machined items of metalwork were produced for the war economy. The Premier Engineering Company in the town processed over ten million metal components for the Forces, as well as carrying out regular welding work on army vehicles and naval craft.

Local machine-tooling work expanded in the run-up to the Allied D-Day landings in France. Scarborough firms mass-produced components for the Allies' Mulberry Harbours and Bailey Bridges. Brogden and Wilson, for example, produced some 20% of the 'keepers' (brackets) required in Mulberry Harbours, in addition to manufacturing frames to transport aircraft engines. H. Pickup Ltd produced over 11,000 components for the prefabricated Bailey Bridges. Another local firm that gained from the D-Day landings was the Trinity Chair Works, which mass-produced wooden crosses for the US Army to take on its European campaign.

Two local companies made a noteworthy contribution to Allied electronic technology. The Electro Manufacturing Co. contributed to the wartime development of radar technology. It supplied the Navy with radar equipment and components, its machine shop turning out over 100,000 parts in the later stages of the war. Erskine Laboratories Ltd developed military radio and radar technology. A former employee remembered that the company employed 'quite a number of clever scientists from all over the country' during the war.[51] Over a quarter of a million component parts were manufactured and incorporated into some 70 different types of equipment, including some used at the naval listening station outside Scarborough. Its most striking work for the war effort was its contribution to the development of the OBOE radar system. Pathfinder aircraft fitted with the OBOE system were used by the RAF to identify and mark targets in Germany for the benefit of heavy bombers. Erskine Laboratories developed and produced half of the OBOE components that were used by the pathfinders.

Scarborough's tourist economy, therefore, experienced serious strains in 1941 and 1942, though making something of a recovery in 1943. Such unstable economic conditions added to the many other stresses imposed on the town by the war. However, the impact of the struggling tourist economy was mitigated to some extent by other economic activities in the town that were stimulated by the military presence and the demands of the war economy. The contribution to the national war economy of smaller-scale industrial production in provincial towns like Scarborough is often overlooked.

Notes

1. *Mercury,* 30 May 1941.
2. *Mercury,* 7 July 1941.
3. Jottings in *Mercury,* 6 March and 5 September 1942
4. See, for example, *SEN,* 25 July 1941 and *Mercury,* 5 September 1941.
5. *SEN,* 1 July 1941.
6. *SEN,* 12 September 1941.
7. *Mercury,* 24 October 1941.
8. *SEN,* 28 October 1941.
9. *Mercury,* 24 December 1941.
10. Chris Sladen, 'Holidays at Home in the Second World War', *Journal of Contemporary History,* Vol.37, No.1 (January, 2002), pp.70-72.
11. *Mercury,* 1 August 1941.
12. Sladen, op. cit., pp.72-73.
13. *Mercury,* 27 March 1942.
14. *Observer,* 31 May 1942.
15. *SEN,* 4 April 1942.
16. *SEN,* 13 April 1942.
17. *SEN,* 25 April 1942.
18. *Mercury,* 6 March 1942
19. *SEN,* 25 May 1942.
20. *Observer,* 31 May 1942.
21. *Mercury,* 5 June 1942.
22. *SEN,* 16 July 1942.
23. *Mercury,* 3 July 1942.
24. NA INF 1/284, Home Intelligence, Monthly Reports to the Cabinet, July 1942. See also Ian McLaine, *Ministry of Morale* (London, 1979), p.254.
25. Chris Sladen, 'Wartime Holidays and the "Myth of the Blitz"', *Cultural and Social History,* 2005; 2: p.239.
26. See *Mercury,* 17 and 31 July and 7 August and *SEN,* 2 July, 5 and 8 September, 1 October 1942
27. *Mercury,* 24 December 1942.
28. *Mercury,* 7 August 1942.
29. *Mercury,* 25 September 1942.
30. *SEN,* 18 May 1943.
31. *SEN,* 24 April 1943.
32. *Mercury,* 30 April 1943.

33 *SEN,* 26 April 1943 and *Mercury,* 30 April 1943.
34 *SEN,* 29 May 1943.
35 *SEN,* 11 May 1943.
36 *Mercury,* 18 June 1943.
37 *SEN,* 11 May 1943.
38 *SEN,* 19 July 1943.
39 *The Times,* 16 August 1943.
40 *SEN,* 31 July and 2 August 1943.
41 *The Times,* 16 August 1943.
42 *Mercury,* 30 July 1943.
43 See *SEN* 31 July and 2 August 1943 for summer season.
44 See *SEN* 6 and 23 October 1945 for a review of the non-tourist wartime economy.
45 See p.172.
46 NAAFI was the Navy, Army and Air Force Institutes, responsible for providing food and recreation.
47 *SEN,* 27 September 1945.
48 *SEN,* 23 October 1945.
49 Hugh Barty-King, *Light Up the World: The Story of Leonard Dale and Dale Electric, 1935-1985* (London, 1985), p.24.
50 Alan Townson and Edward Hirst, *Plaxtons* (Glossop, 1982), p.13. Production was interrupted by a serious fire in 1943.
51 *SEN,* 3 August 2004.

CHAPTER 9

Scarborough Fishermen at War[1]

...I have written this book about the British fishermen believing that their qualities are not exclusive to our race, but symbolise the good in mankind, which in this fight must inevitably triumph.

(Leo Walmsley)[2]

Fishing was a dangerous occupation, in war as in peace. On the night of 24/25 September 1916 the German submarine U-57 came across a flotilla of Yorkshire coast steam trawlers 20 miles north-east of Scarborough. Surfacing, the commander ordered the crews off their boats. The submarines then sank 19 fishing boats with gunfire and explosives, avoiding the expensive use of torpedoes. Eleven of the trawlers were from Scarborough. The U-boat commander arranged for the 126 crew to be transferred to a neutral Norwegian steamer *Laila*, which landed the men safely in South Shields. The Scarborough fishing fleet was nearly wiped out and the port never fully recovered from the blow.[3] Early in the Second World War there were some U-Boat attacks on fishing boats off Britain's west coast. The twin threats to Britain's fishermen in the war to come, however, came from enemy aircraft and sea mines.

Luftwaffe attacks and the threat of mines

During the early months of 1940 there was a spate of *Luftwaffe* attacks on fishing vessels from Scarborough and elsewhere on the Yorkshire coast. The attentions of German pilots became something of a routine menace for Scarborough's fishermen, especially between January and April. After the Scarborough trawler *Persian Empire* was attacked for the fourth time on 7 March, the skipper,

Thomas Robson, may have been forgiven for thinking that the Germans had a personal grudge against him. The reality was that Hitler had decreed at the end of November 1939 that the *Luftwaffe* should contribute to the waging of economic warfare against Britain by cutting off its imports by sea.[4] In the North Sea all British shipping was seen as a legitimate target, as the Germans were aware that British fishing boats were being used by the Admiralty for mine-laying and mine-sweeping, and suspected that they were also being used for spotting enemy aircraft heading for the British mainland.[5] At the beginning of March 1940 Grand Admiral Raeder, the German naval chief, announced on American radio that British fishing vessels were being used as naval auxiliaries, and for that reason were legitimate targets.[6] For individual *Luftwaffe* pilots, attacking vulnerable fishing vessels provided useful combat training.

Date in 1940	Scarborough vessel/s attacked by the *Luftwaffe*
12 January	*Persian Empire, Riby*
9 February	*Hilda, B.S.Colling, Our Maggie, Courage*
22 February	*Persian Empire, Riby, Emulator, Crystal, Aucuba, Cardew*
24 February	*Persian Empire*
1 March	*Courage*
2 March	*Hyperion, Mary Joy*
7 March	*Persian Empire, Aucuba, Emulator*
4 April	*Silver Line*

In most cases *Luftwaffe* pilots attacked in daylight and often quite close to land. Typically, they would circle menacingly before launching machine-gun and bomb assaults from a low altitude. In the first attack, on the *Persian Empire* on 12 January, a Heinkel bomber made two bombing runs, dropping four bombs on each, whilst opening fire with machine guns. The skipper reported that he could clearly see the bombs being released from the aircraft.[7] When the *Courage*, a Scarborough keel boat, was attacked on 9 February 1940, the skipper, Bill Pashby, echoed this: 'The enemy was flying so low that he could have hit him with a catapult.'[8] The experience of the fishing crews was undoubtedly an alarming one. The skipper of the *Hilda*, Harry Sheader, estimated that about 30 bombs were dropped in the vicinity of his coble.[9] He told a *Daily Mail* reporter how his crew had feared the worst:

We were near two trawlers when two planes with black crosses on their wings started to attack us. They seemed to be trying to machine-gun our little boat, and we took off our sea-boots and oilskins, grabbed lifebelts, and crouched under the sheets of the boat for cover.[10]

Thomas Robson of the *Persian Empire*, who had twice survived sinking at the hands of a German submarine in World War One, reflected that he would sooner face a submarine attack than the attentions of the *Luftwaffe*.[11] When the *Courage*, with a crew of three teenagers, was attacked for the second time at the beginning of March, one of the crew suffered from severe shock.[12]

Though the *Luftwaffe* inflicted no direct hits on the Scarborough fishing fleet, there were some close calls. The blast of four bombs damaged the compass, dynamo and wireless of the Scarborough trawler *Riby* in January 1940.[13] When three Scarborough cobles were attacked on 9 February, the *Hilda* was lifted out of the water by bomb blast and lost all her lines.[14] The *Courage* was similarly affected by blast when she was bombed and machine-gunned when fishing near Whitby, subsequently limping home with a split exhaust.[15]

The cook of the Scarborough trawler *Emulator*, George Whittleton, left the crew's dinner out on deck to cool. When the boat was machine-gunned by a German bomber the mutton was drilled full of holes.

The writer Leo Walmsley identified an element of stoical Yorkshire pragmatism that kept such men at sea in the early stages of the war, quoting Scarborough skipper Bill Pashby: 'It would tak mair than that to tuck 'em up in their beds when fish was the price it was.'[16] Fish had not been rationed and price controls were not introduced till mid-1941, so that even ancient boats, according to Angus Calder, could bring in 'uncanny rewards'.[17] There was a pride taken by the fishing crews in their efforts to combat aerial attacks. According to Walmsley: 'There was among these tough old Yorkshire skippers a feeling of intense rivalry as to which of them would be the first to bring a raider down.'[18] An example was set by the *Persian Empire* during the *Luftwaffe's* first attack, when the raider was chased off by the firing of distress rockets.[19] In February the military authorities commenced the arming of east coast fishing vessels with Lewis guns, though the training was hasty: some crewmen reported that they only received a couple of hours of practice. It was not always clear, moreover, who would be responsible for operating the gun. 'The gunner,' according to the *Silver Line's* Tom Watkinson, 'is which ever one of us gets there first.'[20] In late February the Filey-owned trawler *Aucuba*, skippered by Scarborian Billy Normandale, was able to come to the aid of sister trawlers with her Lewis gun, firing 45 rounds and frightening off the German pilot.[21] The fishing crews sometimes benefited also from RAF interventions, though the latter's main priority was the defence of British cities against potential bombing raids. On the 9 February attack an RAF fighter intercepted and chased off the enemy aircraft strafing and bombing Scarborough cobles. Later in the month the RAF came to the rescue of the *Persian Empire* and *Riby*.

The story that seemed to exemplify the gallantry of the North Yorkshire fishermen was that of the Scarborough-based drifter *Silver Line*.[22] The narrative of the crew's exploits helped to stir the nation. On 3 April 1940 she was fishing off the Yorkshire coast when the crew witnessed a dogfight between a Heinkel medium bomber and an RAF Spitfire. The crew of the *Silver Line* joined in with their recently fitted Lewis gun, hitting the bomber at least ten times and wounding the pilot in the leg.[23] Damaged by both the Spitfire and the drifter, and possibly suffering from an earlier engine problem, the Heinkel crashed into the sea. The Spitfire, which had sustained damage, later ditched into the sea and the pilot was rescued. The crew of the *Silver Line* picked up the five German airmen, one of whom was already in the sea, and promised them that they would be well treated. When the vessel returned to port in Scarborough, an injured crewman was taken to hospital and the remainder were handed over to the police. One writer later summed up the spirit of the fishermen:

The German Commander shook the hands of his rescuers on the quayside, in a gesture that suggested chivalry amongst adversaries was still alive, at least in the early stages of the war. Equally, it is testament to the character of the fishermen that once they had landed their human cargo at the quayside, they quickly returned to their routine harbour-side tasks, as if nothing out of the ordinary had ever happened.[24]

The pilot of the Heinkel bomber attacked by the drifter Silver Line is taken into custody. He does not appear to be unduly unhappy about the situation.

Reports of the incident attracted patriotic interest. A humourist at the time, punning on the drifter's name, suggested that in future the *Luftwaffe* might appreciate that not every cloud had a silver lining. The mayor of Scarborough commended the fishermen's actions as 'one more example of the fine courage and determination shown by the men of the fishing fleet'. He also denounced the enemy attacks as 'one of the lowest things possible'. The German airmen, for their part, gave gifts of a watch and a ring to their captors. They were reported as asserting that they had no intention of attacking innocent fishing vessels and one commented, 'We never wanted to fight you anyway.'[25] One of the *Silver Line* crew visited the injured airman in hospital, bringing, in the custom of the times, oranges and cigarettes. The narrative of mutual respect amongst warriors was dented soon after the war when it transpired that one of the German aircrew was exposed, whilst serving as a POW, as a 'nasty piece of work' who worshipped Hitler.[26] But the *Silver Line* episode seems to have generated considerable national admiration for both the fighting-spirit and the magnanimity of the Yorkshire coast fishermen. Lady Astor, for example, an MP representing a maritime Plymouth constituency, congratulated the men: 'Well done, your exploit has thrilled us all. I hope the war will make the people of this country realise that our fishermen are just as important to us as our sailormen.'[27] In a boon to British propaganda in the early stages of the war, therefore, the Yorkshire Coast fishermen were celebrated for their plucky role in the 'front line' of the war against Nazism.[28]

The first half of 1940 was the most dangerous time for the Scarborough fishing fleet, and after this attacks were more intermittent. In June 1941 the *Emulator* received 'more than superficial' damage when she was attacked fishing eight miles north of Scarborough.[29] Predictably, the *Persian Empire*, attacked so many times previously, was struck again in 1941, driving a raider off with her Lewis gun.[30] As the war continued, however, the deadliest threat came increasingly from enemy aircraft laying mines and from stray mines in the North Sea. Mines were to sink more British fishing boats than the German air force. A series of catastrophic misjudgements resulted in a tragic incident in July 1940. The trawler *Connie* caught a mine in her nets. It was landed and, on the assumption that it was harmless scrap, taken in vain to the Corporation Depot and then to a scrapyard. Finally, it was deposited on the South Bay sands, where the army appear to have attempted to disable the mine's detonators before setting it on fire. Eventually it exploded, wounding a nine-year-old boy, Louis Archer, who died of abdominal wounds shortly after being admitted to hospital. This was Scarborough's first war-related death, whilst a further 13 people were injured.[31] In another Scarborough disaster, on 16 October 1940 all four Scarborough crew were lost when the 25-ton keelboat *Pride* hit a mine within a few minutes of putting to sea from Scarborough harbour.[32] The next day, the *Albatross*, another Scarborough keel boat, and her crew were lost whilst fishing from Bridlington, presumed sunk by a mine.[33] On 26 June 1943 the Scarborough-registered steam trawler *Crystal* was sunk by a mine off the Humber and the crew rescued.[34] The lethal threat of mines for Scarborough's fishermen was never entirely overcome. The Scarborough-registered steam-trawler *Ethel Crawford*, skippered by Scarborian Arthur Scales, was probably the last fishing boat to be lost in the war. Striking a mine, she went down with all hands off the West Coast of Scotland on 20 April 1945.[35]

Wartime fishing

The interwar period had witnessed a steady decline in the east coast herring industry, caused by competition from Norway and Germany and by falling prices. North Sea trawling suffered too, from over-production, a slump in prices in the 1930s and the growing domination of the Hull trawling fleet. The vulnerable Yorkshire coast fishing industry was, therefore, ill-equipped to meet the challenges of war. In late 1939 the Admiralty laid a wide band of mines parallel to the east coast, making the North Sea largely inaccessible. The Royal Navy's requisitioning of larger trawlers and drifters was a further blow. In June 1940 the government banned all trawling off the east coast of England, and line fishing at night.[36] Daytime line fishing, moreover, remained handicapped by shortages of bait. Fishing boats required a permit before they could put to sea, which imposed strict controls over their activities. 'For fishermen,' writes Neil Ashcroft, 'the freedom to fish, and to choose when and where to do so, was curtailed as never before.'[37] In the summer of 1941 fishermen faced another setback when the high fish prices of the early stage of the war were brought down by Ministry of Food price controls. Against this backdrop of obstacles and restrictions, English herring fishing virtually came to an end during the war. White fish catches were greatly reduced, prompting the government's purchase of Iceland's annual surpluses of white fish and the mass importation of canned pilchards from California.[38]

In Scarborough, local fishermen complained about government regulations and about the rising cost of bait and equipment.[39] In August 1943 a Harbour Commissioner lamented the unfavourable local conditions for fishermen and the consequent sale of trawlers. This would preclude any post-war recovery in the industry in Scarborough, he feared.[40] As boats were sold and Scarborough fishermen volunteered to serve in the Royal Navy, the remaining crews increasingly comprised the elderly and teenagers, working on ageing boats and increasingly dependent on the support of their womenfolk.[41] By December 1944 there were only four trawlers remaining in Scarborough harbour.[42]

Some local men who were put off by government restrictions or concluded that the seas off Yorkshire were too dangerous opted to relocate to more distant waters. A number of Scarborough boats sailed north to the fishing grounds off the Firth of Forth in Scotland, often returning home weekly. This was far from a risk-free option, as the Scarborough men again found themselves harassed by the *Luftwaffe* and vulnerable to mines. A teenage Scarborough fisherman, Tom Rowley, recalled the perils of fishing off the Scottish coast on the *Emulator*:

> Trawling was now banned in English waters so we had to go to St Abbs and we mainly fished off the Firth of Forth, the nearest we could stop. We used to get frequent visits from enemy planes and lots of mines were trawled up, once we had 3 in the rigging at once, on one occasion we trawled up a body, then some mine-sweeping gear. The war was starting to hot up.

Rowley had a closer shave on the Filey-owned *Aucuba,* trawling off Dunbar in Scotland:

> On another [trip] we were towing just three miles off Barnsness Lighthouse when a mine exploded in the net. We were only in 10 fathoms of water, the ship lifted out of the water aft, only minor damage, broken glass, mirrors etc, but the net, boards and everything had gone. We pulled in 2 empty wires and steamed home.[43]

East Coast fishermen who were determined to remain plying their trade in wartime were most likely to relocate to West Coast ports, and to fishing grounds off Ireland and the west coast of Scotland. Some Scarborough fishermen relocated to Fleetwood in Lancashire, which became the country's pre-eminent fishing port in the war years. Those in Britain who continued to fish made a vital contribution to the country's precarious food supplies in wartime. This was done in circumstances where the usual risks of the fishing industry were supplemented by the threat of enemy aircraft and mines. At the end of the war it was calculated that the fishing fleet had brought back on average 220,000 tons of fish every year of the war, or about 40% of the pre-war catch. This was achieved by about 350 of the older fishing boats, when the fleet had comprised some 1,500 boats before the war.[44]

Fishermen in the navy

Some young Scarborough fishermen, frustrated by wartime fishing conditions, were keen to take the fight to the enemy. Their favoured destination was often the Royal Navy Patrol Service (RNPS), which operated many larger trawlers and drifters as requisitioned auxiliary vessels. Tom Rowley, for example joined up along with his friend Jackie Mann, advancing his age by a year to do so.[45] Another RNPS recruit was the teenage Fred Normandale. He spent the war sweeping for mines and submarines in British waters and the Mediterranean, ending the war escorting German submarines into the Scapa Flow base for scuttling.[46] Proportionately, the RNPS suffered the navy's heaviest losses, the Admiralty losing 361 requisitioned RNPS vessels. In comparison, the fishing fleet lost 136 boats to enemy action in the war. Fishermen serving with the RNPS were commonly deployed in mine recovery. This they were well-suited for, possessing practical skills in handling small craft and on-board machinery. Equally importantly, as a commentator observed, 'their courage, hardened through living daily and nightly with danger in their own profession, fits them psychologically for a task fraught with sudden risks and calling for the steadiest of nerves'.[47]

The Scarborough fisherman Bill Scales followed the well-trodden path of fishing in Scottish waters early in the war, where he learned on the trawler *Star of the East* of the risks involved in minesweeping. When his crew spotted a mine in the sea, the authorities were alerted and the Admiralty minesweeper *Firefly* was sent to the scene. Tragically, the mine exploded on board the vessel, killing all but two of the crew. Bill Scales witnessed the devastation on the *Firefly* when it was towed back to port. Undeterred, he joined the RNPS in July 1940, volunteering for mine recovery. He served on the Admiralty drifter *Achievable*, sweeping for mines in the Humber. Strong nerves remained an essential qualification for the job: 'During one week in 1941 *Achievable* recovered five mines from the Humber and had them all on board at the same time until our "boffins" had examined them and made them safe.'[48]

Another Scarborough fisherman, Dick Sheader, served on two 'sweepers' that were sunk by mines in the Humber area, before he joined the minesweeper *Equerry*, where, writes Arthur Godfrey, 'it was a case of third time lucky'.[49] The loss of minesweeping trawlers along the British coast was a common tragedy. In May 1940 the 290-ton *Charles Boyes* was destroyed by a German mine off the East Coast. All of all the crew were lost, including Scarborough skipper George Reynolds and seaman Richard Adamson.[50] Another trawler, the 505-

ton *Almond,* was struck by a mine off Falmouth in 1941, with the loss of all hands, including another Scarborough skipper, Albert Johnson, and seamen John Clarke and William Eaves.[51] Scarborians Walter Johnson and Billy Hunter served on the Admiralty keelboat *Verbena* and were involved in the extremely risky work of detonating acoustic mines off the East Coast. Those so engaged were known ghoulishly as the 'Suicide Squad'. Walter later played the dangers down, telling an interviewer that they were 'just doing their bit, the same as every other seaman at the time'.[52] The brave contribution of the 'sweepers' to the war effort was used by Lord Woolton to promote the consumption of new varieties of fish: 'After all, is it really important in the middle of a war that a man [sic] should have the particular kind of fish he is used to when our trawlers are fishing for mines in dangerous waters?'[53] The *Daily Mail* compared the 'Battle of the Mines' in 1940 to the RAF's Battle of Britain in ensuring national survival.[54] Scarborough seamen on 'sweepers', then, helped to protect British and Allied shipping and to keep Britain's ports open in wartime, essential elements of the war effort.

The contribution that Britain's fishermen made in the Second World War, both as fishermen and in Royal Naval service, is not always appreciated. Early in the war the *Manchester Guardian* urged support for the country's fishermen:

> It is a strange thing that Britain, which has been saved so often, from the time of Drake till to-day, by its fishermen, has not yet learned the lesson which nearly every country of Western Europe has acted on, that the industry of fishing is one of the main pillars of sea power, and is therefore worth paying for.[55]

As a small fishing port, Scarborough helped to support wartime sea power. Its fishermen displayed many of the qualities they required in peacetime work: practical skill, personal resilience and courage, a spirit of camaraderie. This was in evidence whether they continued to fish in perilous circumstances or served in some of the most challenging roles in the Royal Navy. It looked as though they might be rewarded for their efforts, when there were some spectacularly good catches immediately after the war. Fish stocks had recovered during the underfishing of the war years.[56] But it was not to last, as fish prices tumbled when price controls were removed at the end of the decade.[57] The war, moreover, had taken its toll on an already ailing local fishing industry. The future of fishing in Scarborough was left in some doubt.

Notes

1. In the writing of this chapter, I am indebted to the researches of Arthur Godfrey.
2. Leo Walmsley, *Fishermen at War* (London, 1941), p.256.
3. http://www.scarboroughsmaritimeheritage.org.uk/article.php?article=332 (accessed 4 September 2019)
4. H.R. Trevor-Roper, *Hitler's War Directives, 1939-1945* (London, 1964), p.19.
5. For some evidence of this, see *SEN* 27 March 1986.
6. *SEN*, 8 May 1986.
7. *SEN*, 13 January 1940.
8. *Mercury*, 16 February 1940. A keel boat had a full-length keel (unlike a coble) and was used for most forms of inshore fishing.
9. *Mercury*, 16 February 1940 and 8 May 1986. A coble was a traditional Yorkshire coast inshore fishing boat, typically about 30 ft. It was distinguished by a short keel and a flat-bottomed aft section.
10. *Daily Mail*, 10 February 1940.
11. *SEN* 13 February 1940.
12. *Mercury*, 1 March 1940 and 8 May 1986.
13. *SEN*, 13 January 1940 and 27 March 1986.
14. *Mercury*, 16 February 1940.
15. *Mercury*, 1 March 1940 and 8 May 1986.
16. Leo Walmsley, *Fishermen at War* (London, 1941), p.196.
17. Angus Calder, *The People's War* (London, 1969), p.479.
18. Walmsley, op. cit., pp.188-189.
19. *SEN*, 13 January 1940.
20. *SEN*, 8 May and 6 June 1986.
21. *Mercury*, 3 February 1940 and *SEN*, 8 May 1986.
22. See, for example, *SEN*, 3,4 and 6 April 1940, *Mercury*, 12 April 1940 and SEN 6 June 1986. A drifter was designed to catch herring in a long drift net.
23. Bill Norman, 'First to Fall', *FlyPast*, February, 1988, p.37.
24. Steve Midwood, *First Spitfire Down* (Steve Midwood, n.d.), p.22.
25. The ring (a gold signet ring) was returned to its *Luftwaffe* owner in the late 1980s by the son of Bob Wilkinson, the *Silver Line* crewman that had received it in 1940. See *Daily Telegraph,* 20 May 1988.
26. *SEN*, 19 December 1946.
27. Steve Midwood, *First Spitfire Down* (Steve Midwood, n.d.), p.27.
28. Hence their inclusion in Leo Walmsley's *Fishermen at War*, a book by the Robin Hood's Bay writer, promoted by the Ministry of Information. See also *SEN* 10 February 1940.

29 *SEN*, 9 July 1986 and Police Report, 5 June 1941 in Richard James Percy, *Scarborough's War Years,* p.149.
30 *SEN*, 9 July 1986.
31 *SEN*, 27 October 1944.
32 This was probably a mine dropped from an aircraft near Scarborough harbour on the 10th October 1940 air-raid. See *SEN,* 19 June 1986. The casualties were William J. Colling, William Colling (his half-cousin), Francis Crawford and Jack Robinson.
33 *SEN,* 19 June 1986.
34 *SEN,* 17 July 1986.
35 Ibid.
36 *SEN* 6 June 1986. A long line was a baited line, up to 1,000 yards long. It was used to catch white fish.
37 Ashcroft, op. cit., p.222.
38 Neil Ashcroft, 'The Diminishing Commons: Politics, War and Territorial Waters in the Twentieth Century', in (eds.), David J. Starkey, Chris Reid and Neil Ashcroft, *England's Sea Fisheries* (London, 2000), pp.223-4.
39 *SEN,* 30 June and 3 November 1941.
40 *Mercury,* 20 August 1943.
41 Thank you to Gordon Dent for evidence of similar trends in Newbiggin, Northumberland.
42 In preparation for immobilising the harbour in August 1942, the Army recorded 5 trawlers, 9 keel boats, 30 cobles and 23 yachts at Scarborough, though they would not all have been in use. See NA WO 166/6770 Home Forces North Riding Sub-Area, Scarborough Immobilisation Scheme, Appendix E.
43 From unpublished recollections of Tom Rowley, in the possession of the family.
44 *Daily Mail*, 18 June 1945.
45 Rowley, op. cit.
46 *Mercury*, 7 August 2004.
47 *Manchester Guardian*, 16 December 1939.
48 *SEN*, 19 June 1986.
49 *SEN*, 6 June 1986.
50 Ibid.
51 *SEN*, 19 June 1986.
52 Ibid.
53 *Daily Mail*, 28 September 1943.
54 *Daily Mail*, 10 August 1940.
55 *Manchester Guardian*, 16 December 1939.
56 *SEN,* 24 December 1945.

57 Robb Robinson, 'Steam Power and Distant-Water Trawling', in eds. David J. Starkey, Chris Reid and Neil Ashcroft, *England's Sea Fisheries* (London, 2000), p.213.

CHAPTER 10

Wartime politics and personalities

In 1941 the opinion polling organisation *Mass Observation* (MO) sent one of its observers to Scarborough to cover a parliamentary by-election. The strength of Conservatism was evident in many of the conversations he had with locals. For example:

Labourer, 50 (years old):

'I always give my vote to the people who give me my money. I think it's up to everyone to do that.'

MO 'They don't give you much though, do they?'

'Enough! Enough! If we got the Labour Party in there wouldn't be anything for anyone. Look at the Russians – working themselves to the bone all their lives just for a bit of scram [scran/food?]. That Bolshevism game is played out now and Hitler knows it. Though I must say the Russians surprised me when they didn't collapse.'

MO 'Do you think Hipwell [the anti-Conservative candidate] will get in?'

'He hasn't got a cat-in-'ell's chance. This is always a sure Conservative seat.'[1]

The Constituency

Since the creation of the Scarborough and Whitby constituency at the end of World War One, the Conservative Party had dominated the seat, returning an MP at every election on over 50% of the poll. The resort of Whitby, with about half the population of Scarborough, voted strongly Conservative, whilst in the constituency's rural villages and farming communities voters often took a lead from Conservative-minded landowners. In Scarborough, too, support for the Conservative Party was solid, with hoteliers and shopkeepers forming the backbone of local Conservatism. The resort also possessed an additional middle class of businessmen, professionals and managers, many of whom benefited from the thriving tourism industry. Conservatism was reinforced by a larger than average elderly and retiree population. Some moneyed residents made a home in Scarborough in order to participate in the flourishing social life of bridge, hunting clubs, yachting and the pursuit of 'tunny' fishing. The local community of fishermen in Scarborough was also reckoned to lean towards Conservatism.[2]

The Tories were helped electorally by the periodic splits and disarray of their main nineteenth century rival, the Liberal Party, and, to a lesser extent, by a divided anti-Conservative vote caused by the rise of the Labour Party. The Liberals had a bedrock of support in nonconformist religious communities in the town, but in the interwar period they were handicapped by national and local divisions, failing, for example, to put up a candidate in the 1931 general election. The social basis of Labour support, industrial employment and trade union membership, was slender in Scarborough. Many working-class families took boarders into their modest homes in the holiday season, acquiring something of a business outlook. The *Mass Observation* visitor was keen to record that the town was far from devoid of poorer voters, but 'only a small section of it is actively class-conscious'.[3] The social composition of Scarborough, therefore, lent clear advantages to the Conservative party.

Sir Paul Latham

Since 1931 the constituency's MP was Paul Latham, the son of Viscount Thomas Latham, who had helped transform the British company Courtaulds into a giant manufacturer of man-made fibres and chemicals. Thomas Latham had served Lloyd George in the Ministry of Pensions during the First World War and was rewarded with a baronetcy in 1919. Paul, then, was born into an immensely privileged life, attending Eton and Oxford.[4] He did know some misfortune, at the age of 19 losing a leg in an accident. He grew up, however, to be a lively and engaging character, of impressive physical stature and good looks. Friends and acquaintances tended to note his high-energy personality and his great sense of merriment, one recalling him as being like 'a bounding retriever puppy'.[5] He tended to make a very positive impression on those he met and had a reputation for considerable generosity and extravagance.[6] Paul was a man of great confidence and self-belief, which were channelled from early manhood into a political career. At the age of 23 he became the youngest town councillor in England, representing the London Borough of Lewisham. The following year, in 1929, he commenced his parliamentary apprenticeship by standing unsuccessfully as a Tory candidate in the Labour heartland of Rotherham in Yorkshire. He was on a rapid political ascent, and in May 1931 he was selected as the Conservative parliamentary candidate in a Scarborough and Whitby by-election, following the resignation of the sitting Conservative MP. This he won with a slim majority. Next, he consolidated his position in the constituency with a landslide victory over Labour in a two-cornered fight in the October 1931 general election, triggered by the financial crisis at the time. In the same year he inherited a baronetcy on the death of his father, along with a very considerable fortune. His constituents celebrated in 1933 when he married the glamorous Lady Patricia Moore, daughter of the Earl of Drogheda. Leading figures from the constituency party were brought down to London on a special train and the high society wedding, it was recorded, brought Parliament Square to a halt.[7] The following year saw the birth of a son and heir. Sir Paul went on to win in a three-cornered contest in Scarborough and Whitby in the 1935 general election. His social and political progress led many to conclude that he was one of the rising stars of his generation.

Paul Latham

However, Sir Paul seems to have lost some of his earlier political appetite and ambition after acquiring the Scarborough constituency in 1931. In 1932 he bought Herstmonceux Castle in East Sussex and threw himself into its restoration. It became a venue for regular and lavish social gatherings. In 1937 he separated from his wife and in January 1938 announced that he would not stand as a candidate at the next election. *The Times* reported that he was finding it impossible to reconcile his parliamentary duties in London with a large constituency in the North of England, his restoration work at Herstmonceux and his responsibilities towards his young son and heir.[8] In July 1938 the local Conservative Association selected a prospective parliamentary candidate to replace Latham, a wealthy stockbroker named Alexander Cadwallader Mainwaring Spearman. He was a scion of the Baring banking family, educated at Repton and Oxford and married to the daughter of a baronet. Spearman had acquired a considerable fortune in stockbroking and farming. Coincidentally, he too had lost a leg, in a carriage accident as a boy.[9]

Sir Paul may have been disengaging with public life, but with the approach of war in 1939 it appears that he was keen to do his patriotic duty. He offered his beloved Herstmonceux home to evacuee children and volunteered to join the Sussex Searchlight Regiment (TA). Due to the wartime electoral truce there was no General Election in 1940, but Sir Paul and his Constituency Association underestimated the importance of installing a successor quickly in order to meet some of the considerable challenges facing the constituency in wartime. There were soon rumblings in Scarborough about Sir Paul's absenteeism and lack of commitment. By October 1939 the local paper was complaining that the town had been effectively left unrepresented in the difficult conditions of wartime and in November the new President of the local Hotels and Boarding Houses Association described the constituency as 'like a ship without a rudder'.[10] An angry correspondent in the local paper insisted that all MPs in the Armed Forces should resign their seats.[11] Sir Paul responded to such pressure by taking up some of the pressing concerns of his constituents, especially those of the Hotels and Boarding Houses Association. But complaints were heightened when the constituency was designated as a Prohibited Area for travel in July 1940. One correspondent angrily demanded his resignation and that he forgo his 'nice little salary'.[12]

A further blow to Latham's standing in the constituency came in May 1941 when his estranged wife filed for divorce in a US court.[13] She denounced him for mistreating her, for despising her Irish ancestry and for marrying with the intention only of securing an heir. Her allegations were widely reported in the local and the national press.[14] Sir Paul's credibility as Scarborough's MP had already been seriously dented before a final thunderclap of scandal descended on him in the summer of 1941.

In June 1941 Latham requested that his batman in the Searchlight Regiment arrange leave so that he could accompany him on a trip to London, instructing him to write to him at Battery HQ to confirm this. When the letter arrived it was treated as an official communication and opened. A judge later observed:

'That is undoubtedly, from Sir Paul Latham's point of view, the most unfortunate letter that ever could have been written.'[15] As well as reluctantly confirming his availability, the soldier wrote: 'I don't want to be messed about again. I want to be a man or I want to be treated as a man.' The letter was immediately passed up the chain of command to the Brigadier and higher, though it is not clear why this happened so rapidly. The historian Emma Vickers has documented other cases in the war where similar situations were dealt with informally or a blind eye was turned to them.[16] When Sir Paul was informed that his case had been passed upwards, he quickly realised that his covert homosexual life was about to be exposed and attempted suicide by driving a motorbike at high speed into a tree. He sustained serious injuries.

Sir Paul had been leading a double life. Whilst serving as an MP and as a major in the Searchlight Regiment, he was also enjoying a pleasure-seeking life in London and Brighton. For those with money to spend there was a thriving wartime demi-monde where the contemporary austerity could be evaded and live-for-the moment indulgence pursued.[17] Gay men often found that there were greater sexual opportunities in wartime and less official repression than there had been before the war. Sir Paul was described by one friend as 'sex mad' and he had a reputation for pursuing his preferences recklessly.[18] 'Unfortunately,' commented an old school friend, 'Paul Latham was to grow up believing that there was one law for him and another for his fellows.'[19] Damning evidence from three of his gunners (referred to as Gunners A, B and C at his trial) was provided at his court martial in early September 1941, along with that of a young Cambridge student, whom Latham had met in the Ritz Hotel Bar. Gunner A had been Sir Paul's valet before the war and was then appointed as his batman in the Searchlight Regiment, whilst continuing to be paid a private retainer by Sir Paul. He claimed to have been sexually harassed by Sir Paul on numerous occasions. Gunner C testified that Sir Paul had got him drunk in his flat, taken advantage of him and paid him off with £70. Gunner B, the author of the incriminating letter, told the court that that he had also served as a batman to Sir Paul and had been subjected to sexual advances. Sir Paul pleaded not guilty to all the charges. He was found guilty under the Army Act of ten charges of disgraceful conduct of an improper kind whilst on active service and sentenced to be cashiered out of the army and imprisoned without hard labour for two years.[20] He was also found guilty of the criminal offence of attempted suicide.

By-election

Latham resigned as an MP in August 1941, triggering a by-election.[21] It was anticipated that Alexander Spearman, the existing Conservative parliamentary candidate, would be returned unopposed under the wartime electoral truce. However, by-elections in such circumstances afforded opportunities for publicity-hungry independent candidates. Rumours circulated of an independent standing in Scarborough. Then it was confirmed that Reg Hipwell, a 33-year-old visitor to the town and founder editor of the rank and file soldiers' magazine *Reveille*, was standing. It was not something he had planned, he claimed: 'I only came up here for a holiday – something to make a change.'[22]

Serving as a channel for the grievances and resentments of the lower ranks of the army, the historian Paul Addison has described *Reveille* as 'the private soldier's counterblast to Sergeant-Majors and the War Office'. Hipwell had persuaded most of the British Cabinet, including the Prime Minister, into publicly supporting the publication on the assumption it would be a mouthpiece of the patriotic 'Tommy'. The result, according to a government Director of Public Relations, was as follows: 'So the Cabinet are in the absurd position of endorsing some of the most subversive propaganda now being published.'[23] Efforts were accordingly made to starve the magazine of paper supplies and War Office briefings.[24] Intelligence sources, moreover, alleged that Hipwell was using the publication to make money for himself, or as a 'financial ramp'.[25]

Hipwell had been educated at Rugby School. After this he struck out on a buccaneering life in Australia, pearl fishing and labouring in gold mines and on cattle stations. He returned to England in 1932, selling vacuum cleaners before embarking on a career in advertising and journalism. Before the war he had acquired two convictions for theft.

Taking on the Conservative candidate, who had the unambiguous support of the Prime Minister and the three wartime coalition parties, was something of a David versus Goliath contest. Hipwell lacked the resources of a party machine and was reliant on his own energy and resources, along with his own rumbustious personal qualities. Locally he had few supporters, among them the maverick town councillor 'Johnny' Jackson. He issued a small number of handbills and pasted few wall-posters, deploying only a solitary sandwich-board man in the town centre. However, his skill lay more in attention-seeking and stirring up controversy. A representative of *Mass Observation* said of Hipwell, '… he rushed around the constituency making dynamic speeches with the aim of stirring up the apathetic'.[26] A significant amount of his energy was devoted to the character assassination of his opponents. The first of these, and for many the most shocking, was his attack during his first public meeting on the local landowning grandee Lord Downe, President of the local Conservative Association. Hipwell accused him of cowardice for returning from the Dunkirk evacuation prematurely, having abandoned the men under his command. There is evidence that Hipwell had picked up on a popular current of hostility to Lord Downe locally, and Downe admitted that that there had been criticisms of him over his record at Dunkirk.[27] This electioneering tactic certainly garnered a great deal of attention, *Mass Observation* commenting, 'he thus started off the campaign in a flare of publicity which drew attention to him and his candidature more effectively than any orthodox method.'[28] *Mass Observation* also felt that he had selected his target carefully: '… here was a man, a total stranger to the constituency, who had started his campaign by attacking the most prominent person in it.'[29] Criticisms of Downe struck a chord in some quarters. A 59-year-old Scarborough woman asserted, 'My son was at Dunkirk and he said it was common knowledge that he ran away early.' An elderly man commented, 'I think Hipwell was right to attack Lord Downe … who called him back?' It did not harm Hipwell's attack that Lord Downe's mother, the Dowager Lady Downe, had been active in the fascist movement in the North Riding and Norfolk between the wars.[30] Other locals, however, took a dim view of Hipwell's disrespectful behaviour. An Army Captain condemned him for being a 'cad', whilst an elderly man felt that his accusations were 'very insulting indeed.'[31]

Taking full advantage of Lord Downe's embarrassment over Dunkirk, Hipwell escalated his denunciation by suggesting that Downe was covering up the fact that he had been demoted because of his behaviour. He also questioned why he was so active in Conservative politics when he appeared at the same time to be in military service at the taxpayer's expense. Downe was blamed by Hipwell for the unfortunate selection of Paul Latham as a parliamentary candidate in the constituency, warning of the danger of him selling another 'pup'. Finally, Hipwell made public private conversations he claimed he had had with Lord Downe. Downe, he alleged, had expressed strong anti-Churchill views and had condemned the constituents of Scarborough and Whitby for their stupidity.[32] Such tactics on Hipwell's part undoubtedly had an influence on the local electorate, though late in 1942 Hipwell issued an unreserved apology to Lord Downe for slandering him and paid a small sum in damages.[33]

Alexander Spearman was similarly dismissed by Hipwell in uncompromising terms, as, among other things, 'the Rich Man's Friend' and an opponent of Churchill.³⁴ Whipping up patriotic feelings, he demanded to know why Spearman was not serving in uniform. When a meeting was informed that it was because of he was a one-legged amputee, a Hipwell supporter heckled, 'What about Bader?', who famously had served in the RAF with no legs.³⁵ As a 33-year-old himself and not in military service, Hipwell was not in a very strong position, but he was quick to provide a defence. He asserted cryptically that he had served in the Signal Corps but had had to leave through no fault of his own, explaining to the *Daily Herald* that he had been 'slung' out because of legitimate allegations he had made against a superior officer.³⁶ Hipwell also claimed that army service had so impoverished him that he had had to give up both his greatcoat and his smoking habit.³⁷ However, as evidence of his commitment to the war effort, he reported that he had been involved in fire duties during the London Blitz, and he claimed that *Reveille* had an important role to play in maintaining military morale. He intended, moreover, to return to military service.³⁸ Hipwell had in fact been forced to resign from the Signal Corps as it was felt that 'he did not possess the necessary powers of leadership' and was 'entirely lacking in tact'.³⁹ Earlier in his career he had been drummed out of the 3rd Battalion, the Monmouthshire Regiment for 'brawling in the streets' as well as being 'unscrupulous and dishonest'.⁴⁰

When Hipwell was accused by his opponents of causing an unnecessary distraction from the war effort, he responded by directing the blame on to Sir Paul Latham for precipitating the by-election. He condemned Latham as someone who had bought his way into political advancement and as a 'yes-man' who could be relied upon to toe the party line at local and national level. Predictably, he highlighted Sir Paul's poor attendance record in the constituency. Local politicians and commentators were coy about raising the nature of Sir Paul's 'disgrace' during the by-election campaign. Before the war the popular press in Britain tended to portray the gay man as an enemy within, in the words of one historian, as a 'a social menace, a member of a disreputable underground'.⁴¹ Hipwell had few qualms about exploiting such prejudice and, for example, advised a group of Scarborough fishermen not to vote for his successor, another 'pansy'.⁴²

Hipwell's onslaught on Downe, Spearman and Latham was part of a wider attack on the self-interested politics of the local Conservative machine, which, he claimed, lacked honesty, principle and accountability. Taking on such hidebound political power was an urgent task in the difficult conditions of wartime Britain, according to Hipwell. In this he was backed by Councillor

Jackson, who deplored the succession of nondescript and ineffectual Tory MPs who had represented Scarborough since World War One.[43] Hipwell also shrewdly exploited fault lines in the Conservative Party by shining a spotlight on the alleged hypocrisy of the local party, which harboured a deep-seated hostility towards Winston Churchill whilst at the same time endeavouring to exploit his wartime popularity for their own partisan purposes.

In addition to Hipwell's bare-knuckle personal attacks, he fought the by-election on a populist political platform which responded to a wide range of local and national resentments and grievances. He advocated a more belligerent prosecution of the war, including an uncompromising bombing campaign against Italy. Much greater support for Britain's Soviet ally was desperately needed, he asserted, something of a popular cause in the autumn of 1941. On the war, Hipwell stated:

> I do not think we are giving all the help we can to Russia. If I had my way I would bomb Rome until it looked like the Coliseum and Naples until it could not be distinguished from the last days of Pompeii.[44]

At home, Hipwell's key message was the necessity of providing 'a square deal' for Britain's servicemen and their dependents. He pressed strongly for rewarding the Forces with higher pay and a more generous settlement for their families. In social policy, he backed the cause of family allowances, generous old age pensions and improved War Injury Compensation for women. Hipwell's message was also tailored to more local grievances. He called for guaranteed prices for farmers and a better deal for Yorkshire's fishermen. The *Mass Observation* investigator, however, identified something of a cultural barrier when Hipwell addressed a group of Scarborough fishermen:

> … behaving like an excitable schoolboy or an American announcer and shouting breezy slogans to a group of phlegmatic, weather-beaten old seamen, and as far as the obs. [observer] could see not having the slightest effect on them.[45]

Overall, then, Hipwell's contrived to paint himself as the outsider championing the common man and woman in wartime, pitting himself against the local political establishment and its 'vested interests'.

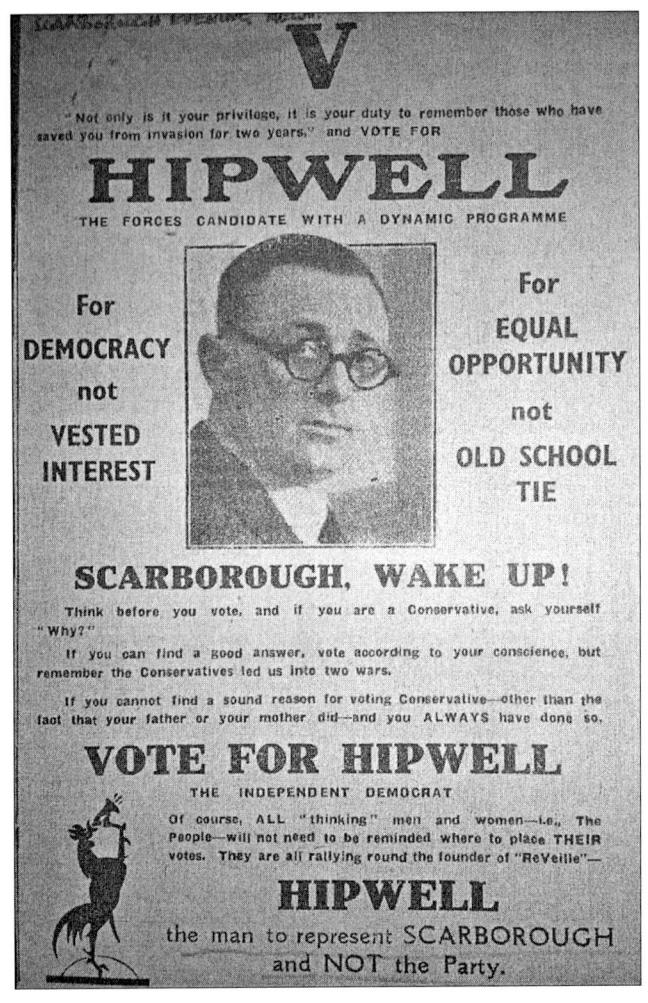

> **V**
>
> "Not only is it your privilege, it is your duty to remember those who have saved you from invasion for two years." and VOTE FOR
>
> # HIPWELL
>
> THE FORCES CANDIDATE WITH A DYNAMIC PROGRAMME
>
> For **DEMOCRACY** not **VESTED INTEREST**
>
> For **EQUAL OPPORTUNITY** not **OLD SCHOOL TIE**
>
> ## SCARBOROUGH, WAKE UP!
>
> Think before you vote, and if you are a Conservative, ask yourself "Why?"
>
> If you can find a good answer, vote according to your conscience, but remember the Conservatives led us into two wars.
>
> If you cannot find a sound reason for voting Conservative—other than the fact that your father or your mother did—and you ALWAYS have done so,
>
> ## VOTE FOR HIPWELL
>
> THE INDEPENDENT DEMOCRAT
>
> Of course, ALL "thinking" men and women—i.e., The People—will not need to be reminded where to place THEIR votes. They are all rallying round the founder of "ReVeille"—
>
> # HIPWELL
>
> the man to represent SCARBOROUGH and NOT the Party.

Hipwell's populist electioneering in the press.

The Tory counterattack was more measured. The Conservatives promoted Alexander Spearman as the respectable antithesis of Hipwell. Spearman, like his predecessor, possessed a refined charm, one Scarborough constituent observing: 'I met him the other day and he seemed a very nice man so I voted for him.' Another reported: 'I was speaking to an old lady today and she said: "Spearman is such a nice looking man and so sincere." She is going to vote for him. Just shows the ignorance of the people here.' To others, he came across as anodyne and dull. The *Mass Observation* investigator was distinctly underwhelmed: 'Spearman, the Conservative candidate, is a typical young Conservative, with no outstanding characteristics.'[46]

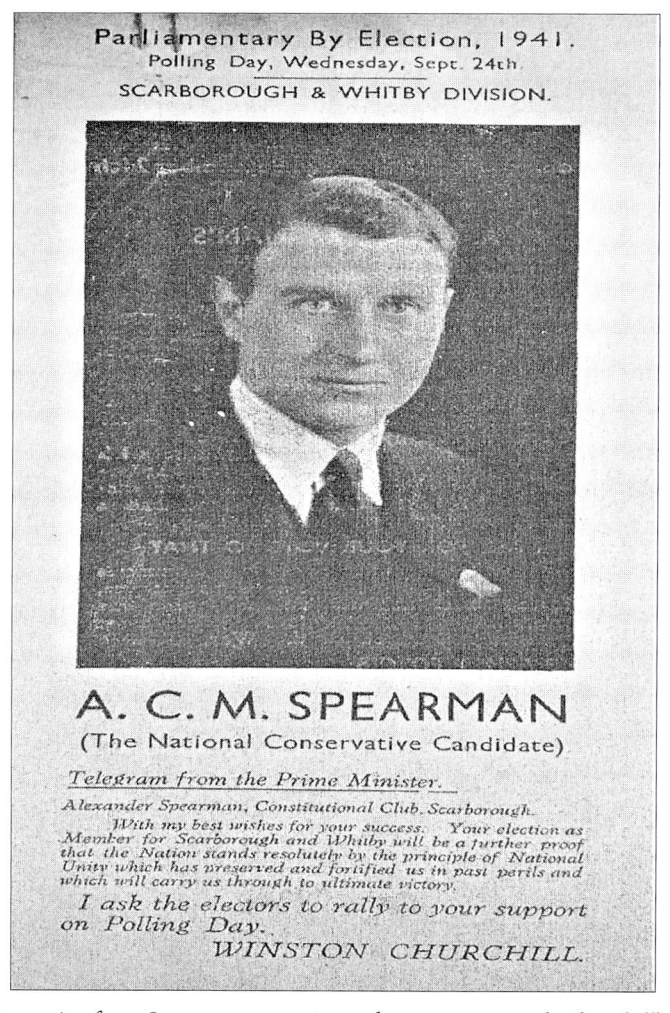

> **Parliamentary By Election, 1941.**
> Polling Day, Wednesday, Sept. 24th
> SCARBOROUGH & WHITBY DIVISION.
>
> ## A. C. M. SPEARMAN
> (The National Conservative Candidate)
>
> *Telegram from the Prime Minister.*
>
> Alexander Spearman, Constitutional Club, Scarborough.
>
> With my best wishes for your success. Your election as Member for Scarborough and Whitby will be a further proof that the Nation stands resolutely by the principle of National Unity which has preserved and fortified us in past perils and which will carry us through to ultimate victory.
>
> I ask the electors to rally to your support on Polling Day.
>
> WINSTON CHURCHILL.

Sober electioneering from Spearman, associating his campaign with Churchill's leadership.

It was made clear by Spearman's supporters that his physical disability debarred him from military service, but that he had voluntarily contributed his business skills to the War Office and the Ministry of Supply. Constituents were reminded that he was already well-known in the constituency, implying that he was not a carpetbagger like Hipwell. In order to reassure the electorate that he would not be a part-time constituency MP like his predecessor, Spearman was keen to publicise the fact that he had bought a property and two farms in the constituency.[47] He pledged to his potential constituents that he would hold regular monthly meetings. At the same time his campaign team highlighted the important contacts he had in Whitehall and Westminster.[48]

Scarborough at War

There were worries early in the campaign that the Conservative Party might fall prey to complacency. However, the Conservative Party organisation in the division remained in rude health and campaigning was effectively stepped up when the seriousness of Hipwell's challenge became apparent. As a long-standing Tory stronghold, there was an impressive reserve of constituency party foot-soldiers to carry out canvassing and electioneering, ably supported by the Tory women of the Primrose Dames. The lead Conservative agents for Sheffield and Yorkshire were drafted in to help with the campaign and some national figures, like the Pensions Minister and the Deputy Chief Whip, were invited to support Spearman at party rallies.[49] Unlike Hipwell, the Conservatives conducted extensive door-to-door leafleting and pasted wall posters throughout the town. For the first time the Conservatives employed a loud-speaker car in the constituency, though this occasioned some irritation in Scarborough.[50] On polling day, a fleet of cars was made available, despite petrol restrictions.[51]

Reflecting national Conservative Party priorities, Spearman stressed that winning the war must be the overriding consideration for all political leaders. Despite his professed interest in pensions and social welfare, Spearmen counselled against raising expectations of social reform at home, implying that Hipwell's approach was irresponsible in wartime. *Mass Observation*, indeed, noted that his campaign included 'little or no reference to social and economic matters', whilst a correspondent in the local paper described his programme as being 'absolutely barren'.[52] The real heart of the Conservative campaign was an appeal for national unity in support of Churchill and the coalition government. Churchill's name was rarely out of Tory electioneering and Spearman claimed to have known him for several years. Churchill's formal letter of support for Spearman was reproduced and read out repeatedly during the campaign, whilst at Spearman's eve-of-poll rally there was uproar in the hall when an attempt was made to read out Churchill's endorsement for a third time.[53] Spearman's supporters went further than the candidate, suggesting that a vote for Hipwell would be a betrayal of HM Forces and would amount to a vote for Hitler and Goebbels.[54]

In the event, Spearman was victorious, but Hipwell secured a surprisingly large minority.[55]

Scarborough and Whitby by-election – 24 September 1941.

	Votes	% vote
A.Spearman	12,518	60.8
W.R.Hipwell	8,086	39.2

Many commented on the disappointingly low turnout (36%). An important reason for this was simply that the electoral register was out of date, having been last revised in 1938 and having failed to keep up with all the disruptions of wartime. The blackout and the petrol shortages, along with the everyday tribulations of wartime, also conspired to depress participation in the by-election. As one woman complained, 'I didn't bother about it at all. I've got enough troubles of my own.'[56] There was also some frustration with the quality of the candidates offered to the Scarborough electorate. Spearman was easily perceived as a staid outsider, whilst Hipwell was dismissed by some as an 'adventurer' and a 'mudslinger'.[57]

The most striking feature of the by-election result was the large number of votes given to a candidate opposing the official coalition candidate. In many ways, the Conservative Party's difficulties in Scarborough and Whitby reflected national developments as well as local ones. By the spring of 1941 there was widespread frustration at the disappointing progress of the war and a tendency to blame the Conservative side of the coalition for this.[58] They were seen as representing the country's elites, who were considered to be an obstacle to the waging of a 'people's war'. Popular concern focused on several issues. Wartime production was failing to meet the demands of total war. It was felt that there was insufficient support being given to the country's 'gallant' Soviet ally after Russia joined the war against the Nazis in June 1941. In autumn 1941 there were military debacles in Greece and Crete and stalemate in the Middle East and North Africa. Frustration mounted regarding the country's inability to take the war to the Nazis in Europe, with the bombing offensive against Germany stalling. Starting with Hornsey in London in May 1941, Independent candidates showed an increasing appetite for standing against Conservative candidates in by-elections, despite the electoral truce. They performed surprisingly well, such that by the spring of 1942 some Conservative candidates were defeated at the hands of maverick Independents. In the words of Paul Addison, 'The by-election independent knew his trade – blame the Tories – and the voters responded.'[59] Other historians have suggested that there was also a more general disillusionment with the established political parties which bolstered the fortunes of Independent candidates in by-elections. This the journal *Tribune* termed at the time the 'movement away from party'.[60]

As an unknown in the area with no party organisation behind him, and facing the constant allegation of disloyalty to the government and the country, Hipwell came within 4,500 votes of the official coalition candidate. His campaign struck a chord. This was recognised by *The Times,* which interpreted the by-election result, and that of a by-election in Wrekin two days later, as an expression of the popular demand for a more energetic and effective conduct of the war. The by-election results, it argued, reflected the popular desire to 'ginger up' the government.[61] As well as being frustrated by the performance of the coalition, voters also appear to have resented the fact that the three main parties tended to rally round the Prime Minister and the government and resist all criticism. A Scarborough barmaid's attitude to Hipwell illustrates the desire to see more independent voices: 'Hipwell did have the guts to stand up to people and say what he thought.'[62] Hipwell's positive advocacy of change on the home front also paid electoral dividends. A Scarborian ex-serviceman, for example, explained: 'I voted for Hipwell because I'm an old serviceman myself and he is out for them and the old age pensioners.'[63]

Hipwell was adept, too, at latching on to any local grievances, whether of fishermen, farmers, hoteliers or servicemen's wives. A commentator in the *Mercury* was perceptive in predicting before the poll that Hipwell would do much better than many people thought: 'Scarborough has its full share of those who will claim that they have one [a grievance]. Some have, and others imagine they have.'[64] A further reason for Hipwell's success was the relish with which he appeared to attack the local Conservative Party, tapping into popular resentment against the complacency of the local Tory establishment. There was a perception that the local Conservative Party was too elitist and out-of-touch, Jottings in the *Mercury*, for example, detecting a 'superiority complex'. A correspondent in the *Evening News* accused the Conservatives of putting wealth before ability in the parliamentary selection process and demanded, 'give us candidates with talent and ideas'.[65] One working-class Scarborian woman voted for Hipwell, 'just to swell the opposition vote. Its [sic] about time we had a change here'. An ex-serviceman judged that Hipwell had 'stirred things up which is what this place needs'.[66] In stark contrast to Spearman, Hipwell certainly stirred things up, though not enough to overturn a long-standing Conservative dominance in the constituency.

Postscript

In the September 1941 by-election the Scarborough and Whitby Conservative Association had exploited the wartime popularity of Winston Churchill, and his endorsement of their candidate, to fend off the challenge from Reg Hipwell.[67] Their victorious candidate Alexander Spearman, however, was a politician of independent judgement, who was far from being an uncritical supporter of Churchill. In early July 1942 he shocked his local party and his constituents by throwing his weight behind an anti-Churchill plot at Westminster at a time of considerable difficulty for the Prime Minister and his government. The war was not going well, and in June 1942 the fall of Tobruk in North Africa was a humiliating defeat. There was widespread discontent in political circles with war production. Then, soon after the fall of Tobruk, the government was heavily defeated by an Independent candidate in a by-election. Meanwhile, the Labour Cabinet Minister Sir Stafford Cripps scented Churchill's political weakness and embarked on hostile political manoeuvres against him. It was at this precarious juncture that two prominent Conservative MPs put down a Commons motion of no confidence in Churchill's government. Despite their inept handling of the attack on the government, 25 members voted for the motion and at least 28 abstained. Spearman was one of only eight Conservatives that voted against the government.[68]

Spearman's stratagems in the House of Commons provoked an angry response in parts of the local Conservative Association and among many of his constituents. At a public meeting called to debate Spearman's behaviour there was applause every time Churchill's name was mentioned and in letters to the press there was widespread condemnation. Why, it was asked, would Spearman know better than Churchill how to manage the war? Spearman was accused of attaching himself to an irresponsible Westminster clique. It was also proposed that it was Spearman's duty, especially as a new MP, to represent the views of his constituents, which were assumed to be wholly behind Churchill. Above all, Spearman was criticised for bringing the constituency into disrepute by his show of disloyalty to the country's war leader.[69] Such criticisms were echoed at a specially convened meeting of the local Party Executive. He escaped official censure, however, receiving vital protection from the Association President, now Sir Kenelm Cayley.[70]

Given the popularity of Churchill, locally and nationally, Spearman's defence stressed that he favoured a reorganisation of the government, not the complete removal of Churchill. He pointed out that the war was clearly not going well, and that something more than 'wishful thinking' was required. Churchill, he lamented, was 'trying to do more than any one man could do'. He also denied playing any part in a coordinated plot against Churchill. To his constituents he maintained that he was entitled to employ his own judgement and conscience in arriving at political decisions, and, therefore, could not always guarantee to reflect the majority view in his constituency, however this may be divined.[71] Despite common criticisms of the local Conservative Party's political docility, it appeared that their new MP had a mind of his own.

Notes

1. Mass Observation (MO), Topic Collection, 46, By-elections 1936-1947, p.2.
2. MO, Topic Collection, 46, p.2.
3. MO Topic Collection, 46, p.2.
4. For an obituary, see *The Times* 26 July 1955.
5. James Lees-Milne, *Diaries, 1946-49* (London, 1996), p.35.
6. Ibid, *Diaries, 1942-1945* (London, 1995), p.183.
7. Matthew Sweet, *West End Front* (London, 2011), p.197.
8. *The Times*, 16 January 1938.
9. *SEN*, 17 September 1941 and obituary, *The Times*, 6 April 1982.
10. *Mercury*, 13 October 1939 and *SEN*, 29 November 1939.
11. *SEN*, 8 December 1939.
12. *SEN*, 11 September 1940.
13. She died in 1947 after falling from a hotel bedroom in Dublin. See *SEN*, 5 March 1947.
14. *SEN*, 2 June 1941.
15. NA WO/1062, Judge Advocate General's Office: Court Martial Proceedings and Board of General Officers' Minutes, 1941.
16. Emma Vickers, 'Queer Sex in the Metropolis? Place, subjectivity and the Second World War', *Feminist Review* 96, 2010, pp.68-70.
17. See Matthew Sweet, *The West End Front*, (London, 2011).
18. Michael Bloch, *Closet Queens*, (London, 2015), Chapter 9, 'Casualties of War'.
19. Sweet, op. cit., p.199.
20. *The Manchester Guardian*, 24 September 1941.
21. Ironically, he followed an arcane parliamentary resignation procedure by applying to be a nominal Steward of the Royal Manor of Northstead, situated in Scarborough.
22. MO, File Report, 902, Scarborough and Whitby By-election, October 1941, p.4.
23. NA CAB 114/1 J.H. Beith letter, 21 November 1940.
24. Ibid.
25. NA CAB 114/1 Intelligence Report on W.R. Hipwell, n.d.
26. MO, File Report, 902, p.4.
27. MO, Topic Collection, 46, p.1 and *SEN*, 23 September 1941.
28. MO, File Report, 902, p.5.
29. MO, Topic Collection, 46, p.1.
30. MO, Topic Collection, 46, p.5. A voter raised the issue of Lady Downe's fascism, but added, 'though that is not anything to do with him [Lord Downe] as he isn't.' On Lady Downe, see also Julie V. Gottlieb, *Feminine Fascism: Women in Britain's Fascist Movement, 1923-1945* (London, 2000), p.296.

31 MO, Topic Collection, 46, p.5.
32 See, for example, *Mercury,* 19 September 1941 and *SEN,* 23 September 1941.
33 *The Manchester Guardian,* 15 December 1942.
34 *SEN,* 22 September 1941 and SEN, 23 September 1941.
35 MO, Topic Collection, 46, p.6.
36 *Daily Herald,* 2 May 1941, in NA HO 144/22710, Disturbances: 'Reveille', unofficial newspaper for the forces.
37 NA HO 144/22710, Disturbances: 'Reveille', unofficial newspaper for the forces.
38 *SEN,* 6 September and SEN, 23 September 1941.
39 NA CAB 114/1, William Reginald Hipwell, n.d.
40 Ibid.
41 Chris Waters, 'The Homosexual as a Social Being in Britain, 1945-1968', *Journal of British Studies,* 51 (July, 2012), p.689.
42 MO, Topic Collection, 46, p.9.
43 *SEN,* 23 September 1941.
44 *News Chronicle,* 4 September 1941 in NA HO 144/22710, Disturbances: 'Reveille', unofficial newspaper for the forces.
45 MO, Topic Collection, 46, p.9.
46 MO, File Report, 902, p.3.
47 *Mercury,* 26 September 1941.
48 *SEN,* 11 September 1941.
49 *Mercury,* 26 September 1941.
50 MO, File Report, 902, p.3.
51 *SEN,* 24 September 1941.
52 MO, File Report, 902, p.5 and *SEN,* 27 September 1941.
53 MO, Topic Collection, 46, pp.6-8.
54 MO, Topic Collection, 46, p.7 and *SEN,* 24 September 1941.
55 *SEN,* 25 September 1941.
56 MO, Topic Collection, p.4.
57 For example, letter to *SEN,* 27 September 1941.
58 Jonathan Schneer, *Ministers at War* (London, 2015), pp.110-112.
59 Paul Addison, *The Road to 1945* (London,1977), p.155 and also Richard Sibley, 'The Swing to Labour during the Second World War', *Labour History Review,* vol.55, no.1, Spring, 1990, p.24.
60 *Tribune,* 3 April 1942.
61 *The Times,* 29 September 1941.
62 MO, File Report, 902, p.7.
63 MO, File Report, 902, p.8

64 Jottings in *Mercury*, 19 September 1941.
65 Jottings in *Mercury*, 26 September 1941 and *SEN*, 29 September 1941.
66 MO, File Report, 902, pp.7-8.
67 See pp.150.
68 Kevin Jeffreys, *The Churchill Coalition and Wartime Politics* (Manchester, 1995), pp.98-100.
69 *SEN*, 13 and 14 July 1942.
70 *SEN*, 13 July 1942.
71 *Mercury*, 3 and 17 July 1942.

CHAPTER 11

The Flyers: the RAF Initial Training Wings[1]

If they learned to obey orders cheerfully, back up their seniors, and be loyal to their unit, then discipline would become a pleasure and not a burden.
(Brigadier-General A.C. Critchley)[2]

Planning

Before the outbreak of the war, and in its early months, the RAF embarked on a large-scale programme of recruiting and training air crews. It was decided that trainee crew would require three months of intensive training in the classroom, along with a fitness and drill regime, before learning to fly. By the end of 1939, accommodation had been found for 10,000 trainee cadets but, on the assumption that the attrition rate would be high, the RAF was keen to train a substantial reserve. Over the next two years the number of trainees increased to between 60,000 and 70,000. During this expansion the man in charge of RAF training, Brigadier-General A.C. Critchley, announced that he wished to use Scarborough, along with nearby Filey and Bridlington, as Initial Training Wing (ITW) bases.

There was some opposition from the military authorities to the use of Scarborough because of the First World War bombardment of the town. Critchley faced the authorities down, stressing the indispensability of the town's hotel accommodation, along with the sands and promenades for drill and sports. Later he wrote with pride that the Scarborough area became one of the 'finest' training centres.[3] 10 ITW was the first to open, in December 1940. It was based at the Grand Hotel, and at the St Nicholas and Manor hotels opposite. Next, in March 1941, came 11 ITW, at the Prince of Wales Hotel on the Esplanade and at the nearby Crown, Weston and Wardorf hotels. Lastly, in October 1941, 17 ITW was opened at Scarborough College, along with the Orleton Girls School and Bramcote Lodge. It also occupied the Astoria, Adelphi and Spa Royal hotels. It has been estimated that at any one time some 2,000 cadets were being trained in Scarborough.[4]

Life in the ITWs

The ITW cadets were young, mostly in their late teens and early twenties, and many came straight from school or university. Some older trainees were transferring from the army to the RAF in the pursuit of more glamorous careers as 'fighter boys'. Though the ITWs had a middle-class feel and recruited from those with an above average education, there was a genuine social mix. The RAF, according to one authority, 'presented itself as essentially meritocratic', and Scarborough veterans testify to such an absence of snobbery and class division.[5] The ITWs were also distinctly cosmopolitan in comparison with other areas of Service life. In Scarborough there were Canadians, Australians, South Africans, French, Belgian, Czech and Polish trainee airmen. It appears that the different nationalities rubbed along well together, whilst the Poles seem to have elicited particular respect and admiration in the town. Though few Scarborough veterans refer to racial differences in their reminiscences, John Harvey remembered three or four black cadets in 17 ITW.[6] He did not recall any racist attitudes in the Wing, though there is some evidence of this elsewhere in the wartime RAF.[7]

The ITW programme was an ambitious one. It aimed to equip trainees with all the knowledge and skills they would require before they commenced hands-on aircrew practice. It also aimed to inculcate key elements of the RAF's ethos. A Scarborough veteran recalled: 'Here is where we were first "programmed" to do what we had to do in the war years.'[8] Alf Wight (later author of the James Herriot novels) quoted his Flight Commander when he arrived at 10 ITW: 'You won't know yourself when you leave here.' Wight added, 'That man knew what he was talking about.'[9]

More than anything else, life in the ITWs revolved around the classroom. For Peter Nevill it was like 'going back to school'.[10] Lectures were given on personal health and hygiene. There was a great deal of maths, theory of flight, meteorology and navigation, along with the principles of aircraft engines and armaments. Courses were attended on aircraft and ship recognition, whilst signals communication was studied in the classroom and put into practice around Scarborough. A common sight was the blinking of Aldis Lamps between the Italian Gardens on South Cliff and the harbour. Cadets were tested throughout their courses, and their aptitude for different aircrew roles assessed (most commonly pilot, navigator or bomb-aimer). There was constant pressure to perform well in order to graduate from the ITW and to become eligible for preferred roles, notably as pilots. John Harvey, for example, was determined to acquit himself well in all his courses as he was 'mad keen to fly'.[11] At the end of the course there were intensive final exams, up to three a day. Failure to pass any of the tests meant that cadets were held back to re-sit courses, and a small number failed outright. Successful students were promoted to the rank of Leading Aircraftsmen and earned a substantial pay rise. Most then progressed to flying instruction in Africa, Canada or the USA.

Second only to mental endeavour in the classroom came outdoor physical exertions. The cadets were a regular sight exercising on open areas of the beaches and jogging around the town, at times providing an agreeable spectacle for holidaymakers.[12] Alf Wight recalled the relentless nature of physical exercise:

> We were never at rest. It was PT and Drill, PT and Drill, over and over. Hours of bending and stretching and twisting down on the prom in singlets and shorts while the wind whipped over us from the wintry sea. Hours of marching under the bellowing of our Sergeant; slow march, about turn. We even marched to our navigation classes, bustling along at the RAF quick time, arms swinging shoulder high.[13]

Cadets were also exposed to regular cross-country running, often up to the top of Oliver's Mount and back. Swimming in the sea was common, as was emergency dinghy practice off the harbour clad in 'Mae West' life jackets. On the curriculum, too, were competitive sports, especially football and rugby. A hint of battle was provided by the RAF's clay-pigeon shooting at Scarborough Castle. All this fresh-air and exercise was designed to enhance mental sharpness as well as physical fitness, whilst square-bashing was deemed to be particularly effective in promoting teamwork and discipline.

Meals were basic and living conditions spartan.[14] Meagre portions at dinner could be supplemented in the town by egg and chips or fish and chips as an 'after supper'.[15] Requisitioned hotels were stripped of most of their carpets, furniture and luxuries. At the Grand Hotel trainees were not permitted to use any of the carpeted areas, nor the entrance hallway or grand staircase.[16] As many beds were crammed into rooms as possible. There was no hot water for washing or shaving. Those who trained in the winter months had the worst memories of physical discomfort, several testifying to the permanent nailing open of windows, regardless of the temperature. Alan Clarke remembers wet boots freezing to the floor at his Orleton School billet.[17]

Although discipline in the RAF was generally less severe than in the other two services, in the ITWs it seems to have been distinctly robust. Some of the NCOs, especially the Drill Sergeants, were remembered as bullies, and nicknames like 'Bill the Bastard' crop up in ITW recollections.[18] Poor standards in parade-ground performance were punished with arduous physical tasks, such as marching up McBean steps from the Foreshore.[19] Other cadets found themselves peeling potatoes or confined to quarters for quite modest lapses in behaviour. Geoff Wright remembers being woken at 5.50 a.m. and being on parade by 7.00 a.m. Morning inspections of bedding, kit, uniforms and dormitories could be pettifogging:

> Before you could go on parade you had strip your bed and pile up your kit in a neat pile at the foot. Blankets, sheets, greatcoat, gas mask container etc. had to be absolutely square, achieved by inserting sheets of cardboard in the front.[20]

Both shoes and flooring had to be polished to a mirror-like state. G.S. Irving of 10 ITW was confined to camp with his comrades for 24 hours when a single hair was discovered in a basin.[21] It can, however, be difficult to generalise about the experiences of trainee aircrew in Scarborough. 11 ITW at the Prince of Wales Hotel had a reputation for 'bull', or petty disciplinarianism, but not all Drill Sergeants were stereotypical monsters. G.S. Irving remembered his as 'a very kind chap, good at his job'.[22] The exercise of power, based on rank, could be performed in a humorous manner, shot through with jocular sarcasm. Peter Yarranton of 11 ITW recalled blurting out an insubordinate question to his Corporal. Why, he asked, was it necessary to stand on guard outside the Crown Hotel in the middle of the night with a .303 rifle with no bullets in it. The Corporal recovered from his shock by repeating the question, then replied:

> I'll tell you why Yarranton – when the Germans invade us they will come across that North Sea out there and they will land in the Spa in the middle of the night. They will climb over the top with those shufty scopes

that can see you through the dark. They'll see you guarding the Crown [Hotel], Yarranton, but they won't know you haven't got any bullets in your gun, and they will open fire – thus alerting the garrison – and your sacrifice will not have been in vain, and you will have saved Scarborough and the Crown.

Yarranton developed a great admiration for the Corporal.[23] In the classroom, it seems, discipline was more relaxed and a more encouraging atmosphere was fostered. It was not, recalled Stan Jarvis, 'a shouting culture'.[24]

According to the recollections of veterans, morale was high in the Scarborough ITWs. Trainees were mostly ambitious about achieving their goal of becoming airmen. 'The Flyer' was perceived as a glamorous figure in wartime popular culture, embracing both exciting new technology and old-fashioned heroic individualism. To many of a population fed in the 1930s on the *Biggles* stories of Captain W.E. Johns, there was no more alluring wartime role, especially after the Battle of Britain in 1940.[25] The ITWs built on this by encouraging a competitive sense of pride in the RAF. The Training Wing dress – grey-blue battledress with a white belt, a white-flashed cap, shirt and tie and shoes – was worn as a badge of status and relative superiority over the brown-clad army. Cadets were, in the words of Ron Mason, 'very pleased with ourselves'.[26] There was also a proud spirit of competition between the town's ITWs, played out on the parade ground and in sporting competitions. Within the Wings, there was a similar rivalry between Flights and Squadrons. 'Everyone,' recalled G.S. Irving, 'did their best to prove we were the number one squadron'.[27] Competition acted as a spur in the classroom too, where comparative test performances were keenly analysed to determine which ITW was the highest achieving. The second annual report of 17 ITW proudly announced that it had attained the best test results for 1943.[28]

The memories of veterans also highlight the key role of comradeship in maintaining morale in the ITWs. The academic pressures, along with the physical hardships, engendered a distinctive sense of inter-dependence and solidarity. 'We found we needed each other,' reported Alan Clarke.[29] Stan Jarvis echoed this, pinpointing an absence of bullying and class snobbery in his ITW.[30]

The culture of the ITWs possessed a current of youthful and masculine bravado. There was much jocular teasing: 'We were a cheerful bunch,' remembers Roy Day, 'always ribbing and being ribbed.'[31] Every squadron would have its comedian or prankster and sexual gossip and innuendo were part of

An RAF march-past on a rather dilapidated wartime Foreshore.

the bonding process. There was a rumour, for example, that a secret passage connected 11 ITW in the Prince of Wales Hotel to the Red Lea next door, and so to the female trainee teachers evacuated from Leeds. The Balmoral Hotel, which was popular with cadets for dancing, was rechristened the 'Immoral'.[32] There was some amusement when the following notice was read by cadets occupying dormitories at the Orleton Girls School: 'If you require a mistress in the night, ring the bell.'[33] Adolescent-style humour could also be used as a form of petty rebellion in the context of enforced military subordination. Some recruits took to signalling rude messages to passing Royal Navy convoys. The Navy complained, and the misbehaviour was stopped. Drill and parades could also be used mischievously to turn the tables on the RAF authorities.[34] Bert Allam remembered a public marching demonstration when cadets conspired to turn a deaf ear to a critical 'about turn' command:

> Those at the rear of the flight duly turned about; from the middle of the group some turned left, mounted a flight of steps and finished up marking time in front of the houses overlooking the Square; others turned right and telescoped upon one another as they arrived at the railings around the gardens in the middle of the square; whilst those who had been in the leading ranks carried straight ahead to eventually disappear around the corner.

Thereafter, the public appearances of Bert and his fellow cadets were 'perhaps noticeably fewer'.[35] Individuals, too, could outwit their superiors in small but satisfying ways. A 10 ITW recruit, for example, developed a technique for catnapping standing up whilst on night-time Guard Duty. He managed this by leaning on the front entrance pillar of the Grand Hotel.[36]

In their spare time the young RAF men liked to take advantage of the amenities available in Scarborough. Gordon Henderson was unlikely to be the only cadet who recalled Scarborough as the place where he, under peer pressure, became drunk for the first time.[37] More innocently, in the absence of hot water at their bases, visits to bath houses in the town were popular. In reaction to their dull meals, many patronised the town's cafés and ice-cream parlours. The cinemas, of course, were a big attraction, as were dancing venues. The Royal Hotel was especially popular with the RAF, holding a weekly dance for each of the three ITWs. Memories of courtship at the Royal were, predictably, mixed. When a local woman, Joyce Boothman, met Harold Foster of 11 ITW in September 1944, 'it was love at first sight'. They married in January 1945.[38] The experiences of A.E. MacDonald of 10 ITW were perhaps more typical: 'The Saturday night dances at the Royal Hotel were well attended but I cannot remember having much luck there!'[39]

Reading the reminiscences of RAF veterans suggests that relations between the cadets and Scarborough folk were generally quite limited. There is some evidence of dissatisfaction locally at the large number of airmen crowding out parts of the town during their regular free time on a Saturday and Sunday. Efforts were therefore made by the RAF authorities to stagger social trips to the town.[40] Memories indicate, also, that the RAF men were commonly short of money, as service pay in the ITWs was poor. Don Williamson, for instance, spent a good proportion of his pay on basic toiletries and laundry.[41] But the most obvious reason that the cadets did not integrate themselves extensively in the local community was simply that they did not have the time. They were granted little time off, and their academic work consumed a great deal of their remaining hours and energies. Alan Clarke remembers cadets testing each other on classroom work and reading up on the next day's learning materials in the evenings.[42] Alex Marshall recorded that his course was so intensive, and that he had so little free time, that he and his peers had no contact at all with local people.[43] John Harvey explained that he and his friends had little time for local girls as they were constantly 'worn out'.[44]

For the airmen there were hazards in training in a town that was in some ways in the front line of the war. A sea mine exploded when it hit the Spa's seawall on a Sunday morning in 1942, near to numerous ITW classrooms. The Spa building was extensively damaged but there were no casualties.[45] As we have seen, incendiary bombs came close to setting 10 ITW's base at the Grand Hotel ablaze (p.103). In May 1941, two months after the opening of 11 ITW, two of the hotels it had requisitioned were hit in an air raid, the Waldorf sustaining considerable damage and the Weston being partly demolished. One of the six RAF casualties died of his wounds.[46] Such dangers could sometimes be brushed off in the self-deprecatory manner of the ITWs. A typical anecdote involved a cadet showing off his newly acquired skills in aircraft recognition, confidently identifying a British aircraft from a long distance out to sea. An explanation was demanded when the aircraft approached, displaying black crosses on its wings and dropping bombs on the town.

Overall, though, the ITW servicemen had a positive memory of their time in Scarborough and appreciated the hospitality they received. They tended to be highly regarded visitors to the town, given their smart appearance and glamorous military vocation. It was well-known, and prompted respect and sympathy, that the casualty rate in wartime for RAF personnel was comparatively high. Local churches would provide tea and biscuits for the young cadets, whilst Rowntree's shop was a source of free chocolates. Organisers of the annual National Savings Weeks were appreciative of the ITWs for their support in fund-raising activities, most conspicuously, of course, in 1943's 'Wings for Victory Week' (see p.204). The cadets appreciated that they were fortunate to be stationed in such an attractive area, offering so many amenities. Robert Hedley, writing to his parents in Kent in June 1941, advised them: 'If you want a decent holiday, Scarborough is the place. In peacetime I should think it would be absolutely super.'[47] Barry Turner of 11 ITW put it succinctly: 'Suffice it to say, I fell in love with Scarborough …'[48]

RAF ex-prisoners of war relaxing on a visit to Scarborough Castle in 1945. The first RAF Resettlement Centre for POWs was established in Scarborough at the end of the war. Time was also spent at lectures on readjusting to civilian life, educational and vocational courses and sport. (© Imperial War Museum)

Notes

1. In the writing of this chapter, I am indebted to the researches of David Fowler.
2. From *Critch*, the memoir of A C Critchley, quoted in David Fowler, *God Bless the Prince of Wales* (Scarborough, 2008), pp.44.
3. David Fowler, *God Bless the Prince of Wales* (Scarborough, 2008), pp.40-46.
4. NA AIR 29/634 Air Ministry: Operations Record Books, ITW, 1940-45.
5. Martin Francis, *The Flyer: British Culture and the Royal Air Force, 1939-1945* (Oxford, 2011), p.15.
6. IWM, John Harvey, Catalogue Number 22617.
7. Francis, op. cit., pp.59-62.
8. Fowler, op. cit., p.112.
9. Ibid., pp.139-40.
10. IWM, Peter Nevill, Catalogue Number 27499.
11. IWM, John Harvey, Catalogue Number 22617.
12. Ted Neale, "A Gastronomic Journey (Experience)," *IBCC Digital Archive*, https://ibccdigitalarchive.lincoln.ac.uk/omeka/collections/document/16359. (accessed 2.3.21)
13. Fowler, op. cit., p.140.
14. Ibid., p.72.
15. Hedley Robert Madgett, "Scarborough postcard from Hedley Madgett to his parents," *IBCC Digital Archive*, https://ibccdigitalarchive.lincoln.ac.uk/omeka/collections/document/11097. (accessed 2.3.21)

    Ted Neale, "A Gastronomic Journey (Experience)," *IBCC Digital Archive*, https://ibccdigitalarchive.lincoln.ac.uk/omeka/collections/document/16359. (accessed 2.3.21)
16. Ibid., p.191.
17. Ibid., p.141.
18. Ibid., p.72.
19. Ibid., p.116.
20. BBC, WW2 People's War, Geoff Wright, A2855702 (accessed 20 June 2018).
21. IWM, Flight Lieutenant G.S. Irving, Catalogue Number 2100.
22. Ibid.
23. *The Crown Hotel: 150 Years of Hospitality* (Scarborough, n.d.), pp.41-42.
24. IWM, Stan Jarvis, Catalogue Number 26947.
25. See Francis, op. cit., pp.14-31.
26. IWM, Ron Mason, Catalogue Number 24729.
27. IWM, Flight Lieutenant G.S. Irving, Catalogue Number 2100.
28. NA AIR 29/634, Air Ministry: Operations Record Books, ITW, 1940-45.

29 Fowler, op. cit., p.82.
30 IWM, Stan Jarvis, Catalogue Number 26947.
31 Fowler, op. cit., p.90.
32 Ibid., p.80.
33 Ibid., p.72.
34 Ibid., p.136.
35 Ibid., p.64-65.
36 Ibid., p.124-125.
37 IWM, Gordon Henderson, Catalogue Number 30629.
38 Fowler, op. cit., p177.
39 Ibid., p.187.
40 Ibid., p.153.
41 Ibid., p.129.
42 Ibid., p.80.
43 IWM, Alex Marshall, Catalogue Number 31044.
44 IWM, John Harvey, Catalogue Number 22617.
45 *SEN*, 5 October 1946.
46 NA AIR 29/634, Air Ministry: Operations Record Books, ITW, 1940-45.
47 Hedley Robert Madgett, "Letter from Hedley Madgett to his parents," *IBCC Digital Archive*, https://ibccdigitalarchive.lincoln.ac.uk/omeka/collections/document/11181. (accessed 2.3.21)
48 Fowler, op. cit., p.203.

CHAPTER 12

Scarborough's Secret War

For the secret listeners, these voices in the air were much more than merely abstract dots and dashes of Morse; they were live commentaries on events.[1]

It you travelled inland from Scarborough on the Pickering road in the later stages of World War Two, you would soon come across a large military installation on Irton Moor. An extensive area was surrounded by a high perimeter fence, patrolled by military police with guard dogs. Some of the land within bristled with aerial masts. Its work was so secret that most of the staff who worked there were not aware of what was being done with their work by the codebreakers at Bletchley Park.

Background

The origins of this installation lay in a First World War Naval Wireless Telegraphy ('Y') station, based at nearby Sandybed Lane. It eavesdropped on the radio communications of the German High Seas Fleet. After World War One the Scarborough 'Y' station entered a period of decline. When a new Officer-in Charge was appointed in 1934 he found a cramped site of 1¼ acres and 25 over-worked naval ratings operating 'junk' equipment. The 'Y' service, he observed, was a 'Cinderella'.[2]

What came to the rescue of the 'Y' station in Scarborough was the escalating international tensions of the second half of the 1930s. The aggressive behaviour of Fascist Italy, the Spanish Civil War and German expansionism increasingly posed a threat to the international order. Scarborough's 'Y' station was instructed to extend and intensify its signals intelligence gathering from the navies of

European powers that were posing a threat.[3] To achieve this the staffing was increased to 45 in 1939 and a new wireless telegraphy room was built with 7 receiving bays and up-to-date radio equipment. A permanent teleprinter link was established between Scarborough and both the Admiralty and the Government Codes and Cypher School (GC&CS.).[4] A Direction-Finding (D/F) station at Scarborough worked in conjunction with other such stations (usually at least two), to establish the location from which a radio transmission was made.[5]

Wartime Interception

During World War II the Scarborough station's primary role was to intercept the radio messages of the German Navy (*Kriegsmarine*) and its U-boats. In doing so it worked hand in glove with the celebrated codebreakers at Bletchley Park. Most of the German communication was encrypted in the German naval Enigma code and sent in Morse code. When the Morse was translated by the wireless operators at Scarborough, it was sent by teleprinter to Bletchley Park. By the summer of 1940 Bletchley was beginning to decode some of the German navy's Enigma signals, but it was not until the summer of 1941 that they were able to do this routinely and speedily enough to be operationally valuable to the Admiralty.[6]

The Admiralty was also interested in the overall pattern of German naval wireless communications. Even when messages could not be decoded, the patterns provided clues, using so-called Traffic Analysis, as to the dispositions and intentions of the enemy at sea. The Direction-Finding expertise at Scarborough also enabled the Allies to locate enemy ships and U-boats. As the lead naval D/F station in the country, Scarborough would determine, from the strength of the signal, the direction that a radio signal was coming from. It would then collate data from other D/F stations and, through triangulation, establish a location, or 'direction fix', on the transmission.

To understand the wartime role of the Scarborough 'Y' station it is important to appreciate that it did not operate in isolation, but that it was a key link in a complex chain of intelligence. Scarborough's role in the sinking of the German battleship *Bismarck* in 1941 provides an excellent illustration of this.[7] Human intelligence, in the shape of the Norwegian Military Attaché in Stockholm, had first alerted the Admiralty to the sailing of the *Bismarck* from the Baltic, an action posing a major threat to British convoys in the Atlantic. The departure was confirmed by RAF photo-reconnaissance over the port of Bergen and by some RAF Enigma evidence. Scarborough intercepts from the *Bismarck* from April were deciphered on 21 May at Bletchley, also corroborating this picture.

Royal Navy ships first made contact by radar. British cruisers and naval aircraft then joined battle with the *Bismarck* in the Battle of the Denmark Strait on 24 May 1941. The battleship was damaged, but the Royal Navy lost contact with her and with the accompanying cruiser, *Prince Eugen*. The *Bismarck* sent 22 radio signals on the 24th, which were picked up by Scarborough and sent to Bletchley Park. It was not possible to decode them, however, until after the sinking of the *Bismarck*. By the end of May the famous Hut 8 at Bletchley was taking three to seven days to decipher naval Enigma. The battleship sailed for the port of Brest in occupied France, to effect repairs after the engagement with British warships.

Three signals sent by the *Bismarck* on the 25th were picked up by British Naval Direction Finding and analysed at Scarborough. These alerted the Admiralty to the fact that radio control had passed from northern Germany to Paris, indicating that the *Bismarck* was heading southwards. This helped visual contact to be made by an RAF spotter aircraft late in the morning of the 26th, whereupon Royal Navy warships and aircraft from Ark Royal attacked the battleship, inflicting further damage. She was attacked again and finished off by British aircraft, cruisers and destroyers on 27 May 1941. Scarborough played its part, therefore, in a complex team effort.

At the beginning of 1942 Britain's military Chiefs of Staff agreed to a major expansion of the country's 'Y' services. Plans were made for the expansion of naval 'Y' work at Scarborough and at the sister station at Flowerdown near Winchester. The case for more naval interception capacity was compelling as Bletchley Park was delivering an increasing volume of intelligence to the Admiralty. There was also an increasing requirement for intelligence on the German navy's expanding activities in the Mediterranean theatre. Finally, there was a desperate need for intelligence on the activities of German U-Boats in the Atlantic. They had to be located, then put out of action, or at least avoided, to ensure the critical passage of essential shipments from the United States to Britain. Therefore, the Admiralty allocated £130,000 to the expansion and improvement of the 'Y' network and proposed employing over 1,000 new staff.[8] Comparing naval wireless interception at the beginning of the war with that of the end illustrates the wartime transformation of naval 'Y' operations. In 1939 the Admiralty had some 200 people manning about 50 sets. In 1945 it had 5,000 people manning 350 shore-based sets and several hundred sets at sea.[9]

In 1942 £35,000 was earmarked for the establishment of a new 'Y' station in Scarborough.[10] The old Sandybed site was replaced by a new, purpose-built one at Irton Moor, near a disused racecourse to the west of the town. The move on 1 March 1943 was accomplished without a stoppage of wireless cover or of teleprinter communication with Bletchley Park.[11] The new site was an impressive 230 acres and included a new Direction-Finding station. Nearly 700 staff were employed by 1944.[12] The Irton Moor station was a testament to the commitment of the military authorities to the secret signals intelligence war against Germany and to the impressive record that Scarborough had already established in wireless interception. Resources were also developed at the nearby village of Snainton, where a group of Wrens were based at the Village Hall. Here they were engaged in training and supplementary work in 'Y' services, whilst the facility had the potential to serve as a back-up in the event of disruption to the work at Irton Moor.[13]

Working at Scarborough

Royal Navy operators at Scarborough intercepting German naval communications in 1944 (the operators are using the National HRO Single Signal Superhet Comms Receiver).
© *Crown Copyright.*

Wireless telegraphy work at Irton Moor was mostly done by naval ratings and members of the Women's Royal Naval Service (Wrens), their work conducted in complete secrecy. Some were collected for work from their billets by buses or army trucks, and a rumour arose in the town that the Wrens were being escorted to their regular daytime picnics.[14] Another Wren recalled a four mile walk to the station, often in the dark and weighed down by a tin hat and a service respirator.[15] The main work at the 'Y' station was done in a submerged, rectangular building, akin to an air-raid shelter or bunker. It had internal blast walls and concrete tops. Over 100 receivers were housed here, together with the D/F control and aerial switchboard. An adjacent teleprinter room had direct connections to Bletchley Park and the Admiralty, and by 1944 to Washington D.C. In the main building naval ratings worked on one side of the chamber, and on the other Wrens, also wearing naval uniform. The work was undertaken in artificial light, the environment was damp and airless and there were regular problems with the heating and water supply.[16] Norah Morgan remembered an atmosphere that was hot and noisy and filled with cigarette smoke.[17]

When a transmission was detected, operators would simultaneously translate from its original Morse code into the unintelligible letters of the alphabet generated by the German Enigma machine, whilst noting any other distinguishing feature of the signal. A charge-hand would then run with the Enigma material to the teleprinter room, where the material was sent by specialist teleprinter operators to the codebreakers at Bletchley. Details of any signal were urgently transferred to the D/F control, which was staffed by civilians.[18]

Wireless interception work imposed a considerable strain on practitioners. The wireless operators worked exhausting eight to ten-hour shifts, with short and infrequent breaks. Their work required considerable skill and formidable reserves of patience and endurance. With their left hands they tuned their radio sets in search of frequencies being used by the enemy. The endless search for German signals could be extremely monotonous, whilst the accurate translation of enemy Morse code at speed added to the stress. As the operators searched for German radio traffic, signals could be very brief or faint and the heavy earphones used were apt to hiss and crackle with interference. Operating the teleprinters was also skilled and exhausting work, 'bashing out' codes and call sign information to be sent to Bletchley Park. Teleprinter operators remembered the main challenge as being a lack of sleep and 'fatigue'.[19]

Wren Pamela Hussey described the work as a wireless operator as 'Absolutely deadly'. 'People used to go off their nut,' she added.[20] Unruly behaviour and gender rivalry sometimes acted as a safety-valve. Hussey recalls, for example, occasions when male ratings bombarded the Wrens in the set room with paper aeroplanes.[21] Another Wren, Cynthia Grossman, who worked at Forest Moor 'Y' station near Harrogate, recalls the difficulty of switching off from the work when off duty. She instinctively found herself treating a dripping tap or a person's cough as a Morse code to be translated.[22]

Servicemen and women at Scarborough, working in great secrecy, tended to see themselves as operating on a front line in the war effort. They therefore felt themselves to be likely targets of *Luftwaffe* air raids in the area. Frieda Bonner recalls the panic, in March 1941, when it was announced that an enemy aircraft was circling the original base on Sandybed Lane. When it dropped a parachute mine, it was assumed that was intended for the 'Y' Station:

> The landmine fell into a newly ploughed field adjoining the station, and the soft ground had absorbed much of the explosion. A miraculous escape for us all. In the morning we saw the enormous crater – large enough to have swallowed the entire station.[23]

However, the assumption that the work being done was of considerable importance also helped in the maintenance of morale. Although naval personnel had no knowledge of the work being done with their intercepts at Bletchley Park, Pamela Hussey, for example, remembers a feeling of pride that they were 'doing their bit in the war'.[24] When an official from Bletchley visited the Scarborough station in May 1944 he paid fulsome tribute to the work being done there:

> There is of course, an air of tension in the set room not to be found at stations of a less operational kind. The watch on U-boats means a great deal of skill and concentration, both in the actual picking up of the signal and in the quick transference of this signal to the D/F networks. Activity by a U-boat often only lasts for one minute, during which time the traffic has to be taken and the signal picked up by the D/F stations for bearings. I was lucky enough to see both operations in progress and the quickness of everyone was a delight to watch.[25]

Such a testament to the working atmosphere at Scarborough is impressive, especially in the light of some of the problems experienced elsewhere. RAF Chicksands 'Y' station, for example, experienced a crisis in morale among its WAAFs (Women's Auxiliary Air Force) in 1942. They suffered from poor accommodation, lack of recreational facilities, staff shortages and overwork. This led to rising sickness rates, 'neuroses among the WAAFs' and 'an act of violence against the CO (Commanding Officer) by a member of the WAAF'.[26]

One reason why it was possible to maintain morale in Scarborough in such demanding circumstances was that the 'Y' station was considered a relatively desirable posting. Its attractive geographical location and amenities offered personnel some recreational relief from the pressures of war work. When off-duty, Wrens enjoyed walking and cycling in the nearby countryside and lunching in country pubs. Many were billeted in seafront hotels and took advantage of the town's eating places and entertainments. The Olympia Ballroom and the Royal Hotel, frequented by other Forces personnel, were favoured venues.[27] Socialising with other servicemen and women helped to relieve the stress of 'Y' station work. Romances developed between Wrens and soldiers and airmen billeted in the area. Hilda Simpson, a teleprinter operator at Irton Moor, for example, met her husband to be, a member of the Royal Signals. They married in 1945.[28] Wrens also gravitated towards the relatively glamorous trainee flyers of the three Initial Training Wings in the town. Hussey recollected putting on a party for Polish airmen at her billet. Reflecting back on this period in the 1990s she observed: '… there was quite a lot of night life. But social life was not as lax as it would be today!'[29]

A striking feature of the naval 'Y' work was the central role of women in the hitherto male world of wireless telegraphy and signals intelligence. As Wrens were doing work of equal value to men, they were all ranked Chief Petty Officers.[30] Their contribution was not, however, always welcomed. Norah Morgan describes her Naval Commander in Scarborough as 'very unpleasant', with an intense dislike of women in the Navy.[31] Training for such work involved intensive study of the practicalities of radio technology and of related academic subjects, such as electricity, magnetism, atmospheres and ionospheres. Training in Morse code was, of course, unremitting. Muriel Davison provides a good example of the scientific and technical accomplishments of Wrens employed at Scarborough. She matriculated in Maths and Physics in her school leaving exam and was consequently trained as a radio and teleprinter mechanic in the Wrens. She was posted to Scarborough in 1943 and worked in the station's mixed-gender radio workshop, testing, repairing and tuning equipment. Receiving an electric shock on one occasion was a reminder that the work could be hazardous as well as highly skilled. She found that a talent for improvisation was useful in preparing lunch as well as in fixing equipment. Cheese on toast was cooked on the workshop's Bunsen burners.[32]

Scarborough's Contribution: A balance sheet

The Scarborough station did face some challenges and difficulties in wartime. It was never easy to find enough qualified wireless and teleprinter operators. Despite the consistently impressive performance at Scarborough, the authorities at the GC&CS and the Admiralty remained eager to see greater speed in getting intercepted material to Bletchley, but the teleprinters at Scarborough remained prone to faults and breakdowns.[33] There was also some criticism of the D/F work performed at Scarborough, as an official recorded:

> We could identify a great many more call signs if Scarborough could be persuaded to regard the D/F part a little more seriously. I am myself continually asking for bearings but in many cases they are not forthcoming.[34]

Morale suffered a temporary body blow when tragedy struck the Scarborough station in 1941. Twelve of the station's Wrens were sent to work in Gibraltar on the civilian ship SS Aguila, but they all perished when the ship was torpedoed by a German submarine on 19 August.[35]

Such difficulties aside, the Scarborough 'Y' station had an impressive record. One of its strengths was its ability to work effectively with other 'Y' organisations. When, for example, Scarborough was having trouble picking up German naval traffic in Norwegian waters, the interception work was passed to Cupar (near Edinburgh) and Shetland.[36] Similarly, Flowerdown acted as a partner station to Scarborough. In the event that Scarborough was disabled by enemy action, Flowerdown was prepared to take over its most vital work. In the Mediterranean, Scarborough concentrated on the German navy, whilst Flowerdown targeted Italian, Spanish and Portuguese traffic. The two stations sometimes practised 'double-banking', where they duplicated interception work in order to compare their respective performances.[37] The relationship was not always harmonious. When Flowerdown was informed in 1943 that it was failing to achieve the high level of performance of Scarborough, its Officer-in-Charge angrily rejected the criticism. He contended that Scarborough had an unfair advantage after its major investment and expansion of 1943. He was not willing, therefore, to enter into an exchange of charge-hands with Scarborough so that Flowerdown might learn from its more successful partner.[38] Nevertheless, Scarborough was given the opportunity to pass its skills on to many new recruits to 'Y' work. By the end of the war some 2,500 personnel had received 'Y' training at Scarborough and Snainton, including Poles, Americans and Canadians.[39]

Scarborough was in receipt of numerous commendations for the effectiveness of its monitoring of German naval traffic. In the early stages of the war the station was proud that 'very little, if any, naval traffic of any importance was being lost'.[40] When U-boat attacks against Allied shipping in the Atlantic were at their height, from August 1942 to May 1943, Scarborough had 65 receivers at work and was intercepting a monthly average of 1,340 incoming messages. This number peaked in March 1943 when 1,800 were picked up.[41] An external authority said of Scarborough's coverage of U-boats that it 'might be described as 100% perfect'.[42] Thus when German naval codes were being decrypted routinely from the second half of 1941 on, with a gap in 1942, the station played a vital role in helping the Allies to hunt down German U-boats and their 'wolfpacks' and to re-route convoys away from danger. Conversely, when Scarborough's intercepts were defying decryption at Bletchley Park in 1942, due to the addition of an extra U-boat Enigma key, U-boat depredations in the Atlantic were at their worst. A further achievement of naval signals intelligence was in alerting the Admiralty in 1943 to the fact that the enemy was breaking Allied naval codes.[43]

As the war progressed, 'Y' intelligence from Scarborough continued to play an important role in providing the raw material of Allied naval intelligence on new theatres of the war. Scarborough's Direction-Finding intelligence remained a vital source of information on enemy dispositions, whilst the successful Allied invasion of Sicily in 1943 was aided by naval Enigma decrypts. By the end of the war Scarborough had been in receipt of further assets: it was operating 128 wireless sets and had had a further three teleprinter lines linked to Bletchley Park. Such investment allowed Scarborough to make a valuable intelligence contribution to the Allied preparations for the D-Day landings, providing intercepts, for example, on the enemy naval and U-boat threat to allied landings and on enemy mine-laying defences.[44] It was a frenetic and exhausting climax to the Scarborough station's wartime signals intelligence work.

Muriel Davison (front left), a 'Y' station Wren outside Chatsworth Hotel, The Crescent, on VE Day 1945. Note the Hammer and Sickle flag of Britain's wartime ally Russia in the background.

The Bletchley Park codebreaking (Ultra) has attracted a great deal of historical and popular attention since it was revealed in the 1970s. Some historians have speculated about the extent to which Ultra shortened the war. Others, like Paul Kennedy, writing of the Battle of the Atlantic, are more sceptical:

> The plain fact was that Ultra assisted in but could never win the hard-fought convoy battles. When the British decision was made to fight the convoys through the U-boat lines, victory went to the side with the smartest and most powerful weaponry, not the one with the better decrypts.[45]

Be this as it may, the 'Y' stations that supplied the raw materials used by the codebreakers at Station X at Bletchley perhaps deserve greater attention. Scarborough's naval 'Y' station certainly provided vital assistance in the decryption of German naval communications and, thereby, in the country's wider prosecution of the war at sea. The town's long maritime history had entered an important new technological phase.

Notes

1 Sinclair McKay, *The Secret Listeners* (London, 2012), p.9.
2 NA HW 8/96 *Historical Review of 'Y' Work on German Naval W/T Communications, 1939-1945*, p.2.
3 Ibid., p.2.
4 NA ADM 116/4088, Institution of teleprinter links between GCCS and RN W/T Stations Flowerdown and Scarborough.
5 See also NA HW 50/15, GC&CS European Naval Section: Extracts and Dossiers Collected Apparently for Historical Purposes and/or Research.
6 F.H. Hinsley, 'British Intelligence in the Second World War: An Overview', *Crypologia*, 14:1, 1990, pp.7-8.
7 For the Sinking of the Bismarck, see F.H. Hinsley, *British Intelligence in the Second World War* (HMSO, 1979), vol.1, pp.339-346.
8 NA HW 14/26, *Expansion of 'Y' Services* and HW 50/15, Records relating to the writing of the history of British signals intelligence in World War II, 1939-45.
9 Hinsley, op. cit., vol.3, p.777.
10 NA HW 14/26, Expansion of 'Y' Services: Appendix, Part II, Material and Apparatus, 5.1.1942.
11 NA HW 8/96, Scarborough, Historical Review of 'Y' Work on German Naval W/T Communications, pp.3-4.
12 NA HW 14/105, Visit to Scarborough 'Y' Station 21 May, 1944 and HW 50/15 GC&CS European Naval Section: Extracts and Dossiers Collected Apparently for Historical Purposes and/or Research.
13 I am indebted to Sid Pearson for first alerting me to this. See also *SEN*, 17 March 2006.
14 McKay, op. cit., p.69.
15 IWM, Dr F B Bonner, Catalogue Number 19649.
16 Muriel Davison, *A Wren's Tale: The Secret Link to Bletchley Park* (Reigate, 2011), *Scarborough News* 29 November 2014 and www.gchq.gov.uk/when-we-are/scarborough/Pages/History (accessed 20 April 2019).
17 https://www.gchq.gov.uk/information/norah-phylis-morgan-describes-her-time-scarborough-y-station-during-wwii (accessed 20 April 2019).
18 McKay, op. cit., p.68.
19 IWM, Mary Elizabeth MacKay, Catalogue Number 17687.
20 Mavis Nicholson, *'What did you do in the War, Mummy?' Women in World War Two* (London, 1995), p.170.
21 *Scarborough News,* 29 November 2014.
22 BBC, WW2 People's War, Cynthia Grossman, A30005696 (accessed 10 June 2018).
23 IWM, Dr F B Bonner, Catalogue Number 19649.

24 Nicholson, op. cit., p.170.
25 NA HW 14/105, Notes on a Visit to Scarborough, 21 May 1944.
26 McKay, op. cit., pp.144 and 172-177.
27 Davison, op cit., p.28
28 *Scarborough News,* 17 October 2013.
29 Nicholson, op. cit., p.170.
30 IWM, Mary Elizabeth MacKay, op. cit.
31 https://www.gchq.gov.uk/information/norah-phylis-morgan-describes-her-time-scarborough-y-station-during-wwii (accessed 20 April 2019).
32 Davison, op. cit., passim.
33 NA HW 25/2, A.P. Mahon, The History of Hut Eight, 1939-1945.
34 NA HW 50/15, GC&CS European Naval Section: Extracts and Dossiers Collected Apparently for Historical Purposes and/or Research.
35 They are commemorated by a memorial bench on Scarborough's Lighthouse Pier.
36 NA HW 8/96, Historical Review of 'Y' Work on German Naval W/T Communications, p.43.
37 NA HW 50/15, GC&CS European Naval Section: Extracts and Dossiers Collected Apparently for Historical Purposes and/or Research.
38 Ibid.
39 McKay, op. cit. p.67.
40 NA HW 8/96, Historical Review of 'Y' Work on German Naval W/T Communications, p.9.
41 Ralph Erskine and Michael Smith, *The Bletchley Park Codebreakers* (London, 2011), p.177 and NA HW 8/96, pp.14-15.
42 NA HW 50/15 GC&CS European Naval Section: Extracts and Dossiers Collected Apparently for Historical Purposes and/or Research.
43 F.H. Hinsley, *British Intelligence in the Second World War* (HMSO, 1979), vol.2, p.229.
44 Hinsley, op. cit., vol.3, pp.91-99.
45 Paul Kennedy, *Engineers of Victory* (London, 2013), p.63. The more sceptical view has been reinforced by an official history of GCHQ: John Ferris, *Behind the Enigma* (London, 2020).

CHAPTER 13

Scarborough Women at War

'The WVS never says no.' The Women's Voluntary Service motto

Women's Work

The Second World War had a significant impact on the status of women in British society, though the extent of this change has been much debated.[1] During the war the role of women received greater recognition in society than it had previously. In the home, the work of housewives and mothers in the straightened circumstances of war was accepted as a patriotic labour which made a vital contribution to the national effort. The importance of the 'Kitchen Front' in providing families with nutritious meals from severely rationed food supplies, helped, some argue, to raise the status of women's domestic role.[2] From the beginning of the war in Scarborough, many housewives and mothers accepted the additional responsibility of looking after evacuee children in the town.

Outside of the home, women earned respect and appreciation for volunteering in countless ways in support of the war effort. They worked through existing organisations like the Women's Institute and the churches and through new wartime bodies like the Women's Voluntary Service (WVS) and the auxiliary military services (WAAF, WRENS, and ATS). The experience of Scarborough women who volunteered to serve in the National Fire Service (created in late 1941) illustrates both some of the restrictions and opportunities that women experienced. Women firefighters often found themselves performing a secondary role. One female firefighter in Scarborough recalled some of the disappointing tasks that were allocated to women: secretarial work, polishing the brass work on the engines ('a job they hated'), rolling up hoses.[3] They were also given driving and pumping duties in order to release men for the 'more strenuous duties of actual firefighting'.[4] However, under the influence of national guidelines and manpower shortages women were increasingly given the same firefighting responsibilities as their male counterparts. There is photographic evidence of women taking an active role in tackling a fire in 1942 at the Grand Restaurant, a building that had been taken over by the army.[5]

Women of the National Fire Service in action at the Grand Restaurant on the Foreshore

Further evidence of the prejudices that women wartime volunteers confronted can be found in the early development of the Women's Land Army (WLA). Founded in 1939, initially there was widespread resistance to the employment of women in agriculture to replace conscripted male workers. This came from both farmers and agricultural workers on the grounds that women lacked both the physical strength and temperament to cope with farm labour. The agricultural workers' union also feared that women volunteers on low wages would depress wages in the sector generally.[6] Testimonies from the Scarborough area, though, point to some of the reasons why such early scepticism began to be broken down, as so-called 'Land Girls' demonstrated a feisty resolve to prove themselves as agricultural workers. To take the example of the teenage Peggy Coopland (of the Scarborough baking family), she was an apprentice shop assistant at the genteel Marshall and Snellgrove department store when, in 1939, she volunteered to join the WLA. She served on farms in the Scarborough area and the Yorkshire Wolds. Peggy recalled that volunteers engaged in a range of strenuous farm labour: threshing, ploughing, tractor driving, reclaiming land, drainage and rat catching. They worked up to 50 hours a week in the summer and 48 in the winter, whilst at harvest time they could work from dawn to dusk. 'It was hard work,' she observed, 'but we were young and strong – we just got on with it.' Even in the countryside the war was never far away. Peggy remembered working with Italian POWs and the startling consequences of local military manoeuvres: 'You would be driving a tractor and the next thing you knew a tank would appear from a dip in the land.' She remained in the Land Army until she married in 1943.[7]

Women replaced conscripted men in other areas of the workforce, taking up jobs in transport, wartime administration and the war industries. In Scarborough male conductors on the buses were replaced by women. One little girl was taken aback on getting on a bus, exclaiming, 'Look Mummy, a man conductress.'[8] Young Scarborough women found employment in local industries engaged in war contracts. Such wartime work could be gruelling. Pat Pickering, for example, recalls work at Premier Engineering:

> We made steel brackets for Bailey bridges [for D-Day] and drilled various parts. These were then dipped in black paint then bagged up and sent to Plaxton's in Seamer Road which was also a munitions factory and employed many female workers. It was very hard, dirty work and a very cold factory with just a stove of some sort in the middle of the building. We used to nip over to warm our hands, but if the foreman caught us we were in trouble. Our treat was a cup of hot chocolate at breaktime. I enjoyed the work but we suffered with our hands and chilblains.[9]

Elsie MacKenzie was employed at Plaxton's as a carpenter. She worked mainly with other women, making crates and boxes for the RAF, after the bulk of the male workforce had been conscripted or redirected to more specialist war production. After a fire destroyed the factory in 1943 the women worked on in makeshift sheds in 'rain, snow and bitter cold.'[10]

Pat Pickering and workmates at Premier Engineering on St Thomas Street in 1944.

Other young women found factory work away from home, commonly in the West Riding, the Midlands and Lancashire. They usually lived in barracks, hostels or lodgings. Marjorie Leppington, for example, left Scarborough at the age of 18 to work at the Royal Ordnance Factory at Chorley, Lancashire, where she worked alongside three other young Scarborough women. Living in barracks and bussed daily into work, she remained there for three years. Her factory work was dangerous, attaching detonators to bombs. A further threat came from German bombers:

> We knew if a plane came over and it was carrying bombs, you could hear it, they sounded different. We didn't bother about them coming over. We were never worried, being young you didn't.[11]

The role of women in the labour market and in hitherto voluntary organisations was expanded from the beginning of 1942 when conscription was introduced for women. Single women, initially aged 20-30, were called up and given the choice of serving either in the auxiliary services and civil defence, or in war-related industries. In 1943 the government began directing married women into part-time employment. Such measures increased further the number of women in work and helped to highlight the indispensability of women to the war effort. It is commonly noted that only the Soviet Union surpassed Britain during the war in the recruitment of women in the war economy. However, it should be borne in mind that before the war most single working-class women in Britain were already working full-time and that during the war most women in employment did low-skilled work at lower rates of pay than men.[12]

Women's Voluntary Service (WVS)

The most conspicuous wartime role that women performed was their work in WVS, an organisation established nationally in 1938 as a branch of Air Raid Precautions (ARP). By the end of 1940 there were over 1,500 WVS volunteers in Scarborough. WVS women, in their bottle green and grey-flecked uniforms, were a constant presence around the town for the duration of the war.

The volunteers provided practical help in the aftermath of bombing raids. They were trained in emergency first aid, firefighting and poison gas cleansing.[13] The organisation operated Emergency Feeding Stations and mobile tea cars, providing hot drinks and snacks to emergency workers, the homeless and the injured. At the time of the raid of 10 May 1941, for example, the WVS fed 82 victims in Emergency Feeding Stations.[14] One of the WVS's central roles was the running of Rest Centres, where those who had lost their homes were able to find a temporary roof over their heads. The volunteers also helped the victims of air raids to get back up on their feet again in the aftermath of raids. Following incidents like that of the March 'Blitz' in 1941, the WVS visited bomb-damaged properties, providing clothing, cooking facilities and advice to residents.[15] For people who had lost nearly everything, volunteers could assist with billeting arrangements, emergency financial aid and obtaining new identity cards and ration books. The WVS Transport Section provided cars and drivers to transport the victims of air raids and their possessions. However, when Scarborough volunteers provided their services in the midst of air-raids, this went beyond official guidelines. Doing so did earn them some popular respect, but also paternalist censure for exposing themselves to the sort of risks that only men should face.[16]

Volunteers also helped those who required support in dealing with the psychological strain of enemy bombing.[17] The WVS aimed to foster a spirit of 'neighbourliness' in a community subjected to air raids, and set an example by visiting the aged and the infirm. The official historian of wartime social services has emphasised the importance of such voluntary post-air raid services in 'absorbing shock' and in encouraging people to feel 'that they had not been forgotten'.[18] Those who lacked the time for full membership of the WVS could sign up to the organisation's Housewives Service, where volunteers concentrated on supporting victims of raids in their own street or immediate locality. Sometimes a word of sympathy or a cup of tea from such a local volunteer could be crucial in the maintenance of morale.

The town's WVS Centre Organiser stressed in 1942 that volunteers were 'first and always there for civil defence, no matter what other special work is undertaken'.[19] Despite the decline in enemy raids from this time onwards, the women of the WVS continued to develop their capacity to deal with aerial attacks. An Information Bureau, for example, was established at the Town Hall in 1943 to provide a full range of post-raid guidance and services.[20] The pride taken by the local WVS in its Civil Defence expertise is evident from the centre's Narrative Report for October 1942:

> A team of Women Wardens challenged the Men Wardens to an A.R.P. Quiz on the evening of the 30th Octr:, at the A.R.P. Headquarters. The Chief Constable was the Question-master & the questions touched on all aspects of A.R.P. and the result was a win for the women by the comfortable margin of 12 marks.[21]

As the bombing threat diminished in 1943, the Scarborough WVS was told to guard against any complacency in civil defence: 'It is still possible for us to have a blitz & even a 'tip-and-run' raid can cause many casualties & harm.'[22] In 1944 the essential civil defence role of the local WVS was redirected when a small group of volunteers travelled to London to work amidst the threat of enemy 'flying bombs'.[23] The same year, the Scarborough WVS adopted the London Borough of Finsbury as part of the national 'Good Neighbours' scheme, collecting and despatching household equipment and furniture to help bombed out Londoners.[24]

The activities of the WVS expanded into new areas of responsibility as fresh challenges emerged on the Home Front. Scarborough's Chief Constable applauded the initiative and adaptability of the local volunteers: 'If he wanted anything doing,' he observed, 'it was always the WVS that he turned to.'[25] By the summer of 1942 the WVS operated 22 departments, devoted, for example, to Air Raid Wardens, First Aid Posts, Ambulance Drivers, Mobile Canteens, School Dinners, Clerical and Ration Card Writers and Clothing Depots.[26]

WVS volunteers were a vital component of Scarborough's wartime medical and social services. They were trained as nurses and helped run the town's Blood Transfusion Service. Other members acted as emergency ambulance drivers and attendants. Behind the scenes, volunteers made up swabs and maternity parcels for the hospital, where they also established a new Outpatients Department for use by the military.[27] When the town was hit by a flu epidemic in December 1943, volunteers stepped in to help tackle the emergency and support victims.[28] The social services role of the WVS also expanded during the war, especially in responding to the needs of evacuees in the town. At the outset of the war volunteers had played a vital part in settling new arrivals into the town. Subsequently, they provided clothes and a sewing and mending service for them. Volunteers organised home visits to evacuees and ran a weekly club for their mothers. When evacuee mothers required the use of a Maternity Home, volunteers provided a Reception Home for any young children in the family.[29] For the community as a whole, members helped with the wartime provision of school dinners and in 1943 initiated a shoe and clothing exchange for local children.[30] Volunteers, therefore, plugged important gaps in wartime medical and welfare services.

As the military buildup in the town developed, volunteers worked closely with the Armed Forces. The ambiguous nature of WVS work in empowering women in wartime is particularly evident in their support for the military. On the one hand, WVS drivers were asked to drive for HM Forces, occupying a role normally reserved for men.[31] On the other, volunteers often performed a distinctly gendered role in relation to HM Forces, as when they visited military posts with refreshments.[32] When the Home Guard was stood down at the end of 1944, some sadness crept into the local WVS monthly report:

> The members of the Home Guard feel that it will cause quite a blank in their lives, and we know also, that we shall miss being called upon to take out the tea car to the different parades and practices that they have held for so long, very often on a Sunday.[33]

Reading the monthly Narrative Reports of the Scarborough Centre (or those that survive), it is striking the amount of time and effort that was devoted to sewing, knitting and mending for the military stationed in the area.[34] In 1942, for example, volunteers were responsible for attaching over 4,500 badges to tunics, battledress and overcoats.[35]

Evidence suggests that the Scarborough Centre was one of the more effective of the WVS organisations. When the Centre Leader Mrs E.A. Thompson-Pegge retired, Lady Feversham, the County Organiser, paid tribute to Scarborough as 'the show centre of the North Riding'. Scarborough's Town Clerk judged that there were 'few towns in which the WVS had had either the strength or the quality of the Scarborough organisation'.[36] Working-class women in Scarborough made a contribution to the WVS. They were most likely to be active in the Housewives Service, where they could operate close to home. The backbone of the body, however, was the respectable middle-aged and middle-class membership which was too old for conscription and which had some confidence and skills in participating in public life.[37] In Scarborough, many middle-class volunteers impressed locals by devoting long hours to the WVS whilst also running businesses in tourism and catering. At the same time many had lost servants or home-helps for the duration of the war. The local Centre Leader was led to comment ruefully that 'the most generous and faithful help has come, as is always the case, from the most occupied people'. In saying this, Thompson-Pegge felt let down by the women of the area's more leisured upper middle and gentry class. In a rebuke at the end of the war, she reproached this group for hanging on to its domestic servants and for participating in voluntary war work 'only in spasms'.[38]

The impact of the WVS on perceptions of women's role in society is not clear-cut. Historians have debated whether the activities of the WVS helped significantly to change attitudes towards the status of women in society.[39] The range and pervasiveness of volunteering in Scarborough made an impression on the wartime community by showing that women were determined to 'do their bit'. Many members developed a confidence in performing a public role in the community. They also won respect by taking over work hitherto deemed to be 'masculine', as some of their civil defence and driving responsibilities were. Nevertheless, many of their duties were undoubtedly of a traditionally 'feminine' nature. Secretarial work, staffing canteens and sewing and mending for the military were common tasks. Women's contributions to auxiliary health and welfare services accentuated their caring 'feminine' skills. Lucy Noakes argues that from its inception, the work of the WVS was seen 'as an extension of women's "natural" abilities to nurture and care for those in need of protection'.[40] To this extent, there were limits to how far the WVS in Scarborough was likely to shift traditional assumptions about men's and women's separate, and unequal, spheres in society.

Women in local politics

In 1944 Jottings, always an astute columnist in the *Mercury*, predicted that women would play a more important role in public life after the war and would enjoy greater representation on the Town Council.[41] He based this judgement on his observation of the increasing influence of local women's organisations in wartime. In addition to the labours of the WVS, one group that made an impression in the town was the National Federation of Business and Professional Women, founded as a local branch in May 1943. It sought to promote the interests of women in the civic, economic and cultural life of the town, whilst women's representation on the Chamber of Trade and equal pay for equal work were two of its more specific goals.[42] In a further step forwards for women, a 'Standing Conference' of women's organisations in the town was set up in October 1943, as part of another national network. Its purpose was to bring together feminist efforts locally in order to achieve the maximum impact.[43] It ran numerous campaigns, mixing some middle-class moralising with practical feminism. Campaigning for a Civic Centre in order to keep young women out of licensed premises, for example, was accompanied by efforts to support women's representation on the Town Council.[44]

One of the most notable advances for women in Scarborough was the unanimous election by councillors of the town's first female mayor in November 1942. Councillor Whitfield had previously served as mayoress when her late husband had been mayor for three terms in the 1920s. She had sat as an Independent Councillor for 16 years, only the third woman member in the history of the Council.[45] As a councillor she concentrated her considerable energies on the educational, welfare, public health and tourist needs to the town.[46] The fact that she had never been put forward for the position of mayor may be related to two factors: prejudice among male colleagues against female political ambitions and her habit of making enemies in the Town Hall. However, when she was elected in 1942 the appointment was regarded as a symbolic recognition of the vital role of women in the life of the wartime community. Councillor Jackson commented that there was 'no more appropriate time' for the appointment of the town's first woman mayor.[47] At a subsequent Civil Defence Day, the WVS was granted a place of special prominence as a tribute to the accession of a female mayor.[48]

In office, Whitfield celebrated women's contribution to the war effort in the town, supported women's organisations that were campaigning for greater equality and presided over the inauguration of the 'Standing Conference' of

Mayor Louisa M. Whitfield

women's organisations in 1943.[49] In her own work, she made a considerable impression at the Town Hall and in the community. 'Nothing was too big for her, nothing too little,' and she worked 'morning, noon and night,' it was said. Mayor Whitfield was clearly over-taxing herself, especially in orchestrating the Wings for Victory Week in 1943.[50] Before her anticipated re-election in November 1943 she fell seriously ill and was unable to continue her official duties. She died on Christmas Day 1943, aged 80.

Alderman Pindar, a former mayor and member of the Council's inner cabal, was elected for the remainder of the civic year.[51] Controversy attached itself to replacing the Independent Mrs Whitfield on the Council. After some argument, it was agreed that the new Councillor should be selected by other Independent members of the Council, as part of the wartime electoral truce. In keeping with the spirit of the times, they decided not to consider any male applicants, provoking some male umbrage, and selected a Mrs Priestley to replace Councillor Whitfield.[52] Mrs Priestley did her best, thereafter, to champion the cause of women from the Town Hall, as her predecessor had done so effectively.

Women in the police

During the war the Home Office encouraged local authorities to enrol women as police officers. This was partly a practical expedient to help tackle 'manpower' shortages on the Home Front. It was also felt that women constables, employing their maternal skills, would be better able to deal with the wartime challenge of juvenile delinquency. It was assumed, too, that they would be equipped to deal with the allegedly wayward sexual behaviour of some young women in wartime. This had been tried out in World War I to keep an eye on women seen in the company of soldiers.[53] In 1940 progress in recruitment was slow, with the Home Office reluctant to take a 'high-handed' approach, regarding the issue as 'primarily a matter for the responsible police authority'.[54] Opposition from some Chief Constables and Watch Committees was extreme, one Chief Constable grumbling, 'We all have quite enough on hand dealing with the Hun without being pestered by females.'[55] However, by 1944 local police authorities were being explicitly ordered to recruit policewomen in any area where troops were stationed, with the aim of countering the spread of promiscuity, venereal disease and prostitution.[56] In March 1944 Councillor Jackson took up the cause of moral policing by women officers in Scarborough. Brandishing the annual Police Report, he listed some of the cases that would benefit from female intervention: sexual assault, bigamy and the concealment of a birth.[57] Later he spoke passionately about the dangers of the military presence in the town and the 'disasters befalling girls aged 14 to 18'.[58] When Jackson's opponents suggested that Scarborough was happily free from the sort of problems exercising minds at the Home Office, Jackson was supported by Councillor Cumberbirch, who found it hard to believe that the town was more virtuous than other places.[59]

The demand for women police officers was backed locally by the Labour Party, the Cooperative Women's Guild and the Standing Conference of Women's Organisations. The latter group demanded an audience with the Council's Watch Committee, which was responsible for police matters. The meeting did not go well. The women argued that their contribution to the war effort entitled them to a more equal role in the community.[60] They were not prepared to be fobbed off with the employment of women in subordinate clerical roles, demanding women in uniform patrolling the streets.[61] The Watch Committee asserted that there was no need for women officers in Scarborough and defended the important auxiliary role that women were already playing in the police.[62] Other local opponents of greater equality in the police force also suggested that feminist pressure groups were posing a threat to democracy in pursuit of 'sectional' interests.[63] The *Mercury* newspaper adopted this line, complaining that, at a national level, the Home Secretary had been pressurised into this policy by the 'feminine [sic] movement'.[64] Locally, Alderman Pindar, mayor in 1944, had to publicly deny that he was opposed to women police officers merely on the grounds that the proposal emanated from a women's organisation.[65]

In June 1944 Scarborough's Watch Committee was instructed directly by the Home Office to appoint women police officers. When it refused yet again, representatives of the Watch Committee were summoned to meet Home Office officials, with the same predictable result. The Home Office took the opportunity of an inspection of the Scarborough force in July 1944 to highlight the Watch Committee's continuing recalcitrance in relation to this issue. Still the traditionalists on the Council held out.[66]

Given such pressure from the Home Office, obstructionists on the Council increasingly framed their opposition around the liberties and prerogatives of local government in the face of overweening central authority. Just because women were enrolled in the police elsewhere did not mean that they should be in Scarborough. Only local representatives, they contended, understood the local conditions and 'facts'. They were not prepared to act as 'a mere yes man' to every whim of the Home Office, nor, in Alderman Whittaker's language, to be 'stampeded' by central government.[67] Labour Councillor Simpson, who embraced the recruitment of women as 'a progressive idea', was scathingly dismissed by the *Mercury* for siding with the Home Office against the town's own Watch Committee.[68]

When supporters of women police officers tried to exploit the juvenile crime figures in the 1945 Police Report to reopen the argument, the mayor merely promised to keep the issue under consideration. 'You can depend upon it we shall not forget that point,' he added mischievously.[69] When the redoubtable Cabinet Minister Margaret Bondfield attended a meeting of the local Standing Conference of Women's Organisations in April 1945, she accused Scarborough's Watch Committee of 'living in the nineteenth century'. Jottings saw red at this insult, exclaiming that no national politician had the right to interfere in the town's local affairs. 'It is our considered opinion,' he declared, 'and that of a very large body of people, that Scarborough is totally unsuited for policewomen for street work.'[70] In October 1945, when the Home Office sent an official to Scarborough as a non-complying police authority, the Watch Committee continued to resist.[71]

Scarborough had no need, it seemed, of women constables. Neither feminist pressure nor central government intrusion would persuade the Council's conservative majority to embrace change on this issue. Progress towards equality was slow-moving, too, in employment, in the WVS and in politics. There were clearly limits to how far gender equality would go in wartime and post-war Scarborough.

Notes

1. Penny Summerfield, 'Approaches to women and social change during the Second World War' in Brian Brivati and Harriet Jones (eds.), *What Difference Did the War Make?* (London, 1995), pp.63-64.
2. Ina Zweiniger-Bargielowska, *Austerity in Britain: Rationing, Controls and Consumption, 1939-1955* (Oxford, 2000), p.100.
3. Jean Wallington in *SEN*, 29 September 2001.
4. *SEN*, 20 November 1941.
5. Les Shannon, *Conflagrations: Scarborough's Firefighting History* (Scarborough, 2003), pp.158 and see also *SEN,* 8 June 1946.
6. Juliet Gardiner, *Wartime: Britain 1939-1945* (London, 2004), pp.448-49.
7. *Scarborough Today*, 5 July 2005.
8. *SEN,* 1 April 1942.
9. Newspaper cutting (n.d.) SMHC, File: Scarborough at War (WW2).
10. BBC, WW2 People's War, Elsie MacKenzie, A4919420 (accessed 12 June 2018).
11. *Scarborough News,* 5 September 2019.
12. Robert MacKay, *The Test of War* (London, 1999), p.226.
13. *SEN*, 11 June 1942.
14. WVS, Narrative Report, Scarborough May 1941.
15. *Mercury,* 21 March 1941.
16. Ibid.
17. For a report on the work of the WVS see SEN 24 December 1940 and SEN 1 January 1941.
18. Richard M. Titmus, *Problems of Social Policy* (HMSO, 1950), pp.346-347.
19. *SEN*, 18 June 1942.
20. *SEN*, 7 January 1943.
21. WVS, Narrative Report, Scarborough, May 1942.
22. WVS, Narrative Report, Scarborough November 1943.
23. *SEN*, 22 July 1944.
24. *SEN,* 20 December 1944.
25. *SEN*, 18 June 1942.
26. *SEN*, 18 June 1942.
27. See, for example, WVS, Narrative Report, Scarborough December 1941.
28. *SEN*, 22 December 1943.
29. WVS, Narrative Reports, Scarborough 1940-45, passim.
30. *SEN*, 3 March 1943.
31. *SEN*, 7 January 1943.
32. WVS, Narrative Report, Scarborough October 1942.

33   Ibid., December 1944.
34   WVS, Narrative Report, Scarborough October 1942 and November 1943.
35   *SEN*, 7 January 1943.
36   *SEN*, 1 December 1945.
37   For the national picture, see James Hinton, *Women, Social Leadership and the Second World War: Continuities of Class* (Oxford, 2003).
38   WVS, Narrative Report, Scarborough May 1945.
39   See, for example, Juliet Gardiner, *Wartime Britain, 1939-1945* (London, 2004), pp.60-64.
40   Lucy Noakes, '"Serve to Save": Gender, Citizenship and Civil Defence in Britain, 1937-41', *Journal of Contemporary History*, Vol. 47, No. 4 (October 2012), p.746.
41   *Mercury*, 3 March and 22 December 1944.
42   *SEN*, 26 May 1944 and *Mercury* 14 July 1944.
43   *SEN*, 5 October 1943.
44   Margaret Elsey, *Scarborough Standing Conference of Women's Organisations: A Brief History* (Trevor Jordan, 2011), pp.5-6.
45   Though she was known as Mrs Whitfield, she changed her name by deed poll to Whitfield-Mansfield when she remarried in 1935.
46   For biographical details see *SEN*, 28 December 1943.
47   *SEN*, 9 November 1942.
48   *SEN*, 12 November 1942.
49   *SEN*, 5 October 1943.
50   *SEN*, 9 November 1943 and *Mercury*, 31 December 1943.
51   *SEN*, 3 February 1944.
52   *Mercury*, 11 February 1944 and *SEN*, 29 February 1944.
53   See Philippa Levine,'"Walking in a Way that No Women Should": Women Police in World War I', *Journal of Modern History*, lxvi (1994), pp.34-78.
54   NA HO/18816, Home Office memorandum, 23 October 1940.
55   Quoted in Clive Emsley, *The Great British Bobby* (London, 2010), p.239.
56   Bernard Donoughue and G.W. Jones, *Herbert Morrison: Portrait of a Politician* (London, 1973), p.308 and Roy Ingleton, *The Gentlemen at War: Policing in Britain, 1939-45* (Maidstone, 1994), p.174.
57   *SEN*, 7 March 1944.
58   *SEN*, 15 August 1944.
59   *SEN*, 11 July 1944.
60   *SEN*, 15 August 1944.
61   *SEN*, 5 April 1944.

62 *SEN*, 14 and 30 March 1944. One historian points out that 'the key image of women in the services [in World War Two] lies in the prefix auxiliary – adjunct, accessory, assisting, subsidiary, supporting.' Philomena Goodman, *Women, Sexuality and War* (London, 2002), p.82.
63 *Mercury,* 14 July 1944.
64 *Mercury,* 16 June 1944.
65 *SEN*, 11 July 1944.
66 *Mercury,* 23 June and SEN 15 August 1944.
67 *Mercury,* 16 June 1944 and SEN 11 July 1944.
68 *SEN*, 15 August 1944 and *Mercury,* 18 August 1944.
69 *SEN*, 14 March 1945.
70 *SEN*, 26 April 1945.
71 *SEN*, 4 October 1945.

CHAPTER 14

Salvage and Savings

Believe me, Sir, to be a loyal, true, and faithful British subject, but I mention one good point re that swine Hitler – he is no waster.
(letter from a workman to *The Times* newspaper, 3 February 1940)[1]

Salvage

During World War Two Britain was starved of many of the imported goods that it took for granted during peacetime. The resources that the country did possess were dedicated above all to the requirements of fighting the war. The British people, therefore, endured a climate of sacrifice and self-restraint on the Home Front, where national resources had to be husbanded carefully and salvaged and recycled wherever possible. According to a hyperbolic statement by the Minister of Supply in July 1940, recycling was vital to the war effort: 'Even old love letters can be turned into cartridge wads, meat bones into explosives, tins cans into tanks, and garden tools into guns.'[2]

In 1939 local authorities were instructed to separate reusable materials in refuse collections and to report monthly to the Ministry of Supply on their salvage efforts.[3] From 1940 on, a concerted effort was made to recycle metal items: aluminium, iron and then other non-ferrous metals. As the nation could no longer rely on the importation of ores and scrap by sea with which to manufacture the weapons of war, ploughshares at home had to be beaten into swords. However, it is difficult to disentangle the morale-boosting dimension of the salvage campaigns from the needs of the war economy, as it was felt by the War Cabinet that popular participation in salvage activity would strengthen a sense of patriotic commitment to the war effort among the civilian population.[4]

On 10 July 1940 Lord Beaverbrook, Minister of Aircraft Production, appealed to citizens to donate household items that were partly or wholly made of aluminium. 'We will turn your pots and pans,' he proclaimed, 'into Spitfires and Hurricanes, Blenheims and Wellingtons.'[5] Scarborough was quick to respond. The Women's Voluntary Service workers threw themselves into the task of collecting the town's aluminium resources, with help from local school pupils, the Boy Scouts and the Girl Guides. By July 27th over 10,000 items had been collected, enough for two fighter planes it was claimed.[6] Though little of the national collection was used for such a purpose, Beaverbrook attached importance to the propaganda effects of the campaign on local communities.

In the summer of 1940, the Ministry of Works requested that local authorities should remove and salvage all non-essential iron railings from public land and property as a further contribution to the war economy. By late October the Council was being congratulated for removing over 40 tons of iron railings, mostly from public parks.[7] In the autumn of 1941 the Council announced a wider culling of public railings, including on bridges and at the Dean Road cemetery. At the same time, the Ministry of Supply, now led by Beaverbrook, instructed local councils to compulsorily requisition iron railings from private houses and gardens. The appeal was accompanied by a propaganda campaign which included images of the royal family stoically observing the removal of railings from Buckingham Palace. To encourage public cooperation from Scarborough householders, the town-crier and a loud-speaker van were deployed.[8] Substantial increases in the salvage of ferrous metals were achieved in 1941 and 1942, but the Ministry of Works applied further pressure on the Town Hall in spring 1942, as the Council was failing to meet national targets.[9] Therefore, at the end of September 1942 the Council announced a further purge of public and private railings, and now iron gates too.[10] The campaign was stepped up in December when the substantial network of disused tramlines was removed from local streets.[11] The activities of the Council towards the end of the year seems to have brought to a head some of the tensions and grievances over metal salvage.

One disincentive to popular effort nationally was the existence of scrap metal dumps across the country, patently making no contribution to war production. In Scarborough's case, there were conspicuous eyesores at the nearby villages of Seamer and Ganton.[12] A further source of public disquiet was the fact that the Government regulations exempted ironwork of historical or artistic importance. The Council therefore incurred some public disapproval for protecting railings at some its municipal buildings, like Wood End and the White House on the Crescent, whilst moving more indiscriminately against private property.[13] There was also widespread dissatisfaction with the way railings were removed from private property. Letters to the press condemned the work of subcontractors employed by the Council in damaging walls and hedges, patching up crudely with concrete and leaving sharp and dangerous metal stumps behind. The makeshift replacements to railings erected by some householders added to the visual disfigurement of the town.[14] The removal of railings from some public spaces served also to heighten fears about juvenile delinquency and vandalism, the security of the cemetery becoming a matter of particular concern.[15] The removal of railings and gates from private property was alleged to have exacerbated juvenile crime in the town, youngsters smashing coping stones to retrieve the remaining iron stumps and trespassing on gardens to steal flowers and vegetables.[16]

As part of the October 1942 salvage drive the Ministry of Supply made a plea for the salvage of non-ferrous metals (brass, lead, aluminium, copper, silver, gold). The Town Hall set an ambitious target of ten tons of non-ferrous salvage. 'Come On Scarborough: Show Us Your Metal,' was the slogan. Volunteers manned stalls throughout the town and homes were offered for the stockpiling of donations. Salvage stewards, reinforced by WVS volunteers, went door-to-door advising and exhorting residents and collecting non-ferrous items.[17] There were high expectations that the fishing community in the Old Town would provide rich pickings of maritime brasses.[18] In the event, many townsfolk patriotically donated highly-valued possessions and heirlooms, including old coins, gold jewellery and silver tankards.[19] From quite early on, however, it became apparent that the campaign had over-reached itself. After a week, less than a ton had been collected and many metal stewards were meeting a negative response on the doorstep. By the end of the month, the collection was 'much below' the government's quota.[20]

Less well remembered nowadays were the wartime campaigns to salvage paper. The country had lost most of its timber imports, whilst there was an increasing demand for paper to feed the needs of a wartime bureaucracy. Paper was also used extensively in armaments production, for bullet cartridges and radio components, for example. Government pleas to recycle paper commenced during the Phoney War in 1939. In 1940 and 1941 the government continued to encourage paper and cardboard salvage whilst, at the same time, restricting the supply of paper to book and newspaper publishers and retail shops. When Beaverbrook became Minister of Supply in 1941, he called for a renewed voluntary effort on the 'paper front', cutting back on consumption and recycling used paper. In January 1942 a national competition was organised to encourage areas to compete against each other in paper salvage. The authorities in Scarborough were enthusiastic about taking up the challenge and the council set an example by cutting back on the circulation of official minutes, though it was criticised for the extensive use of paper in advertising the paper salvage campaign.[21] The mayor asked businesses and offices to clear out redundant paper.[22] The usual panoply of voluntary organisations encouraged households to participate, the recycling of paper lending itself particularly to the labour of children. Scouts, Guides and school pupils helped with house-to-house collections and women, as usual, were to the fore. 750 members of the WVS Housewives Service volunteered their houses as depots.[23] Voluntary effort was backed up by using Corporation collecting vehicles, accompanied by loudspeakers, the town crier and army buglers[24]. A journalist visiting the Corporation's salvage yard claimed to identify, along with the usual types of wastepaper, the remnants of secret documents and, as a song of the time went, 'old love letters tied with a ribbon of blue'.[25]

The January 1942 campaign was a considerable success in Scarborough. In the first week, 25 tons of waste paper were collected and by the end of the month 154 tons had been brought in.[26] In March the mayor was presented with a prize of £50 for the town's performance in the national competition, occasioning considerable civic pride.[27] It was an impressive effort, undertaken by the community in the worst January weather for some 60 years.[28]

Such was the national success of the January paper salvage competition that a second competition was launched for the three-month period May to July 1942. The Scarborough authorities were confident of repeating their earlier success, especially as the rules this time pitted the town against similar sized competitors. The aim on this occasion was to visit all the town's households on more than one occasion and, to facilitate collection, stalls were established across the town. The campaign also benefited from the recent appointment of voluntary Salvage Stewards, largely comprising female volunteers. Considerable progress was made, but it proved to be more difficult to galvanise the community a second time round. A great deal of accumulated wastepaper had already been cleared out and there had been a general decline in the circulation of paper due to government restrictions. The Salvage Stewards also began to provoke some public hostility as interfering do-gooders.[29] By early in the final month of the campaign urgent calls were made for a 'definite spurt' in retrieval efforts and the decision was taken to prioritise the collection of books and magazines as a means of overcoming the dearth of wastepaper.[30]

The urgent quest for books was concentrated into four days in July. The authorities and their helpers pulled out all the stops. Volunteers combed the town offering advice, cajoling locals, sorting books and organising transport. The Deputy Major deprecated sentimentality in disposing of books. The Armed Forces 'were giving their lives, not books,' he reminded people.[31] As a token of the seriousness of the book campaign, soldiers, airmen and firemen were employed as helpers and propagandists. By the end of the campaign, 46,000 books had been collected.[32] This constituted a considerable patriotic sacrifice by many members of the community, with some individuals handing in valuable books, including a sixteenth century Bible. A former member of the Council gave 500 items from his personal library. However, the organisers of the campaign remained frustrated by the sluggish response in the town, as a significant proportion of the books were submitted by a small number of people.[33] The target of at least two books from every man, woman and child in the town was far from achieved. Some townsfolk failed to appreciate the gravity of the book drive, turning up at stalls in the hope of purchasing a bargain. Nevertheless, a substantial amount had been collected over the three-month period.[34] The town had at least put on a good show, even if its salvage goal was not achieved.

In the summer of 1943 the Ministry of Supply instigated another paper salvage drive, the National Book Recovery Campaign. The aim was to organise a nation-wide clear-out of private books. Most would be used for recycling, but some would be donated to the Services for recreational reading and some would be used to re-stock war-damaged public libraries.[35] Local scrutiny committees were to advise on the sorting of books and on safeguarding valuable tomes. Peter Thorsheim, an authority on Britain's wartime salvage, has documented the failure to protect unique books and manuscripts, reflecting that '... the British people paradoxically destroyed part of their nation's cultural heritage in the course of fighting to save their civilisation'.[36] The mayor of Scarborough assured townsfolk that there would be local beneficiaries of the Book Recovery Campaign, like the Children's Hospital. Collections took place between August 21st and the end of September, women and schoolchildren again playing a prominent role in street collections. Children were rewarded with small cardboard badges reflecting the scale of their collections, from 'Private' to 'Field

Salvage and Savings

Marshall'. As a means of coaxing the less civic-minded in the town, entrance to the ever-popular Olympia Ballroom was made dependent on the usual charge, plus at least one book.[37] It was felt important to associate the campaign with military necessity and national survival. Lady Feversham emphasised the contribution the campaign would make to reducing the country's dependence on precarious shipping imports.[38] The mayor, in his appeal to the town, stressed the 'astonishing extent' to which the munitions industry depended on recycled paper.[39] Such pleas seem to have been effective as by the end of September the original target of 100,000 books had been exceeded by about 20,000 volumes.[40]

Recycling books into paper, an appeal outside the Town Hall in July 1942, with Mayor Ireland and Councillor Johnny Jackson on the left. Members of the Armed Forces are present to emphasise the military value of recycling and, typically, a female volunteer is at the centre of activity.

The range and volume of materials salvaged in wartime Scarborough was impressive. When a journalist visited the borough salvage depot in 1942, he marvelled at the bounty of recycled goods stored separately in the yard. There was, of course, ferrous and non-ferrous metals and wastepaper. But the Council, under government directives, had also been salvaging rags, carpets, textiles, razor blades, jam jars and empty bottles.[41] A considerable effort had been made to recover kitchen waste and bones (see page 217). In the first three years of the war, the Town Hall salvaged 3,337 tons of waste, to the value of £13,964.[42] By the spring of 1944 the figures had risen to 4,489 tons, to the value of £19,000. Relative to the rest of Yorkshire, Scarborough's record was impressive, as can be seen from the table below.[43]

Year	Yorkshire average value of salvage per 1,000 of the population	Scarborough average per 1,000 of the population
1940	£51.9	£47.8
1941	£73.8	£100
1942	£115.9	£135.9
1943	£116.6	£157.9

Such levels of recycling were only achieved by firm leadership from the Town Hall and a great deal of voluntarist effort. The mayor described the contribution of women volunteers to salvage collections as 'beyond praise'.[44] Significant adjustments to everyday behaviour and a spirit of patriotism and civic pride were also displayed. Along the way, there was naturally some resistance and backsliding, and, as the end of the war neared, it became more difficult to inspire community effort. However, the anti-waste efforts of Scarborians made a commendable contribution to national wartime self-sufficiency. In 1942 the Borough Engineer, reflecting on the town's wartime ethos of austerity and thrift, expressed the hope that this experience would help to inoculate the people after the war against 'the wastefulness of the past'.[45] This wish proved to be somewhat naïve.

National Savings

A further means of contributing to the war effort through civic responsibility and frugality was participation in the National Savings movement. Individuals and organisations were exhorted to avoid squandering any surplus cash and, instead, to invest in government bonds by buying saving stamps. The effort was commonly made not just by individuals on their own, but by collective effort in places of work and in local streets and neighbourhoods. The primary purpose of the movement was, of course, to persuade people to lend money to the government to help finance the war. In addition, at a time of rising incomes and shortages of consumer goods, such savings served a valuable counter-inflationary purpose. For the participants, the National Savings campaigns gave people the opportunity to get engaged in the war effort, in short to 'do something' and to be seen to be doing something.[46] At the same time, such savings, tax free and with interest, were promoted as a sound financial investment.

Programme cover for the National Savings week in 1941

By the beginning of 1943 the Scarborough organisers could boast £3m in local contributions to National Savings. Such a level was above the national average.[47] In the year 1943-1944 it was found that on average the Scarborough small saver was saving 6s 8½d per head per week, whilst the average for the North-East Region was 5s 8½d.[48] In addition to individual and group savings initiatives, local authorities organised National Savings weeks as part of national campaigns. These were used to raise public awareness of the importance of National Savings and to increase savings in a highly concentrated effort. They provide a valuable insight into the popular mood of Scarborough throughout the war.

The first National Savings Week, War Weapons Week, came in April 1941. The aim was to encourage local investment in war savings to the tune of £200,000. Scarborians were encouraged to contribute by advertisements declaiming 'Scarborough Goes To It!' and a War Weapons Indicator was erected in the centre of the town to keep a tally of donations. At the end of it all, £376,000 was invested, amounting to an average of £9 of national savings per head of population. There was some disappointment that a disproportionate amount of the contributions came from 'big business', but the event was certainly a reflection of, and a boost to, local wartime patriotism.[49] The February 1942 Warship Week aimed to raise £250,000, with the symbolic goal of adopting a Navy destroyer, *HMS Hasty*.[50] This campaign included the national savings generated in the districts surrounding the town. The target was greatly exceeded. Nearly £400,000 was invested, almost a third of this from local businesses and banks.[51] The Wings for Victory Campaign in 1943 aimed to raise £320,000. Some claimed this was somewhat unambitious, given that families and businesses were accumulating idle cash reserves during wartime economic austerity. The goal, it was claimed, was the cost of eight Halifax bombers. This time around, Scarborough and District raised £64,270 above the target, with more than three-quarters coming from small savers, it was proudly announced.[52] Salute the Soldier in 1944, the final wartime savings week, raised £404,047, over half coming from small savers.[53]

Such National Savings drives depended greatly on the wartime volunteering spirit. Nowhere was this truer than with the role of women volunteers, and

Mayor Ireland in front of the War Weapons Week Indicator at Alma Square in April 1941.

especially of the WVS. They played a central role in the planning and running of the savings weeks. A vital part was played by women in forming the nucleus of the street, neighbourhood and office savings groups that badgered people so effectively into buying savings bonds. The *Mercury* newspaper felt that women's groups were the only ones that showed any 'real life' in the challenging circumstances of the 1942 campaign.[54] Women conformed to traditional roles in many ways, organising whist drives, cake stalls and dances. However, one day of each National Savings week was allocated to celebrating women's contribution to the war effort. In 1943, for example, women organised a parade through the town which featured the WVS, the Land Army, women in the Armed Services and local munitions workers.[55] This is not to say that all women threw themselves into the savings events with equal enthusiasm. There were complaints that the same patriotic and activist minority of women shouldered most of the voluntary burden. Lady Feversham, WVS County Organiser, speaking at Scarborough's Warship Week in 1942, complained that 'not all women volunteer as much as they should'.[56]

The contribution of local schools and youth organisations to the war effort was also applauded during National Savings drives. Local dignitaries commended the work of schools in collecting salvage, growing vegetables, knitting for the forces, sending parcels to the troops as well as in promoting national savings.[57] Schools laid on exhibitions about their wartime activities and were visited by military bands. A parade of youth organisations during 1943's Wings for Victory Week gives an impression of the patriotic mobilisation of youth behind the war effort. It included the Boy Scouts, Sea Cadets, Army Cadets, RAF Cadet Band, Air Training Corps, St Peter's Girls' Service, Junior Air Corps, St John's Ambulance Cadets and Red Cross Cadets.[58]

Striking features of National Savings weeks were the celebration of the nation's martial spirit and the promotion of a militaristic ethos in the town. For a week the town was given over to a carnival of military parades, guards of honour, marches-past, military bands and exhibitions of war fighting equipment. 1941's War Weapons Week, for example, was described as 'every schoolboy's dream come true', as local boys got to handle machine guns and anti-tank rifles and clamber over Bren gun carriers. In 1942's Warship Week, a great pride was exhibited in the town's seafaring and naval traditions. However, in the absence of a warship in the harbour, a column of armoured vehicles, howitzers and tanks was driven through the town on the opening day, with a number of civic dignitaries transported in a tank. Throughout the week, in a sort of militarised seaside fun-fare, members of the public had the chance to test their skills on a tank training range, firing at simulated stationary and moving targets, against a desert landscape.[59] In another exercise in patriotic bellicosity, citizens were given the opportunity to attach replica national savings stamps to 500lb. bombs destined for German cities.[60] The Salute the Soldier week in 1944 was conducted against the backdrop of the Allied invasion of occupied Europe. As there were other pressing uses for the usual military hardware, Scarborians had to make do with a display of army petrol carriers. The local Home Guard, however, demonstrated their firepower from a position overlooking North Bay, where machine guns, mortars and anti-tank weapons were deployed against effigies of Hitler and Goering out at sea.[61]

National Savings weeks were also something of a colourful community festival at a time of drab wartime austerity, providing a patriotic licence to engage in distracting public amusements. For a week, the wearying routines of the Home Front were enlivened by street pageantry, musical entertainment and sporting competitions. As the RAF had a strong presence in the town, it was able to make a distinctive contribution to all the wartime savings weeks, and not only to the 1943 Wings for Victory activities. Typically, the RAF laid on impressive programmes of musical and sporting events, exhibitions of its wartime operations and demonstrations of clay-pigeon shooting. Local army units provided similar support. In 1944 the Green Howards drew the largest crowd of the week with a re-enactment of seventeenth century warfare, in 'old-time' costumes.[62] 1944 also witnessed one of the most theatrically effective public spectacles of the war. In the culminating parade of the week, an anonymous soldier from the ranks took the salute from a raised dais, with army top-brass modestly in the background. It was an emotive tribute to the ordinary British Tommy.[63] In addition to the big public performances, dances and other social events could be attended as dutiful citizens. For children, as Norman Longmate observes, such weeks 'perhaps went some way to make up for other wartime deprivations'.[64]

The National Savings campaigns brought figures of national importance to a town that could easily feel cut off from the main momentum of the national war effort. The Wings for Victory Week in 1943 was opened by Lord Keyes, Admiral of the Fleet, who was granted the Freedom of the Borough. The organisers of the 1944 drive exploited national celebrity shrewdly by inviting the son of the former Foreign Secretary, Lord Halifax, to help 'Salute the Soldier'. He had lost both legs in the North Africa campaign. In the same year, they achieved their greatest coup by bringing the Princess Royal (Mary, George V's only daughter) to Scarborough's celebrations.[65] The royal, though, failed to live up to a local schoolboy's expectations of a princess. 'Why Miss,' he declared to his teacher, 'she's nobbut a lass in ATS uniform.'[66]

The Princess Royal, in uniform, meeting military bigwigs at the Salute the Soldier Week in Scarborough, June 1944.

The 1942 Warship Week was exceptional in generating some concerns about the patriotic spirit of the town. Although large sums of money were invested, reflecting a substantial reservoir of surplus capital, attendance at communal events was disappointing. The poor turn-out at the opening ceremony was described by an alderman as 'shocking'.[67] Participation at events remained sluggish through the week. Jottings, in the *Mercury*, complained that townsfolk seemed to prefer to visit cafés than engage in Warship Week events.[68] Women were targeted for pursuing selfish indulgence at the expense of their civic and patriotic responsibilities. A female letter-writer, for example, commended in the local press the small minority of community-minded women in Scarborough, but went on to denounce others who failed to make a contribution, looked after their own comfort and devoted their time to bridge and other recreations.[69] In reality, many of the difficulties attaching to the Warship Week in 1942 can be explained by the depressed state of the local economy and by the severe weather conditions in February.[70]

Salvage and savings provided the people of Scarborough with an opportunity to make a material contribution to the wartime national economy. The campaigns also helped to reinforce the wartime ethos of austerity and self-restraint. Yet perhaps their most significant impact was that they enabled the people of the town to engage in patriotic activity in a way that helped to bring the community together and strengthen wartime morale.

Notes

1. Quoted in Peter Thorsheim, *Waste Into Weapons* (Cambridge, 2015), p.39.
2. Quoted in Peter Thorsheim, 'Salvage and Destruction: The Recycling of Books and Manuscripts in Great Britain during the Second World War', *Contemporary European History*, 22, 3 (2013), p.440.
3. Tim Cooper, 'Challenging the "refuse revolution": war, waste and the rediscovery of recycling, 1900-50', *Historical Research*, vol. 81, no. 214 (November 2008), p.717.
4. Angus Calder, *The People's War* (London, 1969), pp.399-400.
5. Ibid., p.172.
6. See *SEN*, 27 July 1940.
7. *SEN*, 23 October 1940.
8. *SEN*, 9 and 10 September 1941.
9. *SEN*, 31 March and SEN 28 April 1942.
10. *SEN*, 29 September 1942.
11. *SEN*, 5 December 1942.
12. *Mercury*, 7 August 1942.
13. *Mercury*, 20 November 1942.
14. Letters *SEN*, 17, 26 and 31 October 1942.
15. *Mercury*, 16 October and *SEN*, 27 October 1942.
16. *SEN*, 7 August 1942.
17. WVS, Narrative Report, Scarborough October 1942.
18. *SEN*, 17 October 1942.
19. *SEN*, 28 October 1942.
20. *Mercury*, 23 and SEN 28 October 1942.
21. *Mercury*, 9 January 1942.
22. *Mercury*, 2 January 1942.
23. *Mercury*, 2 January 1942.
24. *SEN*, 7 January 1942.
25. *SEN*, 6 April 1942.
26. *Mercury*, 9 January and *SEN*, 2 February 1942.
27. *SEN*, 11 March 1942.
28. *SEN*, 9 February 1942.
29. See for example *SEN*, 22 April and 6 June 1942.
30. *SEN*, 20 July 1942.
31. *SEN*, 21 July 1942.
32. *SEN*, 25 July 1942.

33 *SEN*, 22 July 1942.
34 *SEN*, 10 September 1942.
35 Peter Thorsheim, *Waste Into Weapons* (Cambridge, 2015), p.197.
36 Peter Thorsheim, 'Salvage and Destruction: The Recycling of Books and Manuscripts in Great Britain during the Second World War', *Contemporary European History*, 22, 3 (2013), p.432-33.
37 *SEN*, 21 August 1943.
38 *SEN*, 6 October 1943.
39 *SEN*, 21 August 1943.
40 *SEN*, 6 October 1943.
41 *SEN*, 6 April 1942.
42 *SEN*, 18 May 1943.
43 *Mercury*, 17 March 1944
44 Ibid.
45 *SEN*, 13 June 1942.
46 Rosalind Watkiss Singelton, '"Doing Your Bit": Women and the National Savings Movement in the Second World War' in Maggie Andrews and Janis Lomas, (eds.), *The Home Front in Britain* (London, 2014) p.217.
47 *SEN*, 27 January 1943.
48 *SEN*, 11 September 1944.
49 See *SEN*, 27 February, local press 25-29 April 1941 and SEN, 20 May 1941.
50 Sadly, the destroyer was sunk in the spring of 1942.
51 Local press 21-27 February 1942 and *Mercury*, 6 March 1942.
52 Local press 16-23 June and *SEN*, 20 July 1943.
53 *SEN*, 12 June 1944, local press 15-23 June 1944, *SEN*, 30 June 1944.
54 *Mercury*, 27 February 1942.
55 *SEN*, 16 June 1943.
56 *SEN*, 24 February 1942.
57 *SEN*, 25 February 1942.
58 *SEN*, 23 June 1943.
59 *SEN*, 19 February 1942.
60 *SEN*, 16 June 1943.
61 *SEN*, 16 June 1944.
62 *SEN*, 22 June 1944.
63 *Mercury*, 23 June 1944.
64 Norman Longmate, *How We Lived Then* (London, 1971), Chapter 31, 'Hit Back with National Savings'.
65 *SEN*, 20 and 22 June 1944.

66 *SEN*, 5 July 2005.
67 *SEN*, 21 February 1942.
68 *Mercury,* 27 February 1942.
69 *SEN*, 23 February 1942.
70 Ibid.

CHAPTER 15

Food, fuel and transport

'Food is a munition of war. Don't waste it.'
(Ministry of Food advertisement)

'Is Your Journey Really Necessary?'
(Railway Executive Committee)

Feeding Scarborough

One of Britain's great wartime achievements on the Home Front was the development of a system of food distribution that earned a large degree of consent from the civilian population. The country lost nearly half of its food imports during the war, creating shortages of many everyday foodstuffs, such as sugar and butter. In response, the government aimed to boost food production at home and to ensure a distribution of food that was fair and that provided a healthy basic diet for all. This was achieved by providing government subsidies to keep prices down and by developing a system of rationing where scarce foodstuffs could only be purchased with coupons from an official ration book. Rationing was introduced in January 1940 for bacon, ham, sugar and butter. It was extended as more commodities became scarce and as prices for them rose: March 1940 – meat; July 1940 – tea, margarine and cooking fat; March 1941 – jam, marmalade, syrup and honey; May 1941 – cheese; July 1942 – chocolate and sweets. When in June 1942 nearly 3,000 housewives were asked about wartime food rationing, a majority said that they would like to see the system continued in peacetime.[1]

Under rationing Britain's wartime diet changed substantially. The consumption of vegetables (especially potatoes), milk and brown bread rose, whilst that of meat, fresh eggs, sugar, butter and fats declined. The Ministry of Food and the BBC lectured women on preparing meals in the most economical and nutritious manner and on how to incorporate new commodities into the diet: dried eggs, haricot beans, salt cod and whale meat, for example. Citrus fruits were extremely rare and the odd resident in Scarborough who was fortunate enough to have a lemon posted to them from a relative abroad was treated with considerable envy. It was common for such prized items to be auctioned in aid of a wartime charity.[2] In the summer of 1943 it was considered newsworthy that a shop in the nearby town of Pickering was selling a banana.[3] As is well known, the impact of rationing and dietary changes on public health during the war was beneficial, especially for babies, schoolchildren and the poor in general. By 1943 infant mortality in Scarborough was unprecedentedly low.[4] Reports on the school medical service in the town in 1944 and 1945 found that there had been no deterioration in nutrition or health during the war.[5]

As a pleasure resort, Scarborough experienced difficulties in obtaining food supplies, as hoteliers and caterers often struggled to obtain a sufficient quantity and range of food provisions with which to satisfy their customers. It was ironic that the town, with a long-standing sea fishing heritage, found it difficult to find fish supplies for its fryers.[6] The rationing of sweets in 1942 was a blow to local shopkeepers, hitting small traders selling treats to visiting children. Life in a seaside resort had its drawbacks for residents. Visiting tourists were known to descend on foodstuffs in short supply and carry them off home, earning the epithet locally of 'Shop Crawlers'.[7] Visitors, with money in their pockets earned in war industries elsewhere, could also be resented for crowding locals out of the town's cafés and restaurants.

Rationing had a mixed impact on everyday family life in Scarborough. To a great extent it succeeded in ensuring fair shares for all, but the rations could be meagre and a wartime diet dreary. One 'bottom ender' recalled a diet of carrot and turnip and the odd sheep's head stew.[8] The poet Christopher Wiseman remembered instances of genuine hunger, when 'Our mother went without so we could eat'.[9] He also documents the small ways in which rationing was mitigated by a bending of the rules. The milkman, for example, provided his mother with extra milk and eggs, *'For the kiddies'*.[10] The local butcher kept extra meat under the counter, 'for folk he knew'.[11] The experience of food scarcity and the restrictions of the rationing system also encouraged the development of a black market in some foodstuffs. One of Wiseman's neighbours kept pigs in his cellar without official permission, selling bacon only yards away from the Special Constables' headquarters.[12] There was some concern in the spring of 1942 about the rising scale of racketeering, when a number of cases came before the courts. The problem sometimes arose from the socialising that took place between local women and enterprising servicemen with access to military stores. One woman who ran a small grocery shop for her mother was fined for breaching food regulations when she received jam, corned beef and cheese from 'an RAF man in charge of a big lorry'.[13]

As well as relying on rationing scarce produce, the Ministry of Agriculture aimed to increase domestic food production and exhorted citizens to take more responsibility for producing their own food. 'Dig for Victory' was the refrain. In Scarborough the Corporation and its Parks Department took a lead, from the summer of 1940 ploughing up uncultivated land in the town for growing vegetables. By late August 1940 it had converted over 2,500 square yards of council land to vegetable beds. The harvest that year was such a success that the town enjoyed a glut of vegetables.[14] Thereafter, public parks, the racecourse, school grounds and a holiday camp on the outskirts of the town were given over to the plough. Pupils from the Boys High School lent their support by tending vegetable gardens in the grounds of the newly built Girls High School. The town's two golf clubs cooperated with the Corporation, permitting sheep-grazing and cereal and vegetable planting over large parts of the courses.[15] In the last two years of the war, North Cliff Golf Club yielded crops sold by the Corporation to the value of nearly £1,000. The figure for South Cliff Golf Club was not made public, as cultivation was controlled by the RAF.[16] Small spaces, too, were utilised by the Parks Department. A visitor to the town in September 1942 was impressed to see giant cabbages and seakale in promenade flowerbeds and a large bed of beetroots in the town centre.[17] The town of Scarborough in Ontario, Canada, was keen to express its solidarity, sending vegetable seeds to the Town Hall, including those of the unfamiliar warted squash.[18] The Corporation, then, set an example and made a not insignificant contribution to the cause of local food self-sufficiency. Inevitably, some cynics suggested that Councillors assured for themselves a plentiful supply of fresh produce.[19]

Meanwhile the Council encouraged townsfolk to make their own contributions to self-sufficiency, offering portions of ploughed up land to residents as allotments. In the spring of 1942, Councillor Dennis exhorted all locals to plant vegetables for the next winter and promised an allotment

The RAF managed their own wartime fishery business in Scarborough to help supply their three Initial Training Wings. Here RAF personnel and local fishermen pose with their Yorkshire coast fishing coble.

to anyone who could use one.[20] The Scarborough and District Horticultural Association also promoted the 'Dig for Victory' campaign, encouraging fruit and vegetable cultivation and advising residents on good gardening practice.[21] Horticultural shows were used to promote patriotic competition and to raise money for wartime causes like the Red Cross POW fund.[22] Many individuals and families responded eagerly to Ministry of Agriculture appeals. Throughout the town gardens, allotments and private land were given over to fruit and vegetable production. Amateur gardeners 'dug' for victory and were commonly celebrated in the local press for their skills and resourcefulness, one claiming to be able to foretell the outcome of the war when he dug up a 'V' shaped potato.[23] The ingenuity of a young girl in growing vegetables in her back yard was commended. She grew them in a family pram, which she wheeled into the sun or indoors as weather conditions dictated.[24] Looking back in 1948, the Ministry of Agriculture was fulsome (and distinctly sexist) about the role of the 'Victory Digger':

> He is better in spirit because cultivating his plot took his mind off the burdens of office or workshop; he has benefited his family by providing fresh vegetables that kept them fit and incidentally helped his wife in trying to make ends meet and avoid queues; he and his fellow 'Victory Diggers' benefited their country by contributing in every year a substantial and indispensable quantity of food to the national larder, without which the nation might well have had to go short.[25]

In addition to 'digging for victory', some Scarborians took to small-scale animal husbandry to extend their self-reliance. Families and clubs kept poultry in back yards, rabbits in fields and the odd pig on spare ground. There was initially some surprise when some of the resort's luxury hotels took to pig-keeping, and when pigs were to be seen foraging on the up-market St Nicholas Cliff.[26] In the summer of 1942 the mayor supported the Ministry of Agriculture's campaign to encourage the formation of poultry and rabbit clubs and a local demonstration was organised to advise the uninitiated.[27] The Town Hall staff led by example, forming a pig-keeping club, though they were anxious to reassure locals that the livestock were not kept at the Town Hall.[28] Pupils at the Boys High School also took a lead by rearing poultry, rabbits and pigs at the school.[29] One Scarborian remembers the benefits of such initiatives: 'Like most people we grew our own vegetables, and we kept hens as well as the pigs, so despite wartime we had an adequate diet.'[30]

Young volunteers also made a valuable contribution to bringing in the annual harvests. In the bumper potato harvest of autumn 1942, for example, local schoolchildren helped during their half term, joining farmworkers, evacuees and Land Girls.[31] The Boys' High School made a commendable contribution to sustaining wartime food supplies, as its headmaster recorded:

As in the previous War, the gardeners were busy with the production of food. But in 1939, led by Mr. Turnbull, they went into action at once, dug up the school plots, then the Garden at the White House, then more land at the Girls' High School. They kept pigs and hens, formed Youth Squads for the salvaging of waste food.[32]

Proximity to the coast and countryside afforded Scarborians the opportunity to supplement a bland wartime diet. Fresh-water and shoreline angling were obvious expedients, but there was also a revival of the custom of foraging for birds' eggs in hedgerows and at nearby cliffs.[33] Terry Baker remembers as a boy going 'seagull egging' in wartime at the nearby Cayton Cliffs:

Seagulls' eggs are much bigger than hens' eggs and made good eating. With the rope tied around his waist, Dennis would scramble over the edge and down the cliff face. John and Vic held on tightly at the top with me as an anchor and Pete acting as signal man telling us when to lower or heave up. Trying to avoid looking at the waves 300 ft. below, Dennis would bounce from nest to nest, placing eggs in his home-made pouch which we would share out. That was a treat![34]

Similarly, a renewed vogue for wild mushroom hunting developed, to the irritation of some local farmers whose crops were trampled in the process. Local children and youngsters proved to be especially dedicated foragers. The Boy Scouts organised annual collections of sweet chestnuts and rose hips.[35] Pupils from the Boys High School tracked down sweet chestnuts, rose hips and wild fruit, producing jam for the hospital and donating profits to a POW charity.[36] Local author David Fowler recalls schools encouraging children to participate in wartime 'Hip and Haw' weekends (rosehip and fruit of the hawthorn collecting), after which produce was made into nutritious jams, jellies and syrups.[37] Some youngsters' interpretations of foraging appear to have embraced cultivated as well as wild produce, as Christopher Wiseman testifies:

… we ate what we could find round about –
berries, mushrooms, raw potatoes from the farmer's
field, slitting pods open with bleeding thumb-nails
and eating peas raw.[38]

In order to avoid food waste, the people of the town were encouraged by the Town Hall to leave leftovers and scraps out with their refuse. Unwanted food was then recycled for animal feed, whilst bones had industrial uses. Initially an enormous increase in such salvage took place. In 1940 two tons were collected and in 1941, the first year of official Council collections, 278 tons were collected.[39] It did prove to be difficult to sustain such increases and there was concern amongst officialdom that the town was failing to meet the target set by central government.[40] It may be that residents were increasingly finding their own uses for leftovers, and perhaps, too, they were put off by the mess and smells associated with food recycling. But there was undoubtedly a growing scepticism about the value of food salvage. Dustbin men often appeared to be throwing food scraps in with the rest of their collection, hence negating the good intentions of residents.[41] Overall however, relative to peacetime profligacy, the war years saw a greatly heightened awareness of the importance of food self-sufficiency, recycling and the avoidance of waste.

A 'British Restaurant'?

In late 1940 the Ministry of Food proposed a national scheme of 'communal feeding centres'. They were intended to provide a nutritious and economic meal for citizens who were finding such a meal difficult to obtain in the changing circumstances of war: munitions workers away from home, shift workers, male workers whose wives were working or volunteering. It was felt that vulnerable groups, like the poor and old age pensioners, would also benefit from such centres. They would be run by local authorities, which would receive support from central government for set up and running costs.[42] Churchill judged that 'British Restaurants' would sound more respectable and patriotic (and less socialistic) than 'communal feeding centres'.[43] The idea caught on quickly across the country and by September 1941 the 1,000[th] British Restaurant was opened.[44] Early in 1942 the government decided to tighten financial control of the restaurants to make them more self-supporting.[45] However, the programme continued to expand. In September 1943 there were 2,160 and the majority of municipal boroughs possessed one.[46] It was largely in rural areas that they lacked backing. When it became clear in 1941 that the local authority in Scarborough had no intention of establishing a British Restaurant in the town, the local labour movement initiated an energetic campaign to overcome municipal obstruction. Labour Councillor Sidney Simpson took the lead, writing to the press, canvassing fellow councillors and repeatedly raising the issue at Council meetings. The meeting of June 1942 was described, for example, as 'long enough for Councillor Simpson to give his British Restaurant gramophone record its usual monthly airing'.[47]

In February 1942 the local Labour Party launched a petition to collect evidence of local demand for a British Restaurant.[48] Under some pressure, Town Hall officials conducted research on the experiences of seaside towns like Scarborough, announcing, predictably, that it appeared to vindicate the Council's scepticism about the need for a British Restaurant. Later in 1942 there was some movement on the Council towards Labour's position, with Councillor Walsh, for example, proclaiming his conversion in May, citing the needs of the town's elderly and poor.[49] The Labour Party kept up the pressure in 1943, the peak year of national support for British Restaurants. In September the party conducted a local opinion poll about the restaurants, concluding that there was sufficient interest and support to make such an institution viable in the town.[50] Remarkably, early in October the Council voted in favour of the establishment of a British Restaurant, against the advice of the inner Cabinet, the Emergency

Committee.[51] This was followed by some rapid manoeuvring behind the scenes. The Emergency Committee referred the issue to the Cafés Committee of the Council, which recommended deferring the issue on the grounds that there was no suitable venue in the town, nor a qualified management team.[52]

However, opponents of the restaurants were put temporarily on the back foot when suitable accommodation was identified in the town centre. In what appeared to some as an underhand and conspiratorial ploy, it was then announced that the proposed site had been requisitioned.[53] When a further site was found in March 1944, opponents of British Restaurants enjoyed their final victory when the Council accepted that the expense would be too great and that it was too far into the war to contemplate such a commitment.[54] Councillor Priestley accepted that the time for the town's British Restaurant was 'three years ago'. Councillor Simpson summed up the wounded resignation of supporters:

> Personally, he did not care. He had done his share, and his hands were perfectly clean. The Council must take responsibility for depriving the people of Scarborough of services that almost every town of Scarborough's size, and hundreds smaller, had had for a considerable time.[55]

There was clearly considerable support for a British Restaurant in Scarborough. The case for such a facility benefited from central government backing, and from the whole-hearted support of two popular ministers, Minister of Labour Ernest Bevin and Minister of Food Lord Woolton.[56] Resentment against the Council's refusal to act was fuelled by the fact that so many of Scarborough's neighbouring towns enjoyed the benefits of British Restaurants: Whitby, Malton, York and Hull, for example. Indeed, the North Riding County Council was responsible for establishing a number of British Restaurants, leading Councillor Simpson to express his surprise that the traditionally conservative County Council was proving to be more 'progressive' than Scarborough Council.[57] The evidence seemed compelling to many that the changing conditions in wartime Scarborough made it difficult for a substantial number of people to guarantee at least one wholesome meal per day. When a journalist from *The Times* newspaper visited Scarborough in August 1943, he was surprised that the town had no British Restaurant, concluding:

> … it [a British Restaurant] would be a boon both to local married women in full or part-time employment and to those war workers on holiday who have been able to secure rooms but not board.[58]

There was mounting concern in some quarters, moreover, about the increasing incidence of real economic hardship in the borough, and the inadequate diet of many of those who were suffering. Disquiet centred initially upon pensioners, but it also focused on the many victims of the collapse of the tourist economy in wartime. A letter-writer to the local press, in pressing for a British Restaurant, raised fears about boarding house keepers who were living off tea, bread and butter. Another expressed concern about respectable citizens 'living day to day on the starvation line'.[59]

The spearhead of the campaign for a British Restaurant was the small and energetic Scarborough Labour Party. It saw the concept as an opportunity to revive plans for a municipal socialism, as promoted by the Webbs (Sidney and Beatrice) earlier in the century.[60] A British Restaurant was seen as a stepping-stone towards an expansion of municipal welfare provision and towards a socialist local economy. Thus local Labour persevered in its wartime campaign, despite the obstruction and defeats, and even continued its efforts after the war, despite the much less favourable climate of opinion.[61]

Why, then, was opposition to the setting up of a British Restaurant in Scarborough so determined? Financial considerations were uppermost in many minds. Month after month it was pointed out by senior councillors that such an institution in Scarborough would not be financially viable and that elsewhere, in Sheffield, Hull, Rotherham and Manchester, for example, British Restaurants were running into financial difficulties.[62] Moreover, opponents could not be persuaded that there was any need for them. Local emergency feeding arrangements were in place to support survivors of bomb-damaged properties. There was not a large number of industrial workers in the town who would benefit from the new restaurants, and those that there were, were served adequately by factory canteens.[63] British Restaurants, it was also added, would provide unfair competition for hard-pressed local caterers by monopolising supplies and subsidising prices.[64] The Council's Cafés Committee tried to operate on the principle that it would not run a municipal enterprise that was in direct competition with a local business.[65]

In 1946 the medical journal, *The Lancet*, was among those who viewed British Restaurants as a way of contributing to the transformation of society after the war: 'All of us with a social conscience will wish for a continuance of this service with its possibilities of furthering the health, fitness, and democratic education of our citizens.'[66] However, the ruling groups in Scarborough, in the Town Hall, the press and the business community, were committed to preserving free enterprise in a market economy. A British Restaurant was perceived as a threat to this and as a dangerous socialist experiment. Though the Corporation owned and ran a range of economic undertakings, this was done in the spirit of 'municipal capitalism', to generate a profit and to support other private enterprises in the resort.[67] Such was the weight of the free market lobby in Scarborough that this wartime experiment in communal catering was deemed unacceptable in war and in peace.

Fuel and Transport

Throughout the war there were serious shortages of fuel for transport and domestic purposes. In 1942 the situation was especially critical. Scarborough experienced severe winter weather in the early months and shortages of domestic fuel, notably of coal. In March the government withdrew the petrol ration for all recreational or unnecessary motoring. At the end of June the Ministry of Fuel and Power launched a campaign to encourage the public to cut fuel consumption further and help save fuel for the winter months.[68] Local children in Scarborough took to collecting firewood in nearby woods.[69] There were discussions about the possibility of digging for untapped sources of coal in the local area and of removing peat from the nearby North Yorkshire Moors.[70] Owners of commercial vehicles were instructed by the government to control fuel consumption by sharing journeys with other operators and by ensuring vehicles were filled to the maximum for all journeys. Shoppers were encouraged to avoid deliveries, to carry their shopping home with them wherever possible and to buy in bulk when deliveries were unavoidable.[71] Cycling enjoyed an 'enforced popularity', though some Scarborough riders appeared to have had only a hazy knowledge of the highway code.[72] Private car use incurred particular resentment in the town, townsfolk condemning motorists for making unnecessary journeys and for driving on regular bus routes.[73] One local, employing the pseudonym 'Vigilant', took it upon himself/herself to report such motorists directly to the Ministry of Transport.[74]

The Scarborough buses were particularly badly hit by the fuel crisis. Fuel restrictions and a shortage of drivers had already brought about cuts in bus services, but further drastic cuts in autumn 1942 generated further problems. The General Manager of United Automobiles Services reported in January 1943 that services had been cut by 35% at a time when demand was increasing.[75] As buses became less frequent, anxious crowds gathered at bus stops, forming themselves, in the wartime habit, into queues. There were, however, regular complaints about 'queue crashers' and it was unclear whether some passengers had a priority on the buses, those in uniform or shift workers, for example.[76] By later in 1942 there was mounting anger over the overcrowding on buses, overcrowding which some deemed dangerous.[77] Seats were removed to create more standing room, but the result was greater discomfort for all. Such conditions strained relationships between bus company staff and passengers. By 1942 female conductresses, or "clippies", had replaced males. The work was challenging, dealing with impatient queues and over-crowded buses, at times in near darkness. Some appear to have lacked the patience and diplomacy that comes with experience, finding it difficult to manage tired or irate passengers. It was reported by some unhappy customers that conductresses were 'uncivil', 'surly', 'rude' or 'insolent'.[78] There were allegations that power had gone to the heads of some clippies, who swore at passengers and exercised favouritism in dealing with queues.[79] Passengers were, of course, partly to blame for some of the tensions that arose. The weariness induced by life on the home front in the middle years of the war could make them awkward customers on a bus service that was being stretched to breaking point. There is also some evidence that fare-dodgers tried to take advantage of inexperienced staff and overcrowded buses.[80] In the spring of 1943, a further round of cuts was introduced, the strain on the bus services becoming increasingly intolerable.[81] In the summer of 1943, for example, a conductress was slapped by a passenger, who was subsequently convicted of assault.[82] A Scarborough mother summed up the plaintive feelings of some passengers about the bus company staff: 'They may be tired, but aren't we all.'[83] Problems persisted in 1944. In August, for instance, a passenger appeared in the Borough Police Court for deliberately bumping into the bus driver, who had been summoned by the conductress when she was unable to persuade passengers to move up to make more room for new passengers. The accused had recently been discharged from the navy and was accused of using 'filthy and naval language'.[84] The same year, in a rather desperate appeal to the patriotic goodwill of customers, the bus company resorted to rhyming couplets:

Eliza Jane – she had a dream
Of buses in a constant stream,
With seats to spare and never a queue
Alas, poor Eliza awoke and knew,
That while men fought, they couldn't
Drive her

So, no men – no buses – no seat for
Eliza.[85]

Like local bus services, the country's rail system was put under enormous pressure in wartime. During the war over a third of a million special trains were used for the armed forces alone, goods traffic rose by 50% and passenger traffic by 70%.[86] Scarborough, of course, had to contend with extra holiday traffic at peak periods. On the morning of 10 August 1943, the outgoing train for Hull was waiting at platform 5, the front compartment reserved for soldiers of the Royal Ulster Rifles. The signalman directed the incoming train from Hull to the same platform. It collided with the waiting train, concertinaing the first four compartments. Four soldiers were killed and 31 others, mostly soldiers, were injured. A soldier described a scene of horror, worse than he had seen on the battlefield. Trapped passengers were scolded by the heat and steam of the train engine and the screams were 'terrible' to hear.[87] The consequences might have been worse had it not been for the swift response of the wartime emergency services, including ARP and AFS personnel. At the inquest in September the experienced signalman took full responsibility for the tragedy, confessing that he was 'deeply grieved and sorry'. He denied that he was tired or over-worked, concluding, 'I am unable to say what caused me to do this.' It is not unreasonable to suggest, however, that wartime reductions in maintenance and improvements and the increased volume of traffic on the system should be taken into account in trying to explain the accident. Indeed, the Ministry of Transport Inquiry referred to an increase in rail traffic at Scarborough over recent years and to the antiquated signalling system as possible contributory causes. It concluded its official report with the following observations:

Owing to the short approach view, the driver was unable to avoid the collision. Track circuits on the platform lines, locking the relevant incoming signal levers, would also have prevented the accident; reconstruction will be undertaken at the first suitable opportunity, including the provision of colour light signalling and appropriate safeguards.[88]

Wartime changes, therefore, imposed considerable strains on the rhythms of everyday life. The bus and railway systems struggled to cope with wartime pressures. Whilst the system of food rationing functioned well, diets could be paltry and monotonous. People tried to alleviate the hardships of rationing by 'digging for victory', foraging for food or dipping into the black market. There would, however, be no welfare novelties in Scarborough, such as a British Restaurant. The majority opinion on the council believed in individual self-reliance and in protecting a local market economy as much as possible, both in wartime and under the post-war Labour government.

Notes

1. Paul Addison, *The Road to 1945* (London, 1975), p.161.
2. *SEN*, 27 February 1943.
3. *SEN*, 30 August 1943.
4. Jack Binns, *The History of Scarborough, North Yorkshire* (Pickering, 2001), p.364.
5. *Mercury* 13 July 1945.
6. For the local fishing industry see Chapt.9.
7. *SEN*, 12 August 1942.
8. http://smhc.hqtdevelopment.co.uk/article.php?article=676 (accessed 12 October 2019).
9. Christopher Wiseman, *36 Cornelian Avenue* (Montreal, 2008), p.18.
10. Ibid., p.18.
11. Ibid., p.29.
12. Ibid., p.29.
13. *SEN*, 13 April 1942.
14. *SEN*, 12 October 1940.
15. Paul C. Bang, *North Cliff Golf Club Scarborough* (York, 2015), p.48 and *SEN*, 16 May 1942 and 28 August 1943.
16. *SEN*, 20 February 1946.
17. *SEN*, 29 September 1942.
18. *SEN*, 21 April 1942.
19. *SEN*, 12 September 1941.
20. *SEN*, 10 March 1942.
21. *SEN*, 22 May and 27 August 1940.
22. *SEN*, 28 August 1943.
23. *SEN*, 19 August 1942.
24. *SEN*, 27 May 1942.
25. Quoted in Franklin Ginn, 'Dig for Victory: New histories of wartime gardening in Britain', *Journal of Historical Geography*, 38 (2012), p.300.
26. *SEN*, 29 July 1941 and 4 May 1942.
27. *SEN*, 1 August 1942.
28. *SEN*, 13 June 1942.
29. *SEN*, 7 December 1942.
30. David Fowler, *God Bless the Prince of Wales* (Scarborough, 2008), p.39.
31. *SEN*, 22 October 1942.
32. H.W. Marsden, *The Westwood School at Scarborough: Jubilee, 1902-1952*.
33. *SEN*, 11 May 1943.

34 Terry Baker, *A Merry Dance: Tales of a Scarborough Lad from the 'Bottom End' of Town* (Richmond, 2010), p.15.
35 *SEN*, 23 November 1942.
36 *Mercury*, 18 December 1942.
37 David Fowler, *I've started so I'll finish…A Memoir* (Scarborough, 2017), p.67.
38 Wiseman, op. cit., p.43.
39 *SEN*, 21 April 1942.
40 *SEN*, 18 May 1943.
41 *SEN*, 18 May 1943.
42 R.J. Hammond, *Food, Vol II, Studies in Administration and Control* (HMSO, 1956), pp. 38 and 383.
43 Ibid., p.385.
44 Ibid., p.393.
45 Ibid., p.399.
46 Ibid., p.410.
47 *Mercury*, 12 June 1942.
48 *Mercury*, 27 February 1942.
49 *SEN*, 5 May 1942.
50 *Mercury*, 1 October 1943.
51 *SEN*, 5 October 1943.
52 *SEN*, 5 October 1943.
53 *Mercury*, 11 February 1944.
54 *SEN*, 9 May 1944.
55 *SEN*, 9 May 1944.
56 Letter, *SEN*, 22 March 1943.
57 *SEN*, 9 June 1942.
58 *The Times*, 16 August 1943.
59 *SEN*, 10 and 27 February 1942, *SEN*, 16 June 1942.
60 See Bryan Keith-Lucas and Peter G. Richards, *A History of Local Government in the Twentieth Century* (London, 1978), pp.38-39.
61 *SEN*, 7 May 1946.
62 See, for example, *Mercury*, 4 December 1942.
63 *SEN*, 16 June 1942 and *Mercury*, 27 February 1942.
64 *Mercury*, 15 October 1943.
65 *Mercury*, 22 October 1943.
66 *The Lancet*, 23 March 1946, p.426.
67 On 'municipal capitalism' see John K. Walton, *The British Seaside* (Manchester, 2000), p.170.

68 Siân Nicholas, *The Echo of War* (Manchester, 1996), p.85.
69 *SEN*, 22 April 1942.
70 *SEN*, 15 October 1942.
71 *Mercury,* 23 January 1942.
72 *SEN*, 10 September 1942.
73 *Mercury,* 23 October 1942.
74 Letter, *SEN*, 10 October 1942.
75 *SEN*, 27 January 1943.
76 *SEN*, 1 September and 28 December 1942.
77 *Mercury,* 29 January 1943.
78 See, for example letters, *SEN*, 28 December 1942 and 8 June 1943.
79 *SEN*, 1 September 1942.
80 *SEN*, 8 June 1943.
81 *SEN*, 27 January and *Mercury* 5 March 1943.
82 *Mercury,* 30 July 1943.
83 *SEN*, 17 July 1943.
84 *SEN*, 12 August 1944.
85 Quoted in *SEN*, 4 May 1995.
86 Robert MacKay, *The Test of War* (London, 1999), pp.174-75.
87 Souvenir of the War in Scarborough and the Surrounding Area, unpublished diary of George W. Birley, n.d. p.84.
88 For the 1943 crash see NA RAIL 1053/129/1 and *SEN,* 10,11,12,18,20 August, 15,16 September 1943 and *Mercury,* 13 August 1943.

CHAPTER 16

'Don't You Know There's a War On?'

We must root out all selfishness, for it is destructive of community life. The power to achieve victory does not lie primarily in money, men or machinery but in the enthusiasm and will to accept total responsibility with total sacrifice – to give and not to count the cost.

(Canon A. Linwood Wright, *Leicester Evening Mail*, 30 September 1941)[1]

Wartime Puritanism

The war years were a time of considerable austerity and self-sacrifice in Scarborough. Despite many strains, the community pulled together to an impressive extent and remained conscious of the greater sacrifices being made in the country's bombed ports and cities and by those serving in the armed forces. At the same time, there was a tendency to point fingers at those who, it was felt, were not pulling their weight or were falling short of the patriotic standards expected of them. Some of this fed on traditions of scepticism about the motivations of local politicians. The local press celebrated the cycling Chief Constable, whilst condemning the use of official cars by councillors in a time of fuel economy.[2] Jottings, in the *Mercury*, always with a nose for municipal backsliding and double standards, attacked the Council for sending an empty official car 70 miles to pick someone up, when the journey could have been done by train.[3] In March 1943 the *Mercury* reported 'daily attacks' on the Council for its profligate car use.[4] Similarly, Council habits of hospitality came under scrutiny. In August 1942 the Council was taken to task for providing expensive cocktails at the presentation of an emergency canteen from Canada.[5] When a new school (Scalby) was opened later in the month, councillors were criticised for the extravagance of their civic lunch and refreshments.[6] By the autumn the Town Hall seemed to be adapting to the spartan spirit of the times, as the first female mayor was installed in an 'Austerity Ceremony' devoid of the usual floral display and refreshments.[7]

Those who were especially proud of their belt-tightening and self-denial found the irresponsibility of others galling. Letters to the press in the summer of 1942 complained about youngsters who were wasting their time, and valuable electrical power, in pinball saloons.[8] Questions were asked about the use of electricity to illuminate women's fashions in shop windows and about the use of taxis for shopping whilst merchant seamen risked their lives to bring fuel to the country.[9] Instead, a stoical acceptance of clothes and footwear rationing, and of wartime utility fashion, was recommended. Extravagance and waste were particularly resented when it seemed to some to be accompanied by dubious moral behaviour. Puritanically-minded Scarborians spoke out against extended pub and saloon licenses, the waste of lighting and heating at late night dancing and the use of late-night taxis after such events.[10]

'Good-time girls'?

Against a backdrop of patriotic self-sacrifice and community privation, there was a tendency in some quarters to pass judgement on young women in Scarborough who were deemed to be letting the country down. Whilst the majority made what contributions they could to the war effort, there was a minority in the community, it was suggested, who saw the war as an opportunity to have a good time. The condemnations in Scarborough in 1942 coincided with a frenzy in the national press about the irresponsible behaviour of young women. The newspapers, according to Sonya Rose, were 'fuelling the panic by exciting both outrage and prurient attention'.[11] The alleged sins of Scarborough women were manifold: sexual laxity, eating chocolate, smoking, drinking, 'spilling out of pubs', car driving for recreation, squandering money and frequenting cafés, cinemas and dances.[12] One newspaper letter-writer accused some young women of 'eating, drinking and smoking themselves through a thoroughly good war'.[13] 'Will nothing,' demanded Jottings, 'shame this small batch of youngsters from idling their time away?'[14] Scarborough's dance culture was the target of much moralistic censure, and young local women were seen to be especially vulnerable to its corrupting influences. It was diverting their energies away from the war effort and, according to a correspondent in the local paper, promoting 'selfish pleasure'.[15] To another letter-writer, dances posed a threat to young women's 'health, morals and efficiency'.[16] Jottings expressed concern that girls as young as 14 were participating in such inappropriate recreation.[17] The moral dangers of wartime dances were exacerbated, according to some, by corrupting American dancing styles like the jitterbug. Older residents, it was reported, regarded such exertion as 'a sort of all-in-wrestling-cum-apache display'.[18] Such wartime condemnations of 'good time girls' were common at the time, and were part of an ideological effort to reinforce in young women the feminine virtues of modesty, self-restraint and abstinence in wartime.[19]

Allied to concerns about wartime dances was the wider disapproval of local women fraternising with the military. Some people feared that the morals of young women were being put at risk by the presence of so many young men in the town and surrounding area. Such concerns were echoed by the wife of the Bishop of Selby who gave a talk to the Scarborough and District Moral Welfare Society. She lamented the vulnerability of local girls who not only attended dances but 'hung around' army camps, warning of the difficulties that were arising from this. Servicemen were suspected of winning favour from local women by various means. They supplied cigarettes and other black market goods 'off the back of lorries' and provided social companionship and drinks in local pubs and dances.[20] Young Scarborough women had a predilection, it was claimed, for cocktails.[21] Such fraternisation was liable to be abused. An RAF corporal based in the town met two girls at an amusement arcade. Taking them to a pub, one of the two, a 15-year-old, consumed a half pint of beer, five whiskies and some rum, then collapsed. In court, the corporal claimed that he thought the girls were older.[22] Soldiers billeted in the town were not always what they appeared to be. One local woman married a soldier, only to find that he was already married with a family of six. It would have been better to check with his commanding officer before entering such a matrimonial commitment was the advice from the judicial bench.[23]

Nationally, the war saw some loosening of traditional standards of sexual behaviour. There were several reasons for such a change: the decline in family discipline, the expanding role of women outside the home, marital separation and a 'live-for-the-moment' reaction to wartime dangers. Among the social consequences were an increased incidence of venereal disease, a rising divorce rate and more 'illegitimate' births towards the end of the war. It seems, though, that the notion of a wartime breakdown in family values was an exaggerated worry, ignoring, for example, the wartime popularity of marriage.[24] It is difficult to know how typical Scarborough was of national trends. There were certainly concerns about rising levels of illegitimacy. Scarborough's Medical Officer of Health reported in 1942 that the percentage of illegitimate births was 15%, when the previous highest had been 13% during World War One.[25] A conference was held in November 1943 to discuss the problem in North Yorkshire, resulting in the establishment of a joint committee for safeguarding the welfare of illegitimate children and their mothers.[26] In Scarborough, the local branch of Moral Welfare, which supported single mothers, recognised the challenges posed by the social disruption of wartime and appealed for more financial support.[27] The figures from an annual meeting of Moral Welfare's St Margaret's Home give a pointer to the scale of the problem in Scarborough. As a home for single mothers, in the 1943-44 year it took in 49 adults, three children under 16 and 36 babies.[28] Isolated incidents in the town are also suggestive of the potential for personal tragedy inherent wartime social changes. In May 1943 the body of a new-born baby was found in Valley Gardens. The child had lived for some 10 days before being abandoned.[29] In June 1941 a Scarborough women was jailed for three years for illegally performing an abortion on a 17-year-old Filey girl. The girl died of septicaemia.[30] In March 1944 another local woman was found guilty of performing an abortion. Her client was a widow whose husband had died in Burma the previous year and a soldier stationed in the town paid for the abortion.[31] Yet such fragmentary reports in the press, which failed to take into account pre-war trends, are not sufficient to enable the case to be made for a significant rejection of conventional sexual morals in wartime Scarborough.

In 1943 there was another tragic case which was widely attributed to the moral dislocation of wartime. On 22 March a ten-year-old boy and his two young brothers entered a disused bus station in Vine Street, near the centre of the town. It had been vacated by the army the previous day. He discovered the body of a woman lying face down in two to three inches of water and oil in an inspection pit. When he reported this to his mother, she refused to believe him, assuring him that it must have been a dummy. Two days later, the boy showed the body to a young girl, but only after she then brought an older boy to the scene were the police alerted. The victim was quickly identified, as she had been reported missing on the 22nd by her brother-in-law. She was 33- year-old Mrs Mary Comins, a grocery assistant with a husband serving in North Africa. A post-mortem concluded that she had received a fractured lower jaw and died of manual strangulation. From the start, the victim's relations with the military were seen as providing a key to the tragedy. 'The deceased,' the local paper reported knowingly a week after the murder, 'was seen a great deal in licensed premises and elsewhere in the company of soldiers.' When two senior detectives from Scotland Yard were bought into the investigation, they concentrated on possible suspects in the military. Mary Comins had spent the evening of her disappearance in the company of a female friend and two soldiers, 'Dick' and 'Jimmie'. The soldiers were located, interviewed and discounted as suspects. Subsequently, every serviceman stationed in Scarborough was questioned about their movements on the night of the murder. By early April the investigation had widened to the South of England, where some of the units from Scarborough had been transferred on or after the date of the murder. Altogether, approximately 2,000 men were interviewed, mostly from the Armed Forces. However, no arrests were ever made. All that is known is that she parted company with her friends around 10 p.m. on the Sunday night of March 21st. About an hour later she was seen talking to an unidentified man near her home and around midnight witnesses claimed to have heard screams in Vine Street. The official files on this case remain closed to the public. Some gossip at the time centred on a local man as the perpetrator.[32]

Youth 'Running Wild'

There were concerns that many of Scarborough's juveniles were 'running wild' in the town, showing a complete disregard for the law and respectable standards of behaviour. A rise in youthful bad behaviour prompted considerable discussion in 1940 and 1941, generating frequent references to a 'juvenile crime wave'.[33] This mirrored national concern. In the Manchester region there was such alarm that there was talk of imposing a night-time curfew on young people.[34] Although the scale of the problem was often exaggerated, in the manner of the 'moral panics' of adults, the official statistics in Scarborough indicate an escalation of the problem in the early years of the war.[35] The Chief Constable reported that proceedings against juveniles (under 17s) in Scarborough numbered 63 in 1938, 74 in 1939 and peaked at 113 in 1940, though falling back to 70 in 1941. Many of those proceeded against were, of course, responsible for more than one crime, the 70 proceeded against in 1941, for example, being responsible for 148 offences.[36] The tender age of many of the culprits is striking. When the local press featured the 'crime wave' in February 1941, of the 17 boys that had recently been charged, mostly for theft, the majority were under 12 years old.[37] The criminal behaviour of juveniles and older children remained a preoccupation of the press in Scarborough for the rest of the war.

Some explanations for such juvenile crime merely recycled pre-war anxieties. The courts, it was asserted, were too lenient, or the cinemas were having a corrupting influence on the youth of the country by glamorising crime and gang culture.[38] More persuasive explanations, however, located the problem in wartime developments in Scarborough. The faltering condition of the hospitality industry curtailed employment opportunities for the town's youngsters. Wartime circumstances created new opportunities for criminality: unprotected allotments and food shortages, the blackout, war-damaged properties, abandoned homes and businesses. However, the key reason for juvenile delinquency in wartime Scarborough, identified also in the rest of the country, was the breakdown in the levels of control exerted by parents over their children.[39] The absence of the father on military service, and the increased employment and public service opportunities for the mother, provided youngsters with unprecedented access to unsupervised freedom. This led to what the Chief Constable termed euphemistically 'an adventurous spirit', with the potential to develop into minor misdemeanours, gang delinquency and more serious criminality.[40]

Juvenile delinquency first began to attract public and press attention when the efforts of some Scarborians to 'dig for victory' were sabotaged by destructive thefts of fruit and vegetables from gardens and allotments. Some culprits were so emboldened that they carried off their spoils in handcarts and wheelbarrows. Others were known to have replanted potato plants once they had removed the crop to delay detection.[41] Thieves provoked particular annoyance when they took fruit and vegetables before they had fully ripened.[42] The reluctance of the courts to punish the perpetrators with swiftness and severity only heightened public annoyance, despite trespassing on allotments becoming a criminal offence in 1943.[43] Some patriotic gardeners became so frustrated that they pledged to abandon their horticultural efforts altogether.[44] Others resorted to robust defensive measures, one becoming so indignant that he tarred all the approaches to his private orchard.[45]

There were also angry complaints that youths, freed from adult supervision, were engaging in gratuitous cruelty towards local wildlife. Birds were dragged from their nests, catapults were fired at swans and ducks at the Mere and frogs were inflated, thrown in the air and left to burst on the ground.[46] Of course, misbehaving youngsters was hardly a new social phenomenon in the town.

The heartless mistreatment for frogs, for example, was something of an annual custom for wayward local boys.

Another product of too much freedom was vandalism. Young delinquents were responsible for mindless vandalism against all sorts of municipal property. Air raid shelters were an easy target, whilst windows and gas lamps provided further temptations. Even the cemetery was not spared.[47] When adult passers-by intervened to prevent damage to property, they could be met with expletive-filled hostility. Evacuee children were suspected of committing some of the vandalism, as it was felt that they lacked a sense of loyalty to the town. It is true evacuee children were involved in some juvenile delinquency, but their separation from parental influence was a more plausible reason for this. In a not untypical example in early 1941, three evacuee boys from West Hartlepool were tried for vandalising a Foreshore café. The impression was given that they had led astray an eight-year-old boy from their host family, who participated in the crime.[48]

The most common crimes committed by juveniles were thefts. Homes, shops and businesses were targeted, often under cover of the blackout. Those responsible for blackout robberies were sometimes likened to the *Luftwaffe* menace and referred to as 'Night Raiders'.[49] Air raids provided tempting opportunities for young criminals. There were, for example, instances of thefts from the gas meters of air raid damaged houses in 1940.[50] In 1941 two eleven-year-old boys were found guilty of looting a war damaged house. The penalty in some countries, warned the magistrate, was the firing squad.[51] A worrying development amongst the town's youth in the later stages of the war was the pilfering of dangerous materials from military supplies. Two boys, one 15 and the other 16, were bound over and fined in the Juvenile Court in April 1944 for stealing the following from an army store: 3 'Piat' bombs, 6 mortar bombs, 96 anti-tank gun cartridges, 6 electric detonators, 36 hand grenades, a box of primer detonators, 500 Sten Gun cartridges, 20 anti-tank grenades and another 2 boxes of hand grenades.[52] There were a number of similar, if smaller-scale, cases in the same year, when the equipping of the local Home Guard had reached its peak and the region, like the country as a whole, was inundated with weaponry destined for the Second Front in Europe. The dangers of such criminality were obvious. A gang of juveniles stole ammunition from a Home Guard store and hid it carelessly under a bramble bush.[53] Another group of boys purloined military explosives, including highly dangerous phosphorous incendiary bombs.[54] A 12-year-old stole 12 canisters of explosives from a Home

Guard store that had been left open. He took three to school and gave them to friends.[55] A military detonator injured a Newby boy when it was given to him at school.[56] This combination of criminal opportunism and a boyish fascination with all things military posed a real risk to both young people and the public. The root of the problem was, perhaps, identified by one youth, who confessed in the Borough Police Court: 'I take too much interest in explosives, I am afraid.'[57]

The most common misdemeanours in wartime were often associated with juvenile gangs. Public concern was expressed in letters to the local press lamenting the rise of juvenile bad language, drunkenness, vandalism and other crimes arising from gang culture.[58] The poet Christopher Wiseman provides some insight into the psychology of wartime gang membership in Scarborough. He remembers the freedom from parental control he enjoyed as a young evacuee. Pressurised into joining a local gang, he participated in low-level violence against a rival group. They, he was assured, 'were dirty and mean like Germans'.[59] Gang members egged each other on to behaviour they would not consider engaging in on their own. Reckless bravado was exhibited by gang members who climbed up on washed up sea mines. Some behaviour reported by the press was distinctly menacing and dangerous. Groups of youths were reported to be amusing themselves by hurling missiles at buses on Barrowcliff Road.[60] When a local gang felt slighted by a local shopkeeper in another part of town, they barricaded the shop against customers and terrorised the female shop assistant.[61] In a further disturbing episode, a gang of locals joined battle with a group of evacuees, hurling wood and bricks against each other.[62]

Whilst the majority of young people remained responsible and law-abiding, there were undoubtedly developments in the war years that had the effect of exacerbating delinquency. Tom Johnston, the wartime Secretary of State for Scotland, had a sympathetic appreciation of the ways in which the wartime environment could foster unwanted juvenile behaviour:

> The anxiety and the excitement of the times produces a restlessness which may itself lead to mischief-making, and the destructive instincts aroused by war may also tempt adventurous youths to misguided actions.[63]

The war, then, witnessed some selfish, destructive and antisocial behaviour in Scarborough. It is difficult to quantify how much of this there was. The local press and respectable opinion in the town were probably prone to exaggerating such problems by talking up the 'crime wave' and the misdeeds of young women. It is easy to sympathise with the selfless and patriotic majority which was so exasperated by the irresponsibility of others. It is perhaps also easier now to understand the errant behaviour of those who grew up in the strained and disordered circumstances of the Home Front.

Notes

1. Quoted in Sonya O. Rose, *Which People's War?* (Oxford, 2003), p.71.
2. *SEN*, 8 September 1942.
3. *Mercury,* 31 July 1942.
4. *Mercury,* 19 March 1943.
5. *Mercury,* 14 August 1942.
6. *Mercury,* 28 August *1942.*
7. *SEN*, 9 November 1942.
8. *SEN*, 23 July 1942.
9. *SEN*, 25 July and 2 September 1942.
10. For example, *Mercury,* 28 August 1942.
11. Sonya O. Rose, 'Girls and GIs: Race, Sex and Diplomacy in Second World War Britain', *The International History Review*, 19:1, 1997, p.147.
12. For example, letter, *SEN*, 18 April 1942.
13. Letter, *SEN*, 18 April 1942.
14. *Mercury,* 24 April 1942.
15. *SEN*, 17 September 1942.
16. *SEN*, 15 October 1942.
17. *Mercury,* 24 April 1942.
18. *SEN*, 15 April 1943.
19. Sonya O. Rose, *Which People's War?* (Oxford, 2003), p.83-89.
20. *SEN*, 22 April 1942.
21. *Mercury,* 17 April 1942.
22. *SEN*, 13 April 1942.
23. *SEN*, 24 April 1944.
24. Geoffrey G. Field, *Blood, Sweat and Toil: Remaking the British Working Class, 1939-1945* (Oxford, 2013), pp.201-207.
25. Jack Binns, *The History of Scarborough, North Yorkshire* (Pickering, 2001), p.364
26. *SEN*, 6 January 1944.
27. *SEN*, 26 May 1943.
28. *Mercury,* 5 May 1944.
29. *SEN*, 10 May 1943.
30. *SEN,* 10 and 26 June 1941.
31. *SEN*, 27 March 1944.
32. For the Comins Murder see *SEN*, 30,31 March and 8 May 1943, *SEN*, 23 March 1944 and Alan Whitworth, *Foul Deeds and Suspicious Deaths on the Yorkshire Coast* (Barnsley, 2001), pp. 167-170.

33 See, for example, *SEN* and *Mercury,* February and July 1941, passim.
34 Clive Emsley, *Crime and Society in Twentieth Century England* (London, 2011), p.67.
35 For 'moral panics' see Stanley Cohen, *Folk Devils and Moral Panics* (Routledge, 2002).
36 See Chief Constable's Reports *SEN*, 26 February 1941 and *SEN*, 9 February 1942.
37 *SEN,* 26 February 1941.
38 Chief Constable's Report, *SEN*, 9 February 1942.
39 Victor Bailey, *Delinquency and Citizenship: Reclaiming the Young Offender, 1914-48* (Oxford, 1987), p.270.
40 Chief Constable's Report, *SEN*, 9 February 1942.
41 *SEN*, 5 August 1941.
42 *SEN*, 27 July 1940 and SEN 3 December 1940.
43 *SEN*, 26 September 1943.
44 *Mercury,* 2 August and SEN 8 August 1940.
45 *SEN*, 23 June 1942.
46 *SEN*, 1,5 and 7 July 1941.
47 For example, *SEN*, 26 July and 7 August 1941, 28 March and 27 October 1942, and *Mercury*, 21 January 1944.
48 *SEN*, 26 February 1941.
49 *SEN*, 18 November 1940.
50 *SEN*, 23 October 1940.
51 *SEN*, 2 July 1941.
52 *SEN*, 25 April 1944.
53 *SEN*, 9 October 1944.
54 *SEN*, 1 May 1944.
55 *SEN*, 16 November 1944.
56 *Mercury,* 28 April 1944.
57 *SEN*, 9 October 1944.
58 For example, *SEN*, 23 and 24 November 1942.
59 Christopher Wiseman, *36 Cornelian Avenue* (Montreal Canada, 2008), p.36.
60 *SEN*, 26 August 1942.
61 *SEN*, 20 May 1942.
62 *SEN*, 17 June 1942.
63 Quoted in David Smith, 'Official Responses to Juvenile Delinquency in Scotland during the Second World War', *Twentieth Century British History*, Vol.18, No.1, 2007, p.86.

CHAPTER 17

End of War Tourism: 1944-1945

As the war progressed, with the fear of invasion receding and cash accumulating in the pockets of munitions workers and others, it became ever harder to pretend that families were happy to forgo holidays away from home. By 1944, the sense of 'backs to the wall' urgency was unsustainable ...[1]

Tourism 1944

It was widely appreciated that Scarborough's recovery to economic health depended on a renewal of the tourist economy. As we have seen, 1943 witnessed a reassuring revival of tourism in the resort.[2] In 1944 there were some developments that were favourable to a further upturn. Visitors found a resort that was slowly beginning to return to a peacetime appearance. The removal of some roadblocks and anti-invasion obstacles had been commenced and access to more of the town's beaches had been granted.[3] 1944 also saw the derequisitioning of a few smaller hotels and boarding houses. That many holidaymakers were determined to get to the coast despite the obstacles to travel, ensured that there was no return to the economic doldrums of the early war years. On Whitsun Saturday, amid a heatwave, over 6,000 arrived by train, only 1,000 down on the 1943 recovery. Those who arrived in 1944 seem to have had plenty of money to spend.[4] Council receipts were nearly as good as those of 1943, boosted as they were by price increases and the profitable rental of deckchairs on reclaimed areas of beach.

However, in 1944 Scarborough found it difficult to build on the success of 1943. Recovery remained constrained by the impact of the launching of D-Day and the Allied Second Front in Europe. The Second Front required the government to impose further restrictions on rail travel, as trains were needed to transport troops and supplies before, during and after the June D-Day landings in France. Rail support for the invasion also included special ambulance and POW train services.[5] Scarborough was adversely affected by such travel uncertainties. A conference of sub-postmasters in May was much smaller than expected because of the difficulties of travel from Ireland and the south of England.[6] Though many holidaymakers did arrive in Scarborough for the Whitsun holiday, few travelled from outside Yorkshire, and a high proportion came from Leeds.[7] The Minister of Transport warned in early July that 'military contingencies' were likely to result in further cuts in services nationally.[8] Enjoying the August Bank Holiday in Scarborough, therefore, required no little determination. Those trains that were running were packed full, whilst some passengers were stranded at York, unable to get to the coast.[9] Long queues formed outside the station for returning trains. Restaurants, cafés and pubs endured shortages of supplies.[10]

D-Day made it impossible, then, to take full advantage of the surge in demand for holidays as the war appeared to be nearing its end. But the continuing popularity of seaside holidays provided some reassurance for those with an interest in tourism.

Tourism 1945

In 1945 the holiday season in Scarborough took place against the backdrop of approaching military victory and, finally, the end of the war in Europe. To what extent was the resort prepared for a return to peacetime holidaymaking? The shortages of supplies and labour were now becoming a serious problem for pleasure resorts. Hotels and boarding houses found themselves without essential supplies like cutlery, furniture and bed linen. Some owners had sold equipment during the war due to financial difficulties, whilst other supplies disappeared in the process of requisitioning or storage.[11] At the end of the war a quarter of the country's manpower was in the armed services, and there was an urgent need to get labour into agriculture, coal and textiles. Tourism was not a priority.[12] Labour shortages in Scarborough, along with shortages of building materials, handicapped municipal and private efforts to revive the peace-time amenities available to holidaymakers. The Council, for example, could only partially reintroduce its profitable deck-chair rental due to staff shortages.[13] Only six of the Council's smaller shops and cafés operated throughout the summer, out of a maximum of two dozen.[14] Councillor Cumberbirch sympathised with visitors to the town, who were 'invited to the seaside and unable to get a cup of tea'.[15] The inevitable impact of such a labour shortage, moreover, was rising staff wages. One employer found himself hiring the same waitress on three separate occasions, having to pay 10s. a week more each time.[16] Yet the Ministry of Labour intimated to the country's pleasure resorts at the end of June that there was little that could be done to release labour for at least the next six to nine months.[17]

One businessman who was far from defeatist about labour shortages was Billy Butlin. His new holiday camp near Scarborough had been requisitioned by the RAF at the beginning of the war before it had had the chance to open. When the camp was derequisitioned in May 1945 he persuaded the RAF to deploy some of its personnel in preparing the camp for opening at the beginning of June. He then offered cut-price 'camper-holidays' for those who were prepared to combine their holiday with helping to run the camp. Butlin's commercial manoeuvring provoked some envy and resentment in Scarborough.[18] When the town's MP raised the issue of Butlin's employment of RAF personnel in Parliament, he was lamely reassured that the servicemen had volunteered without official permission, and that it would not happen again.[19]

Derequisitioning of properties by the armed forces remained a bone of contention. There was some progress in derequisitioning hotels and boarding houses in late 1944 and 1945. In spring 1945, about 50 smaller premises were released.[20] However, there continued to be immense frustration at the slowness of the process, especially galling as many requisitioned properties remained empty or half empty.[21] To compound the sense of injustice, some RAF properties that were derequisitioned were then 're-requisitioned' by the War Office, which insisted that it still needed large hotels.[22] Requisitioned properties were invariably treated badly by their wartime tenants. In one, for example, derequisitioning exposed extensive damage. 40 wash hand basins were broken, as were many cisterns and lavatories, whilst ceilings and walls were covered in diagrams. An iron ladder had been run through the floors from the top to the bottom of the building.[23] It was not uncommon for floorboards to be missing from RAF requisitioned hotels, where trainees in the Training Wings used them in the winter to heat their rooms.[24] Repairs and restoration were made difficult because of shortages of labour and materials. It therefore took a significant period between re-possessing a property and re-opening for business. The government made some *ex gratia* payments available to cover this period, but hoteliers often felt that the time covered was inadequate. Scarborough's MP was active in championing the cause of hoteliers in Whitehall and Parliament. Many were 'small men', he protested, who had borrowed money to establish modest hotels and boarding houses in the town and were unable to take on the might of government departments.[25]

The shortage of accommodation in Scarborough made it difficult for the town to take full advantage of the increasing tourist demand in 1945. In early July a honeymoon couple exemplified the problem. Finding no accommodation, they first pleaded with the Police to find them a cell for the night. Rebuffed, they spent their wedding night in an air-raid shelter with eighteen other people.[26] With rooms for visitors at such a premium, reports arose of 'excessive charging' and of the provision of sub-standard, unsuitable and overcrowded accommodation in the resort.[27] It was felt on the Council's Publicity Committee that the accommodation situation 'could make or break the town's reputation.'[28] At the end of the season, the Council's Sanitary Inspector was instructed to make enquiries into the hosting of visitors in unsuitable accommodation.[29]

Following the end of the war in Europe in May 1945, and of the war against Japan in August, Britain's seaside resorts saw record crowds of holidaymakers arriving.[30] Despite the difficulties that the resorts were facing, people were keen to return to peacetime habits and to compensate themselves for the sacrifices of the war years. Easter 1945 came early in April. The end of the war in Europe was within sight, British troops having crossed the Rhine in late March. In Scarborough there was some satisfaction at Easter that more peacetime amenities were being restored. Inshore rowing boats reappeared in the South Bay, prohibitions on pleasure sailing were relaxed and some ninety beach bungalows were reinstated. The availability of accommodation increased, due to an acceleration of government derequisitioning. There was further relief at Easter that the demand for visits to the seaside continued to increase. All the available accommodation was reserved prior to the Easter weekend. The trains were overflowing, with some passengers crowded into brake vans. Despite poor weather, the Foreshore in South Bay was very busy for most of the weekend.[31] Overall, the 1945 Easter week witnessed some 6,000 more visitors than the previous Easter and surpassed any previous Easter of the war.[32] A Cooperative Party conference at the Olympia Ballroom brought a further 800 delegates to the town.[33] Surprisingly, municipal receipts for Easter were down on the previous year's, despite the substantial increase in visitor numbers. Poor weather had hit spending and manpower shortages kept many municipal cafés closed.[34] In general, though, there was considerable satisfaction with the resort's fortunes over Easter. The town seemed to be recovering more quickly than some rival resorts and, with the approaching defeat of Nazism, optimism grew about the resort's post-war prospects.[35]

Whitsun 1945 was the first holiday to take place after the war in Europe had ended. Seaside resorts in Britain enjoyed a bumper recovery. Scarborough continued to restore its peacetime facilities. The Council reopened its miniature golf and its highly profitable miniature railway, whilst local boatmen were greatly in demand for pleasure trips, 'after six years on land'. The transformation was assisted by the reopening of the Spa ballroom and concert facilities after wartime requisitioning. The return of the Spa was a symbolic moment for many residents and tourists, 'battle scarred though it may be', as one local lamented.[36]

The Spa in its post-war splendour, looking across the South Bay.

Visitors arrived in numbers reminiscent of the 1930s. Hundreds had to be turned away from dances at the Spa.[37] Also popular were the Peasholm Park concerts and the Olympia Ballroom, the latter attracting 1,200 customers on

Whit Sunday. Visitors on the Whit weekend were 70% up on the previous year, more than those for the record-breaking Easter of the previous month. The Corporation's takings (£1,891) were the highest Whit receipts of the war years. If the Corporation had had greater access to manpower to staff its amenities, it could have competed with some of the best peace-time years.[38] It was at this time that the local Women's Voluntary Service began to run into difficulties maintaining some of its voluntary commitments, like serving school dinners and collecting for National Savings. Volunteers were dropping out to take in paying guests and capitalise of the tourist surge. '(I)f they now felt that the time had come,' reflected the Centre Organiser, 'to earn some money after a very lean period, there was little I could do about it.'[39]

In the summer of 1945 it appeared that Scarborough was not only enjoying its most successful holiday period of the war but was surpassing some of the best pre-war seasons.[40] The bustle and crowds at the town's railway station were one symptom of this. In early July the station was compared to an 'overturned beehive'.[41] During peak periods in the summer it was not unusual for holidaymakers to spend the night at their home railway stations, before catching the early mail train to the coast. At the busiest times, relief trains were now more generously provided, 25 in one day on the August Bank holiday.[42] Trains invariably arrived in Scarborough crammed full, sometimes with 20 packed into a single compartment which would usually seat ten.[43] On some return trains, passengers were observed getting into crowded compartments through the windows, whilst outside the station there were usually long queues for taxicabs.[44] In August British soldiers and Italian Prisoners of War helped with the incoming luggage.[45] The police advised arriving passengers on accommodation, and a police patrol car with a loudspeaker tried to keep motorists, cyclists and pedestrians moving.[46] Throughout the summer there was a noticeable increase in the number of private cars and 'motor coaches' descending on the town.[47]

The seafront promenades quickly flooded with holidaymakers and large crowds thronged the beaches. Deck chairs were at a premium, long queues formed whenever ice-cream became available and donkeys reappeared on the beach.[48] Good summer weather boosted the demand for nearly 70 pleasure boats, and work for 100 men to sail them.[49] Yacht racing and tunny fishing recommenced.[50] Over 100,000 were attracted to concerts at the Spa over the summer. A major trade union (the National Union of Railwaymen) held its annual conference in the town at the beginning of July and, in another encouraging sign of the resort's return to normality, a cricket festival was held at the end of August, albeit a pared-down one.[51]

Scarborough fishermen taking advantage of the tourist boom in 1945 (Historic England Archive).

The number of visitors in June and July was remarkable. Train arrivals for June were estimated to be 135,000, and for July 178,000. Such numbers far exceeded the 1944 figures and surpassed those of 1938 and 1939.[52] Indeed, it was suggested that the June figures outdid those of the exceptionally good year of 1933.[53] The August numbers were equally pleasing. On the Bank Holiday Saturday, for example, nearly 19,000 visitors arrived at the railway station.[54] In August, overall, there were nearly 182,000 arrivals, down only slightly on the record-breaking August of 1939.[55] This was more than compensated for by an unprecedentedly busy September. The overall number of arrivals by train in September was about 125,000, a spectacular increase in both peacetime and wartime figures.[56] Between May and September inclusive, visitor numbers were estimated to be 137,000 greater than the same period in 1938.[57]

Corporation receipts naturally soared above wartime levels. Revenues from Entertainments and Cafés from 1st April to July 21st (excluding the Easter weekend) were nearly £40,000. In 1944 they had only been in the region of £16,000.[58] Receipts until 13 October 1945 came to £102,624, up by £55,000 on the previous year.[59] The Corporation had never had such a profitable season in the past. The miniature railway was the most profitable municipal enterprise, followed by the North Bay Pool and the Olympia Ballroom.[60]

Overall, then, the summer of 1945 marked a return to peace and prosperity in Scarborough. It seems clear that the long bottled-up demand for a proper holiday outweighed the difficulties faced by holidaymakers during the resort's transition from war to peace. Some of the more distant customers may have been put off. Visitors from Yorkshire's industrial towns and cities, however, poured into Scarborough in large and profitable numbers.

South Bay beach cleared of anti-invasion defences and returned to peacetime appearances in 1945 (Historic England Archive).

Notes

1. Chris Sladen, 'Holidays at Home in the Second World War', *Journal of Contemporary History*, Vol.37, No.1 (Jan. 2002), p.87.
2. See pp.119-121.
3. *Mercury,* 18 February 1944.
4. *Mercury,* 14 April 1944.
5. *SEN*, 19 July 1944.
6. *SEN*, 15 May 1944.
7. *SEN*, 29 May 1944.
8. *SEN*, 5 July 1944.
9. *SEN*, 31 July 1944.
10. *SEN*, 6 July 1944.
11. NA HLG 71/773, Situation Report on Post-war Holiday Accommodation (24 October 1944) and LAB 11/1714, Report of the Catering Wages Commission on the Rehabilitation of the Catering Industry (1944).
12. Alec Cairncross, *Years of Recovery:* Britain's *Economic Policy, 1945-51* (London, 1985), p.385 and J.C.R. Dow, *The Management of the British Economy, 1945-60* (Cambridge, 1965), p.14.
13. *SEN*, 22 May 1945.
14. *SEN*, 21 May 1945.
15. *SEN*, 14 August 1945.
16. *SEN*, 21 May 1945.
17. *SEN*, 30 June 1945.
18. *SEN*, 24, 29 May and 13 June and *Mercury,* 1 June 1945.
19. HC Debs. Vol. 411, 12 June 1945, cols. 1445-6 and 1634.
20. *Mercury,* 18 May 1945.
21. *Mercury,* 11 May 1945.
22. *SEN*, 13 June 1945.
23. *Mercury,* 16 March 1945.
24. David Fowler, *God Bless the Prince of Wales* (Scarborough, 2009), p.221.
25. *SEN*, 4 March 1945.
26. *SEN*, 9 July 1945.
27. *SEN*, 1 August 1945.
28. *SEN*, 14 August 1945.
29. *SEN*, 6 September 1945.
30. James Walvin, *Beside the Seaside* (London, 1978), p.129.
31. *SEN*, 31 March 1945.
32. *SEN*, 2 April 1945.

33 *SEN*, 31 March 1945.
34 *SEN*, 4 April 1945.
35 See, for example, *Mercury*, 6 April 1945, Jottings.
36 *SEN*, 21 May 1945.
37 *SEN*, 21, 22 and 24 May 1945.
38 *SEN*, 21 and 23 May, 2 June and *Mercury*, 25 May 1945.
39 WVS, Narrative Report, Scarborough May 1945.
40 *Mercury*, 22 June 1945, Jottings.
41 *SEN*, 2 July 1945.
42 *SEN*, 4 August 1945.
43 *SEN*, 9 July 1945.
44 *SEN*, 16 July 1945.
45 *SEN*, 6 August 1945.
46 *SEN*, 11 August.
47 *SEN*, 6 August 1945.
48 *SEN*, 18 June and 26 July 1945.
49 *SEN*, 20 June 1945.
50 *SEN*, 21 August, 12 September 1945.
51 *SEN*, 30 August 1945.
52 *SEN*, 25 October 1945.
53 *SEN*, 2 July 1945.
54 *SEN*, 6 August 1945.
55 *SEN*, 25 October 1945.
56 *SEN*, 13 October 1945.
57 *SEN*, 9 and 25 October 1945.
58 *SEN*, 9 August 1945.
59 *Mercury*, 26 October 1945.
60 *SEN*, 25 October 1945.

CHAPTER 18

Peace and Looking Ahead

'Don't you know there's a war off?' Tommy Handley, comedian.[1]

Hinderwell Rd, Edgehill, Scarborough. A typical VE Day party of beaming children, treats piled high, slightly uncertain womenfolk and an improvised 'victory' sign.

Peace

The story of Scarborough's Victory in Europe (VE) Day began in the early hours of 7 May 1945. In a school building in Rheims, northern France, General Jodl signed the unconditional surrender of all German forces. News quickly leaked to Britain. It was not until 7.30 that evening that the BBC interrupted a piano recital to announce that the war in Europe was over and that the following day would be VE Day, a public holiday.

In Scarborough there was a brief civic occasion in the Town Hall Gardens on 8 May, whilst churches organised their own thanksgiving services.[2] Most adults tried to listen to Churchill's radio broadcast at 3.00 p.m. 'The evil doers,' the prime minister intoned, 'now lie prostrate before us.' Despite a shortage of material, some flags and homemade bunting appeared in parts of the town and the Lighthouse was 'dressed', as were a couple of trawlers in the harbour. A large crowd attended a bonfire in the South Bay. When fireworks went off, it was the first time that local children had experienced this since Guy Fawkes Night 1938. The most common form of celebration in the town was the organisation of local street parties for children. After the long sacrifices of wartime, adults strove to provide scarce treats to the town's children: ice-cream, jelly, jam tarts, cakes, fruit and perhaps some Spam sandwiches. The occasion was invariably accompanied by children's games, singsongs and dancing. Some of the grown-ups on the North Side enjoyed a ceremonial burning of an effigy of Hitler.[3] Yet, overall, the mood of the day was surprisingly muted, the local paper describing it as 'calm and peaceful', and far removed from the 'mafficking', or patriotic revelry, that had occurred at the end of World War One. It had, after all, been obvious for quite a while that the war in Europe was coming to an end, whilst VE Day itself was called at short notice. The war against Japan, moreover, was still to be won. In a final dignified public display the following Sunday, 3,000 members of the armed forces marched to the railway station to join a thanksgiving service.

On Victory over Japan (VJ) Day, 15 August 1945, similar celebrations took place, with civic ceremonies, church services and children's parties.[4] However, there was more time to plan for the occasion. The civic ceremony involved a theatrical lighting of the town's ancient beacon on the castle walls, evoking the community's deliverance from foreign threats in the past. A more explicitly patriotic note was struck by the broadcast of the King's speech in several locations in the town and the continuous showing of the film *Henry V* at the *Odeon* cinema. The spirit of VJ Day was more boisterous than that of the earlier

Scarborough's wet Thanksgiving Day Service, Sunday 13 May 1945, outside the railway station. The Armed Forces and civilian volunteers were represented in the preceding parade. The service was conducted jointly by the Vicar of Scarborough and a representative of the Free Churches.

celebration. Crowds, augmented by holidaymakers, seethed through the streets in the rain, with 'dancing, singing, laughter everywhere'. The town centre was mobbed, there was dancing on St Nicholas Cliff and the traffic island near the railway station was a focal point for revelling. Remnants of the crowd remained until 1.00 a.m., singing *Auld Lang Syne* and such like. Elsewhere, the police had to intervene where damage to a shop awning was caused by young men trying to seize a bottle of spirits dangled from the building by a fishing rod. The town's final delivery from the trials of war involved the release of long pent-up emotions and a communal celebration of the prospects of peace.

General Election

On 19 May 1945 the Labour Party decided to end its participation in the wartime coalition. Prime Minister Churchill called a general election for 5 July. On 23 May the wartime government formally came to an end, replaced by Churchill's 'caretaker' administration. The election campaign lasted for the next six weeks. The result was not declared until 26 July, to allow for the Services' votes to be counted. Labour won an historic victory, with a large majority of seats (393). The national percentage votes were:

Conservatives: 36.2%
Liberal: 9%
Labour: 47.7%

The results in Scarborough and Whitby constituency were as follows.

	Vote in Scarborough and Whitby	% of the vote in Scarborough and Whitby	% of vote compared with last election (1935)
Conservative	20,786	50.9	Down 3%
Liberal	10,739	26	Down 13%
Labour	9,289	22.7	Up 16%

The election campaign in Scarborough and Whitby was quite low key. Due to the requisitioning of large properties, electioneering was initially handicapped by a shortage of meeting rooms, until the Council eventually acceded to the use of the Public Library for party political purposes.[5] Polling day was described as 'The Quietest Election Ever'. The absence of party colours and 'noisy bands of youngsters' was attributed to the long lapse in electioneering traditions since the previous general election in 1935.[6]

The sitting MP and Tory candidate, Alexander Spearman, commanded widespread respect in the constituency. He had avoided a conspicuous failing of his Tory predecessor in the constituency by being a highly conscientious MP, attending regular constituency surgeries and vigorously pursuing local casework.[7] Spearman's assiduous work on behalf of the hotel and boarding house interest played a part in shoring up the Tory vote. Even his political opponents had to admit to his diligence.[8]

The Scarborough and Whitby Conservative Association seems to have been in relatively good shape, having benefited from the organisational stimulus of the 1941 by-election. An energetic women's organisation supported the party. With a well-to-do membership, the Conservatives used far more motor vehicles for electioneering than the other two parties.[9]

Spearman had had a difficult relationship with his party during the war (see pp.152-54), but established a reputation in the constituency for intelligence and ability, as well as hard work. For some this seemed to distinguish him from the town's previous Tory MPs who, according to a letter-writer in the press, 'seemed only to require an ability to open charity bazaars etc'.[10] Spearman was an enthusiastic advocate of social reform, championing the 1942 Beveridge Report and the establishment of a comprehensive welfare state.[11] In February 1943 he rebelled against the party whip by voting for an amendment on the Beveridge Report which called for the immediate setting up of a Ministry of Social Security.[12] Despite strong Tory reservations about Beveridge, Spearman insisted the plans would be affordable and good for the country. It was not a time for 'safety first and caution' he declared.[13] By 1944 Spearman had become an enthusiastic advocate of Keynesian economics, believing the state could tackle economic downturns and conquer unemployment by government spending to increase demand.[14] The Conservative candidate, then, was eager to develop a liberal and reformist Toryism. Such an approach was in harmony with dominant currents of wartime public opinion and with popular hopes for a better post-war world.

Spearman's message was not always in tune with old-fashioned Conservatism and with the political instincts of the local party. In the later stages of the war, however, he rowed back on some of his more progressive commitments, emphasising the virtues of free enterprise and vehemently denouncing Labour's post-war plans for economic controls and nationalisation. By the spring of 1944 Jottings noted in the *Mercury* that he 'may have halted a little recently in his trek towards the Left'.[15] The local Communist Party declared that he had come out as 'a true Conservative'.[16] Local Tory traditionalists were reassured.

The Conservative Party had monopolised the Scarborough and Whitby seat since it was formed in 1918, never failing to win less than 50% of the votes throughout the interwar period.[17] In 1945 the party benefited from a strong candidate and a substantial bedrock of support in the constituency. Its support held up well. The party gained more votes than the other two parties combined, and, whilst its vote fell 3% on the previous election in 1935, the party's national vote plummeted by nearly 12%. In a later press profile, the Conservative candidate was praised for 'a personal triumph in a time of country-wide Conservative collapse'.[18]

The Constituency Labour Party adopted Mr Tom Hopperton, an area officer with the National Union of Public Employees, as its parliamentary candidate in 1942. It is not clear why Sidney Simpson, the well-known local Labour activist, trade unionist and town councillor was passed over. It was not because he was too far to the Left of Labour, as Hopperton shared his Marxist brand of socialism, attacking Labour moderates like Herbert Morrison, calling for the abolition of capitalism and extolling the virtues of Soviet Communism.[19] Jottings referred to Hopperton and Simpson as 'our local dilettante Socialist theorists'.[20] It is also uncertain why Hopperton decided to stand down at the end of September 1944. He claimed that he wished to devote more of his time to trade union work.[21] At the beginning of 1945 Scarborough Labour adopted a rather different candidate, Flight Lieutenant Douglas Curry, a 30-year-old schoolmaster from the Darlington area. A socialist from the non-communist left, he was serving as an instructor in the RAF. Curry proved to be a persuasive campaigner, highlighting Labour's commitment to economic planning and social justice, 'not profits for the few'.[22] He promised radical post-war social reform and tapped into dominant local concerns about post-war housing and jobs. The Conservative Party was excoriated in his speeches, caricatured as a party of 'young Guards Officers, amateur steeplechasers, Dukes' nephews out of jobs, company directors and old Etonians'.[23] Conservatives had, he argued, betrayed the British people after World War One and had afflicted them with unemployment and the means test in the 1930s. The party had harboured pro-fascists and pro-Nazis.[24] Labour's rallying cry of 'Never Again' resonated powerfully with the electorate in 1945. Spearman, given his strong local reputation, escaped the sharpest of Curry's wrath. It was the 'powers behind him' that should concern the electorate.[25]

In 1945 the local Labour Party had made it clear that it would not do any deals with the Liberals, who historically had been the main opposition to the Conservatives in the constituency. Curry was confident that the war had transformed the political landscape, elevating Labour to be the main challenger to the Conservatives. He also stressed that between Labour and the Liberals there was a 'wide difference of political aims'. The Liberals, he claimed, lacked the courage to embrace nationalisation, economic controls over the economy and anything more than 'modest' social reform.[26]

The Labour Party benefited from some of its wartime campaigning in the constituency, on local issues like child nurseries and British Restaurants, and on international issues, such as aiding the Soviet Union. In appointing Sidney Simpson' as election agent, Labour acquired an asset of formidable energy and local knowledge. The party, though small, had the committed support of local trade unions and of other small left-wing political groups, like the ILP, Fabian Society, Communist Party and Common Wealth.[27] It has also been claimed that nationally Labour benefited from the armed services' vote, which in Scarborough and Whitby amounted to over 5,000 voters, who had the opportunity of voting by post or by proxy. This was certainly helpful to Labour locally, but generally the services' vote was low, and not exclusively Labour.[28]

The local Labour Party made substantial gains in the 1945 election. Winning over 9,000 votes and 22.7% of the votes cast, this was Labour's electoral breakthrough in the constituency. Before the war the party had come third in all the elections it had contested and its highest share of the vote had been 10.8% in 1929. Following 1945 the Labour Party came second to the Conservatives in the 1950, 1951 and 1955 general elections with an average percentage poll of 28%. Of course, Labour's electoral progress in Scarborough in 1945 reflected the pronounced swing to the party in the country as a whole, particularly among working-class and lower middle-class voters.[29] Labour's increased vote locally in 1945 seems to have arisen from the appeal of its clear-cut message on social justice and economic planning, and not merely from anti-Tory feelings. A large number of voters opted positively to vote Labour in Scarborough and Whitby, and not to vote tactically for the Liberal Party, the main historical opposition to the Conservative Party. This voting behaviour is in keeping with the findings of Peter Sloman who, in examining three-way fights in constituencies in 1945 where Labour had come third in 1935, concluded, '… Labour supporters proved highly reluctant to rally behind the Liberal candidates in 1945. Indeed, many former Liberal voters seem to have peeled away from the party to support Labour, even in seats which Labour had little chance of winning.'[30]

The local Liberals ran a pugnacious campaign in 1945. They, too, possessed a strong candidate. Captain Leonard Razzall of the Royal Marines was a London solicitor and native of Scarborough, educated at its schools and with a local wife.[31] He was a combative politician, eager to seize the initiative from his opponents. Razzall worked hard to persuade anti-Tory activists that he alone should stand as the progressive candidate.[32] When such a proposal was rejected by Labour, he then alleged that many rank and file Labour Party members were planning to vote Liberal to keep the Tories out. This was based on scant evidence, but was intended to sow the seeds of tactical voting in his favour.[33] As election day loomed, he kept the pressure up, repeating the refrain that a vote for Labour was a vote for the Tories.[34] Like Labour, he took a vigorous anti-Conservative line, portraying them as a party wishing to return to the miseries of pre-war Britain and as the defenders of self-serving elites in the economy and society.[35] At the same time, he reminded voters of Spearman's disloyalty to Churchill, claiming that the Tory candidate had been an opponent of Churchill's before as well as during the war.[36] Razzall also enjoyed spotlighting the hypocrisy of the many other critics of Churchill in the local Conservative Party, who were now 'sheltering behind him' in the general election campaign.[37] On policy, Razzall's political offering was in the tradition of Radical Liberalism, criticising Big Business and financial interests. The Liberals would put the people first, he promised, and they would ensure that poverty, insecurity, poor housing and social injustice were tackled.[38] He invoked the authority of the great Liberal reformers to support his case: Lloyd George, J.M. Keynes and William Beveridge.[39] Razzall's campaign received a boost when the latter, a highly regarded and popular figure, came to Scarborough on 26 June to speak on his behalf. The Liberal campaign was, therefore, a lively one, and the party, surprisingly, had more money to spend in the constituency than either of its rivals.[40] The party's policy platform shared Labour and Tory emphasis on the need for post-war social reform. In content, however, the Liberal message lacked Labour's clarity on how to achieve fairness and prosperity by using state economic controls.

The local Liberals performed better than the party nationally, obtaining 26% of the vote. Nationally the Liberals won a mere 9% of the vote, and, humiliatingly, only 12 seats. The Liberals, however, were the real losers of the election in Scarborough and Whitby, despite coming second. They dropped 13 percentage points from the previous election in 1935. In the interwar period Liberals had averaged 40% of the poll. What went so wrong? In Scarborough and Whitby, the Liberals had failed to defeat the Conservatives in any general election between the wars, which had had an adverse impact on party morale and organisation. The party was said to be 'deplorably weak' in Whitby and the rural North Riding in particular.[41] Unkind criticisms were made in Scarborough, a Liberal sympathiser dismissing the local party for its 'fascination of [sic] cards, billiards and idle gossip'.[42] Above all, the Liberals failed to persuade enough Labour sympathisers to vote Liberal tactically in 1945, and they failed to prevent a good number of erstwhile Liberal voters from switching to Labour. Though the Liberals won more votes than Labour, they were no longer the undisputed opposition to the Conservatives in the constituency.

Local Elections

Following Scarborough Labour's success in the general election, the party was optimistic about its prospects in the local council elections in November

1945. There had been no municipal contest since 1938 and an unprecedented number of seats were in contention. The elections were to be fought on a reformed and expanded franchise, based on adult suffrage and not the payment of rates.[43] Labour aspired to success in all wards, save the Tory stronghold of Weaponness. Though most candidates campaigned on similar local priorities, and acknowledged the importance of post-war housing, Labour candidates stressed the critical urgency of the housing situation, 'the crying need of the day', in the words of one.[44] They also highlighted the importance of economic planning for the town's future.

The local election results across the country reflected the national Labour Party's progress in the recent general election. Labour made impressive gains, especially in Yorkshire and the North East. It was a similar story in Scarborough. The Liberals lost votes, falling from three to two seats.[45] Independents slipped from ten seats to eight. The Conservatives came out on top, gaining one seat and finishing with 11. Labour had won its first seat in 1938, but only by a whisker. In 1945 it regained this and won two further seats, in Castle and Northstead wards. In a 1946 local by-election it won another seat in Northstead, which became the first ward in the town to have two Labour councillors.[46] Jottings in the *Mercury*, no fan of Labour, stated that Labour's success was not undeserved, as Labour had 'shown far more vitality than all the other parties put together'.[47] In a subsequent County Council election Scarborough Labour won its first County Council seat.[48] Given that some of the Independents were sympathetic to Labour's priorities on the Town Council, and that the Independents rarely voted as a bloc, Labour was emerging for the first time as the main opposition to the Conservatives.[49]

Another sign that the centre of political gravity was shifting was the election by councillors of the Independent Councillor Jackson as mayor in November 1945.[50] In many ways this should not have come to a surprise to anyone, as the diminutive 'Johnny' Jackson had been a highly active councillor for 20 years and was now over 70. He had served on every council committee except finance and for the previous five years he had also been a member of the County Council. The town benefited greatly from his voluntary efforts as a Baptist lay preacher, on the Public Assistance Committee and on the Harbour Commission. Jackson was, moreover, renowned for his geniality, good humour and unflagging energy. He also possessed, it was said, 'a temperamental inability to bear malice'.[51]

However, his elevation to the mayoralty displeased many and outraged some. On the council he was always his own man and was regarded as the perennial 'odd man out' in local politics. To many observers and colleagues he appeared to be reckless in his judgements and deaf to reasonable argument. He enjoyed the distinction of frequently failing to find a seconder for the stream of motions he submitted to Council meetings. Jackson's priorities were different from those of many councillors, as he tenaciously pursued the welfare of the underprivileged in the town. His tough personal background undoubtedly influenced this. He had attended a Charity School in the town as an orphan, commencing work aged 12, before later setting up his own tailor's business.[52] During the war he continued to act as an 'untiring champion of the underdog'.[53] He backed the establishment of a British Restaurant and the plight of council tenants struggling to pay their rates. In 1941 he supported the rebellious by-election candidate Reg Hipwell, attracted by his populist demands for a better deal for servicemen, their wives and the elderly. Indeed, in autumn 1942 Jackson seems to have entered into unsuccessful discussions with Hipwell about the latter running as an Independent parliamentary candidate in Scarborough and Whitby at the end of the war.[54] Like Hipwell, Jackson had a talent for tapping into popular grievances and for speaking the language of ordinary folk. It is therefore arguable that the currents of opinion that helped strengthen the Labour Party in the town at the local and national elections also helped to persuade councillors to grant the mayoralty to Jackson. Sidney Simpson, his Labour colleague on the Council, saw Jackson as something of a kindred spirit. They were both 'lone voices' on the council and often worked together on shared priorities. 'It was fitting,' reflected Simpson, 'at the beginning of the era of the common people that a common man had been chosen.'[55]

For local Labour, the era of the common man did not last for very long. Its municipal progress, derived as it was from the town's experience of the war, was not sustained for long in peacetime. With the onset of the Cold War in 1947, the local Labour Party also suffered from its association with Soviet Communism. Sidney Simpson lost his seat on the Council that year.[56] By 1949 Labour was reduced to its pre-war presence of one seat on the Council and in the same year it also lost its seat on the County Council.[57]

The collective celebrations on VE and VJ Days signified both relief at the end of the war and hopes for a better post-war world. The prominence given to children's street parties in 1945, captured in innumerable monochrome photographs, was indicative of such hopes for the future. The candidates in the local and general elections in Scarborough tried to capture this public mood, promising jobs, housing and social welfare. Labour was best placed to do this and for the first time made inroads into the Liberal and Conservative votes. But they still had a long way to go in the conservative-minded North Riding.

Notes

1. Quoted in Susan Briggs, *Keep Smiling Through* (London, 1976), p.248.
2. For VE Day see *SEN*, 5,7,8,10 and 14 May 1945.
3. *SEN*, 2 August 2005.
4. For VJ Day see *SEN*, 15 and 16 August 1945.
5. *SEN*, 12 June 1945.
6. *SEN*, 5 July 1945.
7. *SEN*, 20 May 1942, letter.
8. *SEN*, 18 June 1945.
9. *SEN*, 5 July 1945.
10. *SEN*, 20 May 1942.
11. *SEN*, 9 January 1943.
12. Paul Addison, *The Road to 1945* (London, 1977), pp.224-225 and *SEN*, 13 February 1943.
13. *SEN*, 6 March 1943.
14. *SEN*, 17 April 1944 and *Mercury*, 28 June 1945.
15. *Mercury*, 31 March 1944.
16. *Mercury*, 31 March 1944 and SEN 8 May 1944.
17. See p.139-40 on the basis of local Conservative support.
18. *SEN*, 16 January 1947.
19. *SEN*, 6 March 1944.
20. *Mercury*, 18 June 1943.
21. *Mercury*, 29 September 1944.
22. *SEN*, 18 June 1945.
23. *SEN*, 4 July 1945.
24. Ibid.
25. Ibid.
26. *SEN*, 19 April 1945.
27. *SEN*, 4 and 18 June 1945.
28. *SEN*, 5 July 1945.
29. Steven Fielding, Peter Thompson and Nick Tiratsoo, *'England Arise!': The Labour Party and Popular Politics in 1940s Britain* (Manchester, 1995), pp.63-64.
30. Peter Sloman, 'Rethinking a progressive moment: The Liberal and Labour parties in the 1945 general election', *Historical Research* vol. 84, no.226 (November 2011), p.732.
31. *SEN*, 7 June 1945.
32. *SEN*, 25 October 1945.

Peace and Looking Ahead

33 *SEN*, 7 June 1945.
34 *SEN*, 23 and 29 June 1945.
35 *SEN*, 14 September 1944 and 7 June 1945.
36 *SEN*, 26 June 1945.
37 *Mercury*, 13 April 1945.
38 *SEN*, 14 September 1944 and 14 June 1945.
39 *SEN*, 14 June 1945.
40 *SEN*, 30 August 1945.
41 *Mercury*, 27 July 1945.
42 *Mercury*, 21 July 1944, Jottings.
43 *SEN*, 16 October 1945.
44 *SEN*, 30 October 1945.
45 *SEN*, 16 October 1945. The numbers are slightly confusing as previously the Liberals possessed two seats, and one previously Liberal seat had fallen vacant.
46 *Mercury*, 15 February 1946.
47 *Mercury*, 22 February 1946.
48 *SEN*, 6 March 1946 and *SEN*, 6 April 1949.
49 See *Mercury*, 3 August and 9 November 1945.
50 The best sources are *Mercury*, 9 November 1945 and obituary, *Mercury*, 24 April 1953.
51 See pen portrait, *SEN*, 26 September 1946.
52 *SEN*, 12 December 1945.
53 *Mercury*, 24 April 1953.
54 *Mercury*, 4 September 1942 and SEN 14 December 1942.
55 *Mercury*, 9 November 1945.
56 *SEN*, 3 November 1947.
57 *Mercury*, 13 May 1949.

CHAPTER 19

Post-war Scarborough: Housing

We are telling them now that they are heroes for the way in which they are standing up to the strain of the mighty bombardment – and it's true. I think they will keep on being heroes, but when the war is over they will demand the rewards of heroism: they will expect to get them very soon and no power on earth will be able to rebuild the homes at the speed that will be necessary.

(Minister of Food, Lord Woolton,
visiting a blitzed area of London in autumn 1940)[1]

The Housing Crisis

At the end of the war Scarborough, like much of the rest of the country, was faced with formidable housing challenges. The causes were many. During the war there was next to no house building and the town's housing stock was badly maintained. Serious damage had of course been caused by enemy action, and local authorities were not permitted to repair war damaged property till late in the war.[2] By this time there were severe shortages of labour and building materials. Whilst the stock of decent housing dwindled, demand for houses was increasing steeply at the end of the war. The marriage rate in England increased at the beginning and end of the war, whilst the birth rate increased throughout, resulting in an unprecedented number of parents with young families seeking accommodation.[3] In 1946 there were over 700 births in Scarborough, the highest ever recorded.[4] Expectations, moreover, were high. Politicians had given the impression that after the war there would be homes for all and that this time, unlike after World War One, the people's hopes would not be disappointed. It was widely felt that those who had served their country in war deserved nothing less.[5] And after a long period of wartime collectivism, people had increasingly come to expect government to provide solutions to the country's most pressing social and economic problems.[6]

In the summer of 1943 a report to Scarborough Council expressed the fear that by the end of the war there could be as many as 1,000 applicants for Council housing in the town.[7] Concern was felt particularly about the town's responsibility for housing demobilised servicemen.[8] By January 1945 the situation was much worse than anticipated, as there were nearly 2,500 applications for housing, just under 900 of which were from applicants with no current home of their own, often lodging in rooms with friends or family.[9] The Council's entire stock of houses and flats was only 1,495.[10] An analysis in March 1945 found an increase to 3,000 applicants, 2,000 of whom had no home to call their own. Six hundred of this 2,000 were servicemen or ex-servicemen.[11] By the summer of 1945 Councillor Simpson was lamenting 'the growing feeling of hopelessness among people'.[12] In the period 1945-47, the waiting lists remained stubbornly in the region of 3,000.[13]

The government minister responsible for housing in the post-war Labour government, Aneurin Bevan, was alert to the looming housing crisis and was quick to grant to local authorities the powers to requisition empty properties for use by the homeless.[14] Some local authorities in England, especially Labour ones, were keen to do this.[15] At the end of July 1945 160 such properties had been identified in Scarborough, with a further 100 more requiring substantial alteration or repair.[16] However, the Council was not in favour of resorting to the requisitioning of private property in peacetime. The Town Hall saw its requisitioning powers as a means of encouraging property owners to either sell up or arrange for the occupation of their properties as they saw fit. By late 1945 nearly 100 houses hitherto lying empty were re-occupied in this way. When requisitioning powers were terminated in June 1948, only two properties had been requisitioned and given to tenants.[17] The Council also appealed to householders with a spare room to let it to those in need, but this was met with a common criticism: 'men who fought want homes not "digs"'.[18]

'Prefabs'

In March 1944 Winston Churchill had announced that, to deal with a predicted post-war housing crisis, half a million prefabricated steel houses ('prefabs'), designed by the Ministry of Works, would be manufactured.[19] They were to be

Scarborough at War

assembled in aircraft and other war factories and distributed to areas of need. The prefabs were conceived as a temporary expedient, with a life of ten years. In September 1944 Scarborough Council requested 100 prefabs and announced their intention to erect them on the Sandybed Estate on the outskirts of the town.[20] The existing housing here constituted a small middle-class suburb with many elderly residents, and a campaign was quickly formed to resist the influx of a large number of council tenants. The case was difficult to make, as it was known that many of the new prefabs would provide 'homes for fighting men'. 'Cut out the snobbery,' a letter to the press demanded, 'and give these heroes the best.'[21]

The Council started preparing the site of the first 50 prefabs in Sandybed in the summer of 1945, employing German POWs as part of the labour force.[22] In November 1945 it acquired more land and planned for a further 50 prefabs.[23] Meanwhile, preparations were made for five prefabs on Commercial Street, to replace houses destroyed in an air raid. The Council aimed to erect 20 more at Quarry Mount, off Seamer Road, and a further 20 on Seamer Road. However, the temporary homes programme was plagued by delays, to such an extent that in October 1945 the Councillor responsible for housing confessed, 'It is getting me down.'[24] Another councillor commented drily that 'at the speed they were going, they would have permanent houses built before temporary houses arrived'.[25] Some councillors were not very keen on prefab building, preferring to husband resources for the building of larger, permanent homes, Councillor Coates, for instance, dismissing the prefabs as 'snuff boxes'.[26] Progress was slowed also by central government red tape. A councillor in Hull described trying to negotiate with Whitehall on housing as being 'like trying to swim through a sea of glue'.[27] As a consequence of delays, prefabs were painfully slow to arrive and often arrived incomplete. By the end of 1945 no one in Scarborough had benefited from a prefab home.

The first prefabs occupied by tenants in Scarborough were the five on Commercial Street, handed over in March 1946. All were taken over by ex-servicemen and their families, three of the tenants having previously inhabited the sites before their destruction by bombing. According to the press, the new residents were delighted with their new homes. They were appreciative of the high quality of the fittings and decorations, of the 'modernistic' appearance of the interiors and of the large, light-providing windows. A note of nostalgia was also struck: 'All I miss is the cosy look of an open fire.' A journalist felt that they looked as if they could last longer than 10 years. Over 70 years later, three of them are still in use at the time of writing.[28]

Post-war 'prefabs' on the Sandybed estate, the original barrack-like appearance softened by landscaping and tree-planting.

Following these initial completions, progress in receiving and erecting the remainder of the 150 prefabs was relatively rapid. By the end of 1946, 100 had been completed.[29] The target of 150 was achieved a year later.[30] Local opinion was mixed. The smaller developments, like the Spring Hill homes in their orchard setting, drew praise. The large-scale Sandybed scheme was much less popular at first, criticised for its bleak, barrack-like appearance.[31]

Permanent Housing

By the end of the war the Council had anticipated the need for more permanent public housing and had acquired 26 acres of land to the west of the existing Barrowcliff estate on the north-western outskirts of the town.[32] These plans were given a push when the Labour government came to power in July 1945. Aneurin Bevan was not a fan of the prefabs, nor of private house building in a time of labour and material shortages. As a minister he put impediments in the way of private housebuilding, imposing controls on investment and on the use of raw materials. He encouraged the building of permanent council housing and was determined that such housing would be low density, of a good size and of impressive quality. Central government subsidies were made available to councils.[33] The Council aimed to have the first batch of permanent homes ready by March 1946.[34]

In the event, only eight were anywhere near completion by March. The first four tenants occupied permanent new municipal housing at the end of June 1946.[35] Thereafter, completions rose steadily, though in modest numbers. Over the autumn there was something of an acceleration of house building nationally, aided by extra funding from the Chancellor of the Exchequer, Hugh Dalton.[36] By the end of 1946 some 50 permanent houses had been completed.[37] This momentum was largely maintained in 1947, despite a very severe winter and the 'convertibility crisis' in the summer. By March 1948 over 250 permanent homes had been completed.[38] The pace continued to accelerate. In July 1948 the Council was able to announce that 483 permanent dwellings would be completed within the next three months, reaching the target of 633 municipal houses overall, including the 150 prefabs.[39] At the end of 1948, the current building projects in the town were virtually complete, with only six permanent houses still to be signed off.[40]

Progress on permanent housing was, therefore, slow in taking off in the immediate post-war years, and, whilst it did pick up in 1947 and 1948, the number of houses being built hardly matched the numbers in the town in need of a home of their own. The waiting list plateaued at around 3,000.[41] The number of permanent homes completed by the end of 1948 was only about 480. There was ample support on the Council for a greater degree of private enterprise in local house-building and local builders were clamouring to have greater freedom to build, lobbying the 1948 Labour Party Conference in the town to this end.[42] When Corporation housebuilding was at a standstill in 1949, and whilst there was unemployment among builders, the Ministry continued to block the building of private homes. Under Whitehall's writ, this remained a low priority part of the solution to the housing crisis.

The slow pace of permanent house building by the Council bred a great deal of frustration and anger. Locally, married couples and families found themselves sharing with family or friends or cramped in inhospitable rented rooms. The greatest frustration was felt by demobilised servicemen and women. Alderman Wilkinson's frequent insistence that delays in Scarborough were no worse, and probably less severe, than in other comparable towns was scant consolation.[43] The demand for post-war Corporation housing was undoubtedly whetted by the high standards of construction and fittings specified by the Ministry of Health. The majority (70%) of the town's permanent housing, mostly situated on the Barrowcliff estate, was spacious, three-bedroom semi-detached homes, built and finished to a high standard.[44] Although the cost of building such houses had risen by 1948 to £1,400 (four times the pre-war cost), rents remained at 10 shillings a week. This was considered an affordable level of rent, given that the community was in general enjoying increased earnings, high levels of employment and the benefits of Labour's welfare state.[45]

Nationally, the slow pace of post-war housebuilding helped to trigger a squatting movement in the summer of 1946, with some luxury flats in London's West End being illegally occupied. Across the country, disused military camps were taken over. Public opinion was divided. Given the housing situation, there was some sympathy for the lawbreakers, especially if they were ex-servicemen. Other felt that they should 'learn to be *patient* and *wait*'.[46] In the Scarborough area there were some small-scale occupations. In the village of Brompton-by-Sawdon, a family moved into a former army Nissen hut, and some local families moved into an empty military camp in Pickering.[47] Scarborough's neighbouring village of Scalby witnessed a number of ex-servicemen's families, tired of waiting on the housing list, squatting in ex-military huts, whilst in Staxton a dozen families took possession of huts at a former RAF camp.[48] In Scarborough itself, squatting opportunities were limited, especially as empty premises at Burniston Barracks were guarded. There were, however, some isolated incidents. A family took over a condemned Corporation property in the summer of 1946. They were evicted in February 1947.[49] Such incidents, and their attendant publicity, intensified the pressures on central and local governments to come to grips with the housing situation.

With so many applicants for so few Corporation houses in Scarborough, a fair system of allocation had to be worked out. Initially, the Housing Committee of the Council rejected the impersonality of a points system, assuming that they would be able to evaluate judiciously the merits of individual cases. It did not last.[50] After a great deal of frustration all round, it was decided in the summer of 1946 to adopt a points system and by October the details of the system were made public. Predictable criteria were adopted to determine the allocation of housing. Were applicants victims of enemy action? Were they resident locally or had they served in the armed forces? Did they suffer from illness or disability? How large was their family and were they presently suffering from overcrowding?[51] However, given that the root cause of public discontent, an inadequate supply of housing, remained, resentments continued to fester. The points system discriminated against those who were already housed, even if their accommodation was unsuitable. Similarly, those who lacked a year's previous residency in the town felt aggrieved, especially when they had been directed further afield by the state for war work. Women who had been in the Services were rewarded with points, whilst those who had worked in munitions were not.[52]

Subterfuges to gain advantages in the competition for public housing multiplied, with *Mems*, in the *Evening News*, alleging 'dirty work' and 'jiggery-pokery'.[53] Some applicants were said to have temporarily peopled their current accommodation with extended family members in order to claim points for over-crowding.[54] Pressure on key councillors could be intense. The chairman of the Housing Management Sub-Committee complained in March 1948 that he was in receipt of an increasing number of 'scurrilous' anonymous letters, alleging the dishonest housing applications of others.[55] An observer commented that it was 'understandable that candidates for Corporation houses should watch each other like cats watching a mouse'.[56] In an ugly development in 1946, some anti-Polish feeling in the town helped to generate rumours that locals with Polish husbands were receiving preferential treatment.[57]

Eastfield

In the spring of 1946, the Borough Engineer gave the first indication of what would become a revolution in municipal housing policy. Plans were afoot for the Council to commence a major building programme outside of the Borough.[58] It was clear that, once the building developments at Sandybed and Barrowcliff were completed, there would be limited space remaining in the town for further programmes.[59] The business lobby in the town, moreover, were keen to see remaining plots devoted to new hotels, boarding houses and private property.[60] In October a site was announced near Seamer Railway Station to the south of the town (outside the Borough until 1953).[61] The longer-term plan was to build a satellite estate with accommodation for 3,000 to 4,000 families. The inspiration for this sort of scheme really goes back to the utopian principles of Ebenezer Howard's Garden City movement of the early 20th century. After the war planners took a renewed interest in these ideas and aimed to apply them in Labour's post-war New Towns, like Stevenage, Harlow and East Kilbride. Their aim was to build high quality public housing in a healthy and attractive environment in self-contained estates. The development of a strong community cohesion, described by the planning minister as 'a great adventure in social construction', was also considered essential. Scarborough's new estate, therefore, would require not only essential amenities like schools and a shopping centre, but facilities to promote a sense of civic cohesion and pride: a community centre, church, library, public house, cinema, bowling green and allotments.[62]

At the beginning of 1947 the Corporation applied to the Ministry of Housing for permission to make a start on the first 50 houses, receiving approval in March 1947. It was unclear, initially, what the new estate would be called: High Eastfield or Low Deepdale (nearby farms), or Crossgates (a nearby village). A local speculated on Soviet-style Bevanburg. Eventually, plain 'Eastfield' won the day.[63]

When the financial 'convertibility crisis' hit the country in the summer of 1947, the Ministry of Health suspended all new housing projects, 'heartbreaking' for Bevan according to his biographer.[64] To its credit, Scarborough's Housing Committee, under the determined leadership of Alderman Wilkinson, remained committed to the new estate. Preparations, such as roads and sewers, must continue, Wilkinson insisted, so that the Corporation would be ready 'when they received the word "go"'.[65] As the economy recovered in 1948, the Housing Ministry lifted restrictions, as Wilkinson had predicted, and by the summer the Eastfield estate had been given the green light again. However, progress was hard-fought. The emergency surrounding the devaluation of the pound in 1949 hampered finances. The Borough's Chief Engineer blamed government interference and red tape for other delays. Meddling, he complained, came from a clutch of government ministries: Health, Town and Country Planning, Agriculture and Transport. North Riding County Council officials made difficulties over planning regulations. Scarborough Rural District Council had to be consulted on sewers. British Railways and the British Electrical Authority had to be kept happy over the development of the site. Such difficulties were not always appreciated by locals desperate for a home.[66]

In 1951 the initial western development of the estate had been largely completed, easing pressure on Scarborough's housing waiting list. The properties were mostly semi-detached, built to ambitious 1940s planning standards, having three to four bedrooms and an upstairs bathroom. The houses incorporated differences in external design detail and were set in a spacious, landscaped environment. However, as the Conservative governments of the 1950s pursued bold numerical housing targets at the expense of quality, the eastern spread of the estate saw a waning of architectural standards.[67] A sense of community, moreover, was slow to develop. Looking back from the vantage point of 1985, the Town Hall's former Director of Publicity reflected: 'Sadly, amenities lagged far behind the construction of houses, and, for a time, being offered a house at Eastfield was rather like being sent to Siberia.'[68] There was insufficient attention paid, too, to providing employment in the area. It was not until the 1960s that a trading estate was established nearby.

Semi-detached properties on Ridgeway Eastfield, in 1951, with a generous allocation of open space and greenery.

Writing of post-war housing, the historian Paul Addison commented memorably, 'If Rome was not built in a day, neither was Hemel Hempstead,' in reference to the building of Labour's New Towns.[69] Delay also characterised the story of post-war housing in Scarborough. Many families endured prolonged frustration, finding their dream of a home of their own disappointed. In the circumstances, they demonstrated considerable forbearance. The Town Hall, for its part, pursued its house-building goals doggedly, despite the many obstacles. It deserves credit for accepting that its immediate post-war efforts were inadequate and for its consequent decision to build a new estate in Eastfield. This promised a longer-term answer to the borough's housing predicament.

Notes

1. Paul Addison, *Now the War is Over* (London, 1985), p.55.
2. *SEN*, 5 December 1944.
3. This was anticipated in a report to the Council, *SEN*, 1 June 1943.
4. *SEN*, 6 March 1948.
5. *SEN*, 14 August 1945.
6. Addison, op. cit., pp.56-7.
7. *SEN*, 1 June 1943.
8. *SEN*, 12 September 1944.
9. *SEN*, 9 January 1945.
10. *Mercury,* 31 August 1945.
11. *SEN*, 17 March 1945.
12. *SEN*, 10 August 1945.
13. See, for example, *Mercury* 18 October 1946 and 3 January 1947 and SEN 8 August 1946 and 17 February 1947.
14. Addison, op. cit., p.57.
15. John Boughton, *Municipal Dreams: The Rise and Fall of Council Housing* (London 2018), p.56.
16. *SEN*, 31 July 1945.
17. *Mercury,* 17 December 1948.
18. *SEN*, 7 November and *Mercury,* 30 November 1945.
19. Paul Addison, *The Road to 1945* (London, 1977), p.247.
20. *SEN*, 7 September 1944 and 6 February 1945.
21. *SEN*, 11 January 1945.
22. *SEN*, 16 July 1945.
23. *Mercury,* 2 November 1945.
24. *SEN*, 9 October 1945.
25. *Mercury,* 2 November 1945.
26. *SEN*, 14 August 1945.
27. Nick Tiratsoo, 'Labour and the reconstruction of Hull, 1945-51' in Nick Tiratsoo (ed.), *The Attlee Years* (London, 1991), p.128.
28. *SEN*, 28 February, 7 March, 1 April 1945.
29. *SEN*, 1 February 1947.
30. *SEN*, 20 November 1947.
31. *Mercury,* 23 April 1948.
32. *SEN*, 6 July 1944.
33. John Campbell, *Nye Bevan: A Biography* (London, 1994), pp. 156-57.

34 *SEN*, 9 October 1945.
35 *SEN*, 24 June 1946.
36 Michael Foot, *Aneurin Bevan: A Biography*, vol.2, (London, 1973), p.75.
37 *SEN*, 3 January 1947.
38 *SEN*, 18 March 1948.
39 *SEN*, 19 July 1948.
40 *Mercury*, 14 January 1949.
41 *SEN*, 19 July 1948.
42 *SEN*, 17 May 1948.
43 For example, *SEN*, 12 December 1946, *Thursday Profile*.
44 *SEN*, 19 July 1948.
45 *Mercury*, 18 June 1948, Jottings.
46 Quoted in David Kynaston, *A World to Build* (London, 2008), p.123.
47 *Mercury*, 16 August 1946 and *SEN*, 17 August 1946.
48 *SEN*, 27 August 1946 and 13 July 1948.
49 *SEN*, 5 February 1947.
50 *SEN*, 7 August 1946.
51 *SEN*, 2 October 1946.
52 *SEN*, 19 July 1948.
53 *SEN*, 17 September 1947.
54 *SEN*, 7 January 1948.
55 *SEN*, 27 March 1948.
56 '*Mems*' in *SEN*, 26 November 1946.
57 Ibid.
58 *SEN*, 4 April 1946.
59 *SEN*, 17 June 1948.
60 *SEN*, 12 June 1947.
61 *SEN*, 7 October 1946.
62 *SEN*, 11 December 1947, 18 March, 19 July 1948.
63 *SEN*, 3 October 2007.
64 Foot, op. cit., p.95.
65 *SEN*, 28 October 1947.
66 SEN 10 November 1948.
67 See the pioneering work of Stephen Gandolfi, 'The Significance of Eastfield – A 1950s Council Estate', MA Thesis, University of York, 2017.
68 Steve Fewster in *SEN*, 9 May 1985.
69 Addison, op. cit., p.80.

CHAPTER 20

Post-war Scarborough: Who Governs?

It would be disastrous if we allowed local government to languish by whittling away its most constructive and interesting functions.
(Herbert Morrison memorandum to the Cabinet, October 1945)[1]

World War II was a period of 'big' government. Churchill bestrode the country as a presidential prime minister, backed by an inner War Cabinet and an array of emergency powers. The Home Front was managed by powerful government ministries, employing an expanded army of civil servants. As well as handling the economy and manpower, central government increasingly took over the supervision of social policy in war, such as health, welfare and education. Democratic accountability was eroded in the process and local government was weakened as some power shifted upwards to the executive. Other powers went to new power centres created for the purpose of prosecuting the war, like the Civil Defence regional organisations. What would be the implications of all this for post-war local government?[2]

Education

A monument to the wartime spirit of social justice in Britain, and a landmark in the history of English education, was the 1944 Butler Education Act. It arose, in part, from a feeling that ordinary people deserved the greater opportunities in life afforded by a good education. The Act provided for free secondary education in state schools and extended the minimum school leaving age from 14 to 15, with a commitment to 16 when practicable. Depending on performance in an exam at the age of eleven (the Eleven Plus), pupils would be transferred from primary schools to either a grammar, secondary modern or technical school. When Labour came to power in 1945 it implemented the essentials of the 1944 Act. County Councils were put in control of educational provision in their areas, though the central Board of Education was given enhanced powers of direction over local authorities and was 'upgraded in status' to a government ministry.[3] Education in Scarborough was to follow a new central government blueprint, administered by the County Council in Northallerton.

In Scarborough there was some unhappiness about the loss of municipal control over education. The end of jurisdiction over the town's elementary schools, which the majority of the town's children had attended up to age 14, was keenly felt. Mayor Pindar was proud that the town had been 'master of its own house' since the Education Act of 1870 and did not, therefore, receive the Butler proposals with any enthusiasm.[4] Not only would the County Council control public schooling, but also ancillary services like school meals and medical services. The financial implications of County control soon rang alarm bells with Scarborough Council's Chair of Finance. Alderman Whittaker protested in 1948 against the continual growth of education expenditure, complaining that the more extravagant the County Education Committee was, the more Scarborough would have to contribute to county rates.[5] It was true that a Divisional Executive for Education was established in Scarborough, to allow for some local decision-making, but there was not a great deal of confidence in Northallerton's willingness to delegate genuine authority to this body. Scarborough, as a sizable borough with a good educational record, therefore appealed to the Ministry of Education to be exempted from Country Council control, as an 'Excepted Area'. This was rejected.[6]

Butler had predicted that the full implementation of his legislation would take a generation.[7] In Scarborough the County Council's ambitious school building and improvement programme of 1946 was indeed slow-moving, held back by the straitened economic circumstances of the post-war period. An inescapable priority was the building of new primary schools to meet the challenges of the 'baby-boom'. New schools were rapidly completed in the Barrowcliff and Newby areas. However, the majority of secondary pupils continued to be educated in the town's old elementary school buildings, where the senior schools were reclassified as secondary moderns. A few examples will serve to illustrate the poor facilities and resources of the secondary moderns in post-war Scarborough.[8] The Falsgrave County Modern School for Girls, earmarked for closure in 1946, remained open until 1964.[9] In 1948 its site and buildings were felt to 'fall far short of modern requirements'. The Central County Modern School for Girls suffered from overcrowding after the war, requiring overspill teaching in a nearby Wesleyan Chapel.[10] It was described by School Inspectors in 1944 as having a 'grim, prison-like appearance'. In 1954 it was noted that the school was scheduled to close, but it continued in use until 1965. In 1953 Inspectors found that Friarage County Secondary School for Boys also suffered from serious deficiencies in its facilities, having, for example, no library, no woodwork room, no changing room, no showers and no nearby playing fields. The first new secondary modern school to open in the town was Westwood County Modern. It was established in the premises of the old Boys' High School when the Boys' High was moved to a new site on the outskirts of the town in 1959. The first post-war, purpose-built Secondary Modern was Raincliffe County Modern for Girls, opened only in 1964.[11]

In implementing the Butler Act's provisions, the County Council made significant changes to the experience of many young people in Scarborough. Teenagers spent an extra year at school from 1947 onwards, necessitating an extra 400 school places in the first year.[12] Pupils who passed an Eleven Plus exam were placed in an academic stream, attending the town's county grammar schools, the Boys' and Girls' High Schools. These were now non-feepaying. New opportunities were created for working-class pupils who performed well in the Eleven Plus to advance themselves academically. However, middle-class pupils tended to have advantages in sitting the Eleven Plus and were more likely to progress to the grammar schools. Those who failed to gain a place in a grammar school were channelled into a less academic stream, taught at the town's new secondary modern schools. Teaching and learning in the secondary modern schools were little different from that in the old elementary schools, as the Butler Act left the curriculum in the hands of the schools. The work of these schools is sometimes undervalued by commentators, but the schools undoubtedly suffered from a lack of status and resources.[13] Most Scarborough youngsters attended the town's secondary moderns and left with no formal educational qualifications. In theory it was possible for bright pupils who had not passed the Eleven Plus to transfer from the town's Secondary Modern Schools to a local grammar school, but this was rare and discouraged by the North Riding authorities. For example, between 1951 and 1954 only two girls from the Central Secondary Modern School moved to the Girls' High School.[14]

One of the intended effects of the Butler Act was to preserve the strengths of the English grammar schools. After the war Scarborough's well-established grammar schools carried on the traditions (and names) of the Girls' High School and the Boys' High School. The Girls High School had moved into attractive new premises at the beginning of the war, but in the post-war years pupil numbers increased markedly, putting a strain on the new accommodation. There was also a striking increase in the numbers staying on to 17 or 18. In 1937 there were 14 in the Sixth Form, in 1952 60. Despite this progress, girls continued to be educated in preparation for more subordinate roles in the jobs market. The numbers progressing to university remained small – four in 1952, and the most common destinations for leavers in that year were 'clerical posts'.[15]

The Boys' High School now also operated as a county grammar school. It remained in its handsome 1900 premises, despite the County Council's goal of building a new school.[16] During and after the war the school retained a healthy intake and strong academic traditions. The numbers staying on to do Sixth Form work and to sit the Higher School Certificate went from strength to strength. In 1949 there were 76 boys pursuing the Higher Certificate. The most common destinations for leavers were university or further education, followed by commerce, industry and engineering. The continuing success of the school in the post-war period was helped by the retention and recruitment of able and well-qualified staff, whilst it was inspired also by the idiosyncratic leadership of headmaster Henry Marsden, celebrated indiscreetly by a school inspector in 1949:

> The headmaster is a remarkable little man, familiarly known as 'Joey'. He is a bit of an oddity and is apt to end his sentences with a high-pitched nervous giggle which is extremely disconcerting on first impact. There can, however, be no doubt of his quality, and he has impressed his personality upon this large and rather tough school in a manner which few men of his size could have hoped to do. He has suffered in recent years from progressive deafness, and it is uncertain for how long he will be able to continue.[17]

He was to retire in 1961, two years after the Boys' High moved to a its new school building.

One of the weaknesses of the Butler Education Act was its failure to legislate nationally for the types of secondary schools that local authorities were to provide. Most County Councils subsequently failed to recognise the importance of technical education and were reluctant to open secondary technical schools. The North Riding was one such authority and Scarborough had to wait until 1961 before a new Technical College was opened, incorporating the town's old Technical Institute and Art School. The town's Graham Sea-Training School might be regarded as a very successful technical school, albeit a specialist one.[18] Having been identified in 1946 as requiring more suitable accommodation, it was incorporated into a new comprehensive school only in 1973, namely the Graham School.

The pupils of the Queen Margaret's School for girls on Queen Margaret's Drive were evacuated to Castle Howard at the beginning of the war and the building was subsequently requisitioned by the army. Fortunately, the building was empty when a parachute mine severely damaged it in the March 1941 'Blitz'. It was subsequently demolished after the war, the school never returning to Scarborough.

Fee-paying and private education in Scarborough struggled during the war years and failed to flourish in the post-war period. Orleton Boys' Preparatory School went bankrupt during the war. The feepaying Convent of the Ladies of Mary was a church grammar school, which faced challenges also. Its rapid post-war expansion in numbers led to some serious overcrowding and an unsatisfactory staff-student ratio. The academic standards were disappointing, and most pupils left at 16 or earlier.[19] The Queen Margaret's School for Girls never returned to Scarborough after the pupils were evacuated to Castle Howard early in the war and the school building was badly damaged in an air raid.[20] The town's biggest private school, Scarborough College, found itself in a state of crisis. In 1940 the school had evacuated to Swaledale in the Yorkshire Dales, haemorrhaging staff and pupils. In 1942 it had a pupil roll of 35. Returning to Scarborough in 1946, the school was compelled to boost its enrolment rapidly, taking on younger pupils, abandoning an entrance exam and employing many young and inexperienced teachers. The result was that in 1948 Inspectors found that academic standards were very low and in no main subject was teaching satisfactory. The situation was not helped in 1951 by the purchase of a troubled local 'prep school'. Inspectors in 1955 found that academic standards remained depressingly poor and the Ministry of Education only agreed to continue to grant formal recognition of the school 'with some hesitation'.[21]

As a further legacy of the war years, a wartime day nursery in Scarborough became a permanent nursery school, retaining the wartime name Childhaven.[22] In 1948 Scarborough benefited from the post-war teacher shortage, when the North Riding Training College was opened for the training of female primary teachers.[23]

Health

During the war years there was a widespread acceptance that the country's fragmented system of health provision was unsatisfactory. Labour came to power in 1945 promising a comprehensive, publicly funded national health service. Aneurin Bevan, the new Minister of Health as well as Housing, was committed to introducing a service that would deliver high quality provision for all, free at the point of need. General Practitioners were cajoled into joining this new service with guarantees over their professional independence. There were, however, vigorous debates in Cabinet over Bevan's plans to nationalise the nation's hospitals. A minority of ministers, led by the former leader of London County Council, Herbert Morrison, was anxious to keep the hospitals under local authority control, where, it was argued, they would be more accountable to local people and responsive to local conditions. Bevan won the argument for the state control of hospitals, determined to maintain uniformly high standards throughout the country.[24]

Scarborough had acquired an impressive new general hospital in 1936, built in a modern style and set in attractive gardens. The £135,000 cost was raised through local voluntary effort. It provided a full range of services, including three operating theatres and a casualty and out-patients department. The Corporation paid for the building and running of the maternity wing, while the remainder of the finance came from a byzantine system of funding: flag days, voluntary subscriptions, individual and business donations, a contributory health insurance scheme, private pay-beds and means-tested fees.[25] Under the National Health Service Act of 1946 the hospital was brought into public ownership, as were some of the smaller satellite hospitals in the town. It was administered by the Scarborough and Whitby Group Hospital Management Committee, which was answerable in turn to the Leeds Regional Hospital Board, accountable to the Minister of Health. Some miscellaneous medical services were transferred from Scarborough to the County Council in Northallerton, including child welfare, anti-natal, midwifery and health visitor services.[26]

There was some local disappointment that the town's prestigious new voluntary hospital had been given up to the clutches of the state. It was felt that medical services, built upon the self-reliance and civic pride of local people, were becoming the responsibility of a remote bureaucracy. Grumbles were heard that small luxuries for patients, funded by local donations, would no longer be available.[27] Local MP Alexander Spearman lamented the demise of a local institution created selflessly by local effort and generosity.[28] However, disapproval was muted. Bevan's promise of a comprehensive health service, free to all at the point of delivery, was simply too attractive to be resisted. Furthermore, Scarborough Hospital was in debt, like many of the voluntary hospitals, to the tune of £28,000 by 1947.[29]

Fire Brigade

In dealing with the many wartime challenges on the Home Front, the country's emergency services had been increasingly amalgamated into larger units and put, in varying degrees, under centralised control. The national experience of the Blitz in 1940 and 1941 exposed weaknesses in the capacity of the country's fire services to cope with air-raids, especially bombing with incendiaries. Some brigades were badly run and poorly equipped.[30] It was left to the discretion of local brigades how far they would help nearby areas in emergencies and when help was offered there were often incompatibilities between different authorities regarding firefighting practices, equipment and even terminology. Therefore, in August 1941 local fire services were nationalised as the National Fire Service (NFS), under the control of the Home Office. The Home Secretary, Herbert Morrison, described the change as 'one of the quickest administrative revolutions that ever took place'.[31] The Scarborough fire brigade ceased to exist as in independent entity, becoming part of No.1 Region of a national organisation, with the region's headquarters in Newcastle. Concerted efforts were made to standardise employment conditions, training and firefighting methods nationally. Promises were made that locally controlled services would be reconstituted at the end of the war.[32]

A Home Office Inspection of the North Riding Fire Brigade in 1950. The legacy of the war is still evident in the NFS helmets and wartime fire engines. The spirit of wartime improvisation lives on in a converted Land Rover appliance (to the left).

Early in 1947 the decision was taken to proceed with the promised denationalisation. The government resolved to consolidate smaller brigades into larger units. Before the war there were 1,440 brigades, now there would be 147. Much to local displeasure, Scarborough failed to regain its independent fire service and the town's service was put under the authority of the North Riding County Council. It would become, according to the *Evening News* 'another of the multiplying tentacles of the County Council'.[33] The new fire service was inaugurated on 1 April 1948 as the North Riding County Fire Service Brigade.[34] The Town Hall appealed to the Home Office, emphasising that, as a sizeable holiday town in a largely rural county, Scarborough's particular needs would not be served well. This seemed to be borne out when North Riding established a fire service management board containing only one Scarborough representative out of 28 members. After appealing this, Scarborough was given two representatives.[35]

Police

Local resentment about post-war centralising tendencies was stronger still over the reorganisation of the town's police force. Politicians concluded from the experience of war that the country would benefit from consolidating reforms in policing. The Police Bill of 1945 proposed that the Scarborough Borough Police be absorbed by the North Riding of Yorkshire Constabulary. It would therefore, as with education and the Fire Service, be under the control of the North Riding County Council in Northallerton. Supporters of local services were not happy. The Council's Watch Committee and the local Police Federation took a lead in calling for the borough's exemption from this top-down police reform. The Town Clerk wrote to the Home Office warning of the damage that would be done to local policing and threatening that 15 to 20 officers would resign if Northallerton took over from Scarborough.[36] Meanwhile, he encouraged local resistance by talk of 'dictatorship' if the County Council were put in charge.[37] Conveying Scarborough's distrust of the willingness of Northallerton to devolve decision-making, he commented: '… you can rest assured that the North Riding Country Council will limit the delegation so far as they possibly can.'[38] The Town Hall was strongly supported by the town's MP in demanding an exemption. Spearman insisted that local control was essential in a holiday resort which required policing sensitivities that were not required elsewhere.[39] Townsfolk speculated light-heartedly that officers would require Northallerton's permission before they could proffer 'good mornings' to locals.[40]

It was hardly likely that the Home Office would make any exception for Scarborough, as this would set a precedent and undermine the police reforms. One complication was that hitherto the Scarborough police had run the local ambulance service, and Northallerton had to agree to allow this to continue until the service came under the control of the new NHS.[41] As a further concession, the North Riding agreed that that the town's current Chief Constable would be put in charge of a police division responsible for Scarborough.[42]

The merged North Riding police force endured some teething problems, receiving criticisms of its administrative procedures from HM Inspector of Constabulary.[43] Discontent persisted in Scarborough. In the summer of 1947

14 officers were transferred from Scarborough to York to help in the policing of York Race Day. It was alleged that the Scarborough force was left under-strength at the height of the summer season.[44] In 1950 Alderman Whittaker claimed that officers in the town were being recruited from across the county and that 'the individual policeman knows little or nothing about the town'.[45] An enterprising journalist from the *Yorkshire Post* chose to walk around the town for over an hour in the hope of finding policemen who were deficient in such local geographical knowledge. He found the police distinctly thin on the ground (coming across only two officers) and, somewhat to his disappointment, quite well informed.[46] But in the same year the Town Clerk insisted that the 'the decline in police efficiency in Scarborough since the borough force was transferred to Northallerton is very considerable ...'[47]

Nationalisation

The supply of electricity in Scarborough had been provided by the Corporation and managed by its Electricity Department since 1926. The post-war Labour government, in a wide-ranging programme of nationalisation, took the industry into state control, thereby taking over the Corporation's electricity undertaking. Whilst some of the nationalisation programme was politically controversial, the nationalisation of electricity was relatively uncontentious. From April 1948 the British Electricity Authority, along with its 14 Area Boards, ran the industry on behalf of the government. Compensation to Councils for the nationalisation of municipal electricity was, in the words of one historian, 'remarkably generous'.[48] In Scarborough, indeed, it prompted the local authority to abolish the widely resented vehicle tolls on the scenic Marine Drive.[49] As with the town's voluntary hospital, the authorities in Scarborough were proud of their record of electricity supply which, they believed, had served the townspeople reliably and efficiently. The Borough Treasurer was fearful that local prices would be pushed up to pay for the shortcomings of electricity supply elsewhere.[50] Supporters of local ownership complained that the town would lose the modest surpluses generated by the business, resulting in longer-term increases in the rates.[51] A common complaint of the time was that, as the town's enterprise was relatively small, its interests would be overlooked by the distant North-Eastern Board, responsible for the extensive Northumberland, Durham and North Riding areas. Such sentiment was reflected in a local news story, probably inaccurate, that an Area Board official had travelled by car from Newcastle to Scarborough, only to assess whether extra lights could be switched on in Peasholm Park.[52]

Under the Transport Act of 1947 the post-war government nationalised the railways, long-distance road haulage, large bus companies and some other miscellaneous transport. Since 1931, when Scarborough's tram system shut down, the United Bus Company held the contract to provide the town's bus service. The contract was due to expire in 1952.[53] As the Corporation was entitled to a share in the bus company's profits, there was some concern about the financial implications of bus service nationalisation. The loss of annual payments from the bus company would put further pressure on the rates. However, public opinion was hardly stirred. The advantages of a Transport Commission Regional Board coordinating transport over a wider area were apparent to many and such a board, moreover, was perceived to be no less remote that the United Bus Company, headquartered in Darlington.[54] And there was a general feeling that a nationalised service could not be any worse than local people had had before.[55]

Centralisation

In the post-war years Scarborough lost a significant amount of control over its own affairs. Central government, in the shape of the ministries of Health and Education, began to play a more important role in the life of the town. Emerging from the administrative examples of the wartime Civil Defence Regions, regional authorities also became more influential.[56] Regional Health, Electricity and Transport Boards were notable examples. Powers were also transferred from the Town Hall to the North Riding County Council in Northallerton, the process starting at the beginning of the war with powers given to the North Riding over ARP.[57] Distrust towards Northallerton continued after the war. Scarborough's mayor complained about this 'absorption of small local authority units into larger and more remote authorities', whilst Jottings condemned Northallerton for refusing to delegate powers to Scarborough, even when it had the legal powers to do so.[58] Where County Hall appeared to make some concessions to Scarborough, as in education and the fire service, this amounted, according to Jottings, to no more than 'window dressing'.[59] Northallerton, he complained, treated local authorities 'as though they were unreliable and even untrustworthy children'.[60]

What were the driving forces behind this shift in power from smaller localities to larger authorities? Certainly, the war witnessed strong centralising tendencies in the state's prosecution of total war. The ensuing recovery of a country severely damaged by war also required the exercise of strong administrative and political powers at the centre. The war, moreover, had generated optimistic plans for post-war reconstruction, keenly embraced by the Labour Government when it came into office. This required Labour politicians to pull all the levers of power available to the government. Such a climate was not, therefore, sympathetic to the aspirations of a small non-county borough like Scarborough.[61]

The erosion of the borough's powers of self-government in peacetime was a bitter pill to swallow and was perceived to have the potential to be very damaging. Mayor Chapman, amongst others, detected a threat to local democracy: 'The thing I regret most is that this means that local men [sic] will cease to take a great interest in the destiny of their district and that, I think, will be a tragedy.'[62] The town also suffered a loss of some revenues, like those obtained from electricity supply and the buses, and lost its ability to control expenditure on areas like policing and education. When spending was transferred to the more spendthrift county council, the town's contributions to the county purse rose.[63] The Town Hall also faced staffing problems in the post-war period as many experienced employees found that they could earn more in larger organisations like the hospital boards and in the newly nationalised industries.[64] The Town Council did retain important responsibilities. Its role in public housing expanded. And, unlike most authorities of a similar size, the Corporation possessed valuable assets as a holiday resort, managed by its Entertainment, Catering and Parks Departments. In July 1948 it also took control over the town's harbour.[65] Yet, for local observers the general impression was that some of the town's historic independence of action, taken away during the war, would not now be regained in peace.

Notes

1. Quoted in Peter Hennessy, *Never Again: Britain 1945-51* (London, 1992), p.139.
2. On the legacy of wartime centralisation nationally, see Paul Addison, *No Turning Back: The Peacetime Revolutions of Post-War Britain* (Oxford, 2010), pp.7-41.
3. Paul Addison, *Now the War is Over* (London, 1985), p.141.
4. *SEN*, 17 January 1945.
5. *SEN*, 18 December 1948.
6. *SEN*, 9 January 1945.
7. Addison, op. cit., p.141.
8. Evidence for post-war Scarborough schools can be found in: NA ED 109/9203, HM Inspectorate: Reports on Secondary Institutions. Yorkshire (North Riding), 1948-1955.
9. *SEN*, 6 March 1947.
10. SMHC Education File.
11. A mixed County Modern School was opened after the war, but the building had been completed in 1942, as Scalby Senior School.
12. *SEN*, 1 April 1947.
13. David Kynaston, *Modernity Britain, 1957-62* (London, 2015), pp.231-32.
14. NA ED 109/9203, HM Inspectorate: Reports on Secondary Institutions. Yorkshire (North Riding), 1948-1955.
15. Ibid.
16. *SEN*, 21 December 1946.
17. NA ED 109/9203, HM Inspectorate: Reports on Secondary Institutions. Yorkshire (North Riding), 1948-1955.
18. Ibid.
19. Ibid.
20. See p.103.
21. Ibid.
22. *Childhaven Nursery School, Golden Anniversary, 1946-1996*, p.1.
23. *SEN,* 16 October 1948.
24. Kenneth O. Morgan, *Labour in Power* (Oxford, 1984), pp.153-162.
25. Jack Binns, *The History of Scarborough* (Pickering, 2001), p.340.
26. See SEN 8 March, 21 July 1948.
27. *SEN*, 16 September 1947.
28. *SEN*, 5 May 1947.
29. SMHC, File Vol 10, Hospitals.
30. Angus Calder, *The People's War: Britain 1939-1945* (London, 1971), p.241.

31 Quoted in Shane Ewen, 'Preparing the British Fire Service for War: Local Government, Nationalisation and Evolutionary Reform, 1935-41', *Contemporary British History*, Vol. 20, No. 2, June 2006, p.209.
32 Les Shannon, *Conflagrations: Scarborough's Firefighting History* (Scarborough, 2003), pp.153-4.
33 *SEN*, 31 March 1948.
34 Shannon, op. cit., pp.171-175.
35 *SEN*, 5 August 1948.
36 NA HO 45/24277, Minute, 8 June 1950.
37 *SEN*, 13 November 1945.
38 NA HO 45/24277, letter from Town Clerk to Home Office, 8 May 1950.
39 *SEN*, 14 March 1946.
40 *SEN*, 12 January 1946.
41 *SEN*, 5 May 1947.
42 *Mercury*, 17 January 1947.
43 NA HO 45/24277, letter from Town Clerk to Home Office, 8 May 1950.
44 *SEN*, 6 September 1947.
45 NA HO 45/24277, *Yorkshire Post* c. 20 September 1950.
46 Ibid.
47 NA HO 45/24277, letter from Town Clerk to Home Office, 8 May 1950.
48 Kenneth O. Morgan, *Labour in Power* (Oxford, 1984), p.103.
49 *SEN*, 9 May 1985.
50 *Mercury*, 14 February 1947.
51 *Mercury*, 2 April 1948.
52 *Mercury*, 30 July 1948.
53 *SEN*, 9 September 1948.
54 *Mercury*, 3 October 1947.
55 *Mercury*, 2 September 1949.
56 K.B. Smellie, *A History of Local Government* (London, 1957), p.123.
57 See p.18.
58 *SEN*, 10 November 1947 and *Mercury*, 23 July 1948.
59 *Mercury*, 1 April 1947.
60 *Mercury*, 30 July 1948.
61 See, for example, Clifford J. Pearce, *The Machinery of Change in Local Government, 1888-1974* (London, 1980), p.56.
62 *Mercury*, 4 June 1948.
63 *SEN*, 11 March 1947.

64 *Mercury*, 1 April 1949.
65 *SEN*, 1 July 1948.

CHAPTER 21

The Post-War Economy

Still on the terrace of the big hotel
Pale pink hydrangeas turn a rusty brown
Where sea winds catch them, and yet do not die.
The bumpy lane between the tamarisks,
The escallonia hedge, and still it's there –
Our lodging house, ten minutes from the shore.

(from John Betjeman's *Beside the Seaside* (1948),
on returning to a seaside resort after the war)[1]

In 1945 conditions appeared favourable for an economic revival in Scarborough. The country had endured nearly six years of war and there was a pent-up demand for an escape from the privations of wartime austerity. The pleasures of a seaside holiday were an obvious option. There was some optimism, too, that the town's wartime industrial growth would act as a springboard for further expansion after the war.

Industry
During the war, some town councillors began to think about how the town's post-war profits from tourism might be supplemented by the benefits of building on the wartime expansion of industry. In June 1943 the Council's Finance Committee reported on the desirability of attracting light industry to the town.[2] By early 1945 a group of local businessmen had formed a Scarborough Industries Association to promote the development of light industry in the

town, stressing 'the importance of an industrial voice in the town that had almost exclusively put all of its energies into catering for the holiday-maker'.[3] The town's MP was elected President. In support of such initiatives, the Council expanded the remit of its Publicity Committee, renaming it the Publicity and Industrial Development Committee.[4]

The desire for a diversification of the town's economy was understandable. There were opportunities for local firms to convert wartime skills and resources into peacetime enterprise. The post-war Labour government was keen to promote the relocation of industries to areas of economic need.[5] Most importantly, industrial ventures were advanced as a solution to the town's long-standing problem of seasonal, or winter, unemployment. They promised, too, improved job opportunities for the town's young and a year-round boost to the spending power of townspeople.

Progress was made in the post-war years. Local firms expanded. In 1946, the Trinity Chair Works, for example, having done well out of the war, moved into new premises in the town's old Tram Sheds off Scalby Road.[6] Similarly, the Scarborough Hosiery Company moved to a larger site on Seamer Road in the same year.[7] The war had particularly stimulated metal-working industries in the town. The Premier Engineering Company had started the war employing 12 and concluded it employing around 80.[8] The largest industrial enterprise at the end of the war was Plaxton's. A few months after the war it had resumed full peacetime production of motor coach chassis.[9] Such companies benefited from the pent-up demand for peacetime goods following wartime austerity. Dale Electric, too, having profited from wartime contracts with the RAF, used this as a launchpad for an ambitious post-war expansion.[10] Post-war Scarborough also attracted new textile companies to the town. Cockerill and Rew, a men's clothing manufacturer, set up a factory in the old St Mary's School in 1945, employing over 100 young women.[11] The Leeds clothing manufacturer May and Sons established a factory in the old hospital in 1946, employing a similar number.[12] There was, then, some expansion of existing light industry in the town and some incoming business. In December 1947 a report reviewing the progress of industrial development in the town was submitted to the Publicity and Industrial Development Committee. It listed with some satisfaction 15 companies that had been set up or developed during or since the war. Since the drive to encourage light industry in the town in early 1945, some 300 jobs had been created by the end of 1947.[13] Solid progress was being made, but it was far from a revolution.

Plaxton's factory on Seamer Rd returned to coach building after the war.

Obstacles to growth remained. Entrepreneurs were sometimes reluctant to commit to Scarborough, as they anticipated labour shortages, especially at those times of the year when tourism absorbed so much of the town's manpower. May and Sons, for example, were struggling to sign up enough female employees in the spring of 1946.[14] There was disappointment in the Town Hall and business community when the Corporation's application to be scheduled as a Development Area under the Distribution of Industry Act (1945) failed. The government would not, then, provide incentives to industry to locate in the Scarborough area.[15] There was also local opposition to the encroachments of industry in the resort. Catering and tourism interests tended to see industrial developments as a threat to the appeal of the resort to holidaymakers, and as a rival demand on scarce labour.[16] Naturally, they were quick to listen to and recycle outside voices, like that of the Deputy Town Clerk of Leeds, who counselled Scarborough not to sacrifice its charms as a seaside resort in a dash for industrial growth.[17] As usual, the tourism lobby in the town was strongly supported in the local press. The *Mercury*, for example, accepted the desirability of some light industry, as long as it was kept in check and located 'well out of the way'.[18] On the Council, supporters of tourism tended to exhibit a lack of enthusiasm for the spread of industry.[19] The resort's MP was bullish about the opportunities for post-war tourism, recommending that people in the hospitality trades should be spending their time in the winter preparing for the forthcoming holiday seasons. Industrial development, he advised, was a distraction.[20] Others were pessimistic about the prospects of attracting sufficient business to make a real difference to the local economy.[21] Even the Labour Group on the Council, the most committed backers of industrial development, promised to encourage light industries 'provided they were not a nuisance'.[22] Reflecting on post-war developments in 1985, the town's former Director of Publicity concluded:

> It was many years, too, before Scarborough accepted that its hotels did not have a God-given right to a monopoly of the labour market in the town, that light industry would not ruin the amenities of the resort, and that lip-service to its provision was not enough.[23]

Overall, the expansion of tourism, not light industry, was the post-war priority.

Tourism's post-war prospects

What, then, were the prospects for British tourism after the war? Nationally there were grounds for hope. Ernest Bevin, the wartime Minister of Labour with an instinctive feel for the mood of the British people, was prone to repeat the refrain, 'What people want at the end of the war is a holiday.'[24] Professional researchers towards the end of the war identified the reasons for a likely post-war boost in tourism. They also painted a stark picture of the difficulties this might entail.

> The report [of the Post-war Holiday Group of the National Council of Social Service] estimated that 'as a result of the Holidays with Pay Act, higher wages, war savings and war weariness', the number of holiday makers requiring accommodation at the end of the war will be 30 million, including two million family units – that is double the estimated figure for 1937. At the same time the available accommodation, which was strained to its limits in 1937, has probably diminished by 25%.[25]

One solution to predicted accommodation shortages, mooted also before the war, was to spread holidays over a longer period of the year. Scarborough's

MP called for measures to encourage this, whilst the District Chamber of Trade called for an official staggering of holidays in peacetime.[26] The government was sympathetic to such proposals and commissioned research into the existing patterns of holidaymaking, which found that some 68% of holidays in the UK were taken in July and August.[27] The reasons for such a concentration of holidaymaking were clear. It was widely assumed that the best weather in the UK was at this time, whilst a great deal of holiday planning was determined by school holidays in July and August. Many workers liked to extend their holidays by attaching them to the August Bank holiday and in northern towns it was common for mills and factories to close for a common summer break, in so-called 'wakes weeks'. Associated with this was what was described by officials as the 'innate conservatism of industrial workers in their customs'.[28] Workers had always holidayed in July and August, when they enjoyed the thronging crowds and the peak season entertainments, and were loath to lose this.

The Ministry of Labour was keen to tackle the problem of the concentration of holidays in July and August. They aimed to spread holidaymaking more evenly over the four-month period from June to September, confident that this would generate greater profits and lower unemployment rates in holiday resorts. Visitors could avoid over-stretched public transport, over-crowded destinations and inflated prices. It was also suggested that spreading holidays was necessary to boost the quality of the British coastal resort provision. When the demand for accommodation and other services exceeded the supply, there was little incentive to make improvements.[29]

The Ministry of Labour, therefore, launched a post-war 'staggered holidays' campaign in the summer of 1945, renewed in 1948. The key issue was communicated to the public thus:

> Your interests, and national interests, demand that workers should enjoy a holiday away from their usual surroundings, but it will be clearly seen that this cannot be achieved if the slavish adherence to traditional holiday dates continues.[30]

Prospective holidaymakers were informed that the best month for holiday weather was June. They were also reminded that children were entitled to two weeks absence from school on family holidays under the 1944 Education Act.[31] Such messages were supported by a vigorous public information campaign, very much in the spirit of wartime exhortations, employing slogans, posters, leaflets, film trailers and public meetings.[32] Scarborough's tourism chief reinforced the message in 1946 by predicting accommodation shortages and appealing to potential holidaymakers to book for 'June, early July, or September'.[33] The impact of the staggered holidays campaign seemed to be bearing fruit in 1946, as, though the overall number of visitors had not increased significantly from 1945, visits had been spread over a longer season, extending into September in particular.[34] It was not to last, and by 1948 the *Mercury* reported that the staggered holidays campaign was failing.[35] By 1949 the Ministry of Labour, too, admitted that, though some progress had been made, the impact of the campaign was limited.[36] It was always unlikely that the promotion of staggered holidays would transform the patterns of holidaymaking in Scarborough or the rest of the country. Holidaymakers, the *Mercury* reported, continued to enjoy the resort at its busiest and liveliest.[37] It became more difficult to cajole people into early summer and autumn bookings as the seaside accommodation situation eased. And, in the final analysis, the government accepted that holidays were a 'private' affair, and it was not willing to employ any official incentives or compulsion.[38]

Another way of relieving pressure on seaside resorts was by persuading people to holiday in the countryside. The problem was, according to a report, that 'the overwhelming majority, especially those in inland towns, associate holidays with the sea'.[39] The government launched another publicity campaign in the immediate post-war years to highlight the merits of holidays in the countryside. An obstacle, it was reported, was a widespread sentiment about holidays in the country: 'Nothing to do, especially if it rains.'[40] Official literature emphasised the value of walking, climbing, riding, cycling, camping, canoeing and caravanning in the country, but there was no evidence that the supremacy of the seaside holiday was under any threat.

Obstacles to a tourist revival

To cash in on the growing demand for seaside holidays in Scarborough, it was essential to have the hotels and boarding houses occupied by the armed forces derequisitioned as speedily as possible. This was a major operation as in the summer of 1944 some 150 hotels and boarding houses had been requisitioned, or about 75% of the peacetime bedroom accommodation possessed by businesses with more than twenty bedrooms.[41] As the invasion of Europe by Allied forces proceeded, and once peace arrived in May 1945, military personnel began to move out of the Scarborough area, abandoning their camps, billets and requisitioned properties. The special trains that had ferried troops and their equipment back and forward from the requisitioned Londesborough railway station over the previous five years became fewer and fewer. The last of the official troop trains departed in November 1945, 'unostentatiously and without ceremony'.[42] Requisitioning, however, was not entirely at an end, as by the end of 1945 some 50 hotels and boarding houses remained under military control.[43] In the spring of 1946 21 remained so, including some of the largest hotels, including the Holbeck Hall, Grand, Prince of Wales, Norbreck, Clifton and Cambridge.[44] Why was this so? Some military personnel did remain in Scarborough. The Royal Navy School of Music, which had been based in Scarborough since August 1941, signalled its departure early in 1946 with a free concert, whilst the Royal Marines were not redeployed until May 1946.[45] The Air Ministry took advantage of some of its accommodation for the post-war rehabilitation of its airmen and former POWs. However, many delays in derequisitioning arose simply from the foot-dragging of the service departments. Much to the frustration of local proprietors, many properties remained unoccupied whilst the military authorities dealt with the derequisitioning procedures at a snail's pace. 'Can nothing,' complained Jottings, 'free us from the toils of the present red tape?'[46] No government department generated as much exasperation in this respect as the War Office.

Once derequisitioning had taken place, there was often a substantial time lag before the properties were fit for commercial use. Complaints about military mistreatment of requisitioned properties rumbled on from wartime to peace. The damage to the Grand Hotel, occupied by the RAF, was a case in point:

> Thousands of boots had badly eroded steps and stairs. Worse still, the fine cast-iron balustrades surrounding the landing had been completely destroyed. Someone, for reasons intelligible only to himself, had enclosed them in cement, the acidic element of which had corroded them beyond repair, and they were replaced with simple wooden panels.

The owners were determined to return the hotel to its peacetime glory. Altogether, £100,000 was spent on repairs and refurbishment before the Grand re-opened in May 1947, with a new dining room along the full length of the seaward side.[47]

Shortages of labour and building materials continued to slow down the rehabilitation of properties, whilst even soap and other basic cleaning items were in short supply.[48] A final, if more infrequent, hazard of repossessing properties from the military was the discovery of dangerous military ordnance secreted in cupboards and under floorboards. There were reports, for instance, of Mills bombs and anti-tank and anti-aircraft shells being discovered after the military had departed.[49]

Owners of requisitioned properties were generally disappointed by the financial settlement they received from the government. The rent they received was considered to be unfairly low, reflecting the fall in the value of their properties during wartime conditions. Neither did the payments take into account the loss of profits and goodwill resulting from requisitioning. Similar detriments applied when furniture and equipment were requisitioned, where compensation bore little relation to replacement values.[50]

Given that businesses that had not been requisitioned had also suffered badly in pleasure resorts on the south and east coasts, there was considerable concern about the ability of seaside resorts to take full advantage of the return to a peacetime economy. The Catering Wages Commission came to the following conclusion at the end of 1944 about the post-war prospects of the hotel and boarding-house trade:

> Unless some other assistance is made available to them, such businesses will either be driven to bankruptcy or will continue to function on a hand to mouth basis which will be inimical to the maintenance of proper standards in the catering industry.[51]

In seaside towns like Scarborough there were hopes that government financial assistance might be made available. The wartime difficulties of pleasure resorts were, after all, occasioned by circumstances beyond their control. Although there was some sympathy in government departments, action was not forthcoming. It was felt that a special case could not be made for caterers and hotel and boarding-house keepers when so many other people in business had been 'adversely afflicted by war'.[52] Helping those who had fallen into financial embarrassment and debt, moreover, would be unfair on those who had made sacrifices and kept their heads above water.[53] And, given the country's parlous economic situation at the end of the war, tourism was not a top priority. Industry, asserted the Board of Trade, must come first.[54]

Employers in Scarborough and other pleasure resorts had an additional worry about their post-war prospects. During and after the war, conditions of employment in the tourist industry were subjected to an unprecedented degree of central government interference. This had its origins in the controversial 1943 Catering Wages Act.[55] The legislation sought to regulate the wages and conditions of workers in hitherto unprotected and low-paid jobs in hotels, boarding-houses, restaurants, cafés and public houses. Under the Act, a permanent Catering Wages Commission, supported by Wage Boards, was established to impose uniform standards of employment in the areas of both the supply of food and drink and the provision of accommodation.[56] Employers and their supporters (notably on the Conservative backbenches) were hostile. The legislation, initiated by Ernest Bevin as Minister of Labour, was seen by critics as an attack on an ailing industry. It was also damned as impracticable in seeking to impose uniform conditions on such a diverse and fragmented industry. Bevin was the *bête noir* of the critics and was assumed to be motivated by dictatorial ambitions: 'Under the pretext of improving conditions and helping these [i.e., catering] trades,' stated the employers' organisation, 'Mr Bevin is really seeking to obtain absolute control over them in his own hands.'[57]

As the Wage Boards slowly unveiled their regulations for different sectors of the catering trades in the post-war years, there were fears in Scarborough about the impact they would have on catering and tourism. The town's MP believed that the legislation would 'destroy the "give-and-take" between management and staff'.[58] One prominent employer feared a 50% increase in wages, whilst there were complaints that tips were not being taken into account in calculating fair wages.[59] The effect of regulations on overtime pay was a particular concern, one hotelier claiming that he would have to pay a week's wages for an employee to work on Christmas and Boxing Days.[60] Councillor Ireland pointed out that it would be difficult, in a climate of economic austerity, for proprietors to increase prices to offset increased wages.[61] A final grievance was the imposition of unreasonable amounts of paperwork and form-filling, on top of existing bureaucratic burdens. It was the 'small landlady', with only a handful of rooms, that would find this most difficult, it was contended.[62] Dire consequences, then, were forecast for Scarborough's hospitality industry as a result of the new legislation. The list of perceived dangers was a long one: increased unemployment, hotels closed during some of the peak holiday periods, rising prices and declining standards.

The impact of the Catering Wages Act on post-war Scarborough was not as great as employers had feared. Many were already paying at Wage Board wage levels or more, not least because of labour shortages in the town. The

Catering Wages Commission, moreover, was prepared to listen to the concerns of employers in the larger licensed undertakings and make reasonable adjustments. Overtime pay in such establishments, for example, was revised to allow for greater flexibility.[63] There were so many difficulties in introducing regulations in unlicensed businesses that none were applied until the 1950s.[64] For workers covered by the Commission's protection there were, of course, significant benefits. They gained from statutory guarantees concerning wages, hours of work and holidays, whilst the Catering Commission provided effective machinery for the redress of grievances. And it was employees in small hotels and boarding houses than gained most from protections against exploitation at work.

The Town Council faced a formidable challenge in rehabilitating Scarborough as an attractive pleasure resort after the war. Wartime neglect and damage took several years to tackle, even if destruction was slight compared with some of Britain's blitzed cities. Throughout the war the Council, as we have seen, had found itself unable to provide the normal peacetime oversight of the town.[65] Municipal buildings and gardens were deprived of the usual maintenance. The seafront 'bungalows' fell into a state of dilapidation, whilst the Mere on the edge of the town was used as an unofficial tip.[66] The state of the town's roads and pathways continued to deteriorate, as did the town's drainage systems, especially in the Valley.[67] The roadside grass verges at the end of the war were likened to hay fields.[68] And in the absence of the enforcement of many peacetime regulations, residents had taken to building sheds and outhouses 'of all shapes and sizes'. This lent to parts of the resort, it was said, the appearance of a shanty town.[69] When the Grand Restaurant was destroyed by fire in 1942, the ruins were left as a blot on the South Bay. The annex was compulsorily purchased by the Council in 1946 but it remained an eyesore until 1949, when it was demolished to enable a widening of Foreshore Road.[70]

Of course, the Council also had to deal with the more direct legacies of war in the town. The evidence of bomb damage was inescapable. It was at its worst in the Old Town, but bombsites and damaged buildings pockmarked the post-war resort.[71] Fifty static water tanks were removed from the town in the summer of 1945, many finding a use on nearby farms. A further blot on the townscape at the end of the war were the remains of anti-invasion structures and air raid shelters. The Town Hall did its best to pull down such wartime detritus. A start was made in 1944 in dismantling obstructions blocking entrances to the perimeter of the town and obstructing access from the North

Scarborough at War

and South Bays into the town. The last anti-tank concrete blocks to be cleared were removed from the harbour area in late 1946, escalating from the use of pneumatic drills to gelignite.[72] Tackling the unsightly air raid shelters did not begin till the end of 1945. Initially only the smaller brick-built surface shelters were dealt with; by February 1946 177 of these had been pulled down out of 500.[73] In early 1948 some of the larger surface shelters remained, as did the 'big five' public shelters close to the town centre, in Alma Square and at St Nicholas Cliff, for example.[74] Some concrete pillboxes, moreover, seem to have survived into the 1960s.[75] The greatest frustration was expressed about the heaps of rusting barbed wire that disfigured the entire sea front. In 1947 'Mems' in the *Evening News* demanded to know if the Spa had been told that the war was over, given its substantial barbed wire defences. Similarly, early in the following year Jottings suggested that the front looked more like a battle front than a seaside front.[76] Finally, in May 1948 the local press carried photographs of pitchfork-wielding Corporation workers removing barbed wire from the front as if they were gathering in hay.[77] It therefore required a substantial municipal effort and a number of years to reimpose the good order and civic pride in the environment typical of the pre-war resort.

Workmen moving the hugh concrete blocks from the Royal Albert Drive at Scarborough. Each weighs approximately 10 tons.

Post-war tourism

In the post-war years Scarborough recaptured many of the qualities it had enjoyed as a peacetime resort, as modest as well as prominent reminders of peacetime returned. At the top of the town, for example, the aroma of roasting coffee from Rowntree's the grocers filled the air once again.[78] The old rituals of railway travel resumed. In season, the Excursion Station at Londesborough Road, handed back by the army in 1945, disgorged crowds of day-trippers into the town. The trains were then shunted into nearby sidings where, as a local remembers, they remained all day, 'oozing smoke into the air, and frequently into the houses of those unfortunate to live in their vicinity, until it was time to operate the reverse movement in the evening'.[79] In the South Bay, motorboat trips boomed. Long queues formed at the town's cinemas and the other fashionable entertainments reappeared. The Amateur Operatic Society resumed their shows at the Open Air Theatre for example, bringing in audiences of up to 8,000. At the Floral Hall, there were twice nightly performances during the season and a revival of the colourful *Fol de Rols* shows. The Spa offered summer shows in the theatre, dancing to big bands in the ballroom and, in the Grand Hall, concert orchestra performances.[80]

To capitalise on the post-war surge in tourism, some new attractions were developed in the resort. Motorbike racing at Oliver's Mount was a popular innovation. From its first meeting in 1946, it attracted some of the biggest names in the sport. An annual professional tennis tournament was launched in the same year. In culture and the arts, the Town Hall took a striking initiative in 1947, transforming Crescent House, which it had purchased in 1942, into a municipal Art Gallery with public gardens. This was not achieved without some resistance on the Council, one councillor disapproving of 'a tendency to turn Scarborough into a sort of phoney centre of culture and learning'.[81] At the same time the Council made a commitment to converting the new Art Gallery's neighbour in the Crescent, the rundown Wood End, into both a natural history museum and a museum of the Sitwell family, the building's former owners. Councillor Shields, for one, was not impressed, alleging the scheme was merely for the benefit of a few 'highbrows' who wished to study Marxist sociology.[82] Despite opposition, the project was completed in 1951.[83] Another success was the Council's launching of the Treasure Island-themed galleon *Hispaniola* in 1949. It was to take generations of children on a sail across the Mere, on the edge of the town, to a small island where hidden treasure could be found.[84] Children were similarly thrilled by the municipal Tree Walk Wonderland, created on the Peasholm Lake island in 1953. Viewed at night, the trail was lit by fairy lights and featured illuminated scenes from children's stories.[85] It often served as a reward for good behaviour at the end of a family holiday.

Post-war motorbike racing at Oliver's Mount, with the war memorial in the background.

As the post-war national economy faced some headwinds, many seaside resorts feared a continuation of the wartime contraction in business. In the first decade after the war, however, the British people proved to be determined to return to the tradition of a seaside holiday, sometimes, notes James Walvin, spending in inverse proportion to the country's economic misfortunes.[86] Post-war tourism in Scarborough was distinguished by buoyant visitor numbers and strong profits, though Town Hall receipts were inflated by post-war price increases. Having enjoyed a bumper season in 1945, Corporation takings in 1946 surpassed those of the previous year, taking in over £163,000 from April to October inclusive.[87] In 1947, receipts were up again, by a quarter on those of 1946. A new record was set in 1948, benefiting from a particularly profitable summer season.[88] In 1949 the resort enjoyed record municipal takings at Easter and Whitsun and finished the year with a new 'high-water mark' in municipal receipts of over £277,000. Against this backdrop, small guest houses and private hotels began to change hands at ten times their pre-war value.[89]

This post-war revival of tourism in Scarborough had some distinctive features. There was a rising tide of working-class visitors, more now enjoying paid holidays and secure employment. This was perceived as a threat to some of the more socially exclusive parts of the resort. According to the *Mercury*, busloads of day-trippers were arriving in the up-market South Cliff area collarless and in short sleeves, sporting paper hats and plentifully supplied with crates of bottled beer. Such a pursuit of a 'noisy beano' was considered more appropriate to Blackpool than Scarborough.[90] Many new hotels and boarding and guest houses opened to cash in on the boom in tourism. Some were criticised locally for bringing the resort into disrepute by providing sub-standard accommodation and a poor service at inflated prices. In an episode in 1946 that posed a threat to the good name of the resort, customers of one boarding house walked out in a collective protest against unsatisfactory conditions.[91] In such a seller's market, observed one local commentator, 'the bogey of the sour-faced seaside landlady was often no fiction'.[92] Another development of the post-war years was the vast increase in visitors arriving by motor-coach, nearly 500 coaches a day at the peak of the 1946 season.[93] Coaches brought large numbers from further afield than before the war, especially from the North-East and Lancashire.[94] Peace also brought a profitable revival of Scarborough's conference trade, most notably in May 1948 when the Labour Party brought 2,700 delegates to its annual conference in the town.[95] In 1949 the resort hosted the Co-operative Party and three of the country's largest trade unions.[96]

Post-war challenges

The story of tourism in Scarborough in the post-war years was not one of undiluted success and prosperity. Some better-off holidaymakers, embracing the fashion for flying and keen to escape from austerity and rationing, were tempted abroad. The national economy faced recurrent difficulties that affected the spending power of ordinary British families. As wartime savings ran out, and as taxes rose under the Labour Government, some families found it difficult to afford a holiday at the seaside. Others managed, but cut back on so-called 'fringes', like funfairs, whelk stalls and 'fancy goods'. A further shadow cast over seaside tourism was the post-war restrictions on the use of petrol in motor vehicles.

World War Two had had an adverse impact on municipal finances, reducing the money available for investment, whilst expenditure on housing remained a priority well into the 1950s. Even when the Council wished to re-develop old amenities or build new ones, it was difficult to obtain building licences from government departments, who were prioritising housebuilding and industry in the post-war years.[97] Similarly, businesses in the town had been squeezed in wartime, reducing the prospects of private investment in the tourist economy. It would take well into the 1950s, besides, for the resort to feel the benefits of a sustained upturn in the national economy.

Scarborough was destined, therefore, to muddle through with many existing and deficient amenities for holidaymakers. Most of the ambitious recommendations of the 1938 Adshead Report remained unfulfilled.[98] In a speech in June 1948 the Borough Engineer lamented that it would not be possible to preserve the Old Town fishing village as a tourist attraction, as Adshead had envisioned. The extent of war damage and dilapidation was too great.[99] There was a widespread agreement that the Council's Olympia Ballroom in the South Bay, with its spartan interior and decaying wooden structure, was inadequate, but the venue limped on until it was destroyed by fire in 1975.[100] It was a similar story with the subterranean fun-fare, Gala Land. Situated at the south end of the Foreshore, it was also recommended for demolition by Adshead. It remained as an eyesore, struggled to make any money and was, according to Scarborough's historian, 'damp, malodorous and mostly empty'.[101] It mouldered on until 1966, when it was converted into an underground carpark. Adshead had recommended that the resort required a purpose-built conference venue. At the 1948 Labour Party Conference in the town, the party's General Secretary had complained that the conference had had to be conducted in three separate halls at the Spa, with the Prime Minister's address relayed to the other two from the Grand Hall. The resort, though, remained without a large-scale conference facility in the post-war years. The Spa itself struggled to make ends meet and was taken over by the Council in 1957.[102] The Adshead Report had identified the lack of indoor entertainment for wet days as a serious shortcoming of the resort and proposed the building of indoor swimming pools in the South Bay and near the town centre. The resort, however, had to wait until 1973 for suitable indoor swimming facilities. A continuation of the interwar development of the North Side was considered by Adshead to be a key to Scarborough's future as a pleasure resort. His advocacy of an open-air swimming pool at Peasholm Gap had already been realised before the outbreak of war. Also recommended in the Adshead Report for the North Side was the building of a lavish complex of amenities at Scalby Mills, at the north end of North Bay. The Town Hall rejected the feasibility of such a development in 1948, and it was not until 1966 that a bargain-basement development was built on the site.[103] The North Side's Corner Café was another disappointment. Situated at the panoramic Peasholm Gap, its rebuilding was also anticipated in the Report. Though the second-rate building had deteriorated further after wartime military use and damage inflicted in an air-raid, it endured until 2007.[104] Progress in developing amenities, then, was slow.

After the war Scarborough banked on an economic future based on a revival of tourism, and there was ample evidence of a demand for seaside holidays to support such a judgement. Potential obstacles to an expansion of tourism in the immediate post-war years, such as a disfigured townscape and shortages of accommodation, were tackled resolutely. Peacetime amenities and entertainments were restored, and some new ones developed. Yet, given the local disruption and costs of the war, it proved to be difficult to recapture the momentum and confidence that characterised the tourist economy of the 1930s, typified by the boldness of the Adshead Report of 1938. Scarborough, therefore, was not as well equipped as it might have been to compete with the post-war challenges of holiday camps, air travel and foreign package holidays. World War Two was to cast a long shadow.

Notes

1. John Betjeman, *Collected Poems* (London, 2006), p.129.
2. *SEN*, 1 June 1943.
3. *SEN*, 10 February 1945.
4. *SEN*, 5 April 1945.
5. Peter Hennessy, *Never Again: Britain 1945-1951* (London, 1992), p.210.
6. *SEN*, 23 April 1946.
7. *SEN*, 12 December 1946.
8. *SEN*, 28 January 1946.
9. Alan Townson and Edward Hirst, *Plaxtons* (Transport Publishing Company, 1982), p.13.
10. Hugh Barty-King, *Light Up the World: The Story of Leonard Dale and Dale Electric, 1935-1985* (London, 1985), p.24.
11. *SEN*, 28 January 1946.
12. *SEN*, 23 April 1946.
13. *SEN*, 6 December 1947.
14. *SEN*, 23 April 1946.
15. *SEN*, 28 January 1946.
16. *SEN*, 29 January 1946.
17. *SEN*, 11 May 1946.
18. *Mercury*, 9 April 1948.
19. *Mercury*, 10 May 1946.
20. *SEN*, 12 June 1947.
21. Alderman Whittaker, *SEN*, 11 July 1944, for an early example of pessimism.
22. *Mercury*, 31 October 1947.
23. Steve Fewster, *SEN*, 9 May 1985.
24. Quoted, for example, in *SEN*, 1 April 1943.
25. NA HLG 71/773, A Note on the Draft Report of the Post-War Holiday Group of the National Council of Social Service, 22 September 1944.
26. *SEN*, 20 March and *Mercury*, 1 June 1945.
27. NA LAB 9/158, Ministry of Labour Standing Committee on the Staggering of Holidays in England and Wales; Review of the Arrangements for 1948.
28. NA LAB 9/158, The Staggering of Holidays: Report to the Ministry of Labour and National Service by the Catering Wages Commission (HMSO, 1945), p.4.
29. Ibid.
30. NA LAB 9/158, *Holiday Facts*, Home Holidays division of the British Tourist and Holidays Board, n.d.
31. Ibid.

32 NA LAB 9/158, Ministry of Labour Sub-Committee on Publicity for Staggered Holidays, 30 November 1948.
33 Scarborough Tourism Publicity Brochure, 1946.
34 *SEN,* 10 October 1946.
35 *Mercury,* 31 December 1948.
36 NA LAB 9/158, Preliminary Campaign Memorandum, Ministry of Labour, Staggered Holidays – 1949, 5 January 1949.
37 *Mercury,* 31 December 1948.
38 NA LAB 9/158, The Staggering of Holidays: Report to the Ministry of Labour and National Service by the Catering Wages Commission (HMSO, 1945).
39 NA HLG 71/773, A Note on the Draft Report of the Post-War Holiday Group of the National Council of Social Service, 22 September 1944.
40 Ibid.
41 NA LAB 30/34, EC of SHBHA statement to Catering Wages Commission, 19 June 1944.
42 *SEN,* 8 November 1945.
43 *SEN,* 7 November 1945.
44 *SEN,* 3 April 1945.
45 *SEN,* 19 February and 1 April 1946.
46 *Mercury,* 5 October 1945.
47 Bryan Perrett, *'A Sense of Style': Being a Brief History of the Grand Hotel, Scarborough* (Ormskirk, 1991).
48 *Mercury,* 22 February 1946.
49 See, for example, *SEN,* 18 December 1945 and *Mercury,* 8 February 1946.
50 NA LAB 11/1714, Memorandum by Lord Monsell, 19 March 1945.
51 NA LAB 11/1714, Report of the Catering Wages Commission on the Rehabilitation of the Catering Industry, 20 November 1944.
52 NA LAB 11/2051, Note on a Deputation from Holiday and Pleasure Resorts Association to Minister of Health, 5 May 1943.
53 NA HO 186/2250, Meeting on termination of Defence (Evacuation) Regulations, February 1944.
54 NA LAB 11/2051, Note on a Deputation from Holiday and Pleasure Resorts Association to Minister of Health, 5 May 1943.
55 See Alan Bullock, *The Life and Times of Ernest Bevin, vol.2, Minister of Labour: 1940-1945* (London, 1967), p.220-24.
56 NA LAB 11/2444, General Review of the Catering Wages Act 1943, and its effect on the hotel and tourist industry (1949).
57 Bullock, op. cit., p.222.
58 *SEN,* 22 June 1949.

59 *SEN,* 27 January 1948.
60 *Mercury,* 2 July 1948.
61 *SEN,* 9 February 1949.
62 *Mercury,* 1 April 1949.
63 *Mercury,* 11 February 1949.
64 *Mercury,* 23 December 1949.
65 See p.116.
66 *Mercury,* 12 February 1943 and *SEN,* 30 October 1945.
67 *Mercury,* 12 October 1943.
68 *Mercury,* 28 December 1945.
69 *SEN,* 14 February 1946.
70 *Mercury,* 12 July 1946 and *SEN,* 1 February 1949.
71 *SEN,* 25 April and *Mercury* 2 August 1946.
72 *Mercury,* 1 November 1946.
73 *SEN,* 13 February 1946.
74 *SEN,* 17 January 1948.
75 SMHC file, SEN, n.d.
76 *SEN,* 7 August 1947 and *Mercury,* 6 February 1948.
77 *Mercury,* 7 May 1948.
78 Christopher Wiseman, *36 Cornelian Avenue* (Montreal, 2008), p.53.
79 *SEN,* 9 May 1985.
80 Ibid.
81 *SEN,* 15 April 1947.
82 *Mercury,* 17 October 1947.
83 Jack Binns, *The History of Scarborough, North Yorkshire* (Pickering, 2001), p.366-67.
84 Ibid. p.369.
85 Ibid. p.369.
86 James Walvin, *Beside the Seaside* (London, 1978), p.138-40.
87 *SEN,* 24 October 1946.
88 *SEN,* 21 October 1948.
89 *SEN,* 9 May 1985.
90 *Mercury* 27 September 1946.
91 *Mercury* 9 August 1946.
92 Steve Fewster, former Director of Publicity in *SEN,* 9 May 1985.
93 *SEN,* 10 October 1946.
94 *SEN,* 10 October 1946.

95 *SEN*, 10 May 1948.
96 TGWU, AEU and NUGMW, *SEN*, 11 April 1949.
97 *Mercury,* 10 June 1949.
98 For the Adshead Report, see pp.11-13.
99 *SEN*, 3 June 1948.
100 *Mercury,* 4 June 1943.
101 Binns, op. cit., p.382.
102 Binns, op. cit., p.365.
103 *SEN,* 7 April 1948.
104 *SEN*, 19 March and 11 August 1945, *Mercury,* 10 December 1948 and *SEN*, 11 June 1949.

Epilogue

This is no war of chieftains or of princes, of dynasties or national ambition ...There are vast numbers not only in this island but in every land, who will render faithful service in this War, but whose names will never be known, whose deeds will never be recorded.

(Winston Churchill broadcast, 14 July 1940)

Victory Day, 8 June 1946 – Drumhead Service on South Bay (traditionally a makeshift religious service held in the vicinity of the field of battle). The lighthouse is faintly visible top right, and the icehouse chimney rises up from the Old Town above the harbour.

Epilogue

It is appropriate, perhaps, to reflect on some of the themes that have emerged from this study of wartime Scarborough, though it is not always possible to come to clear-cut and definitive conclusions. Firstly, what was the wider significance of the town's experience of the war? Britain's memory of the Home Front in World War II does not always embrace the experiences of the nation's smaller communities. The most evocative images of the war often reflect the ordeal of the country's bombed-out ports and cities. Representations of the war at home also tend to exhibit a bias towards the metropolis and the south east, whether it is images of St Paul's Cathedral defiant amidst the smoke of the London Blitz or Spitfires engaged in dogfights in the skies over Kent. This book has sought to illustrate how Scarborough, as a northern coastal town, not only shared closely in the national experience of the war but also made a distinctive contribution to Britain's struggle. The town served, for example, as a haven for evacuee children and adults. The town's contribution to the training of RAF recruits in Initial Training Wings laid some of the foundations for the air war against the Axis powers. Similarly, the work of the naval 'Y' station at Scarborough assisted the codebreakers at Bletchley Park in cracking the vital German Enigma codes. Fishermen from the Old Town fought back against the *Luftwaffe* during the so-called 'Phoney War'. Britain's war economy benefited, too, from national savings efforts and from war production in Scarborough, including that of pioneering RAF pathfinding equipment at Erskine Laboratories. The town struggled to maintain its tourist business during many of the war years, but, for those who managed a daytrip or a longer holiday, the resort offered a consoling diversion from the strains of war (and from the austerities of the post war years). The contribution of pleasure resorts to national morale in difficult times was far from negligible.

It is difficult to assess the state of civilian morale in Scarborough during the war, as, unlike some of Britain's larger cities, there is little direct evidence available to the historian. To a large degree, therefore, the state of the public mood must be inferred from the behaviour of the community during the war. The picture that emerges is one of solid and patriotic support for the war. The community seems to have taken a pride in 'doing its bit' for the war effort, evident, for instance, in the salvage and 'digging for victory' campaigns. Further evidence can be found in the town's annual National Savings Weeks, which developed as jamborees of patriotic engagement and celebration. The widespread voluntary activity in the town, in the Home Guard and the Women's Voluntary Service for example, is also a testament to the commitment of the town to the national struggle. Throughout the war, too, townspeople appear to have been prepared to make all sorts of sacrifices and adjustments to everyday life with relatively little complaint. A considerable patience and forbearance were required to cope with the blackout, rationing, the fluctuating fortunes of the tourist economy, the impact of evacuees and servicemen on the town, the constant threat of air raids and, after the war, the frustrating waiting list for municipal housing.

Yet, there is a danger of a rose-tinted nostalgia colouring British recollections of World War II. It has been readily apparent in this survey of Scarborough's war that sometimes people found the experience of the Home Front difficult to tolerate. The conflict imposed painful adjustments on the lives of civilians, prompting, at times, communal fears and tensions and some unpatriotic behaviour. There was some ugly opposition to the reception of evacuees, especially those from poorer backgrounds. Juvenile delinquents were part of the local story of the war, as were younger men and women who pursued personal pleasures and rebelled against calls for sacrifice and self-restraint. Tensions arose on the inadequate bus services, as passengers developed sharp elbows and exhibited a lack of community spirit. The one snapshot of local public opinion that we do have comes from the September 1941 by-election, which was a difficult time in the war. The significant vote for the rebel outsider Reg Hipwell suggests the existence of some bloody-minded disenchantment with the state of the country and the progress of the war.

Assessing change and continuity on the Home Front in wartime Scarborough is a challenging task, often involving many variables and imprecise evidence. The economic impact of the war was substantial, if uneven. The fishing industry suffered. Light industry received a boost in wartime but found only lukewarm support afterwards. The vital industry of tourism took a serious hit, some holiday businesses failing to survive the damage inflicted during the first half of the war. Other undertakings soldiered on in a precarious state, depleted of capital. Support for tourist enterprises was provided in wartime by the needs of evacuees and the military, as well as by determined wartime holidaymakers. Crucially, the pent-up demand for seaside holidays helped much of the hospitality economy to recover after the war. Overall, however, the war interrupted the resort's thriving economic trajectory of the 1930s and bequeathed a legacy of commercial and municipal underinvestment.

It is difficult to come to assured conclusions about the effects of the war on the social outlook and attitudes of the people of Scarborough, so a degree of speculation is inevitable. It is hard, for example, to believe that the widespread voluntarism and active citizenship of the war years did not help to bring about a greater degree of social awareness and community involvement after the war. On the other hand, the wartime ethos of thrift and 'waste not want not' was difficult to sustain in a peacetime resort devoted to the pleasures of life. The arrival in wartime of servicemen and evacuees from all over Britain, and Allied servicemen from all over the world, helped to open eyes to a diversity of social outlooks and behaviours, from the children of the slums of Hull to glamorous and uniformed Poles and 'Yanks'. The impact of the war on opinions about women's place in society is a disputed question. It would be surprising if all the work of the WVS and the contribution of female workers did not have a positive impact on women's self-esteem and society's perception of women's social and public role. However, there was also resistance to change. Wartime evidence of opposition to empowering women in Scarborough, in the police and fire service for example, suggests a continuity in traditional male attitudes. This may help to explain feminist reverses in the later 1940s and 1950s when ideas about women's subordinate domestic role found increasing favour.

In addition to welcoming foreign military to the town, the people of Scarborough supported the popular wartime cause of Anglo-Russian solidarity.

Historians have long been interested in the changes in political outlook and values produced by the experience of the Home Front in the Second World War. The war, it is commonly argued, fostered a disaffection with the country's ruling elites and a celebration of the dignity and values of the common man and woman. A greater acceptance of the principle of 'fair shares for all' developed, along with a recognition that state action was essential to the achievement of economic efficiency.[1] It is not possible to come to authoritative conclusions about changes in political attitudes in wartime Scarborough. The vote for Hipwell in 1941, however, can be seen partly as a vote for a champion of social improvement and an opponent of privilege and 'vested interests'. The electoral progress of the Labour Party in the constituency in 1945 also suggests a shift, albeit a modest one, in political opinion. Scarborough, it might be said, experienced a small political tremor as part of the national earthquake of Labour's 1945 General Election victory. Conservatism did, though, retain its electoral ascendancy in 1941 and 1945, benefiting from the weakness of the working class vote in Scarborough and Whitby. Fundamental continuities in Scarborough's post-war politics were thus assured. Yet the war also wrought changes in the Conservative Party locally. The shift from the part-time and patrician habits of Sir Paul Latham to the conscientious, reform-minded attributes of Alexander Spearman perhaps points to a change in the political culture of the local Tory Party.

Social changes in wartime also had an impact on the leadership of the Town Council. The election of the town's first female mayor in 1942 reflected the public contributions of women in wartime Scarborough. The Council's election of Johnny Jackson as mayor in 1945 was likewise a fitting response to the shift of opinion in wartime towards the acceptance of a wider social representation in the running of affairs. In the immediate post-war years municipal politics continued to be more inclusive when Labour Party representation on the Council was increased. Such changes, however, were not enough to alter the direction of most policy on the Council, which tended to remain committed to financial prudence and the interests of local business. The Council's conservative instincts were evident, for example, in its unwavering opposition to the establishment of a British Restaurant in wartime and post-war Scarborough. Nevertheless, the war saw the Town Hall and its councillors playing a more interventionist role in the community. They took a lead when the community faced particular challenges, such as the initial wave of child evacuees in 1939. Throughout the conflict councillors tried to foster a sense of 'civic patriotism' in the town by encouraging, for example, a competitive spirit in national salvage and National Savings campaigns. Municipal activism continued after the war in the race to build much-needed public housing. This record of municipal initiative helps to explain why the Town Hall was so disappointed to lose some of its influence when formal municipal powers were limited both during and after the war.

For many Scarborough families the greatest impact of the war was the loss of a loved one. It can be difficult to establish precise figures for wartime deaths. This author's calculation is that 51 people died in war-related deaths in Scarborough and the surrounding area. Of these, nine were attached to the armed forces and were not permanent residents of the town. The remaining 42 can loosely be termed Scarborians as they lived or worked in Scarborough or nearby, or as evacuees had settled in the town.[2] Of the 42, 34 died as a result of air raids and the remaining eight as a result of war-related accidents (linked mostly to the explosion of land and sea mines). The local press suggested the figure of 57 seriously injured in air-raids, though this is likely to exclude many who also suffered from long-term debilitating injuries.[3] Many more people, of course, left Scarborough and lost their lives on active service. The war memorial, which was unveiled in 1950, lists 661 who died serving in the army, air force and royal and merchant navy, plus civilians killed on active service.[4] For the bereaved families the peace brought a heavy burden of loss. Such a painful psychological legacy of the war is impossible to measure.

In October 1945 the Chief Regional Fire Officer with responsibility for Scarborough spoke in the town of the nation's war effort:

> The war had been brought to a successful conclusion only by the spirit which we British had inherent in us, which only came forth when we had our backs against the wall … What has been our principal armour? The wonderful spirit of the Britisher. We came together.[5]

Such a plucky and patriotic characterisation of the war effort helped to shape how the British people viewed the war in the post-war period. This view remains widely shared, though historical writing is now more likely to take into account the 'spectre of division and difference' also experienced in wartime.[6] Yet, in fundamental ways the people of Scarborough did come together. For most though, as Churchill understood, their names will never be known, nor their deeds recorded.[7]

Scarborough at War

SCARBOROUGH WAR MEMORIAL
OLIVERS MOUNT

The Ceremony of the
Unveiling and Dedication of the
Tablets and Commemoration Seats

To the memory of those who gave their lives in the Second World War
1939 – 1945
Sunday, 12th November, 1950 at 3 p.m.

There was a prolonged debate after the war about how best to commemorate the local victims of World War II. Some argued for something practical, like a community building or sports fields, others for a new monument. In the end it was decided to improve the First World War memorial site and to add new inscribed tablets to the existing monument.

Notes

1. Geoffrey G. Field, *Blood, Sweat and Toil: Remaking the British Working Class, 1939-1945* (Oxford, 2013), p.371-2.
2. This is broadly in line with the national percentage of civilian casualties, if you calculate on the basis of 67,000 civilian deaths out of a population of 41m.
3. For the estimate of serious injuries, see *SEN*, 29 October 1954.
4. Jack Binns, *The History of Scarborough* (Pickering, 2001), p.365.
5. *SEN*, 11 October 1945.
6. Sonya O. Rose, *Which People's War?* (Oxford, 2003), p.286.
7. See Churchill broadcast, p.308.

APPENDICES

Appendix 1

War-Related Deaths in Scarborough and District				
Date	Name	Location	Age	Cause of Death
4.7.40	LOUIS ARCHER	Lifeboat House slipway	9	Died when a sea mine exploded on South Bay beach
15.8.40	ERNEST GATES	Parnell's Wood, off Seamer Rd	8	Killed by bomb blast in single plane air raid
14.9.40	MARY WARDELL	South Bay Beach	25	Shot mistakenly by a sentry
10.10.40	ANN CHAMPLIN nee GODFREY	10 Anderson Terrace, Potter Lane	73	Died in parachute mine air raid
10.10.40	SYDNEY WALKER	10 Anderson Terrace, Potter Lane	7 weeks	Ditto
10.10.40	LILIAN STRAW	Potter Lane	45	Ditto
10.10.40	PATRICIA RYAN	12 Potter Lane	2	Ditto

Appendix 1

War-Related Deaths in Scarborough and District					
16.10.40	WILLIAM J. COLLING	The trawler *PRIDE*, Scarborough Harbour	39	Mine explosion in harbour, probably a parachute mine
16.10.40	JOHN ROBINSON	The trawler *PRIDE*	45	ditto
16.10.40	WILLIAM COLLING	The trawler *PRIDE*	38	ditto
16.10.40	FRANCIS CRAWFORD	The trawler *PRIDE*	35	ditto
18.3.41	ARTHUR TURNBULL	Queens Terrace	79	March 'Blitz' air raid
18.3.41	RODNEY PREVETT	40 Moorland Rd	3	ditto
18.3.41	LOUISA BOUCHER	40 Moorland Rd	?	ditto
18.3.41	SHIELA MCKINLEY (Peggy)	120 North Marine Rd	16	ditto
18.3.41	GEORGE SIDDLE	120 North Marine Rd	48	ditto
18.3.41	LILY SIDDLE	120 North Marine Rd	48	ditto
18.3.41	AUDREY SIDDLE	120 North Marine Rd	15	ditto
18.3.41	GEORGE SIDDLE	120 North Marine Rd	13	ditto
18.3.41	GERALD SIDDLE	120 North Marine Rd	11	ditto
18.3.41	JOE SIDDLE	120 North Marine Rd	5	ditto

\multicolumn{5}{c	}{**War-Related Deaths in Scarborough and District**}
18.3.41	WILLIAM BIGDEN	1 Queens Terrace	26	ditto
18.3.41	ETHEL BIGDEN	1 Queens Terrace	?	ditto
18.3.41	JEAN BIGDEN	1 Queens Terrace	14 months	ditto
18.3.41 (died on 24.3.41 in hospital)	GEORGE CAPPLEMAN	1 Queens Terrace	62	ditto
18.3.41	ARTHUR CAPPLEMAN	1 Queens Terrace	19	ditto
18.3.41 (died 26.4.41)	HENRY CRAWFORD	17 New Queen St	58	Died as a result of the March 'Blitz' air raid
18.3.41	CHARLES GREAVES	Weaponness Farm, Oliver's Mount	55	March 'Blitz' air raid
18.3.41	LAVINIA HALL	65 Commercial St	35	ditto
18.3.41	ALAN HALL	65 Commercial St	2	ditto
18.3.41	SHEILA HALL	65 Commercial St	10	ditto
18.3.41	MARY HESLETINE	69 Commercial St	69	ditto
18.3.41	ELIZABETH HODGSON	69 Commercial St	60	ditto
18.3.41 (died 5.10.41 in hospital)	KATE KING	17a New Queen St.	57	Died as a result of the March 'Blitz' air raid

Appendix 1

	War-Related Deaths in Scarborough and District			
18.3.41	JOAN WALLER	71 Commercial St	17	March 'Blitz' air raid
18.3.41	SYLVIA WILLIS	63 Commercial St	2	ditto
18.3.41	ROLAND SHEARD	Found on Filey Rd outside Wiley's Grocer which was opposite Queen Margaret's Rd	47	ditto
18.3.41	CYRIL HUTCHINSON	Queen Margaret's Road when a parachute mine landed on Queen Margaret's School.	19	ditto
20.3.41	SQUADRON LEADER J WALKER (nationality Canadian)	?	?	Died of a gas leak caused by March 'Blitz' air raid
20.3.41	Mrs WALKER, WIFE OF ABOVE (name unknown)	?	?	ditto
5.4.41	PRIVATE WILLIAM HEWITT	Burniston Bay	30	Killed dealing with a sea mine
5.4.41	PRIVATE EDWARD McGREARY	Burniston Bay	28	ditto

	War-Related Deaths in Scarborough and District			
6.4.41	PRIVATE ERNEST MOORCROFT	Near South Bay Bathing Pool	28	ditto
6.4.41	LANCE CORPORAL GEORGE McALISTER	Near South Bay Bathing Pool	20	ditto
12.4.41	LANCE CORPORAL JOHN ELDER	Holbeck Gardens	30	ditto
4.5.41	CAPTAIN HENRY YORKE	Brompton-by-Sawdon	?	Air raid
10.5.41	WILLIAM STOAT	Weston Hotel	19	Air raid
4.6.41	PILOT OFFICER GEOFFREY MOULD	Allotment gardens near Weydale Ave, North Side	26	Plane crash near his parents' house
4.6.41	PILOT OFFICER WILLIAM THEYS	Allotment gardens near Weydale Ave, North Side	30	Plane crash (above)
29.6.41	PERCY ELVEN	Castle Holms	9	Died entering a minefield
14.9.41	NELLIE THORNTON, NEE CUDWORTH	Woodland Ravine	31	Air raid

Appendix 2

Distribution of High Explosive and Incendiary Bombs landing in Scarborough, 1940-45.

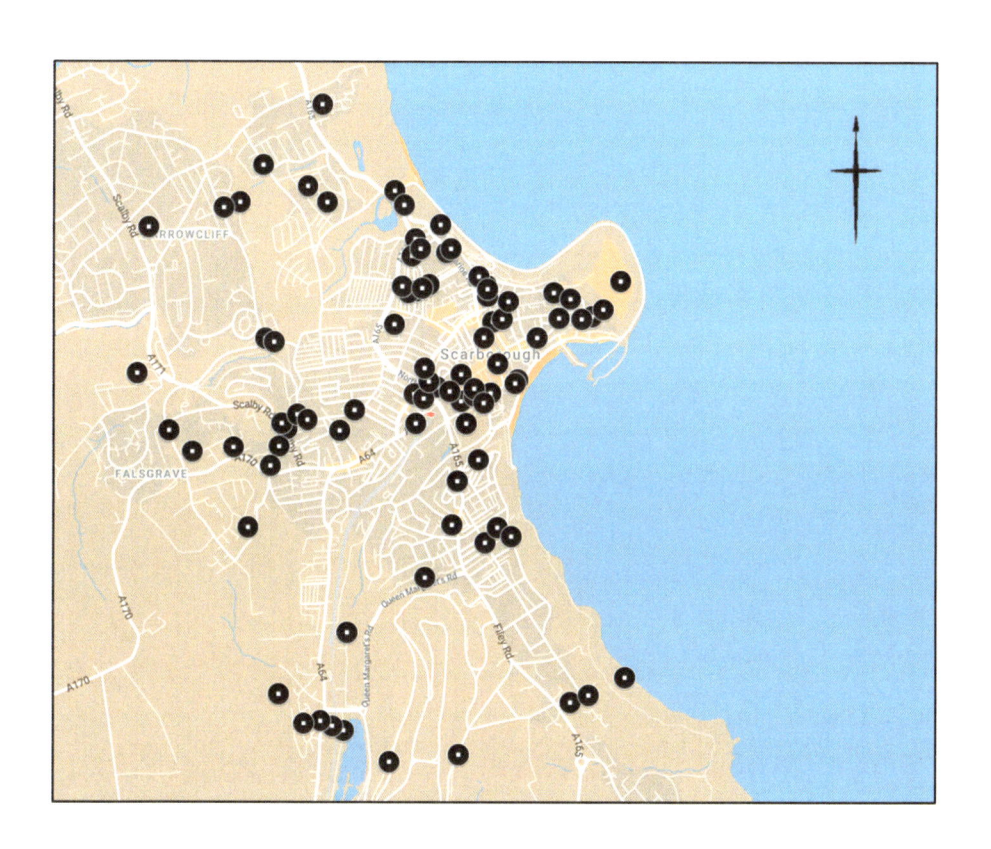

SOURCES *(and abbreviations used in endnotes)*

National Archives, Kew (NA):
Files including material on wartime and post-war Scarborough:
AIR, Air Ministry, RAF
CAB, Records of the Cabinet Office
ED, Board and Ministry of Education, HM Inspectorate
HLG, Local Government, Ministries of Health and Housing
HO, Home Office, Ministry of Home Security
HW, Government Code and Cypher School, 'Y' Stations
INF, Ministry of Information
LAB, Ministry of Labour
WO, War Office, Armed Forces
WORK, Office of Works, Ancient Monuments and Historic Buildings

Imperial War Museum (IWM):
Sound Archive
Department of Documents
Photograph Archive

Mass Observation Archive (MO):
File Report 902 and Topic Collection 46 on the September 1941 by-election

BBC People's War: BBC – WW2 People's War – Archive List (use guidance on archived website to locate individual contributions)

Women's Voluntary Service (WVS):

https://www.royalvoluntaryservice.org.uk/about-us/our-history/archive-and-heritage-collection

International Bomber Command Centre Digital Archive, University of Lincoln:

Material on Scarborough's RAF Initial Training Wings

IBCC Digital Archive (lincoln.ac.uk)

Scarborough Maritime Heritage Centre (SMHC):

Files covering the general history of Scarborough, maritime and fishing history and Scarborough in World War II

Hansard/House of Commons Debates (HC Debs.)

The Second World War Experience Centre:

Memoir of D Goy – LEEWW.2000.698

Scarborough Library:

Topic Files on World War II

Scarborough Evening News (SEN), Microfilm and digital readers

Mercury, Microfilm and digital readers

National Newspapers:

Daily Mail, Daily Mirror, Daily Telegraph, Manchester Guardian, Times.

Select Bibliography

(*for more specialist academic books and journal articles, see chapter endnotes*)

Addison, Paul, *Now the War is Over* (London, 1985).

Adshead, S.D. and Overfield, H.V., *Scarborough: A Survey of its Existing Conditions and some Proposals for its Future Development* (London, 1938).

Baker, Terry, *A Merry Dance: Tales of a Scarborough Lad from the "Bottom End" of Town* (Richmond, 2010).

Bang, Paul C., *North Cliff Golf Club Scarborough* (York, 2015).

Barty-King, Hugh, *Light Up the World: The Story of Leonard Dale and Dale Electric, 1935-1985* (London, 1985).

Binns, Jack, *The History of Scarborough* (Pickering, 2001).

Brivati, Brian and Jones, Harriet (eds.), *What Difference Did the War Make?* (London, 1995).

Brown, Stewart J., *Plaxton: 100 Years, A Century of Innovation* (Hersham, 2006).

Calder, Angus, *The People's War: Britain 1939-1945* (London, 1971).

Childhaven Nursery School, Golden Anniversary, 1946-1996.

The Crown Hotel: 150 Years of Hospitality (Scarborough, n.d.).

Davison, Muriel, *A Wren's Tale: The Secret Link to Bletchley Park* (Reigate, 2011).

Select Bibliography

Elsey, Margaret, *Scarborough Standing Conference of Women's Organisations: A Brief History* (Trevor Jordan, 2011).

Field, Geoffrey G., *Blood, Sweat and Toil: Remaking the British Working Class, 1939-1945* (Oxford, 2013).

Fowler, David, *God Bless the Prince of Wales* (Scarborough, 2009).

Fowler, David, *I've started so I'll finish ... A Memoir* (Scarborough, 2017).

Gardiner, Juliet, *Wartime Britain, 1939-1945* (London, 2004).

A Guide to Historic Scarborough (Scarborough Archaeological and Historical Society, 2003).

Hennessy, Peter, *Never Again: Britain 1945-1951* (London, 1992).

Hicks, John D., *A Hull School in Wartime: Kingston High School's Evacuation to Scarborough* (Beverley, 1990).

Jeffreys, Kevin, *The Churchill Coalition and Wartime Politics* (Manchester, 1995),

Kynaston, David, *A World to Build* (London, 2008).

MacKay, Robert, *The Test of War* (London, 1999).

MacKay, Robert, *Half the Battle: Civilian Morale in Britain during the Second World War* (Manchester, 2002).

Markham, Len, *Homefront Yorkshire*, 1939-1945 (Barnsley, 2007).

Marsden, H.W., *The Westwood School at Scarborough: Jubilee, 1902-1952*.

Morgan, K.O., *Labour in Power* (Oxford, 1984).

O'Brien, Terence H., *Civil Defence* (HMSO, London, 1955).

Pearson, Trevor, *Scarborough: A History* (Chichester, 2009).

Percy, Richard James, *Scarborough's War Years* (unpublished ms., n.d.).

Percy, Richard James, *Anecdotes of Scarborough* (unpublished ms., 2006).

Perrett, Bryan, *'A Sense of Style': Being a Brief History of the Grand Hotel, Scarborough* (Ormskirk, 1991).

Rose, Sonya O., *Which People's War?* (Oxford, 2003).

Shannon, Les, *Conflagrations: Scarborough's Firefighting History* (Scarborough, 2003).

Titmus, Richard M., *Problems of Social Policy* (HMSO, London, 1950).

Todman, Daniel, *Britain's War: Into Battle, 1937-1941* (London, 2016).

Todman, Daniel, *Britain's War: A New World, 1942-1947* (London, 2020).

Townson, Alan and Hirst, Edward, *Plaxton's: An Illustrated History to Mark the Company's Jubilee* (Transport Publishing Company, 1982).

Welburn, Ron, *Full Circle: the jottings of a Scarborian* (Scarborough, 1992).

Wiseman, Christopher, *36 Cornelian Avenue* (Montreal, 2008).

Index

Adshead Report (Adshead, Stanley) 1, 4-8, 11-13, 302-03
Air raids 16-17, 25-26, 89-112, 174, 185, 234, 279, 310, 313
　see also March 1941 'Blitz', Potter Lane
Air raid alerts 90, 96-97, 111-112
Air Raid Precautions (ARP) 16-20, 24, 35, 95-96, 102, 107-08, 185, 223, 283
Air raid shelters 19, 96-98, 108-09, 234, 297-98
　see also Anderson Shelters, 'communal' air raid shelters, public air raid shelters
Aguila SS, sinking 176
Albert Hall 109
Anderson Shelters 97-98
Anti-Aircraft Searchlight Unit, Scalby 64
Army: attitudes to 22, 73-79; 108, 121-22, 131, 162, 182, 206, 234, 241, 277, 294
Art School 109, 277
Art Gallery 299
Austerity 143, 202, 204, 206, 208, 228-29 288-89, 296, 301-02
Auxiliary Fire Service (AFS)16-17, 19, 21, 103, 108

Barker, Kathleen,
　see Fox, Paddy
Barrowcliff 235, 265-67, 274
Bathing (outdoor) 4, 7, 9, 11-12, 25, 64, 116, 119-21, 246
Bevan, Aneurin 263, 265, 269, 278-79
Beveridge, William 253, 256
Bevin, Ernest 219, 291, 296
Bigamy 73, 191, 230

Billeting (military) 27, 72-73, 76, 121, 161 175, 293
Bismarck, sinking 170-71
Black Market 97, 213-14, 224, 230
Blackout 16, 19-20, 22, 75, 91, 96, 233-234, 310
Blackpool 28,116-18, 301
Bletchley Park 169-74, 176-78, 309
'bottom enders'
　see Old Town
Boys High School 111, 214, 216-17, 275-76
Boy Scouts 17, 197, 199, 205, 217
British Restaurants 218-21, 224, 254, 258, 312
Brogden and Wilson (ironfounders) 122
Brompton-by-Sawdon 65, 109, 267
Burniston 90-91, 109
Bus services 117, 183, 221-23, 235, 283
Butler Education Act (1944)
　see Education
Butlin's (Billy Butlin) 84, 241
By-election (1941) 144-152, 252, 310

Cappleman, Winifred 93, 95, 107
Castle (Castle Hill, Castle Holms) 2, 5, 9, 63-64, 66-67, 103, 160, 166, 250
Catering 8, 10, 120, 218-220, 240, 296
Catering Wages Act and Commission 295-97
Cayley, Sir Kenelm 153
Cayton Bay 58-61, 64-65
Change and continuity 310
Chicksands (RAF 'Y' Station) 175
Childhaven nursery school 278
Churches 15,17, 49, 76, 95, 103, 165, 250-51, 277; St Mary's, 6, 94
Cinemas 3, 15, 25, 79, 164, 229, 233, 299

327

Civil Defence,
    see Air Raid Precautions
Cockerill and Rew 289
Comins, Mary
    see Murder
'Communal' air raid shelters 98, 108
Communists 67, 253-254, 258
Conferences (national) 26, 119, 240, 242, 244, 301-02
Conservative Party 4, 139-42, 144-154, 252-57, 312
Cornelian Bay 60-61, 64
Corner Café 4, 9, 12, 103, 303
Council of Social Welfare 28, 41
Countryside, holidays in 293
Crescent 3, 11, 178, 198, 299
Cricket 22, 245
Curry, Douglas 254
Cycling 17, 81, 118, 175, 221, 228

Davison, Muriel 175-76, 178
Dale Electric 121, 289
D-Day 72, 74, 85, 122, 177, 183, 240
Deaths, wartime 313 and see Appendix 1
Defence Area 27-29, 61
Defence of Scarborough,
    see Home Defence
Dennis, ETW 103-04
Derequisitioning 76, 239, 241-42, 293-95
Downe, Lord (Richard Dawnay) 145

Edgehill 3, 10, 149
Education 4, 34, 36, 46, 273-78; Education Act (Butler's) 1944, 273-77; Eleven Plus, 273-74; Secondary Modern Schools 274-75. See also Schools
Elections, local (1945) 256-58
    see also By-election, 1941
Electricity, nationalisation 4, 27, 229, 282-84
Electro Manufacturing Co. 123
Eleven Plus,
    see Education
Employment 10, 27-28, 121-122, 140, 183-85, 191-92, 233, 258, 267, 270, 276, 296, 301

'Enemy Aliens' 67
Erskine Laboratories 123, 309
Evacuation (children) 23, 33-51; arrival 34-36; 'Doodle-bug' Evacuation 48-50; education 36; experiences 40-43; health 37-38, 42-43; hotels 43-47; morals 38, 234; planning 33-34; poverty 37; returning 39; romance 43; teachers 41; 'Trickle Evacuation' 47-48

Fell, John J. and Son, 121
Fire Brigade 16, 19, 60, 108; National Fire Service, 279-80; North Riding Fire Brigade, 280-81
Fishing, 6, 10, 24, 58, 96, 126-135, 140, 198, 213, 215, 244, 310; Boats: *Almond* 135; *Aucuba* 127, 129, 133; 127; *Connie*, 131; *Courage* 127-28; *Crystal* 127, 131; *Emulator* 127, 128, 131,133; *Ethel Crawford* 132; *Hilda* 127-28; *Persian Empire* 126-29, 131; *Pride* 131; *Riby* 127-29; *Silver Line* 127, 129-31;
Fishing Village,
    see Old Town
Fleming, Pat 77, 78, 105
Floral Hall 4, 103, 115, 299
Food 8, 22, 42, 45, 90, 115, 120, 133, 181, 212-221, 223-24, 233; angling 216; animal husbandry 216; diet 213; 'Dig for Victory' 214-15; foraging 217; rationing 212-13; recycling 217; 'seagull egging' 216-17; supplies 213, 240
    see also British Restaurants
Fox, Paddy 77
Fuel 22-23, 25, 84, 150-51, 221, 228-29, 301
Futurist Cinema 8, 77
Fylingdales 121

Gala Land 4, 8, 11, 302
Gates, Ernest 90-91
General election (1945) 251-256, 312
Girl Guides 17, 105, 197, 199
Girls High School 214, 216, 275-76
Glaves and Son 121
Golf Clubs 1-2, 214

Index

'Good Time Girls' 229-231, 310
Government, centralisation 17-18, 273-284
Grand Hotel 7-8, 63, 94, 103, 158, 160-62, 164-65, 294
Grand Restaurant 8, 182, 297
Green Howards 73, 76-78, 206

Hall, Roy 106
Health 4, 11, 35, 37-38, 42, 96, 188-89, 212-13, 220, 273, 278-79; GPs 278; Hospitals 278-79
Hipwell, Reginald (Reg) 139, 144-52, 258, 310, 312
Hispaniola 299
'Holidays at Home' 116-19
Holidays with Pay Act (1938) 10, 291
Holidays, 'staggered' 291-293
Home Defence, invasion threat 26, 72, 79-81, 83-84, 115, 121, 239, 297; UK 56-57; Yorkshire Coast 57-67
'H' (Home) Transmitter 65-66
Home Guard (and LDV) 60, 65, 79-85, 95, 187, 206, 234-35; 'auxiliary unit' 65
Hopperton, Tom 253-54
Hotels 2, 8, 10, 22, 24-27, 29, 35, 43-47 72, 103, 109, 117, 142, 158-160, 165, 175, 216, 240-242, 268, 291, 293-94, 296-297, 300-01; individual hotels: Adelphi 45, 159; Astoria 41-45, 159; Cambridge 294; Clifton 294, Crown 44, 67, 159, 161-62; Fairview 46-47, Holbeck Hall 294; Manor 158-59; Mount 44; Norbreck 294; Prince of Wales 44, 159, 161, 163, 294; Spa Royal 159; Royal 77, 164, 175; St Nicholas 158-59; Waldorf 109, 165; Wessex 46-47; Weston 109, 159, 165 *See also* Grand Hotel
Housewives Service (WVS) 186, 188, 199
Housing 3-5, 8, 92, 95, 254, 256-58, 262-270, 284, 301, 310, 312; allocation, 267-68; Barrowcliff 265-67; Eastfield 268-70; permanent 265-68; 'prefabs' 263-65; private housing, 265-66, 268; requisitioning 263; squatting 267

Industry, war production 121-23, 282, 288-91, 295, 302, 310
Initial Training Wings (RAF) 66, 103, 109, 158-66, 175, 215, 309; and civilian population 164, 206; classroom work 159-160; discipline 161-62; ethos 159, 162-65; living conditions 160-61; morale 162, 165; physical exercise 160; planning 158-59; trainees 159

Jackson, Councillor 'Johnny' 23, 144, 146-47, 189, 191, 201, 257-58, 312
Johnston, Tom (Secretary of State for Scotland) 235
Jottings 19, 26-27, 37, 40, 50, 108, 112, 116, 119, 152, 189, 192, 207, 228-30, 253-54, 257, 283, 294, 298

Killerby Garage, 122

Labour Party 139-140, 191, 218, 220, 251-59, 291, 312
Labour supply 240-41, 244, 290
Labour, Ministry of 118, 241, 292-93
Latham, Sir Paul MP: attacked politically 146; early life 140-41; political career 141-142, 312; scandal 142-143
Leeds Training College 41
Liberal Club 4, 77
Liberal Party 4, 77, 140, 252, 254-257, 277
Living Standards 10-11, 28, 119, 220
Local Defence Volunteers (LDV) *see* Home Guard
London and North Eastern Railway (LNER) 3, 24-25
Lysander, *see* Mould, Pilot Officer

March 1941 'Blitz' 101-109, 115, 185, 277
Marine Drive 9, 63, 120, 282
Marriage 77, 230-31, 262
Marsden, Harry (headmaster) 276
Mary, Princess Royal 207
Mass Observation 139-40, 144-45, 147-48, 150
May and Sons 289-290

329

Mere 2, 4, 233, 297, 299
Mines (land) 63-64, 313
Mines (sea) 24, 64, 126, 131-35, 235, 313
Miniature Railway 9, 243, 246
Morale 58, 79, 85, 118, 146, 162, 174-76, 186, 196, 208, 309-10
Motor-bike racing 299-300
Motor vehicles (cars and coaches) 3, 7, 11, 20, 76, 244, 252, 301
Mould, Geoffrey, Pilot Officer (RAF) 75
Murder (Mary Comins) 231-32

National Federation of Business and Professional Women 189
National Savings 26, 202-203, 244, 309, 312; National Savings Weeks 165, 203-08, 190
Naval 'Y' (Listening) Station, see 'Y' Station
Nellis, Michael 107
North Bay 8-9, 12, 58, 61-63, 83, 302
North Riding County Council 18-19, 97, 219, 257-58, 269, 274-84
North Riding Training College 278
North Side 4, 8-9, 12, 116, 250, 302-03
Northstead Manor Gardens 4, 9, 116

Old Town 5-6, 38, 41, 92-94, 96, 102, 198, 297, 302, 309; 'bottom enders' 5, 94, 95, 98, 213; fishing village, 6, 96, 198, 302
Oliver's Mount 2, 7, 59, 72, 82, 160, 299-300
Olympia Ballroom 4, 8, 12, 22, 25, 41, 94, 103, 116, 120, 175, 201, 242-43, 246, 302
Open Air Theatre 4, 9, 27, 115, 120, 299

Pacifists 67
Peasholm Park 4, 9, 116, 119-20, 243, 282, 300
Pickup, H. Ltd 122
'Phoney War' 15-25, 45, 66, 95-96, 98, 198
Plaxton F.W. and Son 3, 61, 111, 122, 183, 289-90
Police 16-17, 24, 49, 74, 95, 242, 244, 281-82; Special Constables 17, 20, 35, 214, see also Women Police
Potter Lane air raid 92-96

Premier Engineering Co. 122, 183-84, 289
Priestley, Councillor May Lees 190, 219
Prisoners of War (POWs) 76, 131, 166, 183, 214, 217 240, 263, 293,
Public Air Raid Shelters, 20, 96-98, 108, 298

RAF Resettlement Centre for POWs 166
RAF Staxton Brow (Radar Station) 64
Rail transport 3, 22, 24, 25-26, 34, 65, 110, 115, 118, 120, 212, 239-40, 244-45, 294, 299; air raids, 111; train crash, 223
Rates, Council 10, 23-24, 28-29, 258, 274, 282-83
Rationing, see Food
Razzall, Leonard 255-56
Recycling 196-202, 205, 208, 311-12; books 200-201; metal 196-98; paper, 198-200; see also Food
Requisitioning (by military) 22, 117, 121, 240, 243, 252, 294-95
Retirement and retirees 2, 11, 27, 140
Rowley, Tom 133-134
Rowntree and Sons 35, 121, 165, 299
Royal Navy Patrol Service 134-35

Salvage, see Recycling
Sanderson, William 105
Sandybed estate 264-65, 268
Scalby Mills 12, 61, 82, 302
Scalby Rd Sawmills 121
Scarborough and Whitby parliamentary constituency 139-40
Scarborough Hosiery Company 289
Scarborough Hotels and Boarding Houses Association (SHBHA) 22-23, 28-29
Schools: Barrowcliff County Primary 274; Central County Modern 275; Convent of Ladies of Mary 277-78; Falsgrave County Modern 274-75; Friarage County Secondary 275; Graham Sea-Training School 277; Newby Primary 274; Orleton Boys and Girls Preparatory Schools 159, 161, 163, 277; Queen Margaret's School 103, 277-78; Raincliffe County Modern 275; Scarborough College 159, 278;

Index

Westwood County Modern, 275
see also Boys High School, Girl's High School
Sexual relations and behaviour 73, 143, 162-63, 190-91, 230-31
Shops and shop workers 4, 7, 10, 27-28, 35, 118, 120, 140, 165, 213-14, 234-35, 241
Signals Intelligence, see 'Y' Station
Simpson, Sidney 19, 98, 108-09, 192, 218-19, 253-54, 258, 263
Snainton 172, 177
Social attitudes, changing 310-11
South Bay and Foreshore 4, 6-9, 12, 16, 21, 58, 61, 63-64, 72, 82, 84, 92, 95, 115, 131, 161, 163, 182, 242-3, 246, 250, 297, 299, 302, 308
South Cliff, 2, 7, 9, 109, 160, 301
Spa complex 4, 7-8, 23, 115, 165, 243-44, 298-99, 302
Spavin Ltd, 122
Spearman, Alexander MP 142, 144-46, 148-54, 252-56, 279, 281, 291, 312
SS Aguila, *see* Aguila
Standing Conference of Women's Organisations 189-192
Sunbathing 7, 11-12
Supply, Ministry of, 122, 196-200
Swift and Sons 122

'Tip and Run' air raids 89-91, 111, 186
Tourism 3, 6, 10, 13, 21-29, 115-121, 140, 188, 239-246, 290-303, 310
Town Hall (Town Council and Corporation) 3-4, 8, 16, 18-19, 23-25, 28-29, 34-35, 41, 45, 51, 95, 115-116, 119-21, 189-92, 197-202, 214-15, 217-21, 228-29, 242-46, 250, 262-70, 274-84, 290-91, 297-302, 312-13
Trinity Chair Works 121-122, 289
'Tunny' (tuna) fishing 6, 140, 244

Unemployment 10, 24, 266, 289, 292, 296

VE Day (Victory in Europe) 178, 249-50, 258
VJ Day (Victory over Japan) 250, 258

Wages 10-11, 182, 241, 291, 296-97
Walmsley, Leo 126, 129
Wardell, Mary 64
War Memorial 2, 300, 313-14
War Savings
see National Savings
'Watcher' Station (RAF) 66
Wheatcroft Battery 59-60, 82
White House 11, 198, 216
Whitfield, Louisa M. 189-90
Whittaker, Alderman Francis, 19, 21-23, 192, 274, 282
Willis, Margaret 105
Wiseman, Christopher 33, 111-12, 213-14, 217, 235
Women 10, 17, 66, 117, 132, 150, 173-75, 181-190, 199-200, 202, 204-05, 207, 213-14, 229-31, 235-36, 249, 252, 268, 289, 311-12; Women Police 190-92
Women's Voluntary Service (WVS) 17, 35, 41, 48, 95, 181, 185-89, 197-99, 205, 244, 299, 309
Wood End 198, 299
Woodland Ravine 110
Woolton, Lord 135, 219, 262
Working class 2-3, 8, 10, 140, 152, 185, 188, 255, 275, 301, 312
Works, Ministry of 66-67, 197, 263

Yorkshire Wolds 72, 183
Youth 'running wild': crime wave 232-33; cruelty to animals 233-34; gangs 235; theft 233-35; vandalism 234
'Y' Station (Scarborough) 169-78, 309; Direction-Finding 170-74, 176-77; Expansion 171-72; Work 173-74, 176-78
'Y' Station (Flowerdown) 171, 176-77